The Person in the Parasha
Discovering the Human Element in the Weekly Torah Portion

OU**PRESS**

MAGGID

Rabbi Dr. Tzvi Hersh
Weinreb

THE
PERSON
IN THE
PARASHA

Discovering the Human Element
in the Weekly Torah Portion

OU Press
Maggid Books

Person in the Parasha
Discovering the Human Element in the Weekly Torah Portion

First Edition, 2016

Maggid Books
An imprint of Koren Publishers Jerusalem Ltd.

POB 8531, New Milford, CT 06776-8531, USA
& POB 4044, Jerusalem 9104001, Israel
www.maggidbooks.com

OU Press
An imprint of the Orthodox Union
11 Broadway
New York, NY 10004
www.oupress.org

The publication of this book was made possible
through the generous support of *Torah Education in Israel.*

ISBN 978-1-59264-462-9, *hardcover*

A CIP catalogue record for this title is
available from the British Library

Printed and bound in the United States

In Loving Memory of Our Beloved Brother

Jamie Lehmann

חיים מנחם בן מנשה רפאל ושרה

Jamie was an ish eshkolot – a loving, joyful, gentle, brilliant soul;
the embodiment of Torah im derech eretz.
He is missed more every day.

עַל יַד קֶבֶר בְּנִי אֲשֶׁר בְּהַר הַמְּנוּחוֹת

כָּךְ אֲנִי עוֹמֵד דוֹמֵם
אָב גַּלְמוּד מְיֻתָּם
מוּל מַצֵּבְתֶּךָ
הַצְּרוּרָה בִּצְרוֹר
עַרְפִּלֵּי עֶרֶב
הַיּוֹרֵד עַל הָרֵי יְהוּדָה
וּבִצְרוֹר עַנְנֵי בֹקֶר
הַצְּלוּלִים
הָעוֹלְלִים אַט אַט
נֶגֶד פָּנֶיךָ
עִם עֲלוֹת הַשַּׁחַר.

הֵן הֵן שִׂפְתוֹתֶיךָ
הַדּוֹבְבוֹת אֵלַי בַּקֶּבֶר
וְאוֹמְרוֹת
אֵינֶנִּי גַלְמוּד פֹּה, אַבָּא,
בְּאֶרֶץ הַחַיִּים הַקְּדוֹשָׁה.

וַאֲנִי עוֹנֶה וְאוֹמֵר
אָמֵן, כֵּן תְּהִי
נַפְשְׁךָ צְרוּרָה
בִּצְרוֹר הַחַיִּים
בְּנִי אֲהוּבִי.

מנשה רפאל ליהמן
Dr. Manfred Raphael Lehmann

Dedicated by
Yitzchok and Barbie Lehmann Siegel and Family

In Honor of

Rabbi Tzvi Hersh Weinreb

whose wisdom, friendship, and sensitive
leadership continue to guide us

Dedicated by

Lani and Shimmy Tennenbaum and Family

In Loving Memory of Our Dear Parents

Abraham and Sylvia Weinreb
אברהם בן חיים יצחק
טשארנע סאשע בת גיטל

Chaim Yitzchak and Yona Taub
חיים יצחק בן האדמו"ר שאול ידידיה אלעזר
יונה בת עזריאל

who remain our constant inspiration

Dedicated by

Chavi and Tzvi Hersh Weinreb

Contents

Exodus

DEUTERONOMY

Preface

The book you have in your hands is a collection of some of the columns I have written on the weekly *parasha* during the past seven years. These columns have a history, which was initiated by Mr. Stephen Steiner, OU Director of Public Relations, in the spring of the year 2009. At that time, I was preparing to end my tenure as Executive Vice President of the Orthodox Union. It was agreed that I would stay on with the OU in an emeritus capacity, but it was not initially clear to me what that capacity entailed. It was Steve who suggested to me that my new role would allow me to spend more time writing, something I had long dreamed of doing.

Steve further suggested that I might write a weekly column on *parashat hashavua*. He identified a need for a column that would reach all Jews, whatever their educational background and whatever their degree of religious observance.

But Steve went further than that. Because of our many years of collegiality, he was aware of my professional background and abiding interest in psychology, and particularly of my fascination with the inner spiritual lives of human beings. It was out of our initial discussions that

I consented to write such a column and to focus upon the human element contained in every weekly Torah portion. This human element often goes unnoticed or is, at the very least, under-emphasized.

In the early stages of my excitement over the prospect of writing such a column, the title *The Person in the Parasha* occurred to me. That title would allow me to concentrate upon the biblical characters who play a part in the drama of almost every chapter of the Pentateuch. But that title would also allow me to introduce the reader to numerous other individuals, drawn from my own personal life experiences, as well as from the vast world of literature of which I am so fond.

It was after several years of writing these columns that a reader approached me and told me that she had discovered my secret. She knowingly, and correctly, exclaimed, "Why, *you* are the person in the *parasha!*" Indeed, her observation was on the mark. Whereas I only rarely refer to myself directly in the columns, I do rely heavily upon the major personalities who had an impact upon my life. They include my own parents and grandparents, and occasionally my siblings, classmates, and friends. But mainly, I introduce the reader to my religious and spiritual mentors over the years and most especially, my paternal grandfather, Chaim Yitzchak Weinreb, of blessed memory, who was a Talmudist *par excellence* and who inspired me to adopt a lifelong commitment to the study of rabbinic texts.

A preface such as this primarily serves the purpose of thanking those individuals who played a role in the conception of the book and in its writing, editing, and publication. Steve Steiner deserves first mention because he conceived of the idea and prodded me to do it. The many individuals whose lives, works, and teachings provided the material for the columns also deserve to be thanked, although it is impossible to enumerate them all.

A special statement of gratitude is due to Mrs. Yocheved Goldberg, whose remarkable editorial skills, sensitivity to religious language, and commitment to proper English usage in every detail are admirable and laudable and very much appreciated by me. Yocheved has been my loyal and dedicated assistant for many years now, and she and her husband Avi and their lovely children deserve special thanks.

Thanks too to Mr. Matthew Miller, who heads Koren Publishers Jerusalem, for agreeing to co-publish this work and for the many opportunities he has given me to utilize my fascination with the world of books. Matthew's outstanding staff also deserves honorable mention, especially assistant editor Tomi Mager and proofreaders Shira Schreier and Shoshana Rotem.

I am privileged to be on the editorial board of the Orthodox Union's publishing arm, known as OU Press. My dear friends and colleagues, Rabbi Menachem Genack and Rabbi Simon Posner, spearheaded this important undertaking, and I feel especially honored that this book is now numbered among the many excellent contributions that OU Press has made to the world of traditional English-language Jewish learning.

There is one person who heads the list of "persons in the *parasha*." I refer, of course, to my dear wife Chavi. I may never have explicitly mentioned her by name in any of my hundreds of weekly columns, but she has been the inspiration of each and every one of them. Her loving encouragement has enabled me to produce a column every week of the year for many years on end. She has helped me overcome innumerable episodes of writer's block and has been the first reader to see each column after its final draft. Her invariably positive reactions have propelled me to persist with this project and to undertake the writing and editing of other publications.

I extend my blessings to all who have helped me achieve this goal. I close by inviting the reader to share his or her responses to this book with me. I have long ago learned the value of feedback, and I assure those of you who will respond that I will take your comments very seriously.

Tzvi Hersh Weinreb
12 Nissan, 5776
Monsey, NY

Genesis

Creation Conversation

Anyone who has ever taught anything can confirm the adage of our sages, "I have learned from all my teachers, but I have learned most from my pupils." It is especially true that one learns a great deal from his students if one does not limit himself to lecturing to them, but rather engages in face-to-face conversation with them. It is in candid and interactive dialogue that one learns most from his students.

The immense value of simple conversation between teacher and student was brought home to me many years ago in a conversation I had with two very different students. They both attended a series of lectures I gave for individuals with very little prior exposure to the Jewish religion and its teachings. One of them was almost exclusively interested in what he called, "the rules and regulations" of Judaism. The other was far less interested in Jewish law. He was more of the "spiritual" type and had a plethora of questions about the nature of God.

The first individual, let's call him Rick, was interested in a meaningful way of life. He wanted to be part of a congregation, to celebrate the holidays, and to learn how to live daily life as a Jew. The other student, let's call him Seth, was consumed by questions of cosmology and the origins of the universe. He saw God as an almost impersonal force behind nature. He wanted a relationship with God, but questioned whether that was at all possible. Both students had in common an interest in engaging me, their teacher, in conversation after class. Usually, those conversations took place in the local kosher pizza shop.

I vividly recall the evening I gave a lecture on the opening chapter of *Parashat Bereshit* in the Book of Genesis (Gen. 1:1–6:5). Rick and Seth appeared equally eager to corner me in the pizza shop after that lecture.

Rick began the conversation by firmly questioning why the Torah even bothered to give us details about the creation of the world and God's role in it. "As a Jew," he maintained, "I just need to know how to live my life, how to celebrate the holidays, what food is kosher and what is not, and what is right and wrong in the spheres of ethics and morality. I can satisfy my curiosity about the origins of the universe by consulting some scientific book on the matter. For me, this has nothing to do with religion."

Seth, sitting across the table, was absolutely astounded. "What?!" he exclaimed. "This opening chapter of Genesis is precisely what I need to know as I begin my exploration of Judaism. I need to know about God, from beginning to end. And this is His beginning."

I was fascinated by this conversation because it helped me put into a new perspective the conflicting opinions of two of the greatest rabbinic commentators on the Bible, Rashi and Nahmanides.

Rashi (Shlomo ben Yitzhak), in the very first words of his magisterial commentary on the entire Pentateuch, asks the same question that was bothering Rick. He begins by quoting a Rabbi Yitzhak who, some have maintained, was none other than his own father. He avers that the Torah should have begun with the chapter in the later Book of Exodus, which outlines the mitzvot that Jews were supposed to fulfill. Rashi struggles to find a reason for the Torah's description of creation and the detailed narratives of early human history.

"Rick," I was able to say, "your question was anticipated many centuries ago by a great man whom you never heard of." I continued to introduce him to the man who was Rashi and to his indispensable commentary. Rick was gratified that Rashi too seemed to conceive of the Torah as primarily a book of "rules and regulations," so that he felt compelled to seek a reason for its beginning with an account of the creation.

Seth was obviously hard put to restrain himself, but before he began to protest against Rick, and against Rashi, I attempted to placate him. "There was another great rabbinic commentator on the Bible," I explained. "His name was Rabbi Moshe ben Nahman. Some call him Nahmanides. Traditionally, we call him Ramban and consider him second only to Rashi as a rabbinic commentator."

I told Seth, and Rick who was listening reluctantly, that Nahmanides, in his opening paragraph of his commentary on Genesis 1:1, contests Rashi's very question. "Of course," he asserts, "the Torah had to begin with a description of the creation. That is the root of our faith, so anyone who believes that the world always existed but was not created by the Almighty at one specific moment in time, has no share in the Torah at all."

Rick and Seth were gratified to discover that their differing views on what is important in Judaism has precedents in the writings of two great medieval rabbis. I hastened to disappoint them. I told them that it was incorrect to conceive of two mutually exclusive definitions of Judaism. It is not a matter of a "rules-based" religion versus a "God-based" one.

I quoted to them the marvelous passage in the writings of Maimonides in which he speaks of the mitzva to love God, and he explains that there are two ways to achieve this. One way is by studying His Torah and its laws, and the other way is by contemplating His astonishing creation, the world of nature.

I admonished them to carefully avoid reducing our faith to one or the other conception. "Our faith is not a simplistic one," I argued. "As you proceed in your study of Judaism in general, and of the Five Books of Moses in particular, you will come to realize that our religion emphasizes that our God is both Creator and Lawgiver. Any conception of Him as one but not the other is not authentic Judaism."

I thanked them for once again demonstrating to me the great value of conversation between student and teacher. Before we parted that evening, I shared with them a story of another conversation between a teacher and a student that I had read about in philosopher Samuel Hugo Bergmann's memoirs.

Bergmann recounts the story of Hermann Cohen, the German-Jewish philosopher who drew closer to religious Judaism in his later years. The climax of his life's work was his book, *Religion of Reason Out of the Sources of Judaism*. It seems that the philosopher Cohen once entered into a long conversation with an old and old-fashioned Jew who resided in the university town of Marburg with him. The philosopher attempted to explain to the old Jew his elaborate and highly intellectual theory about the nature of God. The old man listened with the respect due to a university professor. When Cohen was finished with his learned and lengthy discourse, his elderly partner in conversation responded in Yiddish, "I understand everything you said, but something is missing. *Vu iz der Bashefer?* Where is the Creator?"

Cohen heard the old Jew's response, and "got it." His eyes welled up with tears, but he remained speechless.

The opening chapter of *Parashat Bereshit* assures that everyone who reads it will not make the philosopher's mistake, but will realize, along with the old-fashioned Jew, that whatever else God may be, He is primarily *der Bashefer,* the Creator.

Self-Control, Marshmallows, and Human Destiny

It didn't take very long after man was created for the history of the world to change its course. It seems clear that the Almighty had a very different narrative in mind for the story of the human race. For one thing, death was not part of the narrative. Nor was the need to earn our bread by the sweat of our brow. We were originally designed to be immortal, and to reside in a paradise that required very little of us. Our immortality and our idyllic abode were assured to us with but one caveat:

> The Lord God took the man and placed him in the Garden of Eden, to till it and tend it. And the Lord God commanded the man, saying, "Of every tree of the garden you are free to eat; but as for the tree of knowledge of good and bad, you must not eat of it; for as soon as you eat of it, you shall die." (Gen. 2:15–17)

As an additional blessing, designed to remove from man the sad state of loneliness, God created woman. The Almighty, who is as benevolent as He is omnipotent, clearly expected man and woman to live up to this single expectation. We can even assume that He was rooting for them to come through this simple challenge successfully. The course of human history was at stake. Would it be a story of a perfect existence or would it be a tale ridden with misery and woe? Man and woman failed the test:

> When the woman saw that the tree was good for eating and a delight to the eyes, and that the tree was desirable as a source of wisdom, she took of its fruit and ate. She also gave some to her husband, and he ate. (Gen. 3:6)

This type of failure has been repeated innumerable times in human history. It is certainly a failure with which we are all personally familiar. But we don't tell our stories in the sublime language of the Bible. In fact, we recently have found a much more mundane way to refer to our moral shortcomings. We now say, "We failed the marshmallow test."

This new term has become part of our parlance because of the many years of research on the subject of self-control by a professor at Columba University, Dr. Walter Mischel. His book, *The Marshmallow Test: Mastering Self-Control*, describes the extensive research he conducted over the course of his long professional career.

It all began with a simple experiment in which he observed how a group of five-year-olds reacted when he placed some tempting marshmallows before them. They were given the choice between consuming one marshmallow immediately or being allowed two marshmallows if they waited fifteen minutes.

Some ate the one marshmallow right away, while others engaged in a range of hilarious attempts to overcome temptation. Some averted their gaze from the marshmallows. Others squirmed in their seats or sang to themselves. Others counted to one hundred repetitively until the fifteen minutes passed by. Some fantasized that the marshmallows were poisoned or that they weren't marshmallows at all, but insects or sugar-coated cardboard.

The point, of course, is that one can use one's mental skills to divert one's attention from the forbidden object. In psychological terms there is such a thing as willpower and it is possible to succeed at the vitally important task of self-control.

Mischel followed the original group of children forty years later and found that the five-year-olds who passed the marshmallow test developed into adults who were much more successful in life than their counterparts who failed the test. More importantly, Mischel used the results of his research to develop a system of guidelines for gaining the ability to delay the pressures of immediate gratification and to exert self-control in a wide range of real life situations.

How different the course of history would have been if Adam and Eve had the benefit of Dr. Mischel's instructions for mastering self-control!

It has occurred to me more than once that the Jewish religion requires a great deal of self-control, perhaps more than any other religion. There are numerous foods that we are forbidden to eat. There are days of the year when we must forego all sorts of otherwise important and often pleasurable activities. There are times of each day when we must interrupt our activities in order to pray. There are urges and passions that we are forbidden to satisfy. We must inhibit tendencies to speak maliciously of others, and it is essential that we deny our very human temptation not to tell the truth (*emet*).

Of course, from time to time we fail, but, by and large, we succeed in controlling ourselves and in avoiding those behaviors that others in our social environment, not bound by the restrictions of our faith, perform without the slightest hesitation. What is the secret of our success?

To some extent, it is the secret that Mischel's five-year-olds knew intuitively. We do go through internal mental processes, either telling ourselves, for example, "This is not kosher," or, "This is a great mitzva." We may even control ourselves to the extent that we physically avoid situations that might confront us with irresistible temptations and compel us to compromise our religious standards.

But I think that the secret of the successful observant Jew lies deeper within us than these exertions of willpower. Dr. Mischel provides us with a clue when he distinguishes between the "hot" and "cool" systems of the brain. The former is designed to deal with immediate rewards and threats, while the latter is designed to deal with long-term consequences.

Although the "hot" system is necessary in certain situations, the practicing Jew learns the importance of the "cool" system. For those born into Jewish observance, it is learned in the earliest formative years, from parents and grandparents, from stories and songs. For those who come to Jewish observance later in life, it is learned intentionally, through study, reflection, and discussion. One way or another, we internalize a world view that looks beyond the immediate present to an ultimate future.

As we read *Parashat Bereshit*, which is all about beginnings, we have the opportunity to begin to be more conscious of our decisions and to appreciate how different and more rewarding our spiritual lives could be if we learn the lessons of self-control. More so, we can ponder how different the world would be if many more of us would learn to pass the marshmallow test.

Parashat Noaḥ

Filling in the Blanks

T he Torah is replete with inspiring stories of its heroes. The lives of Abraham, Jacob, Moses, and David, to name just some, are narrated at great length and in vivid detail. Their noble acts and admirable accomplishments are described, and even their occasional faults or failures are not hidden from us.

It is therefore especially frustrating when the story is incomplete, and facts about their lives that we would love to know are glaringly omitted. Our curiosity gets the better of us, and, not only do we wish to ascertain the facts, but we are additionally puzzled by why those facts were omitted in the first place.

In *Parashat Noaḥ* (Gen. 6:9–11:32), we are introduced to that majestic personality, our patriarch Abraham, originally Abram. We learn of his birth and of his father, Terah; we are informed of the names of his siblings, and of his marriage to Sarai. We are made aware that Sarai was barren and that Terah set out with some of his family, including Abram, for the land of Canaan. We are told that he stopped short of his destination and settled in Ḥaran. That is all that we are told. The Torah is almost teasingly silent about the details of Abram's youth.

In the next *parasha*, and for many *parashot* thereafter, we become immersed in the dramatic story of Abraham's life. That story begins when Abraham, at age seventy-five, leaves Ḥaran for Canaan at God's command.

The gap in the narrative is disturbing. What transpired in Abraham's life from the time he accompanied his father to Ḥaran, presumably as a very young man, until that time when the Almighty saw fit to speak to the now elderly Abraham and enjoin him to leave Ḥaran for the Promised Land?

We also cannot help but wonder why this man, of whose deeds we are told nothing at all, merited to hear the voice of the Almighty. Surely, he must have done something very meritorious to warrant the sacred mission that God assigned to him.

Abraham's early life, his formative years, are a blank to readers of the Bible. But those years are not a blank for the readers of rabbinic commentaries, especially the Midrash. For them, details of Abraham's childhood and early adulthood are not lacking. For the Midrash fills in the blanks, and besides rabbinic scholars, every child fortunate to have a basic Jewish education reaps the benefits of learning the colorful and exciting stories about Abraham's background.

Readers of the Midrash, along with the child in the Jewish kindergarten, learn of Abraham's discovery, at the prodigiously early age of three, of the One God, He who created heaven and earth. They learn too of Abraham's struggle against his idolatrous surroundings, of how he defied his own father and smashed the idols that were Terah's merchandise. They are made aware of how Terah cruelly delivered Abraham to Nimrod, the archetypal combination of king and wizard. They are privy to Abraham's debates with Nimrod, and of how Nimrod was so angered that he cast Abraham into a fiery furnace. And they learn that Abraham emerged from that furnace unscathed.

Now that we have all this information, the question becomes ever more tantalizing: Why is there no mention of all this in the text of the Torah? Why was this dramatic narrative of religious courage not deemed worthy of inclusion in the Bible, instead left to the rabbis of the Midrash to reveal? Many, from the earliest commentaries until this very day, have asked this question.

Nahmanides, for one, addresses this question, but only after providing even more tales of Abraham's early life, surprisingly even drawing from ancient non-biblical sources. His answer is fascinating:

> Scripture avoids describing these wondrous events, because to write about them would have necessitated mentioning the idolatrous views of those whom Abraham debated, and unlike the case of Moses, whose responses to the Egyptian sorcerers are on record, Abraham's responses to his opponents were not made available to us.

I have always felt that somehow Nahmanides' approach begs the question: Why indeed were Abraham's counter-arguments not recorded? Surely they would have been of historical interest, at least, and may even have proved useful in debating contemporary idolatries.

Permit me to share with you a different approach that I once thought was original to me, but that I have since seen advanced by a number of modern commentators.

It is commonly assumed that Abraham's great contribution to the world was his discovery of monotheism. He, as our sages taught us, came to "know his Creator" on his own. He spread the word of God already in Ḥaran where he "made souls."

But it is erroneous, or at least not completely true, that the concept of the One God was Abraham's primary gift to the world. In *Parashat Vayera*, we read what God Himself considered to be Abraham's greatest contribution: "For I have singled him out, that he may instruct his children and his posterity to keep the way of the Lord by doing what is just and right" (Gen. 18:19).

Teaching justice and righteousness to the world was Abraham's greatest contribution. The stories included in the biblical text recount Abraham's ethical behavior, not his theology. He is known for his hospitality, not for his metaphysics. He argues for justice, and not against heresy.

We can thus conclude that the Torah deliberately omits the stories of Abraham's early battles against idolatry because those battles are not representative of Abraham's essence. Rather, his essence is better expressed in the stories of his defense of the sinners of Sodom and Gomorrah, in the compassion he showed to his nephew, Lot, and in his generous demeanor in his encounter with those he thought to be idolatrous wayfarers, but who were, in fact, God's own angels.

True, Abraham introduced monotheism to the world, but that monotheism is best termed "ethical monotheism." The God he came to know was not just One God, but a God who teaches humankind right from wrong, and who expects mankind to abide by that teaching.

While the Torah does not demand that we be theologians, it does demand that we perform acts of righteousness and deeds of justice. Thus, God demands ethical behavior from all of us and that is Abraham's primary teaching. The Torah is quite comfortable in omitting the theological debates, but it will never suppress those stories that illustrate Abraham's historic commitment to eliminate evil from God's world.

Parashat Noaḥ

Easy Spirituality

T he French poet Baudelaire once remarked that the devil's greatest success is his ability to convince us that he does not exist. Whereas Judaism does not believe in the devil quite as Baudelaire does, it does believe that there is a "devilish" force called the *yetzer hara* within each of us, and that that force works in very subtle ways. At the same time, with ambivalence, we definitely do tend to believe that this *yetzer* does not exist.

Jewish writings through the ages have debated the nature of this force. All these writings ultimately trace back to a verse in *Parashat Noaḥ*, "The devising of man's mind are evil from his youth" (Gen. 8:21). And to a similar verse in the previous Torah portion, "The Lord saw how great was man's wickedness on earth, and how every plan devised by his mind was nothing but evil all the time" (Gen. 6:5).

Thus, there most assuredly is an inclination for evil in each of us. He or she who wishes to live the life of a good person is well advised to guard against this natural inclination. This *yetzer*-force rarely commands us directly to do what is wrong. Instead, it tries to craftily delude us into thinking that what is wrong and evil is right and good.

A favorite strategy for the *yetzer* is to persuade us that it seeks the same ends and objectives as God does, but that alternate ways of achieving those ends are also legitimate. Take spirituality for example. How does one achieve a sense of spirituality?

For Judaism, spirituality and the emotions that accompany it, can only be achieved through hard work: prayer, study, sacrifice, and above all, charity and compassion. No easy "grace." The *yetzer*, while not denying the value of spirituality, tempts us with short cuts and cheap and ersatz methods to achieve the same results as the more arduous methods prescribed by the Torah.

A wonderful illustration of this dynamic is found in *Parashat Noah*, just after the story of the great Flood. Noah and his family are beginning anew, rebuilding their lives, and rebuilding the world. What is the first thing Noah does? He plants a vineyard. His grapes grow and ripen, he makes wine and drinks it, and he gets drunk.

What prompted Noah to make wine his first priority? Let me suggest the following imaginary scenario to answer that question. Noah walked with God. He enjoyed the sense of spirituality for which many of us yearn. He experienced a spiritual "high." In the past, he achieved that level of spirituality by virtue of hard work: obedience, construction of the Ark, gathering the animals of the world, tending to them, and offering sacrifices. Along came Noah's *yetzer*-force, and said, "Noah! There must be an easier way! You can achieve the same spiritual high, the same sense of wholeness and holiness, without all that work. All it will take is a few drinks of one of God's own juices. Plant a vineyard, make some wine, drink it, and you will feel all the good feelings you felt before, and then some." For, you see, the *yetzer*, or if you wish, the devil, knows of the connection between addiction and spirituality.

How well I remember the 1960s, and the many gifted spiritual seekers who resorted to alcohol and more potent substances to generate moods of spirituality. Judaism cautions us not to be seduced by facile techniques, even in the service of achieving higher and holier states of conscientiousness. That is why the Torah shifts into the story of Abraham, whose spirituality was based on service, on the courageous search for social justice, and on compassionate concern for others in need. In short, Abraham was dedicated to the very arduous methods that Noah sought to circumvent by drink. From the impressive personality of Abraham can we learn how to achieve a sober sense of spirituality.

Parashat Lekh Lekha

One Day We Will
All Be Together

I picked him up at the airport. He was arriving in Baltimore, where I was then a rabbi, to deliver an address and then return home to New York. The plane was late, so when he finally arrived, I told him that we would have to hurry in order to reach our destination on time. He was already showing signs of age, and walking quickly was hard for him. Nevertheless, we moved rapidly past the gates where passengers of other flights were disembarking, including a number of arriving passengers who were being welcomed warmly by friends and family.

That is where he stopped, transfixed. He could not take his eyes off the scene of the small crowds embracing and kissing each other tearfully and emotionally. Reluctantly, he responded to my rude insistence that we move on, and together we rushed to his appointment.

He was Rav Avrohom Pam, of blessed memory, the late lamented sage, yeshiva dean, mentor to hundreds of rabbis and scholars, and above all, gentle soul. When we finally were in the car and on our way, I asked him what it was about the airport scene that so fascinated him.

His response was the greatest lesson of the many I learned from him. "The saddest of all human happenings is separation," he said. "And the most wonderful of all is reunion. Whenever I see people, of whatever religion or background, who are joyfully coming together after a long separation, I feel spellbound, and I must stand by and witness that pure innocent joy as long as I can."

What a powerful teaching! Separation is the greatest human tragedy, although a very common one. Reunion is the greatest joy, rare though it is.

Parashat Lekh Lekha allows us to further reflect upon the phenomenon of separation (*pereida*). The Torah describes the close relationship between Abraham and his nephew, Lot. It is a relationship that began in the "old country" and continued through Abraham's adventurous journey to and through the land of Canaan. As both prospered, we are told, "Thus they parted from each other; Abram remained in the land of Canaan, while Lot pitched his tents near Sodom."

This decision to separate was a fateful one for Lot. He settled in Sodom, rose to a prestigious position there, and we learn more about his new life in *Parashat Veyera*. He tried to mitigate the effects of the separation by remaining loyal to the precepts he learned in Abraham's tent, a difficult challenge in his new circumstances.

At the same time, Abraham did not forget his nephew. Even after the separation, he stayed in touch with him from afar, and rushed to his aid when Lot was captured by a marauding army.

This dramatic story of the separation of two close companions may be the first on record, but it is certainly not the last. Subsequent separation dramas are themes of great literary fiction, and of real human life, which is even stranger than fiction. Sometimes the separation results in estrangement and alienation; sometimes, despite the distance, the separated parties end up in remarkably similar places.

Personally, I have long been intrigued by the stories of siblings separated at an early age who rediscover each other later in life. Often, they learn how different they have become. One example is the reunion of the ninety-year-old Torah sage, Reb Yaakov Kamenetsky, who, after a seventy-year separation from his sister, rediscovered her in the former Soviet Union. He was steeped in traditional Judaism; she had become totally removed from any semblance of Jewish religion. When one of Reb Yaakov's sons tried to explain to his long-lost aunt what her brother had accomplished in his life, she could only respond that it was a shame that a lad with such youthful promise grew up to become a mere *melamed*, a school teacher.

But there are poignant examples of separated individuals who, despite growing up in radically different environments, end up so similarly. How well I remember an adolescent psychotherapy patient of mine who was adopted in infancy by a professor of physics and his wife, a noted art historian. They were frustrated by this teenager, who was interested neither in intellectual nor cultural pursuits, but whose goal in life was to become a fireman, and who spent all his spare time as a fire department volunteer.

After several years, I received a call from the young man telling me that he had since successfully located his biological father. Wouldn't you know that his father was a veteran fireman!

Separation is part of human life, so much so that in Jewish mystical liturgy this world is called the "world of separation (*alma deperuda*)."

Reunions, planned or serendipitous, are thrilling experiences but are frightening because we fear finding out how different we have become from those with whom we once shared such similarity. Abraham and Lot once were very similar. They separated intentionally, yet there were bonds that linked them, invisible and mysterious. Of some, we read about in the *parashot* of *Lekh Lekha* and *Vayera*, but others surface generations later, with the story of Ruth, the descendent of Lot's progeny, Moav, and her reunion with Abraham's people. Ultimately, King David himself becomes the symbol of the reunion of the uncle and nephew of whose separation we read in *Parashat Lekh Lekha*.

No wonder then that the mystical text that calls this world the *alma deperuda*, calls the next, better world, the *alma deyihuda*, "the world of reunion," the world in which we will all be together.

Walking With and Walking Before

When I was still a pulpit rabbi back in Baltimore, I would meet with a group of teenagers from time to time. The agenda was open-ended and my goal was to encourage the group to freely share their feelings and attitudes. One of the favorite topics chosen by the kids was their school curriculum and what they found wrong with it.

I learned many things from this group of adolescents, whose critique of the curricula of the schools they attended was sharp and accurate. I particularly remember the outburst of one exceptionally creative young man. Let's call him Josh.

Josh was a student in an academically oriented high school that put its major emphasis upon textual study. "What am I supposed to do with my creativity?" he asked. "Where is there room in the school for me to express my artistic talents?"

I was hard-pressed to come up with an answer for Josh's pained query. All I could say was that he was personally experiencing a tension that pervades the history of our religious faith. It is the tension between conformity to the rules and regulations of our sacred texts versus the natural and powerful human need for creative expression and innovation.

Our religion reveres tradition and continuity. Attempts to question tradition and to stake out new spiritual turf have been typically viewed in our history as heresy and rebellion. Is there no room for creative novelty in our faith?

I think that there is room for such creativity, and I think that it is none other than Abraham himself who is the first example in the Torah of innovation and ingenuity within the context of religious service.

In *Parashat Lekh Lekha*, we find God Himself describing Abraham as one who "walks before Me (*hit'halekh lefanai*)" (Gen. 17:1). Our sages contrast this description of Abraham with an earlier description of Noah. There we read, "Noah walked with God (*et haElokim*)" (Gen. 6:9). Noah walked *with* God, whereas Abraham walked *before* Him.

Noah walked *with* God and required divine support to live his religious life. He was not able to walk *before* God. He could not take the initiative and strike out on his own. He needed to be certain of God's will before he could act.

Abraham, on the other hand, walked *before* God. He stepped out on his own and risked acting independently and creatively. He was confident in his own religious judgment and did not require God's prior approval for all of his actions. Indeed, he dared to challenge God's own judgment.

Thus, we never find Noah speaking out in defense of his generation, nor does he pray for their salvation. Abraham, on the contrary, forcefully defends sinful Sodom and Gomorrah and even prays for his adversaries.

It can be said that Moses too walked *before* God. He broke the tablets on his own initiative, and according to our sages, added a day to God's own timetable for giving the Torah. In both cases, we are told that the Lord congratulated him for his bold creative actions.

I remember reading an anecdote about Rabbi Abraham Isaac Kook, the first chief rabbi of the Land of Israel, that illustrates his preference for the creative genius over the conformist. Rav Kook once had to decide a halakhic issue by resolving a disagreement between two great talmudic authorities. The dispute was between the author of

Darkhei Teshuva, a monumental anthology of halakhic dicta, and the Maharsham, who authored many volumes in response to questions arising from the circumstances of new technological inventions.

Rav Kook decided in favor of the Maharsham over the *Darkhei Teshuva.* He argued that whereas the latter was a *gaon me'asef,* a genius at recording the opinions of others, the former was a *gaon yotzer,* an inventive genius. The creative authority trumped the expert anthologist.

One of the areas of psychology that has always fascinated me has been the research on the phenomenon of human creativity. One line of that research suggests that there are two modes of thought of which we are all capable, although some of us are better at one and some are better at the other.

There are those of us who are convergent thinkers. Our ideas connect and ultimately merge with the ideas of our predecessors and peers. Others think divergently and their ideas veer from earlier norms and carve out new paths and different solutions.

The contrast between Abraham and Noah suggests that, although Abraham was the model of ultimate obedience to God's will, he nevertheless was capable of divergent thinking. He was able to walk *before* God. Noah, however, could only think convergently and, figuratively speaking, needed to hold God's hand.

It is important to realize that creativity is not at odds with spirituality, nor with faithful adherence to meticulous religious observance. We must not be afraid of our own powers of creative thinking.

The realization that there is a place for creativity in the worship of the Almighty is especially essential for those who are responsible for the curricula of our educational institutions. They must be on guard never to stifle the wonderful creative impulses that typify youth. They must cultivate those impulses and allow for their expression within our tradition. And we must allow for the development of contemporary Abrahams and not be satisfied to raise a generation of mere Noahs.

Parashat Lekh Lekha

The Reunion

I have always found *Parashat Lekh Lekha* especially inspiring and instructive. It is in this *parasha* that we are told the story of Abraham's *aliya*, of his journey to the Holy Land. What amazes me, and what readers of the Bible over the millennia have found equally amazing, is the total faith in God that Abraham demonstrated by embarking upon this journey.

God tells Abraham to leave his land, his birthplace, and his family. As if that were not a sufficient challenge, God does not even tell him where he is going. He simply says, "Go!" Abraham does not ask where, but is told, "to the land that I will show you."

Why? How? These questions do not even occur to Abraham. He does not ask, nor does the Almighty inform him, about the objective for uprooting himself from his familiar surroundings and intimate personal relationships. Abraham is given the assurance of blessed success, but he is not given a hint as to why he has to venture off into an unknown land and uncertain future in order to achieve this blessing. The question the reader asks, "Why could he not achieve these divine blessings in his own homeland?" is a question that Abraham himself never asks.

I used to think that Abraham was the model of perfect faith whom we ourselves could take as an inspiration, but whose achievements we could never hope to match in our own lives. That is, I used to think that way until…the reunion.

Let me tell you how that reunion came about. In recent years, my wife and I have been privileged to visit Israel frequently, for relatively long periods of time. During these visits, we inevitably encounter old friends, many of whom moved to Israel thirty or forty, and in some cases, even fifty years ago.

One Sunday morning while I was drinking coffee at my favorite Jerusalem sidewalk café, a gentleman sat down at the table next to mine and sipped his coffee while remaining engrossed in a book. I am always curious as to what other people are reading, so I could not resist the urge to peek at the cover of his book in order to ascertain its title. Lo and behold, it turned out to be one of my personal favorites, a lesser known work on the fine points of the Hebrew language by the eighteenth-century philosopher, poet, and mystic Moshe Haim Luzzatto, known by the initials of his name as the Ramḥal.

The fellow was immersed in his reading, but I rudely interrupted his concentration by commenting that I knew that book and that I became familiar with it as a very young man. He lifted his eyes from the page, looked at me carefully, and said, "I know. You and I discovered it together on one of our frequent forays into that old bookstore on the Lower East Side of Manhattan!"

I didn't recognize *him*, but he sure recognized *me*. He was Bernie back then, a classmate in our yeshiva who had moved to Israel soon after we both received rabbinic ordination. He was now Baruch.

A long conversation ensued, during which we caught up with each other's lives and with the whereabouts of other old friends who had moved to Israel long ago. It was his idea to organize the reunion.

We met several weeks later. There were five of them, and I was the only "American." Two of them had gone to Israel to study immediately after high school and never returned to the United States. The other three had made *aliya* a bit later, in their early twenties, after college and after marriage.

We spent quite a few hours together reminiscing about the "good old days," laughing hilariously, and reliving the pranks of our youth. Eventually, the conversation became quite serious as they each in turn described their decisions to leave "their land, birthplace, and house of their fathers," to come to Israel and create new lives there.

The five of them described five unique stories about their journeys. Two had become quite prominent rabbis and authors of noteworthy scholarly works. One had been a musician and now earned his living by giving music lessons to retired adults. One was a physician, himself now retired and, coincidentally, taking music lessons from our mutual friend. The fifth was a very successful businessman who was able to take advantage of the housing construction boom in Tel Aviv.

These were very different personalities with very different stories to tell. But they had one story in common. Like Abraham, but at a much younger age than Abraham, they each heard God's call, "Go forth from your native land and from your father's house to the land that I will show you."

Unlike Abraham, they knew where they were going. But as one of them put it, "We knew where we were going but did not know what we were getting into."

Unlike Abraham, they had no divine assurances that they would be blessed. But they each now felt that they had been abundantly blessed. They each had left family behind, in some cases, never again to see their own parents. But in every case, they built new families, large and diverse, and they all had grandchildren in the Israeli army at the time of this reunion.

Not one of them had the slightest regret about his decision and they all gently teased me for not having chosen the path in life that they courageously chose. I must confess to some guilt and shame, and not a little envy, that I felt in their company that evening.

However, those feelings were outweighed by the admiration and respect I felt for them, and for all the many others who, to this very day, follow in the footsteps of Abraham and Sarah and take seriously the words of God, which open *Parashat Lekh Lekha*, "Go forth, and you shall be a blessing."

Ancestral Decisions

Most people do not give much thought to their ancestral origins, but some do, and I am one of them. I often wonder about my grandparents and their grandparents. Who were they? What was their world like? Most of all, I wonder about the decisions that they made and whether those decisions had any bearing upon my life. Suppose they had made different decisions. Would my life be any different? Would I even be here to wonder?

In my case, I knew all my grandparents and even one great-grandmother. I know a little bit about some of my other great-grandparents, including the man after whom I was named. His name was Tzvi Hersh Kriegel, and I will always remember the portrait of him in a derby hat and long red beard, prominently adorning the dining room wall in my grandparents' home.

Somewhere back in the late nineteenth century, he made a decision. I know nothing of the details of that decision. He chose to leave the Eastern European *shtetl* where he was born and raised, and made his way to the United States. Because of that decision, he and his descendants escaped the fate of most of the rest of his family. Had he not made that decision, I myself would have been one of the millions of Hitler's victims. I would not be sitting at my desk writing this book.

Many of my other forebears, and many of yours, dear reader, made similar decisions in their lives that determined the futures of their children and grandchildren. Reflecting upon this fact leads to many important life lessons, including the need to take one's own decisions very seriously.

In my case, I cannot go back more than three generations, so I'm not familiar with the decisions made by my ancestors much before the late nineteenth century. Others, like my wife Chavi, routinely refer to ancestors who lived in the eighteenth century and even earlier. They are still influenced by decisions made by those who came before them more than two centuries ago.

It remains true, however, that all Jewish people can trace their ancestry much further back than a couple of centuries. I am reminded of the retort uttered by the late Lubavitcher Rebbe to a disciple who proudly reported that he was tutoring several "Jews with no Jewish background." The Rebbe insisted that there was no such thing. "Those Jews," he exclaimed, "have the same Jewish background as you do. They are all children of Abraham and Sarah."

Indeed, we are all children of Abraham and Sarah, and we remain influenced by the consequences of their decisions. Study the weekly Torah portions and you will discover the extent to which we remain influenced by the decisions made by our patriarchs and matriarchs millennia ago.

Parashat Lekh Lekha (Gen. 12:1–17:27), begins with one such decision: Abraham and Sarah's resolve to leave their "native land and father's house" and proceed to the "land that I will show you," the land of Canaan. That decision, which reverberated across the generations, still sustains our commitment to the Holy Land.

There are some lesser-known decisions made by Abraham in *Parashat Lekh Lekha*. The first was his decision to personally intervene in a war conducted by four great world powers against five other kingdoms. What prompted Abraham to do so was the report that his kinsman, Lot, was taken captive by the invaders. Unlike some contemporary world leaders, Abraham immediately sprang into action.

Not having access to jet fighters and long range missiles, he "mustered his retainers (*ḥanikhav*)." He enlisted the help of 318 of those who had been "born into his household," raised and educated by him. He made the decision to draft his disciples into military service.

Was that a good decision? Not according to one view in the Talmud:

> Rabbi Avahu said in the name of Rabbi Elazar: Why was Abraham punished so that his children were enslaved in Egypt for 210 years? Because he used Torah scholars as his army! (Tractate Nedarim 32a)

In Abraham's judgment, enlisting 318 of his disciples to help rescue innocent victims was a no-brainer. For Rabbi Avahu, however, Abraham's decision was a disaster of historical proportions. There is no doubt that Abraham's decision remains relevant down to this very day, perhaps even more urgently than ever before.

The *parasha* continues with the narrative that describes the offer of the king of Sodom – whom Abraham defended and who had Abraham to thank for his survival – to "give me the persons, and take the booty for yourself." Abraham, ever meticulously ethical, declines the booty but also yields the persons to the king of Sodom.

A wise decision? Not according to another opinion in that talmudic passage:

> Rabbi Yoḥanan said that [Abraham's children were eventually enslaved in Egypt] because he impeded the ability of those persons from taking refuge under the wings of the *Shekhina* [the Divine Presence]. That is, had Abraham insisted that the king of Sodom yield those "persons" to Abraham's care, they would eventually have converted to Abraham's monotheistic way of life.

Abraham had a dilemma. Was he to insist on his ethical principles and take no reward whatsoever, not persons and not booty, from the king of Sodom? Or should he have engaged in spiritual outreach and taken those prisoners into his own household? For Abraham, his ethical principles trumped his goal of encouraging pagans to convert to monotheism. For Rabbi Yoḥanan, on the other hand, Abraham missed a critical opportunity. This is yet another of Abraham's decisions with great implications for us today.

We are all children of Abraham and Sarah. In so many ways, their dilemmas remain our dilemmas. Rabbi Avahu and Rabbi Yoḥanan taught us that we cannot merely emulate their choices. We must assess their decisions, determine their validity, and then consider the extent to which our circumstances conform to theirs.

As we study the *parasha* each week, we must remember that we are not just reading Bible stories. We are studying ancestral decisions, which continue to affect our daily lives in an uncanny way.

Parashat Vayera

Abraham the Teacher

I love to teach teachers. I've had a number of opportunities in my career to lead workshops designed to enhance the skills of classroom teachers. Some of the most powerful learning experiences that I've had have occurred during such workshops.

One of the techniques that I use is to ask the participants, all teachers themselves, to close their eyes and visualize their own favorite teacher. After they have "locked in" that image, I ask them to recall the most important lesson they learned from that teacher.

Invariably, a teacher of long ago surfaces in the mind's eye of the workshop members and the lesson that they remember is often surprising to them. When we discuss what this experiment in imagery provokes, most of the participants express the gratitude they have now for lessons they learned long ago. For you see, a lesson that lasts for many years is a valuable lesson, indeed, and one to cherish and for which to be thankful.

In *Parashat Vayera*, we read about a most remarkable man, Abraham. This man had many accomplishments. He rescued his captive nephew, he brought to the world the concept of monotheism, he introduced the practice of hospitality, and he stood up to God Himself in defense of the cause of justice.

Yet, of all these accomplishments, we are told that his most outstanding quality, the one for which he found favor in the eyes of God, was his capacity to teach others, and to teach others the lessons that would last them a lifetime, "For I have singled him out, that he may instruct his children and his posterity to keep the way of the Lord by doing what is just and right" (Gen. 18:19, following Rashi's interpretation).

Of all the reasons to single out and choose Abraham, the Almighty selects his ability to leave a lasting lesson as the greatest of Abraham's many virtues. The text stresses "*aharav*," a *lasting* lesson. The lessons we learn for a lifetime are the true essence of education.

The Hebrew word *ḥinukh* is found in *Parashat Veyera* for the first time. Rashi, the greatest of the rabbinical commentaries, defines the term as setting in motion a process that will last a long time. And that is what education is all about from a Jewish point of view. It is the initiation of a lifelong process.

Plato, in his masterwork *The Republic*, which is arguably the earliest treatise on the subject of education, writes, "The direction in which education starts a man will determine his future life." How well these words capture the concept of education that is expressed in Jewish sources!

Unlike Plato, however, who thought that only the elite could be teachers, Judaism teaches that every person is a teacher. Every one of us can leave a lasting impact upon another, and most of us, for better or worse, do.

I encourage you, dear reader, to reflect upon some of the important lessons you have learned in your life. I wager that you will find that these lessons go back a long way, and that they were taught to you not only by formal classroom teachers, but by men and women from all walks of life.

Personally, I remember lessons of appreciating authenticity taught to me by my father, of blessed memory. And I remember lessons about the importance of time management from a supervisor in the school system where I once served as a psychologist. I remember learning to enjoy reading from my seventh-grade teacher, and I learned to take myself seriously from my Talmud teacher in my early college years.

There is nothing more rewarding to a teacher, rabbi, or parent than encountering a student or child, now grown, to be told how they remember something said long ago, perhaps in passing. Discovering that we have influenced another in a positive manner is one of the most pleasing of life's experiences.

A man who was one of the most perceptive of American educators, John Dewey, once said, "Education is not preparation for life; education is life itself." Dewey was on to something, but he too was preceded in this insight by the Jewish sages who taught that Torah study is the essence of life, and that, as Maimonides put it, "For the wise, a life without learning is no life at all."

Abraham and Sarah were the first Jews, not just because they happened to be born earlier than the rest of us. They were the first Jews because teaching others was their life's mission. They modeled lives of kindness, empathy, justice, and humility. The faithful Jew follows in their footsteps.

Rabbi Joseph H. Hertz, the late chief rabbi of the British Empire, whose commentary on the Bible I commend to each of you, looks upon the verse quoted above as follows, "It is a sacred duty of the Jew to transmit his heritage to his children after him...so that they walk in the way of the Lord and live lives of probity and goodness."

All Jewish parents, indeed every Jew, must primarily be a teacher. The eternal values of our faith are the lessons he or she must teach.

Parashat Vayera

Hospitality Before Heaven

H

e was an old man, frail, tired, and bereaved. News of Hitler's advancing army preoccupied him, and he was overwhelmed, if not broken, by the requests for advice he was receiving from hundreds of troubled Jews. Indeed, he may have already sensed that he had only months to live. His name was Rabbi Haim Ozer Grodzenski, and he was universally acknowledged to be the world's leading talmudic scholar. He lived in the city of Vilna, and the time was late 1939.

The person who told me the story was then a young man, barely twenty years old. He was himself a refugee, along with his fellow yeshiva students. He found himself in the neighborhood of Rabbi Grodzenski's residence during the Sukkot holiday. He decided he would attempt to visit the rabbi, although he knew that he might not be granted an audience.

How surprised he was to find the rabbi alone, studying and writing. The rabbi welcomed him, inquired about his welfare, and invited the visitor to join him in a light lunch. The rabbi told him that because of his age and physical weakness, he deemed himself to be exempt from the requirement to eat in the sukka. He considered himself a *mitzta'er,* one whose physical discomfort freed him from the sukka requirement.

"But you," the rabbi continued, "are a young man and reasonably healthy. Therefore, take this plate of food down to the sukka in the courtyard, and excuse me for not being able to join you."

The young man did so, but soon, sitting in the sukka by himself, was surprised to hear the old rabbi slowly making his way down the many steps from his apartment to join him in the sukka.

"You may wonder why I am joining you," exclaimed the old rabbi. "It is because although a *mitzta'er,* one who is in great discomfort, is exempt from the mitzva of sukka, he is not exempt from the mitzva of hospitality (*hakhnasat orḥim*)."

This anecdote underscores the importance of the mitzva of hospitality and illustrates the fact that even great physical discomfort does not excuse a person from properly receiving and entertaining his guests.

Of course the biblical basis for Rabbi Grodzenski's teaching is to be found in *Parashat Vayera.* In the opening verses, we find that Abraham, despite the fact that he was recovering from his recent circumcision, exerts himself to welcome a small group of wayfarers and tends to their needs with exquisite care. Abraham is our model for the important mitzva of welcoming strangers and seeing to it that they are greeted hospitably.

The seventeenth-century sage Rabbi Isaiah Horowitz, known as the *Shelah HaKadosh,* points out that performance of this mitzva helps us realize that we are all wanderers and merely transient guests in the Almighty's world. We pray that He treats us hospitably during our sojourn in His world, and to earn such treatment, we are sensitive to the physical and emotional requirements of our own guests.

Our sages discovered an even deeper dimension to Abraham's hospitality. The third verse in our *parasha* reads, "And he said, 'My lord, if I have found favor in your eyes, pass not away from your servant.'" The simple reading of this verse is that Abraham is speaking to one of his guests whom he refers to as "my lord."

Another reading, a startlingly provocative one, suggests that Abraham is addressing the Almighty Himself, and that the word "lord" should be spelled with an uppercase "L." According to this interpretation, Abraham is asking that the Lord Himself excuse him and wait for him while he tends to his guests.

The Talmud derives from the story that, "Welcoming one's guests is a bigger mitzva then welcoming the *Shekhina*."

Commentaries throughout the ages have questioned whether it is indeed legitimate for one to abandon his rendezvous with God in order to attend to the needs of mere human beings. Is it right for one to interrupt his dialogue with the Almighty to perform the mitzva of hospitality?

There is a rich literature of responses to this question. One approach is to understand that it is not so much that hospitality trumps the experience of communication with the *Shekhina*; rather, it is that the way to earn such an exalted spiritual experience is by practicing hospitality. One does not achieve a spiritual experience through meditation and prayer. One achieves true spirituality by painstakingly attending to the needs of others.

This is why we give some charity, perhaps even just a few pennies, prior to engaging in prayer. The Talmud suggests that in order to earn the right to address God in prayer, one must first demonstrate that he is not unaware of his obligations to his fellow man. First alms, then prayer. First hospitality, and only then can one come into the Divine Presence.

How important it is that we learn the lesson of religious priorities. Never can we place our spiritual longings above our obligations to our fellow human beings. This is the lesson taught to us so long ago by our forefather, Abraham, when he turned away from God in order to practice the mitzva of *hakhnasat orḥim*.

Parashat Vayera

An Inn and an Orchard

I read the story quite some time ago. It was told by a young woman who boarded an airplane early one winter Friday morning. She was on her way to Chicago from New York to spend a weekend there with friends. She made herself comfortable in her seat, prepared some reading material, and was confident that the plane would take off more or less on time and that she would arrive at her destination in little more than an hour.

But that was not to be. Instead, she experienced what all "frequent flyers" are familiar with – unanticipated delays. At first, the pilot assured the passengers that the delays would be brief and that they would soon be on their way. However, time dragged on, and the young woman, as well as the rest of the passengers, became a bit concerned. They all had appointments in Chicago, or flight connections to make, or were simply upset about the prospect of being strapped into an uncomfortable seat for a longer period of time than expected.

For some of the passengers, however, and our young woman was among them, there was a "higher" concern. It was a short Friday and sundown was early, only six or seven hours away. Would they make it to Chicago in time to reach their ultimate destinations before Shabbat?

The young woman who related the story described the scene. At first, the several Jews aboard the plane took no notice of each other, each minding his or her own business. However, as the delay became more protracted, and the possibility of being stranded became more real, the Jews present began to converse with each other and share their anxieties.

Finally the plane took off, but the worries of the Sabbath observers were not over. About halfway through the flight, the pilot announced that they would not be able to land in Chicago after all. Instead, they were being diverted to Milwaukee.

By this time, there were little more than three hours until sundown. The group of Sabbath observers huddled in the back of the plane, and two of them assured the others, and there were ten or twelve others, that they knew several people in Milwaukee who could host them for Shabbat if they would land in the Milwaukee airport in time.

They asked the crew if they could somehow call ahead and contact their acquaintances in Milwaukee. That was done and the Milwaukee friends assured the group that they would not only put them up and feed them well, but they would have a van at the airport ready to speed them to their Shabbat accommodations.

The young woman had been sitting next to a non-Jewish couple who couldn't help but eavesdrop upon the entire conversation and the arrangements that ten passengers were making to spend a weekend with total strangers. They expressed their astonishment to the young woman, saying, "Are you all going to spend an entire weekend with people you don't know? And why would they put all of you up? Are you sure this is not some kind of a trap? Will you be safe?"

The young woman reassured her co-passengers with this one brief statement, "That's Jewish hospitality."

You, dear reader, are surely familiar with Jewish hospitality, and can anticipate the happy ending of the story. The plane landed with barely an hour to spare, the van appeared, the group was rushed to the Jewish neighborhood, everyone had comfortable accommodations, and the delicious Shabbat meals were especially lively as the group played

Jewish geography and learned about the many connections they had
with each other.

But you may want to know more about what the young woman
told her non-Jewish companions, expanding upon the concept of Jewish
hospitality. She began by explaining to them that Jews read selections
from the Bible in the synagogue each Sabbath. She told them that the
selection that would be read the next day was Genesis 18:1-22:24. She
introduced them to the vocabulary of the weekly Torah portion and
informed them that the name of that week's portion was *Parashat Vayera*.

She went on to briefly introduce them to the inspiring personality of Abraham, our forefather. But time was running out, and she could
not even begin to narrate the stories in this Torah portion that describe
Abraham's hospitality.

She told them that Abraham was the model for hospitality that
all Jews try to emulate, and she shared with them one brief verse, which
appears toward the end of the *parasha*: "Abraham planted a tamarisk
at Beersheba, and invoked there the name of the Lord, the Everlasting
God" (Gen. 21:33).

Of course she had to define "tamarisk," which she did by telling
them that it was a small tree or shrub. But then she went on to relate
the following homily to them:

> I had a teacher at the Jewish parochial school I attended. He
> pointed out to us that the Hebrew word for tamarisk is *aishel*.
> The rabbis of old disputed the meaning of *aishel*. Some said that
> it meant an orchard. But others contended that it meant a hostel,
> an inn. Our teacher shared with us the deeper meaning of this
> dispute, as taught by a much more contemporary rabbi, Solomon
> Joseph Zevin.
>
> Rabbi Zevin held that *orchard* and *inn* represent the two
> qualities that comprise hospitality. The orchard symbolizes life,
> growth, nurturance, and regeneration. This is the emotional
> component of hospitality, the provision of sustenance, of care
> and compassion, and when necessary, of sympathy and healing.
> The other quality is symbolized by the inn – a structure, solid,
> protective, safe, and secure. The hospitable person, and Abraham

was the archetype of such a person, offers his guest both the life-giving sustenance provided by the orchard and the sense of security provided by the home, by the inn.

The two non-Jewish passengers thanked the young woman for the lesson. They added, however, the following remarks:

We too study the Bible and we remember that Abraham was called "the father of the multitude of nations." He modeled hospitality for all mankind. Nevertheless, we concede that there is something special about the Jewish hospitality that we are now witnessing and that you are apparently about to experience. The truly hospitable person opens his or her home even to the total stranger – so much so that total strangers can rely upon that hospitality. You are truly a blessed people, and although we will never meet your hosts, we ask that you share with them our profound admiration.

When the young woman boarded that airplane, she expected a very ordinary experience. Instead, she was blessed with the opportunity not only to benefit from Jewish hospitality, but also to share the lessons of hospitality with others in a way that achieved that highest of all spiritual objectives, a "sanctification of the name of God," a "*kiddush Hashem.*"

Parashat Vayera

Optimism Pays

I t may not have been the first day I reported to my new job, but it was not many days later that I first met Richard Hood. I had joined a team of new PhDs, some trained as psychologists and some as educators, whose assignment it was to breathe new life into a very old-fashioned, one might even say backward, school system in suburban Washington, DC.

It was a rapidly changing community that had been semi-rural up until the late 1960s. At the time I joined the school system advisory staff as senior school psychologist, the area was becoming much more diverse. On the one hand, high-level government employees were beginning to move there, finding the real estate prices more attractive than the neighboring counties. But at the same time, there were a number of areas that were depressed socio-economically and were spillovers from the teeming African-American ghettoes of our nation's capital. It was not long before that Washington had experienced the riots of 1968.

I have many stories to tell about the years I served in that environment. But I want to focus upon the personality of this one colleague, Richard Hood, a tall, burly man in his early thirties with a Southern drawl that originated in small-town Mississippi. His politics were liberal; he was open-minded, tolerant, and most empathic. But he was a cynic. His favorite word was "irredeemable." "This school system is irredeemable," he would say. "The government is irredeemable." "Mankind is irredeemable." "The world is irredeemable." His attitude to life was best expressed in the sign that hung above his desk, "Pessimism Pays."

He felt that people were essentially evil, that a life of pain and frustration awaited us all, and that man was fated to suffer. His spiritual mentor was the philosopher Arthur Schopenhauer, whose writings have been described as the "Bible of pessimism."

Richard had a bone to pick with Western culture, child-rearing, and public education. He felt that we deceive our children into believing that the world is basically a benign and safe environment, that success can be achieved by hard work, and that good health is guaranteed by clean living. He maintained that "we indoctrinate our youth into the belief that the world is a rose-garden, whereas in reality it is a snake pit."

I had long one-on-one discussions with him because he was fascinated by Jews and Judaism. In those discussions, he came to believe that "you Jews are the worst of all. You just emerged from the hell of the Holocaust and you still tell your children that all will be well if they just cling to your tradition."

I think of Richard often, and was sad to learn that he passed away several years ago after having returned to his Mississippi origins upon his retirement from a university teaching post. I especially remember him whenever we read *Parashat Vayera* (Gen. 18:1–22:24).

Why *Vayera*? Because it is in *Parashat Vayera* that we read the story of the *Akeda*, of Abraham's obedience to God's command that he bind his son, Isaac, upon a mountain-top altar, and offer him as a human sacrifice to the Lord. This is surely one of the most troubling passages in the entire Bible, and traditional Jewish commentaries, as well as great secular philosophers, have struggled to understand it. How could Abraham, who so valued human life that he stood up to God Himself to plead the case of wicked Sodom and Gomorrah, unhesitatingly obey God's command that he slay his own son?

That is not a question I will even attempt to address within the limits of this chapter, but another aspect of the story has always troubled me. At the beginning of the story, Abraham was unaware of its happy ending. He did not know that at the last moment, an angel would order him to desist from sacrificing his son. As far as he knew, a terrible, unspeakable tragedy was about to unfold. But in his words to the servants who accompanied him, he was completely reassuring and gave them no inkling of the catastrophe that was about to occur, "You stay here with the donkey. The boy and I will go up there; we will worship and we will return to you."

And he gave Isaac no hint about the fate that awaited him. Did he not owe the lad a glimpse of his imminent death, a chance to prepare himself to meet his Maker? Was it not the height of duplicity for Abraham to reassure his son that all would be well? I could just hear Richard ask these piercing questions. Although to my recollection he and I never discussed the Bible, he was raised as a Southern Baptist and surely knew the story of the Binding of Isaac.

To me, the answer to these questions lies in this phrase, repeated twice in the narrative, for emphasis, "And the two of them walked on together." Abraham conveyed to Isaac this message, "I am with you. I will hold your hand. I will be there for you despite the horror that awaits us both." This is the attitude that Jewish parents have conveyed to their children throughout all of the tragedies of Jewish history. Yes, there are persecutions and pogroms and torture and worse. But I will be there with you. I will be close to you.

This is one of the themes of so many of the Psalms. Rarely is the Psalmist assured that "everything will be all right." More often, he is told, "I, God, am with you." I am with you in your exile, in your wanderings, and in your suffering. I am with you in the hell of Auschwitz and Treblinka. The Psalmist asserts, "Though I walk through the valley of the shadow of death, I fear no evil, for You are with me."

The Talmud teaches us that the *Shekhina* is in exile along with us. Most eloquently, Asaf in Psalm 73 expresses the consoling power of the awareness of God's closeness in the most dire of circumstances, "I have been constantly afflicted, each morning brings new punishments...."

Yet I was always with You, You held my right hand.... As for me, nearness to God is good."

Abraham felt that his duty to obey God took priority over the love for his beloved son. That is one central lesson of the story, although it remains a disconcerting lesson for us. But this much we can comprehend: Abraham's behavior reflected reassurance, trust, optimism, and hope. At the end of the story, that hope proved justified.

Richard could never fathom Abraham's lesson. To remain hopeful in the face of threatening doom, to be able to see beyond the dark clouds of fate, to continue to pray even when "the sharp sword dangles over one's neck" – that is Abraham's lesson and that is the Jewish way.

More than just the "Jewish way," this capability is the secret of Jewish survival. It is a secret that we all must learn, especially in our times, when many challenges sadly still beset us. We can be confident that the *Shekhina* is there for us, but we must be sure that we are there for each other.

Parashat Ḥayei Sara

Mourning Sarah

Grief is the most powerful and most painful of human emotions. Yet it is an emotion that few human beings can avoid in their lifetime. We all face loss and we all grieve. Interestingly, the first death of which we read in detail in the Bible is a murder. And the reaction of the murderer is one of denial and ultimately guilt. I speak, of course, of Cain's slaying of Abel. We do not read of Cain's grief, nor do we know at all of the reaction of Abel's parents, Adam and Eve, to his death.

In *Parashat Ḥayei Sara*, for the first time, we learn in detail of the reaction of a surviving relative to the death of a loved one. I speak, of course, of Abraham and his response to the death of his wife, Sarah.

Much has been written about the psychology of the emotion of grief. It is a complex emotion and is a very long, sometimes life-long, process. It seems that there are at least two components to normal grief. There is an emotional component, consisting of feelings of great sadness and pervasive melancholy. There is also an intellectual component, as the mourner seeks to make some sense of his or her loss and to find purpose and meaning in the death of the loved one, to thus be able to move on in life.

So it is not surprising that when Abraham learned of Sarah's death, and he apparently was not in the vicinity of where she died, he came rushing to make the arrangements for her burial.

We read that he "came to eulogize Sarah and to cry for her." Note the two components of his response. Crying, expressing feelings of loss through sobs and tears (*bekhi*), was one component. The other component was much more cerebral and consisted of a well-thought-out and carefully composed eulogy (*hesped*).

Abraham honored Sarah with his heart – his feelings, but also with his head – with his mind and intellect. Both aspects of this dual response are necessary. Over the first, the emotional aspect, we have little control. Feelings burst forth even when we try to suppress them. But the second aspect, the reasoned and verbally expressed eulogy, is one over which we have great control. We can plan intentionally what we will say and what we won't say in a eulogy.

There is a beautiful eulogy in the homiletic writings of the great eighteenth-century sage, Rabbi Yehezkel Landau, author of the authoritative halakhic work, the *Noda BiYehuda*. In that eulogy, Rabbi Landau speaks about his wife, Leeba, and compares her to the matriarch Sarah.

He notes that in our text, Abraham cries "for her," the pronoun "her" being used instead of the proper name. However, he "eulogizes Sarah." No pronoun here, but her personal name – the name by which she was known to him and to all of her acquaintances.

Rabbi Landau insists that Abraham was setting an example for all eulogies to follow, for all time and eternity. A eulogy must be specific and speak in detail about the particular and unique qualities of the deceased. One should not just eulogize "her," but must eulogize "Sarah." Those listening to the eulogy must come away with a better sense of who the deceased was, and with some details about what made the deceased special.

Too often at funerals, we hear clergymen make very impersonal remarks about death and eternity, and they do not leave us with even an impression of the biographical details and significance of the life that was just lost.

Abraham set the tone for a proper eulogy. He eulogized the Sarah that he knew, not some abstract description that could fit any woman, but an exquisitely detailed portrait of the real Sarah, from the perspective of one who shared his life with her.

There is so much that careful students of Torah have learned from the lives of Abraham and Sarah. One lesson that I personally cherish is the lesson of Abraham's eulogy for his life's companion. The actual words of this eulogy are not recorded, but the message is clear. It was not an anonymous "her" that he mourned, but a real, flesh and blood, deeply beloved life-long spouse, Sarah.

Parashat Ḥayei Sara

To Eulogize and To Weep

Kindergarten children are delightfully oblivious to the distinction between what adults call reality and the imaginary world. For these young children, there is no difference between the people in their actual lives and the people they learn about in the stories they hear.

For most adults, the heroes of the Bible stories are historical figures, and although they exist in our imagination, we know that they are long gone. These heroes and heroines, however, are as real to kindergartners as their parents and siblings.

This hit home for me many years ago when my eldest daughter was a kindergarten student. She is now herself a grandmother, so that tells you just how long ago this was.

As all children in a Jewish religious kindergarten, she had heard many stories about our matriarch Sarah. She knew about Sarah's journey to the Promised Land, of her trials and tribulations in Egypt, of the fact that she was barren, and of the joy she experienced with the birth of Isaac.

On the Friday before the Shabbat of *Parashat Ḥayei Sara*, she came home from school distraught, with tears flowing down her little cheeks. "Mommy, Daddy," she cried. "Did you hear? Sarah died, Sarah died!" She was in the grips of a sadness very close to real grief; for Sarah had become a living figure for her, much to the credit of the teacher who told her Sarah's story. Few of us adults will exhibit emotion when we read of Sarah's demise, but I wager there are numerous kindergarten age boys and girls in Jewish schools who will shed tears.

For those of us who study the Torah portion weekly, death and dying are not unfamiliar. From the first human being who died, ironically through murder, until the near death of Isaac at the *Akeda*, the Bible has reported dozens of deaths to us.

But there is something especially poignant and moving about Sarah's death, even to us jaded adults. This is partly because, for the first time in the Bible, we have the report of another person's reaction to the death of a loved one. We read of a bereaved Abraham, a loving husband who comes "to eulogize Sarah and to cry for her" (Gen. 23:2). For the first time, we learn of the human capacity to express emotions through eulogy.

The Talmud has a fascinating discussion over the nature of eulogy. "Is a eulogy designed to benefit the dead," asks the Talmud, "or is it for the benefit of the living survivors, the mourners?"

The Talmud has its own conclusion, but there can be no doubt that, from a psychological perspective, the eulogy does both. It honors the dead and it provides the mourner with the opportunity to give vent to his grief and to achieve a degree of catharsis. Perhaps this is why Abraham both "eulogizes" Sarah and "cries for her." In his "eulogy," he honors her person, her character, and her achievements in life. By "crying for her," he gives voice to his profound sense of the loss of his life's partner.

I can never forget the powerful experience I had long ago in a workshop led by the famed psychologist, Virginia Satir. She asked us to each retreat to a private corner of the large room and to devote a quiet hour to meditate upon, and if we wished, to record in writing, the eulogy that we imagined would be written for us when we died. I remember silently adding to those instructions the words "after 120 years."

This exercise forced us to look deeply within ourselves and to determine what was permanent and worthy in our lives and how we wished to be remembered by others. After a few moments into the exercise, the initial silence was broken by sobs, sighs, and weeping. After that hour, the group gathered, and many shared extremely moving feelings and reported much self-discovery and self-revelation.

I don't recommend this experience to you, dear reader, unless you can do so in the presence of a trusted friend, preferably a person trained in coping with the feelings that can possibly emerge from such an exercise. But I do draw upon the experience I had that day to understand what others go through in the inevitable process of grief and mourning. I do continually go back in my memory to that day to understand myself and to evaluate my own life and its successes and failures, accomplishments, and frustrations.

And I do rely upon the reactions I witnessed and personally underwent that day to understand our patriarch Abraham and his need to both "eulogize Sarah, *and* to cry for her."

Parashat Ḥayei Sara

Spiritual Slavery

I grew up, as I imagine most of you did, believing in the basic principles of democracy. My parents and grandparents deeply appreciated the freedoms that they experienced in the United States. My mother especially raised me to cherish the values of our country. Among the beliefs that I firmly held from as far back as I can remember was the conviction that slavery is evil. I remember being asked by my fourth-grade teacher to write a composition about Abraham Lincoln's statement, "As I would not be a slave, so I would not be a master." When I looked up this quotation, I found that Lincoln continued to say, "This expresses my idea of democracy. Whatever differs from this, to the extent of the difference, is no democracy."

My lifelong belief in the illegitimacy of slavery has been continually tested by the fact that our Torah recognizes a place for slavery in our society. The slave takes such a central place in our halakhic system that Maimonides devotes an entire section of his code of law to the laws of slaves.

It is comforting to those of us for whom slavery is repugnant to learn that the institution of slavery within Jewish law and practice has been obsolete for many centuries. However, slavery as an institution, and slaves as individuals, play a major role in the stories of the Bible. For instance, in *Parashat Ḥayei Sara*, we read of Abraham's slave and of the important mission upon which he was sent, the mission to find a suitable wife for Abraham's son, Isaac.

This slave proves to be quite persistent and ingenious. He may be a slave, but he is not slavish. He is successful in his mission, and he brings back a bride, Rebecca, for Isaac. The Torah tells us this slave's story at great length. Indeed, our rabbis wonder why this story is told over dozens of verses, whereas there are only brief phrases dedicated to important ritual laws. In answer to this question, our rabbis say, "More beautiful is the conversation of the slaves of the patriarchs than is the Torah of their sons." The narrative of this slave is in some way superior to Torah commandments.

The great hasidic rebbe of Gur, Rabbi Yehuda Leib Alter, writes in his masterwork, *Sefat Emet*, that he finds the above statement "wondrous." "How can the slave," he asks, "be superior to the son?" Rabbi Alter led his flock from the 1860s until the early twentieth century, and in his discourses on *Parashat Ḥayei Sara*, he returns to this theme again and again.

He begins by pointing out that there are two modes of religious worship, two types of spiritual experiences. The first mode is that of "the slave," who obeys his Master from a distance, without really understanding Him. But this mode is a preparation for a higher one, in which the relationship is far more intimate, based upon deeper understanding. In this manner, we all begin to worship the Almighty as slaves. And as slaves, we prepare ourselves for the next step, to worship God as His children. This is the meaning, says the *Sefat Emet*, of the rabbinic statement, "More beautiful is the conversation of the slaves of the patriarchs than is the Torah of their sons." More beautiful is the stage of preparation than the stage of achievement.

This approach helps us to understand how our sages can also say, "More beautiful is a moment of repentance and good deeds in this mundane world than is eternal life in the World to Come." The spiritual preparations, which are possible only in this material world, are in some ways superior even to the delights of paradise.

One can take this idea further and come to realize that the six days of the week, with their ordinary concerns of work and profit, are "more beautiful" than even the Sabbath itself. Without the precedent of six days of the profane (*ḥol*), we could not achieve the hallowed (*kodesh*); in this case, the sacred Sabbath.

There is such a profound lesson for all of us in this approach. We seek instant gratification in all of our objectives, even within the realm of spirituality. We all desire spiritual "highs." But the reflections summarized above teach us that we must first go through a long period of servitude, of hard religious work, before we can attain the experiences of true spirituality.

Slaves of the Almighty have a place even in Abraham Lincoln's world, even in a democratic society. We must be servants of God before we can become His children.

Parashat Ḥayei Sara

Better the Servant
than the Student

Y ou can't find decent help these days!" This is a common complaint heard in middle-class homes, particularly in Jewish kitchens during the season of preparations for Passover. Happily, my wife and I have been blessed over the years with some excellent domestic help. Usually, they were African-American women who were not only honest, efficient, and reliable, but also surprisingly knowledgeable about traditional Jewish practices.

I fondly recall a woman named Mildred. She had spent many years working as a maid for an older rabbi in the community. We'll call him Rabbi Rosenkrantz. Although I was but a young rabbi when she began working for us, I had already amassed a considerable library of sacred Jewish books, including some precious antique volumes that I had inherited from my grandfather. Needless to say, I was extremely careful about how those books were handled.

How astonished I was when I returned home late one spring afternoon to find all of my bookshelves empty. In a panic, I began to search the premises and, much to my chagrin, discovered that the books were lying in disarray on a long table in the backyard. Mildred was systemically turning them all upside down and shaking them vigorously. I couldn't contain my disapproval and yelled, "Mildred, what on earth are you doing?"

Mildred gently replied that she was making certain that there was no *hametz* inside any of the books. You see, it was just before Passover and many people carefully inspect their books for breadcrumbs or cookie bits that may have found their way into the holy volumes during the course of the year. I am generally quite careful to avoid bringing any food into close contact with the books I use, but apparently Rabbi Rosenkrantz was much more meticulous about inspecting his books for *hametz* than I was.

When I told Mildred that she really didn't have to do that, she responded, "Rabbi! I am not going to allow a young upstart like you to tell me how to prepare for Passover. I learned about *hametz* from Rabbi Rosenkrantz, and he was old enough to have been your grandfather!"

No question about it. Sometimes a gentile maid can take Jewish customs more seriously than an ordained rabbi. This lesson is not a new one. It can be learned from *Parashat Hayei Sara* (Gen. 23:1–25:18). Eliezer, Abraham's servant, is the hero of the entire chapter 24. The story of his mission to find a wife for his master's son, Isaac, is narrated at length and in great detail. We learn of how Eliezer identified Rebecca as a proper wife for Isaac. Eliezer then reviews the story, at length and in detail, to Rebecca's father Bethuel and brother Laban. Finally, in verse 66, we read that Eliezer retold the story yet again, this time to Isaac himself.

The rabbis see in this repetitive detail an indication of the Almighty's attitude toward Eliezer's words: "The idle conversation of the Patriarchs' servants is more precious than the Torah of their descendants."

A much lesser known but even more impressive illustration of the superiority of a servant's wisdom is to be found in a passage in Talmud, Tractate Moed Katan 17a. There, the story is told of the maidservant of Rabbi Judah the Prince, usually referred to simply as "Rabbi," or "Rebbe."

She once observed a father disciplining his adult son by striking him. She censured the father, convinced that the son might not be able to resist reacting to the provocation by striking his father back. In her judgment, the father was guilty of "placing an obstacle before a blind man." So critical was she of the father's behavior that she placed him under a ban (*nidui*), effectively ex-communicating him. The rabbinical courts of that time let three years pass before they lifted that ban.

The great medieval halakhic authority, Rabbenu Asher, known as "the Rosh," questions the courts' failure to nullify the ban sooner, which was their usual practice in response to bans imposed by non-credentialed individuals. In response, he quotes the words of an earlier authority, Rabbi Avraham ben David, or "the Raavad," who writes, "The rabbis were reluctant to overturn a ban imposed by this woman because of her superior wisdom and piety. They did not consider themselves her equal until they found an outstanding sage who was demonstrably qualified to nullify her ban!"

We can learn quite a few powerful lessons from the story of Rebbe's maidservant; from Eliezer, the servant of Abraham; and yes, even from my family's beloved housekeeper, Mildred. First of all, we can learn the timeless lesson that we must be ready to gain knowledge from every conceivable source. "Who is wise? He who learns from every person" (Avot 4:1). One can learn a great deal even from unexpected sources and must revere every potential source of knowledge, even in matters of religion.

But there is another lesson to be derived from these anecdotes. There are many ways to learn. Some learn by studying books; others learn by listening to lectures. These are important tools to gain knowledge and they cannot be minimized. However, one also learns through experience. If one is fortunate to grow up in a home rich in spirituality, he or she will become knowledgeable about spirituality, even if no explicit lessons were taught. A process of osmosis occurs by which anyone who spends time in an environment in which high ideals are exemplified will absorb those ideals.

The Talmud used the example of Eliezer, and the medieval rabbis used the example of Rebbe's maidservant, to teach us that sometimes what the "mere" servant absorbs from his experience in Abraham's company, or her years of service in the palace of Rabbi Judah the Prince, is of greater value than the erudition of great scholars. Precious indeed is the idle conversation of the servants of the Patriarchs!

What I learned that pre-Passover day so long ago was that the capacity to learn from unexpected sources was not limited to times gone by, or to lofty souls such as the biblical Eliezer, and the unique personage who was Rebbe's maidservant.

Even Mildred, who passed away long ago, had a lot to teach me. She taught me about the importance of the scrupulous observance of Jewish customs, particularly those that have to do with Passover. She taught me that, even with regard to matters of religious observance, one can learn a great deal from unexpected sources. Above all, she taught me a lesson about humility. That's a lesson that requires lifelong review. Thank you, Mildred.

Parashat Toledot

Disillusionment

Disillusionment. I first learned about it on a park bench on the Lower East Side of Manhattan where I attended high school. I learned about it from three old gentlemen, each affected differently by disillusionment, and each with a different lesson to teach.

Some of my classmates and I frequented that park daily for a round or two of basketball. Few of us noted the shabby elderly trio who joined each other on a park bench near where we played and engaged in heated conversation in Yiddish and in another language that we later learned was Russian.

A friend and I decided one morning to inquire of these gentlemen as to who they were and as to the topic that so excited them. They told us that they were Mensheviks and expected that we were familiar with that term. We weren't, but they soon enough educated us about the Russian Revolution and about a group of early communists who split from Lenin and the Bolsheviks, who were known as the Mensheviks, the Russian word for minority. After the Russian Revolution in 1917, this minority found itself in grave danger. Many, including the park bench companions, emigrated from Russia in the early 1920s. These three settled in the United States, in New York City, on the Lower East Side.

We listened for several weeks to their magnetic story of youthful dreams and grand plans for changing the world. They helped overthrow the Czar and looked forward to a new order of freedom, peace, and total economic equality.

But they became disillusioned. Their youthful dreams came to naught and the utopia they envisioned turned out to be nightmarish. One of them never gave up on the dream, and told us that he was certain that the day would soon come when he could return to Russia and help lead the ultimate reform. Another, darkly depressed, had turned to alcohol and was only sober in the early morning. And the third, abandoned his former beliefs and became, of all things, a hasidic Jew. Each experienced disillusionment and each dealt with it in his own unique way.

Many years later, I became inspired by another story of disillusionment, the story of Rabbi Yissachar Teichtal, martyred by the Nazis. This man was a disciple of one of the most virulently anti-Zionist pre-World War II Jewish leaders. He was raised to think that Zionism was equal to apostasy and that participating in the creation of a Jewish State was a terrible sin.

When World War II broke out, Rabbi Teichtal was witness to all the horrors of the Holocaust. He found himself questioning and eventually re-examining his earlier beliefs and rejected them. Instead, he developed the contrary perspective, namely, that the failure to adopt Zionism and build a Jewish State was the root cause of the suffering of the Jewish people. Rabbi Teichtal's erudite treatise, *Em HaBanim Semayha,* is a fascinating and rare example of a courageous retraction of an earlier held worldview, a public confession of disillusionment.

In *Parashat Toledot,* we learn of the disillusionment of none other than the patriarch Isaac who labored under the lifelong illusion that his son Esau was righteous and good. He was ready to bestow his blessings upon Esau and not upon Jacob.

Jacob, disguised as Esau, ultimately received those blessings. When Esau appears and asks for those blessings, Isaac realizes that the Divine Hand has intervened and that he has been wrong all along in considering Esau to be the son who deserved those blessings. He is, quite literally, disillusioned.

He is stunned to learn that he has been mistaken all along in his assessment of this son, and his shock is expressed in Genesis 27:33 with these powerful words, "And Isaac trembled an exceedingly great trembling." The great trembling of a disillusioned father.

How apt and poignant is Rashi's comment here, "He saw the gates of Hell open before him." It is indeed hellish to have one's dreams shattered and to have to re-examine the fundamental assumptions that one has made in life. Yet, in ways significant and trivial, we are all occasionally called upon to do so.

Knowing that even Isaac was proven to be in error about the assumptions he made, and that he was dramatically confronted with his mistake, can be of some solace to us all. It is difficult and painful to garner the courage to turn our disillusionment to advantage and start life again under new assumptions. But it is a choice we are inevitably called upon to make.

Parashat Toledot

Friday Night with Grandpa

My paternal grandfather, Chaim Yitzchak Weinreb, was an old-school Jew, with roots in the region of eastern Poland known as Galicia. He had studied under renowned Talmudists back in the old country and his fervent wish was to see his grandchildren grow up to be dedicated Talmud students.

I was his oldest grandchild and discovered from a very early age just how determined he was to steer me in what he was convinced was the right direction. I particularly remember the time he visited my parents' home when I was in the seventh or eighth grade. I had just received my report card and proudly showed it to him. I felt it was a pretty good report card, but for him, anything less than perfection was inadequate. After one glance, he noticed just how uneven my academic performance was.

He spoke to me in Yiddish, unadulterated by English phrases – pure, old-fashioned Yiddish. He protested that my grades were spotty. "You did very well in Ḥumash (Five Mosaic Books), but not nearly as well in Talmud. How can one truly know the Bible if he is ignorant of Talmud?"

I responded defensively by saying that I saw no connection between the Bible portions of *Bereshit* that we were then studying and Tractate Bava Metzia, our Talmud text that year. "The Ḥumash is full of great stories, but the Talmud is only about legal arguments, some of which are over my head."

He smiled and said that if I would give him an hour on the upcoming Friday night, he would give me kugel and soda, teach me a song, and demonstrate how the Talmud elucidates the Bible in an "amazing" way. Only he didn't say "amazing," he said "*vunderbar*."

That Friday, true to his word – and he was always true to his word – he personally served me the kugel and soda, taught me a song that he had learned from the old rabbi of his now-extinct *shtetl*, and asked me to review with him a short passage in *Parashat Toledot* (Gen. 25:19–28:9). You know the story. Esau, the older brother, comes in from the field, famished. He finds his younger brother, Jacob, cooking a pot of stew and asks for some of it. Jacob is willing to give it to him, but for a price. He demands that Esau first sell him his birthright; that is, the material and spiritual privileges that come with being the first-born. Translated literally, he says, "Sell me your birthright, like today (*kayom*)!"

Whereas nowadays kids will call their elderly grandfather Zaidie or Saba, we called ours Grandpa. Despite his old-fashioned demeanor, in many ways he was as American as apple pie. He asked me if I found anything problematic with the story.

I did. "The phrase '*kayom*' seems strange, Grandpa. Why does Jacob insist that the sale should be 'like today?'"

He responded, "Good! Maybe you have a *gemara kopp* (a talmudic intellect) after all! But let's see if you can ask a question on the whole transaction based on the Talmud texts you are now studying in school. Here's your volume of Talmud. I'll give you ten minutes to come up with a really good question."

To say that I was frustrated would be putting it mildly. Not only was I going to be stuck studying all Friday night – I was actually being asked to think! But one did not say no to Grandpa. So I opened the large book, pored over it, and focused on the task with great concentration. I was searching for a connection between a fascinating story and what I then experienced as some very boring rules and regulations.

After some time, probably much more than the allotted ten minutes, I had an "aha" experience. I really got excited. "Grandpa! It can't be! How could Jacob purchase the birthright from Esau? The privileges of the birthright are way off in the future. They include privileges like a dual portion of their inheritance of their father Isaac's estate, and Isaac was alive, if not entirely well, at that time. We studied in the Talmud that one cannot buy or sell objects or privileges that do not yet exist!"

My grandfather was thrilled, but no more than I was. Finally, I saw a connection between my Bible stories and the legal terminology of the Talmud that I had begun to resent.

He then sat back, asked me to relax, and took the role of the teacher. "If you reached page 16 of the tractate you are studying, you know this scenario. A fisherman wishes to sell the fish he will catch that day to a customer. He doesn't have the fish yet. Can he sell them? Yes, answers the Talmud. He can sell them if he desperately needs the money to feed himself that day. But if he wishes to sell the fish, he will catch in thirty days or in a year, he cannot do that. If one is desperate, he can sell even objects that he does not yet possess, even fish that are still in the sea."

There is a logical rationale for this legal principle, which I will omit from this chapter in the interest of brevity. Suffice it to say that I now saw the connection between the story and the talmudic principle:

> Of course Jacob said *kayom*. Sell me your birthright even though its privileges will not be realized until the distant future, but do so in your current state of desperation. Do so because you are famished, and in your desperation have the legal ability, much like the fisherman, to sell something that is now non-existent, because you need it for your urgent immediate needs. Sell me the birthright *kayom*.

Grandpa was proud of me that day, but I was even prouder of myself. He told me that the concept that I had discovered on my own was to be found in the commentary *Ohr HaḤaim*, which he studied assiduously every Friday night.

He then leaned back, stared at me with his gentle blue eyes and said, "I am trying to think of a prize, a reward for your willingness to sit with me for a few hours on a Friday night, for exerting your young intellect, and for seeing the connection between the Written Torah, Scripture; and Oral Torah, Talmud."

I sat there imagining all sorts of possible rewards, certain that he would ask for my input. Kugel and soda would have been acceptable, but lowest on my list of suggestions. I was thinking big bucks, or at least tickets to a baseball game.

Then he told me his idea. "From now on, every time I visit you, we will study together. And we will make it our business to discover connections. Our motto will be the verse in Psalms that says that God's Torah is perfect, soothes the soul, and brings joy to the heart."

What a disappointment for a twelve-year-old. But today, many decades later, each time I sit down before a folio of Talmud, I experience Grandpa's reward. I can now appreciate Grandpa's willingness to risk his popularity with his grandchildren, instead using every means at his disposal to get us to sit and learn with him.

Two Meanings of Maturity

How do you define "maturity"? The dictionary definition is: a state of being full-grown, ripe, or fully developed. But I think that the common man gives a subjective definition to maturity in one of two other ways.

Maturity, depending upon whether one tends to be idealistic or cynical, seems to carry one of the following meanings:

Either one takes the position that maturity is associated with the wisdom gained from experience over time. From this point of view, the mature person is one who has learned from all that has happened to him, and has developed, if not an infallible system that answers all questions, then at least an approach to life that is practical, informed, and wise.

Or, one takes the position that maturity is the state reached when one realizes that childhood dreams were just that: dreams, and no more. One who is mature has learned to abandon youthful ideals, surrender impractical hopes and plans, and settle for reality and its limitations.

Which definition of maturity is yours, dear reader? Is maturity associated with wisdom? Or is the mature person the one who has learned to live a practical and cautious life, without ideals and utopian dreams?

In *Parashat Vayetzeh* (Gen. 28:10–32:32:3), we have the opportunity to read about the maturation of our patriarch Jacob. The portion begins with a dream, a sublime dream. Toward the middle of the portion, Jacob dreams again, this time a very businesslike, down-to-earth, practical dream.

Jacob's first dream, the sublime one, envisions a ladder firmly rooted into the earth, but extending heavenward. However one interprets it, and creative interpretations abound, it is a majestic glimpse of infinite possibilities, of ideals of immense significance. If anything, it is a grand imaginative symbol of the relationship between man and God, and of the former's potential to connect with the latter.

But then, Jacob spends his years working for his uncle, Laban. He is busy with mundane affairs; in his own words, "scorched by heat all day, and freezing at night." He is busy, nay preoccupied, with business affairs, with profit, and with practical material matters.

And he dreams again. But the second time, his dream is far from sublime. He sees that "the he-goats mating with the flock were streaked, speckled, and mottled." Things are going his way in the world of sheep-raising. Every trace of another higher world is missing.

If Jacob's second dream had ended at this point, we could say that he matured in the second, cynical, sense. His initial dream was a lofty one; his subsequent dream, a come-down. His vision was diminished, from a glimpse of Heaven to earthly things.

But his second dream does not end with his vision of goats, speckled or otherwise. Rather, an angel appears to him and says that he, the angel, has observed Jacob's dream and has "noted all that Laban has been doing to you." The angel in the dream is the better part of Jacob himself, the part that realizes that Laban's environment has contaminated his dreams.

The angel in the dream then goes on to say that he represents the God of Bethel and that it is time for Jacob to "leave this land and return to his native land." It is time for him to become mature in the first sense. It is time for him to reclaim his first dream and to do all that he can to make that dream real.

Jacob reaches true maturity when he decides not to yield to the temptation to compromise upon his original dream. When he realizes that his dreams are not what they once were and that he has lost his youthful vision of a ladder connecting heaven and earth, he does not merely settle for his new reality.

Rather, he learns, and this lesson is imparted to him by God Himself, that one must not surrender to mundane dreams, abandoning old ideals. He learns that he can return to the dream of his youth. And he learns not only that he *can* go home again, but that he *must* go home again.

There is, of course, another lesson that he learns, and this is an eternal lesson for the Jewish people. The dreams of our national youth, the visions of our biblical heroes and of the patriarchs and matriarchs, can only be achieved in the Land of Israel. The dreams of the Diaspora are apt to be mundane, short-sighted, and a bit selfish. The dreams of the Land of Israel are noble dreams, exalted dreams, and dreams that ultimately connect us to heaven. Indeed, the dreams of Israel ideally connect all of the earth's inhabitants to their Father in heaven.

We can revisit the dreams of our youth. We can go home again. The Land of Israel is the land of our dreams and it is home. This is one lesson learned from *Parashat Vayetzeh*: a lesson about being a Jew, and a lesson about true maturity.

Parashat Vayetzeh

What's in a Name?

Who am I?" This is the most powerful question that a person ever asks himself. For many of us, there are no easy answers to that question. We are uncertain of our own identities.

Social scientists believe that this question is typically asked by adolescents. After all, it is legitimate for young people to be unsure of who they are. The task of the adolescent is to begin to define his or her identity, to formulate tentative answers to the question, "Who am I?" Often, however, individuals persist in struggling to answer the "Who am I?" question long after they have passed the stage of adolescence. The so-called "midlife crisis" can be understood as a time in life when one again asks himself the question, "Who am I?" and a crisis arises when no clear answer to that question emerges.

An important component in the formulation of an answer to the "Who am I?" question is the answer to another question, "What's in a name?" Each of us has a name, almost invariably given to us very early in our lives by our parents or parent figure.

I would like to suggest that our sense of personal identity is in a large part determined by the names that we have been given. Our names were chosen for us because they have a certain meaning to those who named us. When our parents gave us our name, they also gave us a message about who they expected us to be. Whether we ourselves are conscious of that message depends on how explicit our parents were in their choice of our name. But on some level, we know that our name was not randomly chosen, and to a greater extent than we realize, our self-concepts are shaped by our names.

In *Parashat Vayetzeh*, no fewer than eleven newborns are given names. In every case, these names are given by women, by Leah and by Rachel. Each name is carefully crafted by these women and is designed, not only to reflect the emotions of the moment, but to shape and give direction to the destinies of each of these children.

Let us consider but two examples: Leah gives her third son the name Levi, which means "connected" or "attached." This reflects her confidence that with the birth of a third son, her husband, Jacob, will become more attached to her. But it is also a message to the baby Levi that he will grow up to be "attached" to others. In his lifetime, he is typically number two of the duo "Simon and Levi," secondary to his brother. And his progeny become "attached" to the Almighty and to all things sacred as the tribe of priests for the rest of Jewish history.

Leah then names her fourth child, Judah, which means to praise or to thank, because of the special gratitude she experiences with his birth. And Judah ultimately, in his own life and through his descendants, gives praise to the Lord in his actions and with his words.

In more recent times, it has become rare for a Jewish parent to invent a new name for his or her child. The prevalent custom is to name a child for a deceased ancestor or for some other revered personage. The child who carries the name of a grandparent surely internalizes the message that in some way, his life should reflect some of the values of that grandparent.

I know for whom I was named. He was my great-grandfather, my mother's mother's father, Tzvi Hersh Kriegel. He was an immigrant to America, hailing originally from Galicia. His portrait adorned one of the walls of my grandparents' home, and it showed an immaculately dressed, bright-eyed but old-fashioned middle-aged man with a luxuriant red beard. As a child, I learned much about him from his widow, my great-grandmother. I learned of his commitment not only to Jewish observance, but to all aspects of the *Galitzianer* culture, especially to its wry humor and nostalgic hasidic tunes.

I visit his grave ever more frequently as time goes on. And I both consciously and unconsciously model myself after him. When I ask myself, "Who am I?" – a significant part of my answer relates back to him and to his name bequeathed to me.

I have found myself preaching over the years, to those parents who would listen, that they should choose the names they give their children carefully, and that rather than choose a name because they like the way it sounds or because of its popularity, they should select a name of a real person, someone who stood for something, someone their child could eventually emulate.

In my Torah study and in my readings of Jewish history, I have noticed that during different eras, different names seem to predominate. I find it fascinating that the names Avraham, Moshe, David, and Shlomo are today quite popular and have been certainly since the days of that second most famous Moshe, Maimonides. Yet, in talmudic times, those names seemed to have been quite rare. We find no major rabbis in the Mishna or in the Talmud who carry the names of the aforementioned four biblical heroes. No Rabbi Moshe, no Rabbi Avraham, but strangely more than one Rabbi Yishmael. And, of course, returning to the *parasha*, Yehudas and Shimons aplenty.

"What is in a name?" A message to help answer the persistent and challenging question, "Who am I?" As is so often the case in rabbinic literature, one question answers the other.

There is a passage in the works of our sages that tells of the three names we each have. There is the name we were given at the time of our birth, but there is also the name that we earn by our own deeds, the part of the answer to the "Who am I?" question that we ourselves provide.

And finally, there is a name that others give us, the reputation that we deserve. It is that name to which King Solomon in his Ecclesiastes (*Kohelet*) refers when he remarks, "A good name is better than fragrant oil, and the day of death than the day of birth." And it is that very name that the Mishna, in Avot, has in mind when it concludes that, of all the crowns of glory that humans can achieve, there is one that stands supreme: the *keter shem tov*, the crown of a good name.

Parashat Vayetzeh

The Thankful Jew

He may or may not have been an anti-Semite, but he sure was an abrasive personality. He was my seatmate on an Amtrak train, returning to Baltimore from New York, some years ago.

As I recall, it was at the end of a particularly long and grueling day for me. I had a series of rabbinical meetings, delivered a talk during lunch, which provided me no opportunity to eat, and was involved in an unsuccessful attempt to keep the marriage of a young couple from breaking up. I was looking forward to the respite of some quiet time on the return trip to my home in Baltimore, but even that luxury was denied to me that evening.

I sat down, as I always try to do, in the window seat. This fellow entered the railroad car and walked past me in search of a seat for himself. There were several seats that he could have chosen, but for some reason he returned to where I was sitting, glared at me, and sat down with a gesture of dissatisfaction.

I immediately sensed that I would not experience the peaceful train ride that I had anticipated. I tried burying my head in the book I was reading, but that was not sufficient insulation from my neighbor's insistence upon conversation.

"You are obviously Jewish," he began. "Your yarmulke for one thing is a dead giveaway. Plus, I see that you are reading a Hebrew book."

Of course, I admitted to being Jewish and slanted my book in his direction so that he could verify that it was indeed in Hebrew. I asked him, as I typically do in such conversations, whether he was Jewish.

I can only describe his instant response by saying that he snorted. "Look, buddy," he growled. "I've got my bunch of problems and burdens, but being Jewish is thankfully not one of them."

I was at a loss as to what to say next, but there was something about his use of the word "thankfully" that prompted me to comment to him, "But surely you have other things to be thankful for besides not being Jewish."

He seemed to be taken aback, having expected some defensive statement on my part, or perhaps some indication that I was offended. I was hoping that I had succeeded at changing the topic from my Jewishness to his life and the things he had to be thankful for. It worked. That is, at least for a while. He went on to say that he didn't have much to be thankful for, although he was happily married, had several children, and held a well-paying job. He also insisted that these beneficial facets of his life were merely the result of good fortune and did not call for any expression of thanks on his part.

He then pressed on with his almost obsessive interest in my Jewishness. "You seem to be proud of the fact that you are a Jew. Why? What is it about you Jews that makes you want to wear your Jewishness on the outside? Why do you dress so differently, and why do you persist in reading those old-fashioned books in that outdated language?"

I was about to launch into a major lecture but restrained myself from doing so, knowing full well that my efforts would be in vain. As I hesitated, pondering my next move, he surprised me.

"Forget those questions," he said. "Instead, give me an answer to the following question. It is one that I've asked many Jews before, but none were able to give me a satisfactory answer. My question is, What does the word 'Jew' mean? What is its origin, and what is its significance?"

Once again, the word "thankful" proved useful. I responded that the word "Jew" in English is related to the word "*Jude*" in German, which in turn derives from the Hebrew word "Judah," one of the ancestors of the Jewish people.

I then asked him whether or not he was familiar with the Bible, particularly the Old Testament. His face, which up until this point projected hostility, suddenly took on a different aspect. His facial muscles seemed to relax at first and then his eyes clouded over with tears.

"Are you kidding? I was the child of a preacher whose father was a preacher before him. We read from the Bible at the dinner table and studied it regularly every single day. I grew up resenting the Bible and all that it stood for, although I remember much of it against my will. I guess one can't forget words that were ingrained in him since his childhood."

I now had my opening. And this is the connection to *Parashat Vayetzeh* (Gen. 28:10–32:3). "Then you must remember the stories of Genesis. Do you recall the passage in which Leah names her children? Do you remember the name she gave to her fourth son?"

The words came out of his mouth as they would from a recording, "Genesis 30:35: And she conceived again and bore a son, and said, 'This time I will praise the Lord.' Therefore she called his name Judah. Then she ceased bearing."

He looked at me with a big grin, his face finally indicating a small measure of friendship. "Impressive, wouldn't you say? I remember every word. I even remember Grandpa explaining that 'Judah' sounds like the Hebrew for 'praise.'"

I responded by congratulating him for his excellent memory, and further remarked that he had his old Grandpa to thank for his biblical expertise. I indicated that Leah's reaction to her fourth child's birth was usually translated in our tradition as, "This time I will *thank* the Lord."

"Now you have your answer. We are called Jews because of our ancestor, Judah, whose very name means to praise, or to thank. By definition, the Jew is a person who feels thankful, who expresses gratitude for all his blessings to the Almighty, who provides those blessings to other humans without whose help those blessings would never be realized."

He didn't seem convinced. "Why then," he pressed on, "is it so hard to feel thankful and ever so much more difficult to express it?"

I told him that to answer that question, I would have to give him a further lesson in the Hebrew language. I explained to him that the word *hodaa*, while it is the Hebrew word for thanks, is also the Hebrew word for admission or confession. I went on to explain something to him that I had learned in the writings of Rabbi Isaac Hutner, who taught that when we are thankful to another person, we are in effect admitting that we couldn't do it alone, but were dependent upon the other person for the favor.

Gratitude to God entails the recognition of one's own insufficiency and the confession that, without God, we would not have achieved that for which we are grateful.

"It is difficult to be thankful," I concluded, "because it is difficult to admit to ourselves that alone we are inadequate and we must always rely upon the Divine or the human to achieve whatever we wish to achieve in life. We don't like to admit that we need another and that we can't 'go at it alone.'"

At that point, the train was fast approaching Wilmington, Delaware. My companion was about to get off. He didn't say goodbye and certainly did not thank me for my words. But he did give me a small bit of satisfaction. He said, "You're different from other Jews. You actually make sense."

I spent the rest of the train ride pondering the adequacy of my responses to this stranger and feeling thankful to the Almighty for giving me the words I needed to earn this dubious compliment.

Parashat Vayishlaḥ

Unheralded Heroes

Y ou don't hear much about them and sometimes you don't even
know their names, but they are the true heroes and heroines in our lives
and in our times. As I hope to demonstrate, it was also true in biblical
times that very important characters in the narrative are hardly mentioned, perhaps only hinted at.

I first became interested in this phenomenon shortly after the
events of September 11, 2001. I was listening to one of my favorite radio
talk shows while driving. The guest was a professor of sociology who
was insisting, much to the chagrin of the talk show host, that the firemen who lost their lives saving others at the World Trade Center were
not true heroes.

He maintained that a true hero does something very unusual,
something neither he nor anyone else typically does. These firemen,
he argued, were simply doing their duty. They showed up to work in
the morning, went through their usual routine, and responded to this
assignment as part of their job.

The announcer was horrified by this professor's opinion and pronounced it a typical example of "academic snobbery." My gut reaction

was identical to the announcer's horror. Of course those firemen were heroes, great heroes. And they were heroes by virtue of the very fact that they carried out their life-saving duties with such astounding courage.

Continuing to drive, I began to reflect upon the question of the definition of "hero" in the Jewish tradition. From the Jewish perspective, is a hero some kind of Superman who behaves in some extraordinarily dramatic fashion, or is the true hero the person who, day in and day out, does what is expected of him in a faithful and diligent manner, humbly and anonymously, never making the headlines?

My research soon convinced me that the latter definition is the accurate one from a Jewish point of view. He or she who dutifully and loyally does his or her job, be it in the mundane or the sacred sphere, is the true hero or heroine.

As an example, let me introduce you to a personage who is mentioned in *Parashat Vayishlah*, although even if you read the portion carefully, you may not have noticed her name. Her name was Deborah.

Open your Bible and turn to Genesis 35:8. Jacob, his wives, and their many children have returned to the Land of Israel. They have reached Bethel, Jacob's original starting point. Jacob erected an altar there. And then we read, "And Deborah, Rebecca's nurse, died and she was buried...under the oak, and it was called the 'Oak of Tears.'"

Who was this woman never mentioned by name before? Why did her demise evoke such grief? Why is she important enough to "make it" into the biblical narrative?

Now turn back a few pages to Genesis 24:59. Here we read that when Rebecca left her birthplace to journey to the Land of Israel and marry Isaac, she took her nurse with her. A nurse with no name, whom we know nothing about until we learn of her death in *Parashat Vayishlah*.

Our rabbis speculate that nurse Deborah was a major part of the entire epic drama of Rebecca's life with Isaac and Jacob. They suggest that she was the one sent by Rebecca to retrieve Jacob from his long exile. Our rabbis tell us too that she was nurse to Rebecca's many grandchildren who shed many tears under the old oak tree. Jewish mystical sources even aver that nurse Deborah was reincarnated into the much later Deborah who was a Judge and Prophet in Israel!

Deborah is an excellent example of someone who "just did her job," regularly and consistently, and who had an impact upon three generations of major biblical characters, including a matriarch, two patriarchs, and the forbearers of the twelve tribes. She exemplifies the type of person that the Talmud refers to when it asks, "Who deserves a place in the World to Come?" and answers, "He who slips in silently and slips out silently."

Rabbi Akiva, one of the great Jewish heroes and sages, taught us a similar lesson. At a critical juncture in his life, he was inspired by the fact that a stone is impenetrable by ordinary means. But when a gentle waterfall drips upon stone for hundreds of years, it succeeds in boring a hole in the stone. Quiet consistency and persistence are the true ingredients of heroism and strength.

In the Bible, as in all of life, there are major figures who work behind the scenes but who are indispensable to the important events of history. They are unheralded and often anonymous. They are real heroes too.

In the words of the poet John Keats, they are the children "of silence and slow time." They help us see the truth in that poet's exquisite words, "Heard melodies are sweet, but those unheard are sweeter."

Parashat Vayishlaḥ

Nameless

There is something special about meeting up with an old friend whom one hasn't seen in years. I recently had just such a special experience when I spent a weekend in a community where a friend I hadn't seen in ten years resides.

Of course we spent much of the time catching up with each other's lives. He showed me a book he had just written, the product of many years of research on his part. He gave me the book as a gift, and I opened it to find that it was dedicated to a rabbi who had passed away some years ago, who had made *aliya* to Israel together with the famed *alter*, or old man, of Slobodka, Rabbi Nosson Tzvi Finkel, in the mid-1920s.

I asked him what his connection was to the old rabbi. He told me that this rabbi was one of those anonymous scholars who can be found only in Jerusalem. He was someone with no official position, who lived in poverty, but who would gladly teach any young yeshiva student who would ask for time with him. He was almost nameless, and in the world's eyes, was insignificant, although my friend attributes all of his considerable talmudic erudition to the old rabbi. In gratitude, he dedicated his book to this sad soul, who now has a "name."

Reflecting upon this, I soon realized that I have had similar experiences, and that many people have influenced me who are, in a sense, nameless. I recall, for example, the rabbi, diminutive in stature but superlative in pedagogical skill, who was retained by my parents to teach me Talmud during summer vacations. I studied with him intensely in my early teens and then forgot about him until relatively recently when I came to realize how much of my modest skills in Talmud I owe to him.

In *Parashat Vayishlaḥ*, we encounter just such a person. She unobtrusively walked onto the stage of drama of the biblical patriarchs and matriarchs in the portion of *Ḥayei Sara*. There we read (Gen. 24:59), "And they sent away Rebecca, their sister, and her nursemaid, and Abraham's servant." We learn of this nursemaid's existence, but we are not told her name. Indeed, we do not hear of her at all again.

That is, not until *Parashat Vayishlaḥ* where we read (Gen. 35:8), "And Deborah, Rebecca's nurse, died, and she was buried below Bethel under the oak; and the name of it was called, the 'Oak of Weeping.'" We learned that her name was Deborah and that Jacob and his family sorely grieved and mourned for her.

It is left to our imagination, and to the Midrash and commentaries, to speculate about her activities and relationships during the many years from the time she escorted her mistress to the land of Canaan until her sad demise so many years later.

Our rabbis tell us that she was sent by Rebecca to bring Jacob from his long exile in the land of Ḥaran back to the land of Canaan. After all, when Rebecca encouraged Jacob to flee, she promised him that when it was safe, she would "send for you and fetch you" (Gen. 27:45). It was Deborah whom she sent to retrieve Jacob, to bring Jacob back.

Deborah then spent much time, probably many years, with Jacob and Rachel and Leah and their growing family. As is evident from the fact that her death occasioned such profound grief that it is memorialized in *Parashat Vayishlaḥ*, she must have been much loved. I always imagine that she served as the grandmother figure for all the sons and the daughter of Jacob who grew up without the advantage of a nearby *bubby*.

For me, as for the old friend with whom I was briefly reconnected this past weekend, Deborah is an archetype of the nameless soul who makes a powerful impact upon us, and who is forgotten for a very long time until we finally remember him and "name" him. Rebecca's nurse-maid had no name when we first learned of her existence. Only when she passes on, do we finally learn, under the "Oak of Weeping," that her name was Deborah.

The name of my summer time teacher from so long ago? We called him "Rabbi Abramchik," and although I remember him fondly, and he clearly was a major influence in my life, I cannot remember his full name anymore.

Perhaps it is of Deborah and of Rabbi Abramchik that the prophet Isaiah spoke when he said in the Name of the Almighty:

> I will give them, in My House
> And within My walls,
> A monument and a name
> Better than sons or daughters.
> I will give them an everlasting name
> Which shall not perish. (Is. 56:5)

Parashat Vayishlaḥ

See You Later

Them here is an expression that we often use when we say goodbye. Most of us pay no attention to what we are saying. I doubt that very many of those who use the expression really mean it.

I refer to the words "See you later." I am quite confident that everyone reading this chapter has said these words of farewell to someone whom he wished he would never see again. Seldom do we consider "See you later" as a promise of a reunion or a commitment to a subsequent encounter.

I find it fascinating that this expression has its equivalent in other languages. In Hebrew, for example, we say, "*Lehitra'ot,*" which implies that we anticipate seeing each other again in the future. The German, "*Aufwiedersehen,*" conveys an even stronger degree of intention to meet again.

It is not surprising that we ordinary folk occasionally use language loosely and do not literally mean to fulfill every casual remark that we make. But it is surprising to find a biblical character using the same expression. Surely the Bible does not trouble itself to record casual remarks.

In *Parashat Vayishlaḥ* (Gen. 32:4–36:43), we find the patriarch Jacob using just such an expression. The careful reader of the *parasha* faces the dilemma of either viewing his remarks as mere empty words, or worse, seeing in them a deliberate attempt at deception.

I refer to the passage at the very end of the narrative of the dramatic encounter between Esau and Jacob after a separation of many years. Surprisingly, the encounter concludes on a peaceful note, in which Esau suggests, "Let us take our journey and let us go together."

Jacob's response, which I have rendered into contemporary conversational English, is, "You go first, and because of the children and cattle, I'll follow slowly. I'll see you later, in Se'ir, your mountain retreat."

The reader of this passage cannot help but anticipate that we will read, at some point in the narrative, of how Jacob indeed sees Esau later, in Se'ir. After all, he promised to follow, albeit slowly, and to reunite with Esau at Mount Se'ir, his home base. But we never read of such a reunion; not in the *parasha* and not anywhere else in the entire Bible. Jacob says, "See you later," but that "later" never occurs.

Our sages were troubled by this seeming gap in the narrative. They provide us with several explanations. Rashi suggests that Jacob was trying to avoid any further encounters with his brother, assuming that he would treacherously abandon his feigned brotherly façade. In other words, he told Esau to go ahead, with no intention of following him all the way to Se'ir. Jacob's "See you later" was thus a ruse. He was justifiably resorting to deception in the interest of self-defense.

The Talmud, in Tractate Avoda Zara 25b, actually advises all who find themselves threatened by suspicious companions while on the road to resort to Jacob's tactic. The Talmud counsels that when one is confronted by such a companion, he should inform him that his destination is far off and not disclose that his true destination is a much closer one. This is not an uncommon example of the practical advice that the Talmud often gives to those who face the difficulties that Jews have faced throughout our history.

But the rabbis have an alternative approach to Jacob's "See you later." This approach insists that Jacob used those words in all sincerity, with no guile whatsoever. Rather, he was predicting that, whereas a true reunion of Jacob and Esau was not likely to happen in their lifetimes, there would come a time when that reunion would happen. That time would be in the distant future. Then, the descendants of Jacob, the Jewish people, and the descendants of Esau, the historical enemies of the Jews, will indeed meet again, at the time when the Esaus of the world will be judged, finally and fairly.

This ultimate "reunion" was foretold by the prophet Ovadia in the very last verse of his book, "For liberators shall march up on Mount Zion to judge Mount Esau; and dominion shall be the Lord's" (Ob. 1:21).

In this light, we come to see that Jacob was not using the expression "See you later" loosely or casually, and certainly not deceptively. Rather, he was peering into the messianic future and envisioned a time when Jacob and Esau would come together, if only for a final reckoning.

Does this final reckoning mean victory for Jacob and defeat for Esau? It is often assumed that this is exactly what is meant, and such a conclusion is warranted by a literal reading of some of the concluding verses of the Book of Ovadia, for example, verse 18: "The House of Jacob shall be fire.... And the House of Esau shall be straw."

But Rabbi Joseph H. Hertz, in his (regrettably underutilized) commentary on the Pentateuch, suggests otherwise and makes the following hopeful statement, "There is no record that Jacob went to Se'ir to see his brother. But, add the rabbis, Jacob will yet visit Esau on the day of the Messiah, when the reconciliation between Israel and Edom will be complete."

The medieval commentator Rabbenu Baḥya finds a hint in the Hebrew words that Jacob uses to say "See you later" (until I come unto my lord unto Se'ir), which suggests the messianic meaning behind the words. He points out that the final letters of the words that constitute that phrase spell out the name Elijah, who, in our tradition, is the herald of the Messiah.

It is safe to conclude with the assumption that most uses of the term "See you later" have no significance. However, Jacob's use of the term had great significance. It gives us occasion to reflect upon the millennia of hostility that existed between Jacob and Esau and upon the prophecy that that hostility will eventually end.

Parashat Vayishlaḥ

The Better Angels

D o you believe in angels? Have you ever met one? I do and I have. Let me tell you about the ones I've met.

But first, why do I believe in angels? Well, it is because I believe in the Bible, and the Bible speaks of angels. An angel of God instructs Hagar to return to Sarah's service (Gen. 16:7–12); it is an angel who assures Hagar that her son Ishmael will survive (21:17–18); and an angel calls out to Abraham from heaven and prevents him from harming Isaac (22:11–12).

Parashat Vayetzeh began with Jacob's dream, in which angels ascend and descend a ladder to heaven (Gen. 31:11), and concluded with the "angels of the Lord" whom he encountered upon his return to the land of Canaan.

Not once in any of these incidents is the angel described, and we are left wondering whether these angels are humanoid but winged creatures (as they are described elsewhere in the Bible) or heavenly bodiless spirits, emissaries of God who heed His command and perform His will. Either way, if you take the Bible literally, you must believe that there is such a thing as an angel.

But what do I mean when I say that I have met angels? Surely you would scoff if I told you that I encountered a winged creature that descended from heaven and spoke to me on my way to the subway yesterday. I wouldn't try to convince you of that without fear that you would question my sanity, and indeed, that is not what I mean when I say that I have met angels.

In order to explain what I mean, I must quote that central masterpiece of Jewish mysticism, the Zohar, in a passage in its commentary on the Book of Ruth. There, it is written, "If you perform mitzvot, you will find that out of each mitzva, a beneficent angel is created." That good angels are created out of our good deeds, and that evil angels are produced by our sins, is a popular notion in our tradition – so much so that many commentators find sources in the Mishna and Talmud for this idea.

Take, for example, this passage in the fourth chapter of Ethics of the Fathers (*Pirkei Avot*):

> Rabbi Eliezer b. Yaakov said: One who performs a single mitzva acquires for himself an advocate. One who commits a single transgression acquires for himself an accuser.

No less an authority than the Gaon of Vilna understands that the advocate is the good angel created by the performance of the mitzva, and the accuser is the evil angel resulting from a sinful act.

What are these angels like? Are they the winged creatures flying from place to place as they are often depicted in illustrated Bibles? I think not. I think these angels are representations of the influence that our deeds have upon others in our environment. If we perform a good deed, it has an effect on those around us, and this effect is termed a good angel. I've known some very pious individuals and have seen the "angels" they produced in their lifetimes, reflected in their offspring and disciples even long after they themselves passed away. And we all have witnessed the lasting impact of the "evil angels" created by the misdeeds of fiends and knaves.

We have all suffered as we witnessed the tragic murders of fellow Jews – in synagogues, at bus stops, and upon battlefields. As we read about these individuals, we cannot help but be impressed by the impact and influence they had on others. Even in the cases of very young victims, we learn of the effect they had upon parents and siblings. Each of these *kedoshim*, holy martyred souls, left behind numerous angels who will live on long after the death of those whose good deeds created them.

These are the angels whom I have met. I met some of them on those occasions when I paid condolence calls upon bereaved families who embody the teachings of their lost beloved parents and teachers. And I have met others in print as I read the numerous stories of the lasting impact that young soldiers (*hayalim*) had upon their fellows and friends.

We create angels, and I believe that these are the kinds of angels whom we read about in *Parashat Vayishlah* (Gen. 32:4–36:43). It begins, "Jacob sent messengers ahead to his brother Esau." The Hebrew word here generally translated as "messengers" is *malakhim*, or *malakh* in the singular. Yet this is the same word that, in the verses cited earlier, is invariably translated as "angels." Did Jacob send angels or did he send messengers?

Those who translate *malakhim* in this verse as messengers do so because they cannot fathom that Jacob, a mere mortal, would have angels at his beck and call. Yet Rashi, the greatest of our commentators, insists that Jacob sent *malakhim mamash*, real "tangible" angels. How could that be?

I would not be the first to suggest that Jacob's angels were of the second type of angel that I have been describing. Jacob's "angels" were the product of his many good deeds: of his faithful adherence to his duties as Laban's shepherd, of his acts of charity, and fervent prayers to God. The angels he created out of his good deeds are the ones he sent to appease his fearsome brother, Esau.

Some have found a hint of this interpretation in the words *malakhim mamash*. *Mamash* means real, actual, and literally tangible. But its letters comprise an acronym for: *Min Mitzvot She'asa*, from the good deeds he performed; or *Malakhim MiMitzvot She'asa*, angels from the good deeds he performed.

Jacob was not the only one capable of creating angels. We all are capable of performing good deeds. Our good deeds may not reach the level of those of Jacob, so our angels may be less "angelic" than his, but we all can cultivate angels within ourselves. We can step outside the Jewish tradition and learn that others have discovered this secret – namely, that we have spiritual abilities within us that cry out for expression. There are potential angels within us all.

Abraham Lincoln knew this and expressed it in his majestic First Inaugural Address: "The mystic chords of memory, stretching from every battlefield ... all over this broad land, will yet swell the chorus of the Union, when again touched, as surely they will be, by the better angels of our nature."

Long before Lincoln, our father Jacob taught us that we all have mystic chords of memory within us, waiting, desperately waiting, to be touched by the better angels of our nature. These better angels, whom we create out of our own good deeds, will stand us in good stead as we encounter the Esaus of our own time.

Parashat Vayeshev

No Favorites on Ḥanukka!

Envy is surely one of the most insidious of human emotions. It is a self-destructive emotion because it often leads a person to act against his own best interests as he attempts to redress the situation that caused him so much envy. It is also damaging to relationships with others and can have disastrous social effects.

Our sages include envy, along with lust and the search for glory, in their list of items that are sure "to drive a person from this world."

That envy can lead to great national tragedy is one of the lessons of Jewish history. *Parashat Vayeshev* describes the deterioration of a family brought about by the envy that Joseph's brothers had toward him. This envy led to the hatred that motivated them to sell him into slavery.

Hatred between brothers, and the consequences of this hatred, is sadly at the root of Jewish history. *Sinat ḥinam*, unwarranted hatred, remains a stubborn problem in the ongoing story of our people.

Interestingly, the Talmud blames Jacob for the brothers' treacherous deed, and for the future course of the history of his descendants. It comments:

One should never favor one child over his other children, for it was the mere two shekels worth of silk, which Jacob gave to Joseph over and above that which he gave to his other children, that caused the brothers to be envious of him, leading eventually to our forefathers' descent into Egypt.

The multicolored garment with which Jacob showed special favor to his son Joseph provoked the envy of the other brothers, and the rest is Jewish history.

Parashat Vayeshev coincides with the holiday of Ḥanukka. Can we discern any connection between the favoritism demonstrated by Jacob, and condemned by our sages, and the festive holiday of Ḥanukka? I think we can, and I share this admittedly novel idea with you, dear reader.

The central mitzva of Ḥanukka is, of course, the lighting of candles on each of the eight nights. Strictly speaking, this mitzva can be fulfilled by the head of the household lighting a single candle on behalf of the entire family – *ner ish ubaito*, a candle for the master of the house on behalf of the entire household.

However, the prevalent custom is that every member of the family, every child, every boarder, and every guest, kindles his or her own menora. No favorites here. Everyone gets to light a menora.

Can it be that this custom arose as an antidote to the tendency some parents have to play favorites among their children? Can it be that the central message of Ḥanukka is that all children have an equal role to play in this holiday, and moreover, in the very destiny of the Jewish people?

I have found no source in our literature for this interpretation, but nonetheless, it feels right to me. I personally find it dramatically significant that on the very Sabbath in which we read of how Jacob singled out Joseph from his other children, we also celebrate Ḥanukka and light candles in a manner in which no one child is singled out as superior, in which all have an equal share.

The lessons of Ḥanukka are many, but here is one novel lesson and a very important one. Envy can wreak havoc in a family. One way for parents to avoid this poisonous emotion is by treating all their children fairly and equally, and by not playing favorites.

One of the wise sayings of Ben Sira, the Jewish sage whose work did not quite make it into the Bible, but which has much to teach us, is that "envy and wrath shorten life."

Wise parents will take this lesson to heart and not discriminate among their children. Instead, they will learn the lesson of Ḥanukka and give all their children equal roles in celebrating this beautiful holiday, the "festival of lights."

Parashat Vayeshev

Man Plans, God Laughs

Y ou thought your life would run smoothly, right? We all do. Then something occurs, tragic or happy, that proves to us that life is not smooth at all, and probably is not supposed to be.

Somehow, each of us has a personal script that envisions what our lives will be like in the near and even distant future. I remember a friend from college who had his life planned out. He knew who he was going to marry, what his career path would be, where he would live, and which friends would be loyal to him.

My friend, like all the rest of us, soon found out that life had many surprises in store for him. His fiancé ended their relationship, he was offered a very different job than the one he was trained for, he moved to a part of the country he had previously never heard of, and his friends soon became but memories.

There is a passage in Psalms 30, one of my favorite biblical quotations, which says this better than I can. It reads, "I said in my tranquility (*shalvi*), I shall never fall down." Of all the fifty-plus weekly Torah portions, it is *Parashat Vayeshev* that conveys this message most powerfully, in a manner designed to leave an impression upon us all.

"And Jacob dwelled." Rashi comments that Jacob sought to dwell in tranquility. He thought that he had finally made it home, the dwelling place of his fathers, and that his encounters with Laban and Esau were now over. It was clear sailing from here on in.

But wouldn't you know, his troubles with Joseph soon "jumped on him." He never anticipated that his life would be completely disrupted and changed forever because of his favorite son and his internal family dynamics. From this point on, Jacob experienced no tranquility, only surprises, which eventually climaxed in exile to Egypt. Not only could he not live in the land of his fathers, but he was destined not even to die there.

There is a Yiddish saying that captures this lesson in four succinct words, "*Mentsch tracht, Gott lacht.*" Literally this means, "Man plans, God laughs." I have seen it paraphrased as, "Man proposes, God disposes."

Nahmanides, the second most important traditional Jewish biblical commentator after Rashi, uses the narrative of Joseph's search for his brothers and their plot to sell him into slavery as a primary example of how man's plans usually go awry. He too formulates a four-word phrase that conveys this idea, but his is in Hebrew, "*Hagezera emet, vehaharitzut sheker.*" This means that God's design is true while man's efforts are futile. Sounds pessimistic, but it has the ring of reality.

Nahmanides points out that Joseph was sent by Jacob to the brothers but could not find them. Ordinarily, if he was convinced that his search for them would be unsuccessful, he would have returned home. But lo and behold, a strange man (an angel according to rabbinic legend) appeared on the scene and guided Joseph to his brothers, who promptly sold him to the next passing caravan.

This lesson is a profound existential one for all of us. It comprises needed implications for the way we tend to raise our children in this day and age. Many of us parents are guilty of trying to arrange our children's lives so that they will never experience problems or difficulties. We are protective to an extreme in the hope that our children will never have to face the challenges and obstacles that we faced. But we delude ourselves and, more importantly, are not fair to our children. Their lives will contain unpredicted and unpredictable circumstances, negative and positive, and we cannot make their lives fool-proof.

How much better off they would be if we taught them not how to avoid problems, but how to cope with problems. Problems are unavoidable. They are the very stuff of life. A good parent, and a good teacher, conveys the lesson that life will have its challenges, but that these challenges can be met, and that by meeting them, the individual grows.

We, as observers of current youth, particularly in the Jewish community, have identified a sense of entitlement in our children. They feel entitled to leisure and comfort and an environment free of restriction. We would be well advised to dispel this sense of entitlement, and instead, enable them to face the surprises that life has in store for all of us.

Parashat Vayeshev

The Wisdom of the East

T here are jokes that are very funny on the surface, but that, upon reflection, can be quite painful and disturbing. One of them, which was told frequently twenty years ago or more, concerns a matronly woman from the Bronx who seeks to visit a famous guru somewhere in the Far East, perhaps in the mountains of northern India or Tibet.

She boards a plane at JFK airport and begins the long and arduous flight, which necessitates several stopovers and the changing of planes. She lands at the closest airport to the remote ashram, or temple, where the guru has his mountain retreat. She finds a bus that takes her part of the way to the ashram and, although she's never even seen a donkey before, summons a donkey cart to continue her trek to her encounter with the guru.

Totally exhausted, she finally arrives at the guru's quarters. To her great disappointment, she learns that the guru has just begun a three-day period of fasting and meditation and cannot possibly be interrupted. Anything but total solitude is forbidden.

She pleads and begs and finally resorts to one of the strategies of persuasion that she learned back in the Bronx. She tells the guru's guards that she only wants to say three words to him.

On the condition that she limit her message to just three words, they allow her access to the guru's inner chamber. There she finds him sitting in the lotus yoga position, totally entranced in his meditation.

She approaches him, but he remains unaware of her presence. Finally, she bends over him and whispers in his ear, "Melvin? Come home!"

I used to tell this story many times not so long ago when so many young Jewish men and women, from the Bronx and from elsewhere, traveled to the Far East in their quest for spiritual truth and a meaningful path in life.

The story always drew laughs from the crowd, but the laughs were inevitably followed by a contemplative silence as the audience began to reflect upon the point of the story. Young Jews by the thousands had become alienated not only from their Jewish roots, but from Western civilization in general.

Although this phenomenon is no longer as prevalent as it once was, Eastern religions remain attractive to many, and not just to young Jews but to a wide variety of individuals in search of a New Age alternative to Western culture.

The reasons so many are dissatisfied with the Western way of life center around the relentless pressures and frantic pace that this way of life entails. Eastern religions offer an alternative that involves serenity, tranquility, and inner peace.

This leads us to a question that, surprisingly, connects to *Parashat Vayeshev* (Gen. 37:1–40:23). The question is, "Is there anything wrong with seeking tranquility and inner peace? Are they not highly desirable components of a healthy and meaningful lifestyle?"

An answer can be found in the words of the Midrash Rabba that appear in most contemporary editions of Rashi's commentary, although they are absent from earlier manuscript editions.

The first words in *Parashat Vayeshev* read, "Now Jacob was settled in the land where his father had sojourned." The Bible then narrates the story of Jacob's son Joseph and how he is sold into slavery by his brothers.

Rashi, quoting the Midrash, comments, "Jacob wished to dwell in peace and tranquility but immediately was beset by Joseph's troubles and tribulations."

These words imply that it was somehow improper for Jacob to desire a calm and serene existence. The comment even suggests that Jacob was punished for his wish by suffering the disappearance, and supposed death, of his favored son.

Why? What possible sin would Jacob have committed by hoping for tranquility? Had he not suffered enough during his years of exile? Were the family crises described in detail in the previous *parasha* not sufficient torture?

Rabbi Yehuda Leib Alter (the second rebbe of Gur), the author of the *Sefat Emet*, a profoundly insightful hasidic work, suggests that the calm and peaceful life is not necessarily the religiously desirable one. Such a life is conducive to complacency.

"What God wants from the Jew," he writes, "is for him to have a life of constant toil in the service of His Blessed Name, because there is no limit to striving for perfection."

The Torah's ideal is a life of action and involvement in worldly affairs. The Torah rejects the attitude of detachment and passivity, which is implicit in the teachings of Eastern religions. The Torah cannot envision the good life if that life is without challenge. Achievement of inner peace is not the ultimate value, especially not if it results in withdrawal from responsible action within society.

The author of the *Sefat Emet* led his flock and wrote his works in the latter half of the nineteenth century. But the important lesson he taught was expressed about a century before, in the words of the Ramḥal, whose work *Mesillat Yesharim* (*The Path of the Just*) contains the following demanding passage:

> A man must know that he was not created to enjoy rest in this world, but to toil and labor. He should therefore act as though he were a laborer working for hire. We are only day laborers. Think of the soldier at the battlefront who eats in haste, whose sleep is interrupted, and who is always prepared for an attack. "Man is born to toil" (Job 5:7).

The teaching of both of these authors was anticipated by this passage in the Talmud (Berakhot 64a), as translated and elucidated in the *Koren Talmud Bavli*:

> Torah scholars have rest neither in this world nor in the World to Come, as in both worlds they are constantly progressing, as it is stated: "They go from strength to strength, every one of them appears before God in Zion" (Ps. 84:7).

The differences between the ideologies of Judaism and other religions are sometimes subtle and hard to define. But in contrasting Judaism with the religions of the Far East, the differences are quite clear. The latter promise inner peace and serenity and advocate detachment. Judaism makes no such promises. It tells us that life is all about struggle and challenge and it demands that we be actively involved in improving the world.

Parashat Vayeshev

Thinking and Dreaming

When I recall the great teachers I was blessed with over the course of my lifetime, I realize that one thing comes to mind: they were a diverse group. This eclectic group included the gentle man who introduced me to the study of Bible when I was in fourth grade; the seventh-grade teacher who inspired me to read great literature and to try my hand at writing; the talmudic scholar who turned me on to rabbinic study when I was about eighteen-years-old; and the devout Roman Catholic psychiatrist who was my mentor when I trained to become a psychotherapist.

What did they all have in common? They all were thinkers and intellectuals, each in his own distinct field. And they were all imaginative. They combined *sekhel* with *regesh*, intelligence with emotion, information with creativity.

My fourth-grade teacher used pictorial materials, which he had personally designed using his own substantial artistic skills, to illustrate the biblical stories we studied.

My seventh-grade teacher read to us as a reward at the end of a long day, made longer by the strain of a double curriculum. He read with great drama, moving us sometimes to tears, and at other times to fits of laughter.

The rabbi who made Talmud study so exciting did so using stories of great Talmudists over the ages, employing vivid imagery to convey the meaning of the most abstract texts.

And my mentor taught us how to understand people. He especially taught us the importance of the dream. But he was not interested in the dreams of our patients. He was interested in our own dreams, and he insisted that we pay attention to our dreams as one way to know ourselves better, something that he considered an absolute requirement for an effective psychotherapist. "The way to cultivate the imagination necessary to know another person," he would insist, "is to be aware of your own dreams and what they might mean."

In *Parashat Vayeshev* (Gen. 37:1–40:23), we meet Joseph, the dreamer. He was not the first person in the Bible to dream. His great-grandfather Abraham dreamt and his father Jacob dreamt several times. But Joseph not only dreamt himself. He paid attention to the dreams of others: the chief baker and chief cup-bearer in this *parasha*, and Pharaoh in the next *parasha*.

Joseph, though, was the first person in the Bible to attempt to interpret dreams. In modern terms, he was the first to use intellect in order to analyze the quintessential product of the imagination, the dream. It is no wonder then that Joseph was the first person in the Bible who is referred to as a *ḥakham*, a wise man.

Jewish tradition has always revered the intellect. The paramount mitzva in our religion is *Talmud Torah*, Torah study – an intellectual pursuit if there ever was one. We are proud of the towering geniuses in our history: Rabbi Akiva, who could "uproot mountains and grind them together" with the power of his intellect; Maimonides, who composed his commentary on the Mishna while still in his teens and went on to write his magisterial code and his awesome philosophical treatise; and the Gaon of Vilna, whose genius encompassed every aspect of Torah and extended into the fields of mathematics and astronomy.

But what about the imagination? What place does that have in our tradition? Is it suspect because it is not bound by reason? Is it acceptable but clearly secondary to rational thought? Is it in some way superior to the intellect?

The answer to these questions lies buried in the vast and daunting writings of two of our greatest philosophers: Maimonides, in his *Guide to the Perplexed*, and Rabbi Yehuda Halevi in his fascinating work, the *Kuzari*.

I can only briefly summarize the differing positions these two sages took on the subject of the power of the imagination (*koah hadimyon*). I trust that the reader will understand that I am simplifying very complex ideas.

For Maimonides, reason is the essential quality of man. Intellect is all-powerful and all-important. Philosophical expertise is a prerequisite for spiritual achievement. The imagination, according to Maimonides, is clearly secondary. It is limited to the sensory world and cannot transcend it. It is inadequate when thought is required. Even the prophet, whom one would think exemplifies the imaginative person, is basically a philosopher blessed with an additional skill: imagination.

Rabbi Yehuda Halevi, on the other hand, sees the imagination in very positive terms. For him, it is an alternate way of perceiving the world, and in some ways, is a superior method of perception. The intellect can perceive the world of physical reality, whereas the imagination has access to spiritual reality, to the *inyan eloki*, the "God factor." The prophet, according to Rabbi Yehuda Halevi, is essentially a mystic, not a philosopher.

At this point, the reader might be wondering about the relevance of these philosophic discussions to our everyday lives. It is here that I resort to yet a fifth great "teacher" that I was blessed to have. This teacher is the product of the decades I have amassed in working with educators, psychologists, and the pulpit rabbinate. After all, is not experience the best teacher?

Experience has taught me that our imaginations help us achieve some very important interpersonal goals. First of all, our imaginations enable us to put ourselves in the shoes of another person, to sense what he or she is going through. This is the skill of empathy, which is so essential if we are to get along with others. To be able to feel what another person is feeling requires an active imagination. Too often, we are limited in our ability to empathize with another because we only know our own feelings and reactions, and fail to comprehend that the other has different feelings and different reactions, even to the very same circumstances.

Imagination is important not only if we are to get along with others. It is also necessary if we are to succeed in life, for success requires the ability to envision new possibilities and creatively discover the options that are available in challenging circumstances. Problem-solving cannot be done with intellect alone. Flexibility and creativity and an imaginative vision are absolutely essential counterparts.

What made Joseph great? He was, as we will read next week, a *ḥakham* and a *navon*, a wise and discerning man. But he was also, as we read in this *parasha*, a dreamer, who could inquire empathically after the well-being of his fellow prisoners and ask them, "Why are you so downcast today?"

It was Joseph's imaginative capacity that allowed him to develop new options and to plan to avert the famine that threatened to annihilate the entire then-known world. His role in the history of our nation is a model of the exquisite blending of intellect with imagination. This balance is required of all of us if we are to understand each other, if we are going to succeed in life, and if we are to experience personal growth. Joseph's example is one that we are challenged to emulate and that we are assuredly capable of following in our own lives.

Parashat Miketz

Joseph, Ḥanukka, and Wisdom

Wisdom is the rarest of all important human qualities. Observers of the contemporary state of affairs often remark that wisdom, which is especially necessary in this day and age, is now particularly lacking.

Yet at the same time, we are told that there is an age in life when most of us finally do obtain wisdom. Erik Erikson, the famous psychologist and thinker, believes that the course of the lifespan is marked by a series of developmental stages. At each stage of life, we master different developmental tasks. In late middle age, about age sixty, one begins to achieve wisdom. Erikson's book, *Childhood and Society*, devotes an entire chapter to defining wisdom and to detailing the process by which one achieves it or fails to achieve it.

What is wisdom from a Jewish perspective? And what does wisdom have to do with the theme of Ḥanukka?

The search for wisdom is a frequent biblical theme. King Solomon was once assured by the Almighty that he would be granted the fulfillment of one wish. He wished for wisdom, obtained it, and is therefore termed in our tradition the wisest of all men.

Reading this story of Solomon and other sacred texts leads to the conclusion that there are at least two components to wisdom. There is a knowledge base: mastery of the facts and its data. There is also, however, the essential ability to select from this database those bits of knowledge that apply to the situation at hand. There is the mastery of material, and there is the ability to advance that material and make it relevant.

One of the early twentieth-century masterpieces in the field of Jewish ethics is a book by Rabbi Yosef Hurvitz of Novardok, entitled *Madregat HaAdam* (*Man's Stature*). Torah wisdom is one of Rabbi Yosef's themes. He insists that mastery of the corpus of Jewish law, in and of itself, does not constitute wisdom. Knowledge in "matters of the world" is also necessary; abstract knowledge must be interrelated with concrete reality.

The symbol of the Ḥanukka festival is, of course, the menora. The original Menora in the Holy Temple was situated in the southern end of the inner Temple shrine and consisted of seven branches. The menora symbolizes the light of wisdom, and its seven branches, the seven classical areas of wisdom, include not only knowledge of the Divine, but also mathematics and music.

Combining the wisdom symbolized by the menora with Rabbi Joseph's insights, we begin to appreciate the complexity of the concept of wisdom. It encompasses theoretical and practical knowledge and it involves the seven major areas of human inquiry.

It is in *Parashat Miketz* that we encounter the first man to be known as wise, to be recognized as a fount of wisdom. That man is Joseph and it is the Pharaoh of Egypt who calls him wise.

You know the story. The Pharaoh has his dreams, Joseph interprets them and suggests a plan of action. Pharaoh is pleased by the plan and says to his courtiers, "Could we find another like him, a man in whom is the Spirit of God?" And he continues and says to Joseph, "Since God has made all this known to you, there is none so discerning and wise as you."

Pharaoh recognizes that wisdom is not only mastery of facts and the ability to apply them; it is more than familiarity with the seven branches of worldly wisdom, and it is even more than life experience. Besides all that, it is a gift of God.

I have had the good fortune of meeting several wise people in my life and I am sure that most of you have as well. Whenever I have met such people, I have been struck by how their words seemed to come from a higher place. Their insights reflect that they have access to a source beyond my ken.

This was Pharaoh's experience when he heard Joseph's interpretation. He realized that no course of study – no training, no mastery of expertise – was sufficient to account for the good counsel that he was hearing. He knew that the man in front of him was blessed with the Spirit of God.

There is no better time than Ḥanukka when we read the story of Joseph to reflect upon the quality of human wisdom and to fully appreciate this lesson: Whatever else wisdom comprises, it has one indispensable ingredient. It is ultimately the inspiration of the One Above.

Parashat Miketz

But By My Spirit

It is a common scene in the United States at the time of year when *Parashat Miketz* is read. The shopping malls, television commercials, and all public venues are transformed visually. As December 25 approaches, we see the evidence that we do indeed live in a predominantly Christian country. Images of Santa Claus and his reindeers, evergreen trees with dazzling decorations, crucifixes illuminated by bright lights, and depictions of the Nativity are everywhere and are inescapable. The sounds of the songs of the season fill the air.

True, in recent times, and especially in cities where Jewish people are a significant presence, consideration is given to Ḥanukka. Symbols of our holiday and its music are also in evidence. We are thankful for that.

It is also true that many of our Christian friends, including the gentleman I am about to introduce to you, find all this public fanfare objectionable. They think of it as garish, commercially motivated, and inconsistent with the spiritual message of their faith.

But the reaction of many to this situation is similar to the one that my gentile friend Paul, with whom I worked closely during the years I was employed by the public school system, expressed to me some time ago. It was on a day in the middle of December and we were walking around one of the malls in suburban Washington, DC. He remarked, "Don't you and other Jews feel a bit outnumbered and overwhelmed at this time of year? It seems to me that your Ḥanukka candles make little impression in contrast to the lights on our trees and the jingle of our bells." I told him that I appreciated his candor and that he gave me cause for reflection.

At the time, I did not think that it would be tactful for me to tell him the truth; namely, that I had long ago reflected upon this phenomenon. And I had long ago concluded that the relatively modest manner in which Judaism celebrates Ḥanukka is nothing less than the essence of our religion.

When *Parashat Miketz* coincides with Shabbat Ḥanukka, we supplement the *parasha* with verses from the Book of Numbers that relate to the *ḥanukka*, or inauguration, of the Tabernacle. But for me, the highlight of the scriptural readings for this Shabbat has always been the words of the prophet Zechariah in the *haftara*.

Zechariah was a man who saw many mysterious visions. He would typically ask either the angel to whom he had access, or he would inquire of the Almighty Himself, to tell him what these visions meant. And so we find, near the end of the *haftara*, the following vision, "I see a lamp-stand full of gold, with a bowl above it. The lamps are seven in number; each has seven pipes above it, and by it are two olive trees."

Characteristically, Zechariah asks the angel who talked with him, "What do these things mean, my lord?" The angel, like a good psychotherapist, asks him what he thinks the dream means. But the prophet confesses that he has no clue. The angel finally responds, "This is the word of the Lord: 'Not by might, and not by power, but by My spirit, says the Lord of Hosts.'"

This is the lesson of Ḥanukka. The mighty are subdued by the weak and the many by the few. As a public demonstration of our holiday and its miracle, we eschew lavish displays and extravagant celebrations. Instead, we kindle humble *ḥanukkiyot* in the windows of our homes.

It is true that the mitzva requires *pirsum ha'nes*, a public ceremony to publicize the miracle. To that extent, our celebration is not totally modest and discrete. However, as the Talmud tells us, when the outside world is especially hostile, we are permitted to take the menora "and place it on our table, indoors, and that is sufficient." For many centuries, Jews did just that, so that their celebrations of Ḥanukka were painfully private.

But even today, when most of us can practice our religion publicly, a few modest candles suffice. We wish to make the point, to ourselves if not for the rest of the world, that "a little light can drive away much darkness." We are content to let other religions celebrate their holidays as they wish; colorfully, dramatically, and publicly. We understand the power of the ubiquitous symbols and of the songs loudly sung. But for ourselves, we prefer the softer sounds of the spirit and the quiet environment of our own homes. The mitzva is *ish ubeito*, every man and his house, each person with his family.

The lesson of the power of the single little candle is especially important in this day and age. We are bombarded by the images and sounds of cyberspace and their message is often pernicious and malicious. The negative effects of most of what we hear and see on the Internet and via other media are typically devastating to our hearts and souls, if not to our minds.

How do we counteract the immense influence of such overwhelming forces? We can only do so if each of us is committed to use the power of modern technology to assert tolerance, kindness, morality, and ethical behavior. Our voices may be soft, but they will be heard. The positive images that we present may be dim, but they will be seen.

The year after my encounter with my gentile friend, we met again and wandered through the same shopping mall in the middle of December. This time I decided to put my inhibitions aside. I openly shared my reflections about the discrepancy between the commercially motivated displays of the symbols of his faith and the softer, smaller, and gentler displays of our tradition's symbols. He heard me, although I cannot say that he fully agreed with me.

He did agree with me about one thing though. "A little light can dispel much darkness."

Forgiveness: A Jewish Value

T his has got to be one of the oldest "rabbi" jokes in the entire repertoire of American Jewish humor. It tells us of the young rabbi, fresh from rabbinical school, who addresses his first several sermons to his new congregation on the varied subjects of meticulous Sabbath observance, refraining from malicious gossip, honesty in business, and the avoidance of inappropriately familiar behavior with other men's wives.

After these first several homiletic salvos, the president of the congregation approaches him with the suggestion that these topics are much too sensitive and have upset many of the synagogue's members. The president urges the rookie rabbi to try to find some more acceptable topics to speak about.

The rabbi objects and asks, "But what, then, do you suggest that I speak about in my sermons?" To which the president replies, "Judaism! Why not just talk about Judaism?"

Those of us with experience in the pulpit rabbinate typically do not find this story very funny. Each of us has, on more than one occasion, taken on causes in our sermons that our audiences have felt were not in our rabbinic purview and indeed were somehow "not Jewish."

One of my favorite examples of this phenomenon in my own career has been my attempts, in sermons to the entire congregation and in more intimate counseling sessions, to encourage forgiveness. I will never forget the first time I made "forgiveness" the theme of one of my sermons, only to be accused by one of the more prominent members of my congregation of preaching Christianity. I urged people to forgive those who have offended them, only to find that for many Jews, forgiveness is a Christian not a Jewish, virtue. Of course, this is not true. Forgiveness is a major teaching of our own faith. We are encouraged to forgive others who may have sinned against us and we must seek forgiveness from those against whom we have sinned.

In *Parashat Vayigash*, we have an outstanding biblical example of forgiveness. Joseph, after putting his brothers through tests and trials, finally cannot contain himself. He exclaims, "I am your brother Joseph, whom you sold into slavery in Egypt." And immediately after identifying himself, he unequivocally forgives them: "Now, do not be distressed or reproach yourselves because you sold me hither...it was not you who sent me here, but God."

It is true that the brothers were "blown away" by this unanticipated revelation of the true identity of their tormentor and even more astounded by this assertion of total forgiveness. But this is not the first example of human forgiveness that we find in the Bible. Joseph may have learned about this value from his great-grandfather Abraham's precedent. Abraham, back in Genesis 20:17, not only forgives his adversary, Avimelekh, but offers prayers on his behalf.

What then can be the basis for the misconception that forgiveness is a Christian virtue and is not preached by Judaism? I think that the answer can be found in a precious book called *The Sunflower*, by Simon Wiesenthal.

Wiesenthal relates his personal experience of being brought to the bedside of a dying Nazi officer by the officer's own mother, who pleaded with him to forgive her son for killing Jews. Wiesenthal had been an eyewitness to this officer's murderous brutality. He found himself confronted with a moral dilemma. Could he deny a mother's tearful entreaties? On the other hand, could he possibly forgive such unspeakable cruelty? And could he forgive on behalf of others, the victims?

I will leave it for you, dear reader, to discover for yourself what Simon Wiesenthal actually did. But long after the event, he submitted this excruciating dilemma to several dozen philosophers, writers, and political leaders, asking them what they would do. Some of his respondents were Christians, some were Jews, and I believe one was a Buddhist.

The results were astounding. By and large, the non-Jews were able to find justification for forgiveness. On the other hand, most of the Jews could not express forgiveness for this soldier's heinous crimes, convinced that certain crimes were not subject to forgiveness.

For me, the lesson here is one that Judaism teaches well. Forgiveness must be earned, it must be deserved, it must be requested, and above all, it can only be granted by the person who was offended. I cannot forgive you for a sin you committed against my brother.

In a sense, Joseph goes beyond the call of duty in expressing forgiveness to his brothers. They did not even know who he was, let alone beg forgiveness from him. But he knew from close observation of their concern for each other that they had long transcended their previous petty jealousies and rivalries. He was convinced that forgiveness was in order.

Joseph is an exemplar of how important it is for each of us to forgive those who have offended us. Forgiveness is a practice for all year long and not just for the season of Yom Kippur. After all, it is not just on that one sacred day that each of us stands in need of the Almighty's forgiveness. His forgiveness is something we need at every moment of our lives.

The prophet Micah (7:18) says, "Who is God like You, tolerating iniquity, and forgiving transgression." Upon which the Talmud comments (Rosh HaShana 17a), "Whose iniquities does God tolerate? He who forgives the transgressions of another."

Wagons, Calves, and Responsibility

I have been blessed with many fine teachers. She was one of the best. Her name was Mrs. Lachmann. I no longer recall her first name. She taught an advanced course in world literature at the college I attended and she insisted that we call her Mrs. Lachmann, although as I later discovered, she had earned a doctorate with honors at a very prestigious European university

The course was an elective and I was motivated to take it because of my fondness for literature, which I developed quite early in my childhood. I was already familiar with some of the authors of our assigned readings, all of whom were nineteenth-century Russian or German writers, and assumed that the course would be an easy one for me.

I was a philosophy major, then, and was particularly impressed by Mrs. Lachmann's assertion, in the very first class session, that great literature is an important source of philosophical ideas. In fact, she insisted that a work of literature bereft of philosophical lessons could not qualify as great literature.

As the course progressed, two things became apparent. First of all, it was not going to be nearly as easy as I had anticipated. Furthermore, it was not philosophy in general that was her *sine qua non* for great literature. It was one specific concept that mattered so much to her. That was the concept of ethical responsibility.

I can still hear her, with her central European accent, making the case that great writers of fiction portray their characters in light of whether or not they meet their responsibilities.

"Several central questions are posed in all works of literature," she would say. She would then proceed to list those questions: "How do the heroes or villains of the novel define their responsibilities? Do they consider the long-term consequences of their actions? Do they feel accountable to others? To what degree is their sense of responsibility central to their personalities?"

She would quote the words of Fyodor Dostoevsky, who wrote *The Brothers Karamazov*, which was, in her opinion, the greatest novel of all time: "We are all responsible for all ... for all men before all, and I more than all the others."

I remember her remark at the end of her final lecture, "The theme of all great literature is the theme of responsibility."

Over the years, I have come to realize that Mrs. Lachmann's insight was not limited to the Russian and German writers of the nineteenth century. It applies even more to biblical literature. Indeed, I am convinced that the theme of personal responsibility is the core theme of the Book of Genesis.

One example of the theme of responsibility can be found in a verse in *Parashat Vayigash* (Gen. 44:18–47:27), as explicated by Rashi.

In the story, Joseph finally revealed himself to his brothers. They journeyed back to Canaan and informed Jacob that Joseph was still alive. Initially, Jacob did not believe them. The verse then reads, "But when they recounted all that Joseph had said to them, and when he saw the wagons (*agalot*) that Joseph had sent to transport him, the spirit of their father Jacob revived. 'Enough!' said Jacob. 'My son Joseph is still alive! I must go and see him before I die.'"

Rashi wonders what it was about the wagons that convinced Jacob and revived his spirit. Rashi tells us that these wagons were a sign sent by Joseph to Jacob, recalling the subject of their learned conversation when they first parted ways so long ago.

That subject is the ritual of the "calf with a broken neck," the details of which are described in the first several verses of Deuteronomy 21. Joseph was apparently confident that Jacob would see the connection between the word for wagons and the word for calf (*egla*).

The reader of Rashi's words cannot help but ask with astonishment: Is this some game, some bizarre wordplay? *Agala* calls to mind *egla*? What connection can there be between the ritual of the calf and Jacob's parting words of instruction to Joseph before sending him off on his mission to his brothers, never to see him again, or so he had come to believe?

To answer this question, we must reflect upon the meaning of the ritual of the "calf with a broken neck." It is a ritual that is performed by the elders of the city nearest to a discovered murdered corpse whose murderer is unknown. The elders must wash their hands over the calf whose neck was broken and declare that they did not shed this blood.

The Mishna asks, "Can we possibly suspect the elders of the city of murder?" The Mishna answers that the elders must declare that they did not allow the victim to pass through their city unfed, nor did they allow him to depart their city without escorting him along his way.

The early seventeenth-century commentator *Keli Yakar* understands this to mean that the elders must declare that they treated the victim decently and humanely. Had they not done so, they would be, however indirectly, responsible for the murder. Their failure to treat their fellow properly would render them responsible for his tragic end. The theme of responsibility for the long-term consequences of one's interactions is the dominant theme of this ritual.

As the *Keli Yakar* explains, if the elders of the city are not hospitable to the wayfarers who frequent the city, the criminals who populate the environs of the city will assume that this wayfarer is of no import and they will therefore take liberties with him, even to the point of shedding his blood. Were these villains to observe that the wayfarer was significant enough to the elders of the city to be treated graciously, they would have refrained from harming him.

This is the nature of responsibility. The elders are not suspected of actual murder. But if they treat their guests improperly, they set in motion a process by which those guests are dehumanized, becoming easy prey to malicious persons. That is how far the demands of responsibility extend.

When Jacob sent Joseph on his dangerous mission, continues *Keli Yakar*, he escorted Joseph part of the way. By doing so, he was teaching Joseph the lesson of the "calf with a broken neck," the lesson of the importance of escorting the traveler, thus demonstrating the human value of that traveler. Joseph signaled to his father that he learned that lesson well and knew the responsibility entailed in dealing with one's fellow.

Jacob realized that it was Joseph who personally had a hand in sending the wagons of Pharaoh, thereby escorting his brothers part of the way back to Canaan. Jacob took note of those wagons and therefore knew that Joseph had learned that a minor gesture of considerate behavior to others may have long-term consequences. He signaled that he had learned the crucial importance of taking responsibility for all one's actions, however insignificant they may appear. And so, "The spirit of their father Jacob revived."

Agalot and *egla* are not just words in a linguistic game. Rather, they allude to the profound lesson about personal responsibility, which is the basis of the requirement of the elders to proclaim their innocence of murder.

Let's return to Mrs. Lachmann, may God bless her soul. The reunion of Jacob and Joseph contains the implicit theme of which she spoke with such lasting impact so many years ago. Recall the questions that Mrs. Lachmann listed. "How do the heroes or villains of the novel define their responsibilities?" Joseph defines his responsibilities in terms of the need to be sensitive to other human beings. "Do they consider the long-term consequences of their actions?" Joseph certainly does. "Do they feel accountable to others?" Again, Joseph can answer with a resounding "Yes." "To what degree is their sense of responsibility central to their personalities?" Joseph demonstrated that his sense of responsibility was part of his very essence.

If, as Mrs. Lachmann contended, a profound sense of responsibility is the test of the true hero, Joseph certainly passed that test.

Parashat Vayigash

Reconciliation

I have known more than my share of families that are torn by discord. I think most of us, perhaps even all of us, are familiar with families in which brothers and sisters have not spoken to each other in years, sometimes even having forgotten the original reason for the destruction of their relationship. My background and experience in the field of family therapy has given me even broader exposure than most to this unfortunate phenomenon.

Colleagues of mine in the practice of psychotherapy will concur that helping clients overcome feelings of hatred and urges toward revenge is one of the most difficult challenges that they face in their practice. Reconciling parents and children, husbands and wives, is a frustrating process for those of us who counsel families. The successful reconciliation of ruined relationships is a rare achievement, especially after the misunderstandings have festered for years.

The Ramḥal contends that these difficulties are intrinsic to our human nature. Thus he writes:

Hatred and revenge. These, the human heart, in its perversity, finds it hard to escape. A man is very sensitive to disgrace, and suffers keenly when subjected to it. Revenge is sweeter to him than honey; he cannot rest until he has taken his revenge. If therefore he has the power to relinquish that to which his nature impels him; if he can forgive; if he will forbear hating anyone who provokes him to hatred; if he will neither exact vengeance when he has the opportunity to do so, nor bear a grudge against anyone; if he can forget and obliterate from his mind a wrong done to him as though it had never been committed; then he is, indeed, strong and mighty. So to act may be a small matter to angels, who have no evil traits, but not to 'those that dwell in houses of clay, whose foundation is in the dust.'" (Job 4:19) (*Mesillat Yesharim* [*The Path of the Upright*], chapter 11)

Granted that one must approximate the angels in heaven in order to overcome the natural human inclinations to hate and take revenge. How then do we explain the astounding reconciliation between Joseph and his brothers which occurs in this *parasha* (Gen. 44:18–47:27)?

Joseph's brothers came to hate him because of what they saw as his malicious arrogance. Joseph certainly had reason to hate his brothers who cast him into a pit full of snakes and scorpions. We can easily understand that he would attribute his years of imprisonment to their betrayal of him. And yet, in *Parashat Miketz*, we learned that the brothers came to regret their actions and to feel guilty for what they did to him. "Alas, we are at fault…because we looked on at his anguish, yet paid no heed as he pleaded with us" (Gen. 42:21).

In *Parashat Vayigash*, we learn of the forgiveness that Joseph demonstrated toward his brothers. We read of a dramatic reconciliation – a total triumph over hatred and revenge. What inner strengths enabled Joseph and his brothers to attain this rare achievement?

I maintain that quite a few such strengths helped Joseph's brothers to rejoin him harmoniously. One was their ability to accept responsibility for their actions. Over time, they reflected introspectively and concluded that they were indeed wrong for what they did. Self-confrontation and a commitment to accepting the truth when it surfaces allowed them to forget whatever originally prompted them to hate Joseph.

I further maintain that the underlying dynamics of Joseph's ability to forgive were very different. He came to forgive his brothers because of two fundamental aspects of his personality: his emotional sensitivity and his religious ideology.

Joseph's sensitivity becomes apparent to the careful reader of this and the previous Torah portions. The most reliable indication of a person's sensitivity is his ability to shed tears of emotion, his capacity to weep. Joseph demonstrates this capacity no fewer than four times in the course of the biblical narrative.

Subsequent to his initial encounter with his brothers, we read that, "he turned away from them and wept" (Gen. 42:24); when he first sees his younger brother Benjamin, "he was overcome with feeling.... He went into a room and wept there" (43:30); unable to contain himself after Judah's confrontational address, "his sobs were so loud that... the news reached Pharaoh's palace"; and finally, in *Parashat Vayeḥi*, in response to his brothers' plea for explicit forgiveness, "and Joseph was in tears as they spoke to him" (50:17).

No doubt about it. The biblical text gives us conclusive evidence of Joseph's emotional sensitivity. But there is another secret to Joseph's noble treatment of his brothers. It relates to his philosophy, not to his emotional reactivity.

If there is one lesson that Joseph learned from his father Jacob during his disrupted adolescence, it was the belief in a divine being who ultimately controls man's circumstances and man's destiny. When a person wholly has that belief, he is able to dismiss even the most painful insults against him. He is able to attribute them to God's plan and not to blame the perpetrators of that insult. Thus was Joseph able to say, "So, it was not you who sent me here, but God" (Gen. 45:8).

The power of genuine faith to instill the awareness that even hurtful circumstances are part of the divine plan is, in my opinion, best described in this passage from the anonymous thirteenth-century author of *Sefer HaḤinukh* in his comments on the commandment to desist from revenge:

At the root of this commandment is the lesson that one must be aware and take to heart the fact that everything that happens in one's life, whether it seems beneficial or harmful, comes about because of God's intervention.... Therefore, when a person is pained or hurt by another, he must know in his soul...that God has decreed this for him. He should not be prompted to take revenge against the perpetrator, who is only indirectly the cause of his pain or hurt. We learn this from King David who would not respond to the traitorous curses of his former ally, Shimi ben Gera.

The author of *Sefer HaHinukh* sees King David as the exemplar of this profound religious faith. In these final Torah portions of the Book of Genesis, we learn that Joseph was King David's mentor in regard to the capacity to rise above the misdeeds of others and to see them as but part of God's design.

It is not easy for us lesser believers to emulate Joseph and David, but we would be spared much interpersonal strife if we would at least strive to do so.

No Two Snowflakes Are Alike

I live on the eastern seaboard of the United States, which at the time of writing this particular piece, had recently been hit by a severe snowstorm. Most people find snowfall a nuisance. But for me, a snowfall is a chance to reflect on one of the Almighty's greatest wonders, the little snowflake.

The snowflake, held under a magnifying glass, is an exquisitely intricate and beautiful creation. Furthermore, every snowflake is unique. No two snowflakes are alike.

The uniqueness of each snowflake is but one example of an amazing fact, which is true of the entire natural world. No two blades of grass are identical, no two leaves are exactly the same, and every individual member of every animal species is unique in some way.

This is true of human beings as well. None of us has the same fingerprint, and no matter how closely one of us might resemble another, we are different from the other in some respect.

The Talmud recognizes this when it comments that "just as no two faces are alike, so too no two personalities are alike." We are different from each other physically, psychologically, intellectually, spiritually, and in every other way.

Any person who has parented several children knows that each child is different from the get-go. Mothers tell me that even while still pregnant with their children, they were aware of the potential differences that unfolded later in life.

Woe to the teacher who treats all of his or her students alike. The so-called cookie cutter method of education is doomed to failure. Each of us has different learning styles and differing intellectual strengths and weaknesses. The secret of successful pedagogy lies in the recognition of individual differences and in the ability of the teacher to be flexible enough to adapt his or her lessons to each individual and his or her learning needs.

In *Parashat Vayeḥi*, we find that our patriarch Jacob was well aware of this secret.

Jacob blesses the two sons of Joseph, and later proceeds to bless each one of his sons, the twelve tribes. Reading these blessings, we cannot help but notice how each one is fundamentally different and seems tailor-made to the character traits and emotional makeup of each tribe.

Jacob blesses one son with power and dominion, another with agricultural wealth. One is compared to a lion, one to a wolf, and yet another to a serpent. Jacob knows his children and knows how diverse and heterogeneous his family is. He knows how to bless them with the particular resources that they will need as they march forward with varying talents and dispositions into their historical roles.

The Bible underscores this when it summarizes the entire episode of the blessings with the following words: "All these were the tribes of Israel, twelve in number, and this is what their father said to them as he bade them farewell, addressing to each a blessing appropriate to him" (Gen. 49:28). To each a different blessing, to each his own parting word.

The fact that each of us is uniquely gifted is a basic component of the thought of Rabbi Abraham Isaac Kook, the chief rabbi of the Land of Israel, who passed away in 1935, but whose written legacy keeps him very much alive.

Rav Kook insists that the very purpose of education is to help each person discover his or her own individuality, to learn what he or she can do best. Self-discovery, for Rav Kook, is the essence of the educational endeavor.

Rav Kook, besides being an educator, was also a mystic. From his mystical perspective, he views the world as being a unified whole, to which every individual is necessary, because each individual contributes something utterly unique to the cosmos.

Each snowflake is different from the other because the beauty of each snowflake is equally essential to nature's beauty. Each human being is unique because the contribution of every one of us is absolutely necessary for the accomplishment of humanity's ultimate mission.

Like Jacob's children, we all are uniquely blessed. Appreciating our uniqueness, as that of every one of our fellow men, is an essential component of Jewish spirituality.

Each One Is One of a Kind

I was very embarrassed by her sharp rebuke, but looking back, I realize that the lesson I learned from her brief criticism was more valuable than most of my other training experiences.

It happened about forty years ago. I had the good fortune to attend an intensive workshop designed to teach young mental-health professionals the basic skills of the method known as psychodrama. The workshop leader was a world-famous psychodramatist, expert in both the complexities of the human psyche and the art of improvisational theater.

Psychodrama is a technique whereby a person's inner emotional conflicts are acted out in dramatic fashion under the direction of a skilled clinician. It is similar to what is known as role-playing, but more powerful.

Early on the second day of the workshop, I volunteered to play the therapist for another member of the group – let's call him Charles – who played the patient. Charles told of the challenges he was facing with certain key persons in his life. I suggested that he act out one of these conflicts in a particular fashion. I, of course, was convinced that my suggested strategy was brilliant and insightful until, only about two or three minutes into the exercise, the workshop leader thundered, "That's your psychodrama! That's not Charles' psychodrama!"

At that precise moment, I learned to appreciate that what was going on inside of me was based upon who I was and was very different from what was going on within Charles' mind. Those words of rebuke taught me a lesson to remember forever: I am different from you and you are different from me. We are all very different from each other, exquisitely and irrevocably different.

This lesson was well understood by our forefather, Jacob. In *Parashat Vayeḥi*, just before Jacob dies, he blesses all of his sons and two of his grandsons. He bestows these blessings upon them separately, fully aware that no one blessing fits them all.

The Torah sums up the entire deathbed drama with these words, "Their father spoke unto them and blessed them; every one according to his blessing, he blessed them" (Gen. 49:28). No two blessings were alike.

I have often thought that the greatest blessing that they each received was the message, "You are special. You are not the same as your brother. You have different personalities, different strengths, different talents, and therefore you each have a different destiny."

When I read this *parasha*, I am struck with wonder by the dazzling array of metaphors that Jacob uses: "unstable as water...weapons of violence...a lion's whelp...a colt bound to a tree...the blood of grapes... the shore of the sea...a large-boned donkey...a hind let loose...a bowed shoulder...a judge...a serpent on the road...a troop upon their heel...fat bread." Diversity, uniqueness, complexity, and individuality. That's the message.

Every parent and every teacher must learn this basic lesson. Teachers and parents must treat each child individually and must assure that each child comes to know his or her specialness.

Our sages throughout history have imparted this lesson to us. For example, Maimonides, in his fascinating review of the early life of Abraham, writes, "and he reasoned with each and every person according to that person's intelligence, until he convinced him of the truth" (*Mishneh Torah, Hilkhot Avoda Zara* 1:3). Again, when instructing us of our duties at the Passover Seder, he tells us that it is a mitzva to relate the story of the Exodus to each child according to his or her intellectual ability. A very young child must be told stories, one with limited mental capacity must be given concrete examples, and older and wiser children can be taught in a more abstract fashion. "Everything must be done according to the particular intelligence of the child" (*Mishneh Torah, Hilkhot Ḥametz UMatza* 7:2).

Among my favorite essays on the subject of education is the one written by the late Rabbi Elimelech Bar Shaul, once the Rabbi of Rehovot. He wrote, "If we give more to one who is only capable of receiving less, then we have given him nothing. And if we give less to one who can receive more, we have failed our mission, and worse – the student may come to think that there is no more, or that there is no more for him."

Giving too much to one with a lesser capacity can frustrate him irremediably. Giving too little to one with a greater capacity shortchanges him and cheats him, and worse – may alienate him forever.

Jewish mystics see human differences as but part of the Almighty's cosmic design. Thus, Rabbi Yaakov Moshe Charlap, a mystic in the tradition of his master, Rav Kook, writes, "There is no duplication in the universe. Just as no two people are perfectly alike, so there are no two things in all of the universe that are alike. Each person, like the grains of sand on the seashore, has a special quality and a special novelty."

Mystic or realist, appreciating our differences is our vital task as Jews, as human beings, and as residents of the Almighty's cosmos.

Parashat Vayeḥi

The Horse Thief

T hey called him a horse thief. That was the worst possible epithet that one could hurl at a young man in the early nineteenth-century *shtetl*, or village, of Czernovitz. Back then, a horse was a necessary item, and many of the townspeople spent all of their hard-earned savings to procure one. Losing one's horse often meant losing one's livelihood.

Truth to tell, he really was a horse thief, and he had other "virtues" as well. He desecrated the Sabbath regularly in a community where such desecration evoked horror. He was also a womanizer, a drunkard, and a gambler to boot.

The townspeople regularly attempted to have him expelled from the *shtetl*. But he had a powerful ally who blocked every attempt that the townspeople made to rid their community of this rascal. That ally was his father.

You might wonder why his father had such an influence in the small town. The answer is quite simple. His father was the rabbi of Czernovitz, and no ordinary rabbi at that. He was Reb Haim, one of the earliest hasidic masters, who came to be known in later generations by the title of his commentary on the Pentateuch, *Be'er Mayim Ḥaim*.

One year, on the eve of Yom Kippur, the townspeople had had enough. They approached the three most influential citizens of the town: Yankel, the chief of the City Council; Berel, the sexton of the synagogue; and Moshe, the cantor.

The entire town clamored around the three and insisted that they must confront the rabbi and demand that he banish his son from the *shtetl*. The councilman, the sexton, and the cantor had no choice but to proceed to the rabbi's home and tell the rebbetzin that they must have an appointment with her husband, even if it meant intruding upon his Yom Kippur spiritual preparations.

The rebbetzin politely requested that they be seated in the anteroom of the rabbi's modest study. "The rabbi is praying to the Creator," she explained. "He will certainly come out to see you when he is through."

The wall between the anteroom and the rabbi's study was paper thin. Yankel, Berel, and Moshe could not help but overhear every word of the rabbi's conversation with the Master of the Universe. At first, they were unperturbed and remained adamantly committed to demanding that the rabbi send his son away.

Then they heard the specifics of the rabbi's prayer, "Oy, dear Father in Heaven," he cried. "Yom Kippur, the day You sit in judgment, is almost here. I beseech You to have mercy upon the leaders of our little community. First of all, there is Yankel. He is in a position where he is tempted daily to take bribes, and he frequently submits to these temptations. Secondly, there is Berel, who regularly dips into the *tzedaka pushka*, the charity box, thereby stealing alms from the poor. There is also Moshe. I can't even bring myself to speak about his many misdeeds, any one of which would disqualify him from serving as our cantor. I know that You, dear God, have good reason to expel them from this world and could justifiably punish them severely."

At this point, the three gentlemen felt thoroughly ashamed and prepared to retreat from the rabbi's ramshackle abode one by one. But then they heard the rabbi conclude his entreaty, "But remember, dear God, that I too have a son who has failed me in so many ways. I have good reason to disown him and chase him from my home. I have not done so because I am a merciful father. Yankel, Berel, and Moshe are Your children, and if I can show mercy to my child, then surely You, the most Merciful One, must pardon them."

You know the rest of the story. The horse thief remained in the *shtetl* with no further protest from Yankel, or Berel, or Moshe, or anyone else.

I have often felt that Reb Haim of Czernovitz learned the proper behavior of a good father from the patriarch Jacob in *Parashat Vayeḥi* (Gen. 47:28–50:26). In this *parasha*, the Torah narrates the story of Jacob's final words of blessing to his sons.

Jacob had sufficient cause to withhold his blessing from quite a few of them. Besides Benjamin, they had all participated in the sale of Joseph, deceiving their father and causing him many years of grief and worry. Reuben was far from perfect – just turn back the pages to Genesis 35:22 to recall how he interfered with his father's marital relationships. And Simon and Levi disappointed him greatly with the violent act that they committed against the population of Shekhem, an act he never completely forgave.

Jacob does indeed rebuke them in his words of farewell. But he never rejects them totally. He sends none of them away.

He criticizes Reuben for being as "stable as water" and tells him explicitly, "When you mounted your father's bed, you brought him disgrace."

To Simon and Levi, he directs these words, "Cursed be their anger so fierce, and their wrath so relentless."

But the Bible ends the poignant episode of Jacob's parting words to his sons with this assertion, "All these were the tribes of Israel, twelve in number, this is what their father said to them as he blessed them, giving each one his own particular blessing."

He blessed all twelve. He disowned no one. He offered fair words of criticism, but uttered no words of rejection. Jacob thus taught a lesson to all parents for all time. Never close the door, no matter what faults you find in your child.

Reb Haim of Czernovitz learned that lesson, as we saw in the story of that Yom Kippur Eve approximately two hundred years ago.

He also recorded it so touchingly in his masterwork, *Be'er Mayim Ḥaim*, commenting near the end of *Parashat Vayeḥi*, "Jacob began his blessings with the words, 'Assemble and hearken, O sons of Jacob. Hearken to Israel your father.' He wanted them to listen well and feel assured that each of them, individually, had the spiritual vigor necessary to absorb and put to good use the blessed rays of light that he conveyed to them from the blessed lights of the Living God."

Parashat Vayeḥi

Changing the World

I have always been impressed by something my grandfather told me many years ago. I believe he quoted the following in the name of Rabbi Yisrael Salanter, the nineteenth-century founder of the Musar movement, which advocated the perfection of our ethical behavior:

> When you're young, you think you can change the world. As you get older, you realize that you can't do that, but you're still convinced that you can change the town in which you live. Then, there reaches a point where you realize you can't do that either. But you're still sure that you can change your family. Finally, you become aware that the most you can do is change yourself.

What's amazing to me, however, are the rare examples of individuals who have been able to change their worlds. I remember, for example, the older couple who lived in a community in which I once lived. We were a group of young married couples, most of whom were in the final stages of their professional training. The older man and his wife were both Holocaust survivors. We were certain that they felt out of place in our youth-oriented community. But eventually we realized not only that they fit in with us, but that they had an impact on each of us individually and upon our group as a whole. One couple was able to subtly but profoundly change an entire community.

I also recall the relatively few young men and women who were able to galvanize the American Jewish community to heed the plight of Jews in the Soviet Union. The adult religious and political establishments belittled those efforts, thinking them futile, even counterproductive. But a handful of young, committed individuals were able to change the attitudes of masses of Jews, finally achieving nothing less than the freedom of millions of our brethren.

Individuals can impact entire societies. This lesson can be learned from a careful study of *Parashat Vayeḥi* (Gen. 47:28–50:26). For, as I hope to demonstrate, Jacob alone changed his social environment at least twice in his life. Once, early on, he influenced the small town of Beersheba. Then, during the last stage of his life, he performed the feat of changing the culture of the most powerful nation of his time: Egypt.

We learned of his first achievement when we read the first verse of the *parasha* of *Vayetzeh*. "And Jacob left Beersheba and set out for Ḥaran" (Gen. 28:10). Rashi notes that the text emphasizes Jacob's departure from Beersheba. With his departure, "gone was the glory, gone was the beauty, gone was the prestige," which Jacob's presence bestowed upon that town. His very presence added so much to the town that when he left, the town was altered.

Vayeḥi is one of only two *parashot* that carry the Hebrew word for life, *ḥayim*. The other is *Parashat Ḥayei Sara*, which we read a while ago. It begins, "Sarah's lifetime [the span of Sarah's life] came to 127 years." *Parashat Vayeḥi* begins with the verse, "And Jacob lived seventeen years in the land of Egypt." Ironically, both narratives immediately continue with accounts of the deaths of the two protagonists, those of Sarah and Jacob.

But there is a difference. *Ḥayei Sara* indeed begins with an account of Sarah's death and burial. On the other hand, our *parasha* refers to the life Jacob lived in his final seventeen years, near his beloved Joseph. Those final seventeen years parallel the years that Jacob shared with Joseph, until they were tragically separated as Joseph turned seventeen.

How different these seventeen years were from the earlier ones. The initial seventeen years of Joseph's life were full of difficulties for Jacob: the trickery of Laban, the enmity of Esau, the seduction of Dinah, the violence of Simon and Levi, the death in childbirth of Rachel, Reuben's misconduct, and the heartbreaking disappearance of Joseph.

But his final seventeen years, spent in Egypt of all places, were full of life for Jacob – a vibrant and peaceful life, a renewed life, a life lived in the bosom of his family, surrounded by his children and grandchildren.

Remarkably, however, Jacob did not sit back idly and simply enjoy those years. Rather, he acted to bring blessing to the land of Egypt. As Rashi states in *Parashat Vayigash*, "Although Joseph predicted five more years of famine, great blessing accompanied Jacob when he came to Egypt. The people began to plant, and the famine ended." Other rabbinic sources tell us that it was because of Jacob's encouragement that the people resumed their agricultural activities, trusting him that they would be productive.

In hasidic literature, we learn even more about Jacob's role in Egyptian society. Hasidic sources are fond of quoting the holy Zohar, which notes that never in the lengthy narrative of Jacob's life is the phrase "and he lived" mentioned, because his life was full of trials and tribulations. Only when he descended to Egypt do we find this precise phrase.

One early twentieth-century hasidic sage, Rabbi Israel of Modzitz, the author of the homiletic work *Divrei Yisrael*, suggests that the verb in the phrase *vayeḥi*, "and he lived [in the land of Egypt]," can be interpreted as a transitive verb, "and he brought life to [the land of Egypt]." He revived Egypt.

Let us not forget that Egypt was, until this famine, the most fertile land on earth, the breadbasket for the world. We recall Lot's description of the plain of the Jordan, which he believed to be "like the garden of the Lord, like the land of Egypt" (Gen. 13:10). But when Jacob arrived in Egypt, it was no longer "like the garden of the Lord." It was not a source of life. It reeked of death, as Egyptian farmers complained, "nothing is left...save our bodies and our farmland. Let us not perish before your eyes.... Provide the seed, that we may live and not die."

Rabbi Israel probes deeply in his attempt to understand the spiritual powers that enabled Jacob to vivify a dead land. His analysis is a fascinating one. He points out that in order for a seed to develop into a source of food, the seed must go through two processes. It must first decay in the earth, losing all resemblance to the seed it once was. Then it is stimulated to grow. It must have what he calls the *koakh habitul*, the capacity to negate itself, to efface itself. It must also have the *koakh hatzemiḥa*, the ability to come alive, to sprout, to flourish.

Rabbi Israel continues to demonstrate that these two capacities were characteristic of Jacob, essential to his personality. Firstly, he had the *koakh habitul*, the capacity to demonstrate humility. He once exclaimed, "I am too small to deserve all the kindness that you have so steadfastly shown your servant" (Gen. 32:10). Jacob's ability to model self-effacement for the rest of Egyptian society was crucial in its revival.

Secondly, Jacob possessed the *koakh hatzemiḥa*, the capacity to flourish. Here, Rabbi Israel demonstrates his homiletic ingenuity and keen psychological insight. The secret of *tzemiḥa*, the ability to transform oneself, to blossom, is the ideal of truth. As the Psalmist says, "Truth will sprout forth from the earth." Truth has a generative power. It can cause genuine transformation and authentic change. And truth, as Micah teaches us at the very conclusion of his prophecy, is Jacob's hallmark, "You have granted truth to Jacob, loyalty to Abraham, as you promised on oath to our fathers in days gone by" (Mic. 7:20).

Jacob's humility and his commitment to truth were his two secret powers that enabled him to foster growth in others and to single-handedly transform an entire culture.

Thinking back to the elderly couple who lived among our group of inexperienced twenty-somethings, it was that couple's sincere humility and their absolute authenticity and truthfulness that enabled them to penetrate our naïveté and teach us lessons for a lifetime.

And it was the selflessness and genuine commitment of a small group of young people that helped them change the minds of an entire society and eventually even change the minds of the Soviet tyrants.

We can use the occasion of the conclusion of the Book of Genesis to rededicate ourselves to those two primary Jewish values: humility and truth. We can thus cultivate in ourselves the *koakh habitul* and the *koakh hatzemiḥa*, the capacity to humbly cause others to flourish.

But Jacob teaches us that we can go beyond changing ourselves. We can influence our families and impact our communities, and perhaps even change the world.

Exodus

Parashat Shemot

Sleepless Nights

Can you sleep at night? There is so much trouble in the world. Violence, wars large and small, natural disasters, disease. We all personally know many who are suffering at this very moment. Some are friends and acquaintances living in plain sight. Others are individuals in the media, people whose pain we see portrayed daily on the evening news.

It is perfectly understandable to be unable to sleep at night. Yet most of us do manage to sleep quite well. We all have developed a repertoire of defense mechanisms designed to enable us to keep these troubles from our consciousness. We have compartments in our minds into which we can deposit the suffering of others, somehow sealed and kept from immediate awareness.

But there are those among us who cannot sleep, for the pain of others keeps them awake. Their empathy is so great that the suffering of others is their own suffering and cannot be compartmentalized, or even temporarily forgotten. Indeed, rather than try to shield themselves from others' travails, they seek out those others in order to witness their suffering. They do not stop with mere observation and compassion, but actively attempt to alleviate the suffering they witness.

Such a person was Moses, to whom we are introduced in *Parashat Shemot*. Moses was raised in the very lap of luxury. He was reared as a prince in a royal palace, his foster mother the daughter of Pharaoh himself. He grew up in a protected environment in which he was able to remain unaware of, and could certainly ignore, the plight of his enslaved brothers.

But he chose to do otherwise. The very first self-initiated action of which we read in the account of Moses' life is his inquiry into the condition of his enslaved kinsfolk. "When Moses had grown up, he went out to his brothers and witnessed their labors" (Ex. 2:11). He did not have to go out; he could have remained in his protected royal quarters. He did not have to "witness"; he could have shut his eyes or used any of the methods we use to shield ourselves against seeing what we do not want to see. But that was not Moses. In Rashi's poignant phrase, "He gave over his eyes and his heart to suffer along with them." He could not sleep.

We often wonder about what qualified Moses for the leadership role he was destined to attain. For that matter, more generally, we speculate as to what qualifies anyone for leadership.

Theories of the elements of good leadership abound. Stephen Covey has written a book on this very subject entitled *The Eighth Habit*. In it he offers a chart, briefly summarizing no fewer than twenty such theories, with a list of hundreds of books on the topic.

The theories range from "great man" theories, which contend that leaders are born to leadership because of their innate gifts. But Moses had innate handicaps, which included a speech defect (*aral sefatayim*). Other theories stress the motivations of leaders to lead. Moses insistently and consistently shunned the leadership role. Still other theories stress the powers of persuasion and the gift of popularity. Neither characterized Moses. He had no apparent charisma, no formal leadership training, no career aspirations, and no special vision other than the one shown to him by God.

Of all the theories on Covey's comprehensive list, one seems to fit: the theory of "servant leadership," which implies that leaders primarily lead by serving others. The primary characteristics of such a leader include listening and empathy. These were demonstrated by Moses in his very first venture out of the royal palace.

The characteristics of such leadership also include a commitment to others' growth. Moses' leadership can be seen as a life-long process of commitment to others' growth: to their freedom from slavery, to their spiritual conditions, to their ordinary needs, and to their moral and ethical education.

Some of us strive to be leaders. Most of us are content to leave leadership to others, yet strive to know God, to know our own souls, and to benefit others in some small way.

The lesson of the life of Moses is that both the grand leadership that some of us seek and the more modest goals of all who are spiritually motivated can be achieved by "going out to our brothers and witnessing their condition." It may cost us sleepless nights, but it will bring us enlightened days.

In the words of an anonymous poet:

I sought my God and my God I could not find.
I sought my soul and my soul eluded me.
I sought my brother to serve him in his need,
And I found all three – my God, my soul, and thee.

Open Eyes and an Open Heart

I was always taught of the advantage of simplicity in language. My favorite author during my adolescence was Ernest Hemingway and I remember reading comments that he made criticizing those who used multi-syllable words when shorter words would suffice.

Then I went to graduate school in psychology and learned quite the opposite lesson. There I learned that if one could invent a word with multiple syllables to describe a simple phenomenon, he could gain credibility as an expert, even without real expertise.

Take, for example, a word with seven syllables: compartmentalization. Sounds impressive, but what does it mean? The dictionary that I consulted offers two meanings. One, "the act of distributing things into classes or categories of the same type." A simple definition, but one having nothing to do with psychology.

The second dictionary definition that I discovered is "a mild state of dissociation." Of course, to understand this definition, one must know that dissociation is a psychological process by which one splits two sets of perceptions or emotions into two separate inner worlds so that one does not affect the other.

All of us practice compartmentalization in this sense when we turn on the television, see some news events that are especially troubling to us and simply turn off the TV. Many of us did this, for example, when we witnessed the terrible forest fires in northern Israel and the horrible deaths of more than forty people. Watching the agony of the families whose loved ones were consumed by that fire was, for many of us, too much to bear. And so, perhaps after a minute or so, we turned off the TV to avoid being confronted with such human suffering.

This might be normal human behavior, and perhaps even necessary to avoid being overwhelmed with negative emotions. But it is not the behavior of a true leader. And it was not the behavior of Moses here.

Rather, "he went out unto his brethren, and looked on their burdens" (Ex. 2:11). Upon which Rashi comments, "He gave his eyes and his heart [in order] to be troubled about them." Not only did he not avoid the scene of Jewish suffering, but he made sure that he beheld it ("his eyes"), and that it affected him emotionally ("his heart").

Two very important, albeit very different, early twentieth-century commentators have much to say about our verse. Rabbi Joseph H. Hertz, in his sadly neglected commentary, writes, "He went out *to* his brethren. In later ages it must alas be said of many a son of Israel who had become great, that he went away *from* his brethren." How well this former chief rabbi of the British Commonwealth captures the notion of compartmentalization. It is the process by which we *look away* from upsetting scenes, rather than carefully looking *at them*.

Rabbi Simha Zissel Ziv, known as the "Alter" (old man) of Kelm devotes the opening sermon of his remarkable collection of ethical discourses to our verse and to the criticism of the psychological process that we call "compartmentalization."

The "Alter" points out that Moses was not content simply to hear about the suffering of his brothers while he sat comfortably in the palace. Rather he "went out" to see for himself. Moses wanted to witness the suffering of his brothers personally. Moses knew the secret of the power of direct sensory perception. Moses wanted to have the image of the burdens of slavery impressed upon his mind's eye.

For the "Alter," who was one of the earliest leaders of the Musar movement, ethical behavior demands the use of imagery to arouse emotions and thus stimulate proper ethical behavior. Moses used his eyes to inspire his heart to motivate his actions. Vision, feeling, and behavior are the three essential components of the truly ethical personality.

The lesson for all of us here is that to be a truly ethical person, one must invest in the effort of becoming familiar with the plight of others. One must avoid the temptation of "looking away." From a psychological perspective, compartmentalization might be a healthy defense mechanism, necessary to avoid being flooded by images of evil. From an ethical perspective, on the other hand, compartmentalization is a seven-syllable word, which, in simple terms, means avoidance of one's responsibilities to another.

How instructive is the hasidic tale of the rabbi who met the village drunkard in the town square. The drunkard asked him, "Rabbi, do you love me?" To which the rabbi replied, "Of course I love you. I love all Jews!"

The drunkard then responded, "So tell me then rabbi. What hurts me?" The rabbi had no answer, and so the drunkard exclaimed, "If you truly loved me, you would know what hurts me."

To know what hurts, we must be sure to open our eyes and hearts to see and feel the pain.

Parashat Shemot

Spiritual Time Management

The two old men couldn't have been more different from each other. Yet they both taught me the identical life lesson.

The first, a cagey old Irishman, was one of my mentors in the postgraduate psychotherapy training program in which I was enrolled many years ago. He wrote quite a few books in his day, but they are all out of print now and nearly forgotten, like so many other wise writings.

The other was an aged rabbi, several of whose Yiddish discourses I was privileged to hear in person. He was but moderately famous in his lifetime, but is much more widely known nowadays because of the popularity of his posthumously published writings.

The lesson was about the importance of time management. Neither of these two elderly gentlemen used that term, which is of relatively recent coinage. Yet their words, while far fewer than the words of the numerous contemporary popular books on the subject of time management, made a lifelong impression upon me.

It was long after my encounter with these elderly gentlemen that I first realized their lesson was implicit in a verse in *Parashat Shemot*.

The Irishman, we'll call him Dr. McHugh, was a master psychotherapist with fifty years of experience under his belt. A small group of us gathered in his office every Tuesday evening. We went there not only for his wisdom, but for the warm and comfortable furnishings and splendid view of the city of Washington, DC.

Dr. McHugh was an existentialist. He was heavily influenced by his encounters with Martin Buber, and because of this, he felt a special affinity to me, thinking that since Buber and I were both Jewish, we must have had much in common. He wasn't aware that my Judaism was very different from Buber's, but I wasn't about to disabuse him of his assumption.

He was a diligent and persistent teacher and, true to his philosophical perspective, doggedly encouraged us to appreciate the human core of the patients we were treating. He was convinced that he had a foolproof method of comprehending that human core. "Tell me how the patient uses his time, how he organizes his daily schedule, and I will tell you the secret foundation of his soul."

Dr. McHugh firmly believed that you knew all you needed to know about a person if you knew how he used his time. Or, as he put it, "if he used his time and how he used it." He would then make his lesson more personal and would ask, carefully making eye contact with each of us, "How do *you* busy yourself?"

In the summer following that postgraduate course, I took advantage of the rare opportunity of hearing the ethical discourses, the *musar shmuessen*, of the revered Rabbi Elya Lapian. He too spoke of the fundamental importance of one's use of time and he too, though he did not even know the term, was quite an existentialist.

He began his remarks quietly, almost in a whisper. Gradually his voice reached its crescendo, and when it did, he uttered the words I will never forget, "*Der velt sagt*," he said in Yiddish, "the world says that time is money. But I say time is life!" I was a young man then, but not too young to appreciate the profound meaningfulness of that simple statement. Time is life. He went on to say that we all allow ourselves to become busy and busyness detracts from life.

It was quite a few years later that it dawned upon me that the Irish psychiatrist and the Jewish spiritual guide were preceded in their teaching by the Ramḥal, who was himself preceded in antiquity by none other than Pharaoh himself.

In the second chapter of his widely studied ethical treatise, *Mesillat Yesharim* (*Path of the Upright*), the Ramḥal writes of the tactics of the *yetzer*, the personification of the evil urge, which is buried within each of us:

> This is, in fact, one of the artifices of the evil inclination, which always imposes upon men such strenuous tasks that they have no time left to note whither they are drifting. He knows that, if they were to pay the least attention to their conduct, they would change their ways instantly…. This ingenuity is somewhat like that of Pharaoh … for Pharaoh's purpose was not only to prevent the Israelites from having any leisure to make plans or take counsel against him, but to deprive them also of the very opportunity to reflect.

To become so busy and have no time to reflect, no time to really live, is bondage. Ramḥal's insight into Pharaoh's scheme epitomizes the essential nature of our years of exile in Egypt. To have no time, that is slavery.

How prescient were the words of Rabbi Elya Lapian. Time is life. And how germane is his teaching for contemporary man, who despite the "time-saving" technological devices that surround him, is even busier than those who came before him. Contemporary man has no time for himself, certainly no quality time, and thus no life. Time is life.

Millennia ago, an Egyptian tyrant knew this secret. Centuries ago, an Italian Jewish mystic was keenly aware of it. Decades ago, I learned it from a gentile existentialist psychiatrist and a gentle and pious rabbi.

It is the secret of spiritual time management and it is the secret of life. Would that we would learn it today.

Reading the Footnotes

I often find myself disagreeing with the phrase, "It's just a footnote in history." I have found some of the most interesting and important facts buried, unseen by most people, in the footnotes of the books I read.

Recently, I have begun to use a pocket-sized edition of the Talmud in my daily study. I have been doing a lot of traveling lately and this miniature edition suits me well.

I find that the print of the main text and major commentaries in this edition is in sharp focus and although quite small, is perfectly legible. However, this edition, known as *Oz VeHadar*, contains an innovative feature. In the margins of every page are footnotes in very fine print, indicating variant readings of the traditional text. These footnotes supply minor corrections based upon ancient manuscripts or early print editions of the Talmud.

These footnotes are so small that I can hardly make them out, even with my glasses. I resort to the use of a magnifying glass, which enlarges the size of the letters by four or five times. In one corner of the glass is a small circle with an even more powerful magnifier, which enlarges the size of the letters to ten or perhaps twelve times their size.

I find these footnotes extremely useful in my study. Invariably, they suggest changes to the text that seem minor but are not at all trivial. Passages in the Talmud that I previously found vague or puzzling are elucidated with the change of a word or sometimes even the addition of one single letter.

Often I am tempted to ignore these footnotes, passing up the opportunity to use the magnifier. But when I do so, I forfeit the opportunity of gaining surprising and edifying insights. These marginal footnotes, together with this magnifier, have literally opened my eyes to the authentic meaning of the text, and have given me a fresh understanding of passages that I had previously found challenging.

In *Parashat Shemot* (Ex. 1:1–6:1), we encounter a phrase in Rashi's commentary that my experience with the footnotes and the magnifying glass has helped me appreciate anew.

The Bible has just concluded the account of baby Moses' rescue by Pharaoh's daughter. It is about to proceed to narrate the story of the mature Moses. It begins, "Sometime after that, when Moses had grown up, he went out to his brethren and he saw their labors" (Ex. 2:11).

Rashi comments, "He saw their labors: He directed [literally, 'gave'] his eyes and heart, to feel troubled for them." Rashi's comment is prompted by the words "he saw." Of course, if he went out to his brethren, he "saw" their labors.

Rashi, therefore, suggests an alternative and deeper interpretation of the words "he saw." He is telling us that he didn't merely see visually. He saw deeply. He took notice. Metaphorically, he used his "magnifying glass" to discover every footnote, to absorb every detail of his brethren's toil. What he saw troubled him and he suffered along with them.

The Midrash, serving as our "magnifying glass," provides an expanded picture of every "footnote" in the scene that Moses saw:

> He saw their labors, and he wept, saying, "Woe is me, I am willing to die for them." He extended his shoulders to help carry the burden of each and every one of them. He saw the weak carrying heavy burdens, and the strong carrying lighter ones. He saw manly burdens being carried by women, and feminine burdens carried by men. He saw tasks appropriate for the elderly assigned to the

young, and tasks befitting the young passed along to the elderly. He put aside his royal equipage and eased their labors.... So that the Holy One, blessed be He, said to him, "You left behind your concerns, went to observe Israel's pain, and reacted like a good brother. So too will I, God, leave behind My upper and lower celestial spheres and speak to you."

The Midrash's implication that the Almighty, so to speak, took his cue from Moses is a daring one. But even more daring from a theological perspective is Rashi's comment on a later phrase in the *parasha*, "God looked upon the Israelites, and God knew."

What can "and God knew" possibly mean? After all, He is all-knowing, omniscient.

Targum Onkeles, troubled by this question, renders the phrase "God knew" into Aramaic as, "and God gave His word that He would redeem them." A widely-used English translation renders the phrase "and God took notice of them." Rashi offers a theologically daring comment, "He directed [literally, 'gave'] His heart toward them and did not hide His eyes."

Returning to the metaphor I introduced above, God, so to speak, used His divine magnifying glass to scrutinize every footnote, to attend to every detail, of Israel's enslavement. Rashi dares to apply the same terms that he used to describe Moses' empathic response, "eyes" and "heart," to the Almighty Himself. Rashi leaves his readers with an image of a God who demonstrates human-like sympathy for His suffering people.

There is much more to these two passages in Rashi's commentary than an account of Moses' compassion. There is more to them than just a glimpse of God's merciful ways. There is a lesson here for all of us.

We often "see" our brothers in difficulties of one sort or another. Typically, matters stop right there. We "see" them, but we do not extend ourselves in the ways that Moses did. Quite the contrary: we tend to look away.

But there is another, much more worthy, option. We can utilize our magnifying glass to look at the footnotes. We can pay careful attention to the plight of our brothers, noting all the details of their plight. We can direct our eyes to the scene that is before us and can then open our hearts so that we feel the pain of others who suffer. Finally, like Moses, we can shed our inhibitions and plunge right into the fray, extending our shoulders to help bear our brother's burden.

Moses is called *Moshe Rabbenu*, Moses our Teacher. We can learn many things from him, but the very first lesson, one that he modeled by his own conduct, is: Direct your eyes and your heart to your brother's suffering.

Parashat Va'era

On the Shoulders of Giants

T hey don't make them the way they used to." We have all heard this comment with reference to all sorts of things, usually tools and utensils. Despite all the technological advances from which we benefit, we often are convinced that certain things were of superior quality in the old days. We believe that the old hammer Grandpa once used was stronger, and the snow shovel he wielded more effective, than the new-fangled "throwaway" junk that they produce nowadays.

We even extend this belief of things being better back in the old days to human beings. Today's leaders cannot be compared to those of old, and today's athletes are cheap imitations of the Babe Ruths and Ty Cobbs of yesteryear.

In the Jewish tradition, there is a concept of "the generations get progressively smaller (*nitkatnu hadorot*)." Talmudic sages are no match for biblical heroes, and the great rabbis of recent times cannot compare to the rabbinical leaders of centuries ago.

Like any other belief, this one requires a healthy dose of skepticism. Surely technological progress has provided us with tools that are superior to those we once used. And whereas every generation has its outstanding heroes, not everyone in the past was a perfect person. Furthermore, there are plenty of people today who can stand up to the best of previous generations in their courage, in their erudition, or in their piety.

In *Parashat Va'era*, we encounter what might be the first example in history of the comparison of a current personage with previous ones, in which the former comes off poorly.

Rashi shares with us, and ultimately rejects, the Talmud's version of what the opening verses in our *parasha* tell us. The Talmud understands these verses in the context of the concluding episodes of the previous Torah portion, in which Moses challenged the Almighty and asked Him why He has "mistreated this people," thereby questioning his very mission. Indeed, somewhat earlier in *Parashat Shemot*, he asked God, "What will I tell the people if they ask me for Your name?"

With this background, the rabbis understand the opening verses of our Torah portion as follows: God compared Moses to Abraham, Isaac, and Jacob. From this perspective, the patriarchs were much more trusting in God and demonstrated greater faith than Moses. They did not question God in spite of their frustrations. Moses did.

"A pity that they are gone and no longer to be found." This statement, which the rabbis attribute to the Lord, closely resembles the opening statement of this essay, "They don't make them like they used to."

Personally, I have come to appreciate the opinion of those other commentators who defend Moses, and who point out that Moses challenged God not out of faithlessness, but out of a profound and powerful empathy for the suffering of His people.

Abraham, Isaac, and Jacob were individuals. At best, they were heads of families, whereas Moses was the leader of a nation. In his circumstances, blind faith would have been irresponsible.

When comparing later generations with earlier ones, we must take into account the changed circumstances of those later generations. We must judge them, not by the standards of those who came before them, but in their own contexts.

In the reading that I do about victims and survivors of the Holocaust, I often ask myself whether I could possibly have struggled to remain alive in the conditions of torture and horror that they experienced, retaining their will to live. And I am certain that had I personally suffered the Holocaust experience, I would not have been able to emerge from it with the faith commitment of so many of the survivors, who came to these shores with recreated families, practicing their faith punctiliously, and reconstructing vibrant religious institutions.

It is not, I believe, that we are innately inferior to them. Rather, our circumstances have softened us, whereas their circumstances strengthened them. There is indeed a theme in our tradition that sees a generation as diminished in comparison with the previous one, the later generation in fact becoming "smaller." But our tradition also encourages us to realize that later generations have one great advantage over previous ones: We stand on their shoulders. We benefit from their precedent.

Moses had this advantage. He could learn from Abraham, Isaac, and Jacob and could model his faith and leadership capacities upon them. From this view, Moses' confronting the Almighty in defense of his people was simply something he learned from Abraham, who similarly confronted God in defense of the people of Sodom.

It might be true of us that "they don't make them the way they used to," but that need not stop us from asking ourselves, as our sages did, "When will my deeds approach the deeds of my fathers?" For we have the deeds of our fathers to learn from as we build our own spiritual lives.

We stand on the shoulders of long generations of giants. Perhaps future generations will similarly look up to us.

Parashat Va'era

Work and Will

There was a time in my life when I was fascinated by the works of the great psychoanalytic thinkers. Chief among them, of course, was Sigmund Freud, whose attitude toward his Jewish origins piqued my curiosity.

Although Freud's work has now fallen out of fashion, he unquestionably had some profound things to say about humanity. There is one remark of his that has remained with me over the years. He said, "Love and work are the cornerstones of our humanness." He considered the ability to love and the ability to work the two criteria of mental health.

There was a lesser-known psychoanalyst, a disciple of Freud, whose writings also fascinated me. His name was Otto Rank, and he disagreed with his mentor in many ways. He left "love" out of the formula for the healthy personality. Instead, he inserted his concept of "the will." For him, our ability to work productively and to express our will creatively were the cornerstones of our humanness.

Rank wrote entire volumes about the nature of man's will and of its importance. In simplified terms, the will is the directive intention by which we get things done in life. In his words, "It is a positive guiding organization of the self which utilizes creativity" to accomplish one's objectives.

In a much more recent time in my life, I have come to ponder the nature of spirituality. I have become convinced that the ability to engage in meaningful work and the capacity to exercise one's will creatively are two essential components of spirituality.

In *Parashat Va'era* (Ex. 6:2–9:35), we read about the first stages of the redemption of the Children of Israel from bondage in Egypt. We learn that freedom from slavery does not come easily. A measure of spiritual preparedness must first be achieved.

Were the Jewish people spiritually ready for redemption? When we read *Parashat Shemot*, we were inclined to believe that they may very well have been ready. "Aaron repeated all the words that the Lord had spoken to Moses... and the people were convinced... they bowed low in homage" (Ex. 4:30–31).

In *Parashat Va'era*, however, we learn that that level of spiritual readiness was short-lived. "But when Moses told this to the Israelites, they would not listen to Moses, because their spirits were crushed [literally, 'out of shortness of breath'] and their bondage cruel [literally, 'out of difficult labor']" (Ex. 6:9).

Two factors stood in their way. "Their spirits were crushed." In Otto Rank's terms, their "will" was crippled. They could not dream, they could not plan, and they could not utilize their creativity. In no way could they "get things done" in their lives. A person without will is a person paralyzed. Such a person cannot transition from slavery to freedom.

Their "bondage was cruel." Freud was correct that productive work was one of the "cornerstones of humanness." Meaningful work nourishes the soul. But the work that the Jews were forced to do in Egypt was far from meaningful. Besides being physically tortuous, it was purposeless. Our sages teach us that the labor that Egypt forced the Jews to do was not only unbearably strenuous; it was belittling and demeaning. Such work is poison for the soul, and a poisoned soul is not ready for redemption.

Pharaoh knew all too well how to thwart the initiative of his slaves, how to assure that they would take no effective steps to attain their freedom. "Let heavier work be laid upon the men; let them keep at it and not pay attention to deceitful promises" (Ex. 5:9).

Denied the access to their creative will and deprived of the rewards of meaningful work, the Jews were spiritually handicapped. They could not hear the words spoken to them by Moses – not because their hearing was impaired, but because they were spiritually deaf. Moses had his work cut out for him, and only with divine assistance, could he hope to advance his people to the point where they would be ready to hear the clarion call of incipient redemption.

There is a lesson here for all of us. We too are deaf to God's redemptive messages. Our spiritual condition is woefully inadequate to prepare us to hear higher callings.

The Ramḥal puts it so well in the second chapter of his *Mesillat Yesharim*:

> This is, in fact, one of the artifices of the evil inclination, which always imposes upon men such strenuous tasks that they have no time left to note whither they are drifting. He knows that, if they were to pay the least attention to their conduct, they would change their ways instantly…. This ingenuity is somewhat like that of Pharaoh…for Pharaoh's purpose was not only to prevent the Israelites from having any leisure to make plans or take counsel against him, but to deprive them also of the very opportunity to reflect.

Nowadays, it is as if each of us has an "inner Pharaoh" whose malicious intent it is to entrap us into a lifestyle where we not only overwork, but where our work is unfulfilling and therefore spiritually unrewarding. This "inner Pharaoh" is also shrewd enough to know how to stunt that creative human will that is such an essential component of spirituality.

Mankind's struggle against "crushed spirits" and "cruel burdens" is a historical struggle, one that is certainly relevant in our times. There are obstacles to finding and defining a work-life that is meaningful. There are impediments to our ability to exercise our creative wills. But we must use whatever tools are at our disposal to lift those cruel burdens and free our crushed spirits. Those tools include introspective reflection, contemplation of pertinent religious texts, conversation with like-minded friends, and dialogue with experienced spiritual mentors.

Parashat Va'era

Hopeless

I remember the conversation very well. It was a discussion among a group of assorted friends, from a variety of backgrounds. One or two were true scholars. The others were not scholars by any stretch of the imagination, but were familiar with those Jewish texts frequently read in the synagogue.

The discussion revolved around the question, "What is the saddest verse in the entire Bible?" The opening candidate for the saddest verse was the passage in *Parashat Vayetzeh*, which reads, "The Lord saw that Leah was unloved." But that phrase was soon rejected in favor of the second half of that same verse, "but Rachel was barren." No question about it. Both the lack of love and infertility are very sad human conditions.

Others quoted various verses from the curses in the weekly portions of *Behukkotai* and *Ki Tavo*. There is no paucity of horribly sad verses in those two *parashot*. Here are just a few: "I will set my face against you…your foes shall dominate you"; "I will heap your carcasses upon your lifeless fetishes"; "You shall eat your own issue, the flesh of your sons and daughters." For these phrases, the adjectives "frightening" or "terrible" seem more appropriate than "sad."

For most of the discussion, I remained silent. For you see, I had long before concluded which Torah verse was the saddest for me. The verse appears in *Parashat Va'era* (Ex. 6:2–9:35). It reads, "But they would not listen to Moses because of their crushed spirit and difficult toil" (6:9).

Let's understand the context of this verse. In *Parashat Shemot*, we read of the first time Moses delivered the message that the redemption was near. The people were convinced. They believed. They trusted Moses. They "bowed low in homage." They had hope.

Parashat Va'era, however, begins after the Jews knew bitter disappointment. Moses had intervened with Pharaoh, but his intervention backfired. Pharaoh reacted by increasing the burden he placed upon the Jews. He said, "Let heavier work be laid upon the men; let them not pay attention to deceitful promises." After such disillusionment, the eloquent promises with which our *parasha* begins evoked a very different reaction. Moses' words were met with disbelief, with a despair that is the result of *kotzer ruah*, a crushed spirit, and *avoda kasha*, painfully difficult toil.

For me, hopelessness is the saddest of human emotions, especially when it follows upon the excitement of hopefulness. The moment when hopes are dashed and dreams abandoned is for me the saddest moment of all.

Ironically, this saddest of all verses gives us the opportunity to learn important lessons about hope, and its opposite, despair. To learn these lessons, we must scrutinize these two phrases – *kotzer ruah* and *avoda kasha* – which I have thus far translated as "crushed spirit" and "difficult toil." Our great commentators give these phrases different "spins."

For example, Rashi understands *kotzer ruah* to mean "shortness of breath," the result of strenuous physical labor. Can a man who is gasping for air be expected to hope? Of course not. He is so panicked that hope for a better future is totally beyond his capacity.

Whereas Rashi translates *ruah* as "breath," Rabbi Ovadia Sforno, the great Jewish commentator who lived in Italy during its Renaissance, prefers to translate it as "spirit." For him, it is not "shortness of breath" that deprives a person of hope. Rather, it is the "shortness of spirit," the absence of a "spirit of faith," which makes hope so difficult. The Jews lost faith in Moses. He had let them down by failing to provide them with an instant solution to their plight. Thereby they lost their faith in the God of Moses. Without faith, argues Sforno, hope is impossible.

The Ramḥal understands our verse differently. For him, Pharaoh was the expert par excellence about the processes of despair and discouragement. He knew how to squash hope. He knew why genuine hope is so rare. To keep man from hope, Pharaoh knew, you must keep him so busy with all sorts of tasks and chores that he is too distracted to take the few moments necessary to begin to think of hopeful possibilities.

This is how the Ramḥal puts it in *The Path of the Upright* (*Mesillat Yesharim*):

> This is, in fact, one of the artifices of the evil inclination, which always imposes upon men such strenuous tasks that they have no time left to note whither they are drifting. He knows that, if they were to pay the least attention to their conduct, they would change their ways instantly.... This ingenuity is somewhat like that of Pharaoh ... for Pharaoh's purpose was not only to prevent the Israelites from having any leisure to make plans or take counsel against him, but to deprive them also of the very opportunity to reflect.

Without this opportunity – with "shortness of time to reflect (*kotzer ruah*)" – hopefulness is out of the question. One would be too busy to hope.

Another insight into the possible meaning of *kotzer ruah* is found in a most unusual source. There exists a collection of brief homilies, authored by Rabbi Kalonymos Kalman Shapira, the hasidic rebbe of Piacezna in pre-Holocaust Poland. He recorded these homilies, delivered in the early years of the Warsaw Ghetto, in a little notebook, which miraculously survived those fateful years.

He writes that under conditions of very difficult toil (*avoda kasha*), one loses the "spirit of life." Rabbi Shapira knew all too well the meaning of difficult toil, enslaved as he and his "congregation" were in that horrible ghetto. And he knew how he and they struggled to do God's will despite their dire straits. He witnessed their attempts to help each other, to maintain faith in God, and to perform whatever ritual mitzvot they could. But furthermore, he observed that their tortured souls could not muster the "spirit of life" necessary for religious action. *Kotzer ruaḥ* for him meant the absence of a "spirit of vitality." For him, religious actions performed without enthusiasm were defective.

Like the Jews of the Warsaw Ghetto, the Jews of ancient Egypt suffered from *kotzer ruaḥ*. They could not respond to Moses with a "spirit of vitality." No vitality, no life, no hope.

These commentators lived centuries apart from each other and in very diverse circumstances. But they all teach us this: there are many factors in life that render hope impossible. Some of these factors are cruel and unusual, as exemplified by the slaveries of Egypt and Nazi Germany. But some of these factors are common today. They relate to our busy lifestyles, to our work routines, even to the ways we play. We are consumed by "busyness." There may be little that slaves can do to free themselves for the possibility of hope. But there is much that we can do to avoid our own "slavery," to at least limit the *avoda kasha* that leads to *kotzer ruaḥ*.

Reflect upon it. Where there is time for reflection, there are opportunities for hope.

Parashat Bo

Flow

Sometimes we feel inspired. We may be working hard, but we don't seem to mind because we love the work we are doing and believe in it. Our objectives are based on our heartfelt convictions and our labors are consistent with our deepest attitudes. No task feels onerous because time flies by and we have a constant feeling of accomplishment.

This sense that everything is just right and the ability to do all that is expected of us effectively and enjoyably is called "flow" by some psychologists. One such psychologist, Mihaly Czikszentmihalyi, has written a book entitled *Flow: The Psychology of Optimal Experience*, where he reports his research on this vital feeling of how the work we do conforms with our innermost beliefs and highest principles.

Other times, however, there is also a very different manner in which we work. We feel unhappy with our jobs, not merely because they are difficult, boring, or stressful, but because we don't really want to be doing what we are required to do. We perform out of a sense of obedience and duty, but we would prefer that someone else take up our task.

In this instance, we often do not feel competent to perform our labors. We are certain that there are others much more capable than we are who could do much better. We feel unworthy and uncertain of our success.

In reading *Parashat Bo* and *Parashat Va'era*, we encounter one man, Moses, working very hard at some complex and almost impossible tasks: leading the Jewish people and challenging Pharaoh to free them.

I often ask myself about Moses' inner experience while carrying out his mission. Are his feelings like the first set of emotions described above? Does he feel inspired, happy, and eager? Does he experience this sense of "flow"? Or does he find himself reluctant, uncomfortable, and perhaps even awkward, at least at times?

Does he experience thrill in his comings and goings into Pharaoh's royal court? Is he excited by the words he finds to challenge Pharaoh and to debate with him? Or does he approach these experiences with trepidation and suffer in agony as each successive attempt to free his people is disturbed?

In *Parashat Bo*, there is a transition in Moses' role. Moses' initial role is being an advocate for freedom, but by the end of the *parasha*, he becomes a law giver and teacher as well. And his role further expands to that of master of logistics and desert-travel guide as he prepares his people for their journey and embarks upon it.

Is Moses in "flow"? Or is he struggling inwardly with reluctance, resistance, and perhaps even resentment?

The answer lies in Moses' initial reaction to his assignment, in his ongoing expressions throughout his life, in his disappointments with his people, and in his willingness to shed his leadership role.

Initially, he asks God to send another in his stead. He insists that his handicaps disqualify him from God's mission. He does not trust his people to respond to him and he is certain that Pharaoh will mock him. He never seems comfortable with his many tasks, even at the end of his life .

What then does motivate Moses to stand before Pharaoh, suffer his taunts, threaten him repeatedly, and teach his people lessons they often do not wish to hear? What motivates him is his sense of duty and his commitment to a life of responsibility. He models for us – for all of us – a life of obedience to a higher authority. He teaches us that we each have a vocation, a mission, and a part to play in life's drama.

More importantly, he teaches us that our tasks will often be frustrating and painful. We may not experience "flow." Our careers may not go smoothly and may not bring us gratification. But we will, nevertheless, prevail if we recognize the truth of our calling and respond dutifully and faithfully, even if it doesn't "feel good."

Obedience is a major value in Judaism. It may not be trendy these days, but it was certainly the hallmark of the life of Moses, and we are all challenged to emulate him in our own lives.

Parashat Bo

Tell Me a Story

The Book of Genesis is a dramatic story extending over many centuries. It begins with the creation of man and proceeds with the narrative of the transformation of a small family into a large nation.

In the Book of Exodus, the plot thickens. That nation becomes cruelly enslaved. In *Parashat Bo* (Ex. 10:1–13:16), the story takes a suspenseful turn. We sense that the redemption from slavery is imminent. But before redemption begins, the narrative is interrupted.

The Torah shifts gears. It is no longer a story that we hear, but a set of God given commands: "This month... shall be the first of the months of the year for you. Each member of the community shall take a lamb.... Your lamb shall be without blemish.... You shall keep watch over it until the fourteenth day of this month and... slaughter it at twilight, eat the flesh that same night... not eat any of it raw... not leave any of it over until morning" (Ex. 12:1–10).

Whereas the novice reader of the Torah is jolted by this drastic transition from the narrative mode to a set of laws, Rashi and Nahmanides were not surprised by this sudden shift. They wondered why the Torah would focus at such length on storytelling and not proceed directly to this passage of ritual law.

"Is the Torah a story book?" they ask. "Is it not, rather, a set of instructions for ritual and ethical behavior?" They each answer these questions differently, but both conclude that much of the Torah, perhaps even most of it, is one long and fascinating story.

Why does a book designed to teach the reader about proper religious belief and practice take the form of a narrative?

I think that the reason is quite simple. The Torah recognizes the power of the story to influence the minds and hearts of men. An author who wishes to profoundly impact his reader will do well to choose the narrative mode over other modes of communication. In secular terms, a good novel is more powerful than the best law book.

Taking note of this important lesson enables us to understand an otherwise puzzling phenomenon. Despite the fact that the Exodus from Egypt was, and remains, the central experience of Jewish history, there were at least two Jews alive at the time of the Exodus who did not experience it directly. I refer to Gershom and Eliezer, the two sons of Moses. They remained behind in Midian when Moses struggled with Pharaoh. They did not witness the ten plagues. They missed the thrilling flight from Egyptian bondage. They did not personally experience the wondrous miracle of the splitting of the Red Sea. They were brought back to Moses by their maternal grandfather, Yitro, so it is not at all clear whether they were even present at Mount Sinai when the Torah was given.

The early twentieth-century hasidic master, Rabbi Yehoshua of Belz, wonders about this puzzling fact. His answer is a most instructive one. God wanted Moses to tell his sons the story of the Exodus. He wanted Moses to be the storyteller par excellence, the one who would model storytelling for every subsequent father in Jewish history. Gershom and Eliezer were denied witnessing the Exodus because God wanted them to serve as the first Jewish children who would only hear its story, who would not know the real-life experience of the Exodus but only hear its narrative told to them by their father.

This, teaches the Belzer Rebbe, is the simple meaning of the verse in *Parashat Bo*, "So that you [singular in the Hebrew] may tell the story, in the ears of your son and son's son, of how I made a mockery of the

Bo

Egyptians and how I displayed My signs among them – in order that you may know that I am the Lord" (Ex. 10:2). The singular "you" at the beginning of the verse, explains the rebbe, refers to Moses himself. He is to tell the story to each of his sons individually, because he is the only father then alive whose sons would hear the story of the Exodus second hand. In this manner, Moses set the stage for all subsequent Jewish fathers. A Jewish father must be a storyteller!

A good story's power is familiar to all of us. The secret of the hasidic movement's success was not its texts or teachings, but the inspiring stories it told to its early adherents. To this day, Hasidim maintain the tradition of storytelling in their *melave malka*, or post-Shabbat repast, every week.

Personally, I long ago became familiar with an approach to psychotherapy called narrative therapy, in which the patient uses his or her own personal narrative as the basis for curative change. My favorite mentor would emphasize that when a therapist first encounters a patient, his opening question should not be, "What's your problem?" but rather, "Please tell me your story."

As I reflect upon those of my teachers who left a lasting impression upon me, I recall that they all told stories. Indeed, I remember those stories better than the academic lessons they taught me.

I remember a youth-group leader named Shmuli who told us stories and gave us cupcakes every Shabbat afternoon. I later learned that he obtained those stories from an early Chabad publication entitled *Talks and Tales*. Those tales left me with a taste for religion that even surpassed the taste of those delicious cupcakes.

I remember my seventh-grade teacher who read us the stories of William Saroyan at the end of each class, laying the foundation for my abiding love of literature. And of course, there were the stories my unforgettable Talmud teacher told us about the heroes of rabbinic history, which ultimately inspired me to pursue a career in the rabbinate.

Frankly, I fear that storytelling is becoming a lost art with the rapid change of our modes of communication. Grossly abbreviated electronic messages have replaced the face-to-face encounters that are essential for storytelling. The absence of the good story will effect personal development negatively and will impede the spiritual development of our children and grandchildren.

For me, Torah is but the most outstanding of the many stories that shaped my Jewish identity. I can think of only one modality that rivals the narrative as a basis for emotional growth. That modality is music as we will see in *Parashat Beshallaḥ*.

2icli · pass on stan of ancestar, peg·0, owela an bort to next guide. softly rut idoad, + spirit elevated.

Parashat Beshallaḥ

Song of the Sea

T eaching young children has always been a joy for me. One of teaching's special advantages is the clarity that emerges from conversation with people under the age of ten.

A cute and oft-told story describes the reaction of one fourth grader to the lesson in which he first learned the difference between poetry and prose. He remarked, "Wow! I have been writing prose all of my life and didn't even know it!"

I guess it was in the fourth grade when I first learned the distinction between prose and poetry, and when I became aware not only that I was writing prose, but that much of what I was studying in Jewish day school was prose, not poetry.

We were taught that prose is ordinary writing, language that portrays everyday events. Poetry, on the other hand, is the language of the extraordinary. Poems are for special events and rare emotions. Poetry is a song and we only sing when special feelings well up within us.

In *Parashat Beshallaḥ*, we finally encounter poetry. From the beginning of the Book of Genesis until this *parasha*, we have been reading prose. Surely, much of what we have been reading has not been ordinary, and we have even read about some miracles. But the language, with the possible exception of Jacob's blessings to his children, has been prose. It is only in the narrative of the crossing of the Red Sea that the poetic bursts forth.

One of the lesser differences between poetry and prose is that the words of the former are surrounded on the page by much blank space. Prose, on the other hand, consists of written or printed words with a minimum of space between them.

You will notice that in the Torah scroll, too, the prose of all of Genesis and of Exodus until this *parasha* consists of words written by the scribe with only minimal space between them. Look at the Torah scroll for *Parashat Beshallah* and you will see long columns of white space parallel to the holy written words.

These white spaces are found wherever the language of the Torah or of the Prophets makes use of poetry and song. It has been said that these blank spaces are symbolic of feelings so deep and inexpressible that they cannot be reduced to words of black ink and are instead word-lessly conveyed in the white empty spaces.

It is with the crossing of the Red Sea that the powerful feelings of the redemption experience emerge from the hearts of the former slaves. Words of poetry come to the surface. Song and music demand expression. These feelings have no precedent in all that has come before in the biblical narrative.

Today, many of us live lives of prose. Day fades into the night, and even years seem to march along uneventfully with only rare episodes of drama. Few of us sing and even fewer would feel capable of poetry.

That is what is so amazing about the Song of the Sea in our *parasha*. Everyone sang. All of Israel joined in the expression of poetic exultation. Our sages tell us that even the "lowly maid servant at the sea saw more than the prophet Ezekiel" and sang! Moses led all the men in the song, and Miriam, all the women.

Perhaps it was the contrast between centuries of oppressive slavery and the sudden experience of utter freedom that evoked song in everyone. Perhaps it was the release from the deadly fear of the approaching Egyptian army that gave vent to unanimous poetry. Or it might have been the sight of the hated and dreaded enemy drowning under the waves that inspired all present to sing out triumphantly. Most likely, it was all of the above.

As readers of the weekly Torah portion, each of us struggles to relate what we study to our daily lives. It is therefore important that we use the narrative in *Parashat Beshallah* to nurture our own poetic urge.

The Talmud compares the miracle of the Red Sea to quite ordinary processes, such as finding a spouse and earning a livelihood. The Talmud does this to inspire us to see the miraculous even in everyday events. Our sages realize the importance of poetry and soul, and wish to motivate us to respond with poetry and song even to mundane events. They want us to see the extraordinary in the ordinary.

Of all the many Torah portions until this point, beginning with Genesis and continuing until *Beshallah*, no biblical text is fully incorporated into our daily liturgy. Finally, from *Parashat Beshallah*, the Song of the Sea was made part of the daily Jewish liturgy, recited every single day of the year, weekday or Sabbath, ordinary day or holiday.

The message is clear: Poetry and song are vital for you. They are evoked by the experience of something very special. Every living moment is very special.

Horse and Rider

P haraoh was just the first. One way of looking at Jewish history is as a series of encounters with evil rulers. Pharaoh was just the first tyrant who persecuted us. Over the millennia, he was followed by Nebuchadnezzar, Haman, Antiochus, Titus, Hitler, Stalin, and others too numerous to mention.

Each of those men, without exception, did not act alone. Rather, they represented an entire culture, a comprehensive ideology, which opposed the Jewish people and its religion. They enlisted the assistance of huge constituencies who believed in their teaching and who followed their example. Without the support of the masses they led, they could not have wrought the havoc they did.

An excellent illustration of this is the book *Hitler's Willing Executioners* by Daniel Jonah Goldhagen. In this book, the author demonstrates clearly that only because Hitler had the cooperation of so many of his followers, all of whom believed as he did in the need to exterminate our people, was he able to be so tragically successful.

Pharaoh, at the beginning of our history, and Hitler in our more recent past, were each able to create a culture, a belief system, that pervaded their societies and that enabled them to execute their heinous schemes.

Throughout our history, the enemy was not just one individual, king, or dictator. Rather, it was an entire culture that opposed each of us and everything we stood for.

One lesson of our history is that just as these individual leaders were vanquished, so too did their ideologies fall into oblivion. This is the meaning of the statement of our sages, "The Holy One, blessed be He, does not bring about the downfall of the enemy until He first defeats its gods."

The gods of a nation, and in some versions, the ministering angels of that nation, represent what we would call today a nation's culture, its *weltanschauung*.

Where is this idea expressed in *Parashat Beshallah*? Long ago, I heard a lecture from the late Rabbi Ahron Soloveichik on *Beshallah*. He based it on the phrase near the very beginning of the Song of the Sea (Ex. 15:1): "I will sing unto the Lord, for He is highly exalted; the horse and his rider hath He thrown into the sea."

What is the significance of the horse being thrown into the sea? Why do the Israelites, led by Moses, open their song of praise to the Lord, the theme of *Shabbat Shira*, by singing of the horse's downfall?

Rabbi Soloveichik answered that the horse was the symbol of the culture of Egypt. When the Israelites sang of the downfall of both horse and rider, they were expressing their appreciation that not only were Pharaoh and his slave masters being removed from the scene, but so too was the culture of Egypt coming to an end.

Throughout the Bible, we find the culture of Egypt identified with the horse; the horse is a symbol of militarism, of the ideology that might makes right. The horse is also a symbol of arrogance and pride, fitting companions for militarism.

When God brought down Pharaoh and his cohorts, He was also in effect removing from the world stage a belief system that justified crushing and enslaving other human beings.

The removal, not only of the dictator but of his doctrine, and not only of the tyrant but of his theology, is part of the pattern of history from a Jewish perspective. On Purim, we do not just celebrate

Haman's hanging, but rather the triumph over a culture that had arbitrarily planned to commit genocide. On Ḥanukka, we honor a victory over Hellenism and the Greek way of life, not just a victory over an alien occupier of our land.

In more modern times, the triumph over Nazism was not just the defeat of hordes of brutal and sadistic men and women. It was a triumph over a racist and bigoted worldview, and for a short while, many believed that that triumph was permanent.

An excellent example of the horse and the rider both being thrown into the sea is the fate of the ideology of communism. True, the communist foe was personified in Joseph Stalin and his henchmen, and his several successors. But what eventually came about was the sudden and unexpected total abandonment of the communist approach to economics, to the organization of society, and to the religious and spiritual aspects of humankind.

It is so instructive to read the writings of men who were once avowed communists, but later abandoned that philosophy when they realized how corrupt it really was. There is a book edited by Arthur Koestler, who had Jewish roots, entitled *The God That Failed*. He and the other famous thinkers who contributed essays to that book all saw communism as a kind of god. Long before their god met his final defeat, they foresaw that defeat was not far away.

When our sages say that the Holy One, blessed be He, first brings about the downfall of the gods of our enemies, they are already using a term for a failed ideology that Arthur Koestler and others used centuries later.

Our sages spoke of the downfall of the enemy and of its gods, and in our *parasha*, the Bible speaks of the downfall of the rider and of the horse. Different metaphors, but the same idea.

Today, we confront not only "evil kings" and "evil kingdoms" but evil ideologies and systems of belief, masquerading as sacred religion, that call for murder and mayhem, torture and genocide. We pray to be able to witness both the horse and the rider being cast into the depths of the sea.

Parashat Beshallaḥ

An Ounce of Prevention

I couldn't believe it. One of my trusted old reference books failed me for the first time. You see, I am an old-fashioned guy and I still use books for reference rather than resorting to the electronic high-tech alternatives. Therefore, on the shelf next to my writing desk, I have three reliable works: *Webster's Collegiate Dictionary*, *Roget's Thesaurus*, and *Bartlett's Book of Familiar Quotations*. It was the latter that disappointed me as I prepared to write about *Parashat Beshallaḥ*.

Parashat Beshallaḥ (Ex. 13:17–17:16) contains the following verse: "If you will diligently hearken to the voice of the Lord your God, and will do that which is right in His eyes...I will put none of the diseases upon you that I have put upon the Egyptians; for I am the Lord that heals you" (Ex. 15:26).

That is how Rabbi Joseph H. Hertz, late chief Rabbi of the British Empire, phrases it in the translation that accompanies his excellent commentary to the Pentateuch. However, Rashi's commentary suggests a different translation.

This is what Rashi says, "Simply put, I am the Lord your physician, who teaches you Torah and mitzvot so that you will be spared illness, much as a physician would instruct his patient not to eat certain things because they may lead to his getting sick." Thus, For Rashi, the more accurate translation of the end of our verse is not, "I am the Lord that healeth thee," but rather, "I am the Lord thy physician."

At this point, you must be asking yourself, "What's the big deal? Is there any difference between "I heal you" and "I am your doctor"?

Rashi would respond, "Yes, there is a great difference between the two. 'I heal you' means that you are sick and I make you better, whereas 'I am your doctor' means that I have the ability to prevent you from getting sick in the first place."

For Rashi, this is fundamental. The Almighty has the power to prescribe for us a lifestyle that will protect us from illness; from spiritual illness certainly, but arguably from physical suffering as well.

Rashi, of course, never knew the great physician who was Maimonides. But Rashi's conception of a good physician as one who does not merely heal the sick, but who counsels those who are well about how to avoid disease, is identical to Maimonides' definition of a good doctor.

Maimonides was the court physician for the Sultan Saladin in medieval Egypt. The Sultan was never ill and once called Maimonides on the carpet, as it were, and demanded of him proof that he was a good doctor. "I am never ill," said Saladin, "so how am I to know whether you in fact deserve the reputation that you have for being a great physician?"

Reportedly, Maimonides answered:

> The greatest of all physicians is the Lord, of whom it is said, "I am the Lord thy physician." As proof of this, it is written "I will not place upon you the illnesses that I have placed upon ancient Egypt." Who is truly the good doctor? Not the person who heals the sick from their diseases, but rather the one who helps the person from becoming sick and sees to it that he maintains his health.

As Maimonides writes in one of his medical works, *Essay on Human Conduct*, "Most of the illnesses that befall man are his own fault, resulting from his ignorance of how to preserve his health – like a blind man who stumbles and hurts himself and even injures others in the process due to not having a sense of vision."

As I was contemplating the merits of the translation suggested by both Rashi and Maimonides, I couldn't help but think of the old adage: "An ounce of prevention is worth a pound of cure." My memory told me that this was another wise saying of crafty old Benjamin Franklin. But these days, I have grown increasingly distrustful of my memory and so decided to confirm the origin of those words.

Here is where the reference books with which I opened this column came into play. I reached for my trusty and well-worn *Bartlett's Familiar Quotations*. I searched under "prevention," "cure," and even "ounce," but to no avail. Then I looked up "Franklin, Benjamin," and found all sorts of words of wisdom but nothing about "an ounce of prevention."

Google was my next resort. And there I indeed confirmed that it was Benjamin Franklin who echoed an important Jewish teaching when he said, "An ounce of prevention is worth a pound of cure."

But there is more to be learned from the verse in *Parashat Beshallaḥ*, which we have been pondering: That the Almighty describes Himself as a healer or physician is more than just a lesson in the importance of living the kind of life that avoids the very real physical suffering that is often the consequence of an immoral life. The metaphor of "physician" also makes a strong statement about the nature of the relationship between the Almighty and us, his "patients."

If the verse had read, "If thou wilt diligently hearken to the voice of the Lord … for I am the Lord thy Master," that would suggest that He demands our obedience in order to assert His own authority. But by urging us to "hearken to His voice" because He is "our physician," we gain an entirely different view of why we should be obedient. As Malbim, a nineteenth-century rabbinic commentator, puts it, "A physician, like a master, demands obedience, but only for the purpose of securing the patient's welfare." Thus, the divine commandments are to be seen as being for our own benefit, for our own ultimate well-being.

The image of a divine healer is one of the special gems to be found in *Parashat Beshallaḥ*, which is a rich treasury of such images. How helpful it is for the Jew to experience a life of Torah and mitzvot as a gift given to him by a divine being who is concerned with his benefit, and how meaningful it is to know that the observant life is designed to avoid every manner of illness and to promote spiritual health and material wellness.

Don't Forget the Tambourines

I t is a familiar domestic scene, one that we have all experienced. The family is about to leave on a well-deserved long vacation. All the suitcases are packed and ready to go. Then, someone, usually the mother, shouts out, "Did we all remember everything? Once we get started, we're not turning back!"

Then the cross questioning begins, "Sally, did you remember your toothbrush?" "Sam, did you remember your sneakers?" "Dad, did you remember your reading glasses?" And so on.

All is well if the answer to all those questions is, "Yes!" Things are not too bad then if Sally has forgotten her toothbrush, but rushes upstairs to fetch it. The real crisis begins when the family car has progressed five miles down the road when Dad suddenly realizes that, although he did remember his reading glasses, he forgot to bring along the book that he had looked forward to reading on this vacation.

Now, a decision is called for. Will the family turn around and return home? Or is it not important enough to waste precious vacation time retrieving Dad's book? After all, one can always buy another one somewhere down the road.

Whether or not the forgotten object justifies a U-turn depends very much upon its significance. Toothbrushes and sneakers can easily be replaced. Reading glasses, less so. And books? Well, it depends. Some books are easily replaced, for others, a U-turn is required.

Parashat Beshallah (Ex. 13:17–17:16), calls this little family drama to mind. The Jewish people are finally leaving Egypt. They are packing their belongings. It is likely that they limited what they took with them just to what they could carry. Do we have any idea what they took and what they left behind?

They certainly took with them the gifts that the Egyptians themselves pressed upon them. As we read in the previous *parasha,* "The Children of Israel did according to the word of Moses; and they asked of the Egyptians jewels of silver, and jewels of gold, and raiment. And the Lord gave the people favor in the sight of the Egyptians, so that they let them have what they asked" (12:35–36).

Did they take anything else along? They surely left behind their ragged clothing and those tools and utensils that would only remind them of their enslavement. But allow me to demonstrate to you that several items besides the "jewels of silver and jewels of gold and raiment" were carefully included with their baggage.

One of these "items" is explicitly mentioned in the Torah. "And Moses took the bones of Joseph with him." Moses faithfully fulfilled the oath that the Children of Israel swore to Joseph when he said to them centuries before, "God will surely remember you; and you shall carry out my bones hence with you."

The Midrash (Exodus Rabba 20:19) sharply contrasts Moses' "baggage" with the booty that the other Children of Israel stuffed into their suitcases: "All of Israel busied themselves with silver and gold, but Moses was preoccupied with Joseph's bones, to which the Holy One, blessed be He, applied the verse, 'He who is wise of heart accepts mitzvot'" (Prov. 10:7).

From a spiritual perspective, the silver and gold that the Jews took with them were not very different from Sally's toothbrush and

Sam's sneakers. Moses, however, carefully took along something far more significant: Joseph's sacred bones.

Did anyone besides Moses pack items in their baggage aside from jewelry and clothing? Scripture tells us nothing in response to this question. But our oral tradition, as recorded in the Midrash, records other items that were, in fact, taken along on the journey.

Later in the *parasha*, we read the Song of the Sea, at the climax of which, "Miriam the prophetess, the sister of Aaron, took a timbrel in her hand; and all the women went out after her with timbrels and with dances" (Ex. 15:20). Where on earth did these timbrels, an ancient form of tambourine, come from? Tambourines don't grow on trees, and even if they did, trees don't grow in the desert.

Did it ever occur to you to ask this question? It never occurred to me until I encountered it in a collection of ancient midrashic fragments (*Yalkut Shimoni Shemot* 253), which answers that Miriam, and many other righteous women, left Egypt fully confident that they would one day have occasion to sing and dance. Thus, they brought musical instruments with them out of their place of enslavement.

Moses left Egypt dedicated to preserving the history of our people. So he took with him the bones of Joseph, and according to the Talmud, the bones of all of Joseph's brothers. Miriam and her companions anticipated a hopeful future and took with them the wherewithal to celebrate it in song and dance.

Moses and Miriam were not the only ones to their suitcases with more than just "jewels of silver and gold and raiment." Others did too. For this, we turn to yet another midrashic passage (Genesis Rabba 94:4). It comments upon a verse that we will read in *Parashat Teruma*. There, the Torah describes the component parts of the Tabernacle and the boards of acacia wood that comprised its walls. One of these boards was known as the *briaḥ hatikhon*, the middle bar: "and the middle bar in the midst of the boards, which shall pass through from end to end" (Ex. 26:28).

On this verse, the Midrash asks: "Did acacia wood grow in the desert?" The answer is a fascinating one. The Midrash maintains that Jacob brought these trees out of Canaan to Egypt, prophesying that, eventually, they would be necessary for the construction of the

Tabernacle. As they were about to finally depart from Egypt, several of the newly freed slaves foresaw a time when those trees would be needed to help build a house of worship. They therefore stowed a large haul of lumber along with their baggage. The uprooted trees were also "packed into the suitcase."

Moses took Joseph's bones, Miriam carried out tambourines, and some unnamed Israelites loaded huge trees onto their wagons. Nothing essential was forgotten. The family of Israel could proceed on its journey without having to make that unwanted U-turn.

What great symbolic significance these three items have for our people today! Moses knew how vital it is for us to revere our ancestry and preserve our past. Those who took the trees knew the importance of houses of prayer and study.

With her womanly wisdom, Miriam grasped what we often forget. Tradition and ritual are necessary but not sufficient. The capacity for joyous celebration must also be assured. Let us thank Miriam for "schlepping" those tambourines into the desert. Let us credit her for enabling us to celebrate Shabbat Shira, the Sabbath of Song.

Fathers-in-Law

Very much has been written about most family relationships. There are books about fathers and sons, fathers and daughters, and mothers and sons and daughters. Many volumes have been written about relationships, typically rivalrous, between siblings. But comparatively little has been written about the relationship between father-in-law and son-in-law. Often, admittedly, there is little or no relationship between them, but just as often, the relationship is an important and rewarding one.

I know that I personally have benefited immeasurably from my relationship with my father-in-law, of blessed memory. As is most often the case, I did not know him at all until my young adulthood, when I began to date his daughter. Unlike the father-son relationship, the relationship between father-in-law and son-in-law usually begins in maturity and is therefore more of a relationship between equals, more man-to-man.

My father-in-law modeled his relationship to me after the precious relationship he had with his father-in-law. He would often joke that, whereas a father couldn't choose his son, he could choose a son-in-law, to which I would usually respond, "Yes, true, and a son cannot choose his father, but a son-in-law can choose his father-in-law."

In *Parashat Yitro*, we read of a very rich relationship between a son-in-law, Moses, and his father-in-law, Yitro. Of course, we first read of their connection much earlier on in the Book of Exodus. But in our *parasha*, the relationship begins to sound much more familiar to those of us who have "been there."

Yitro travels to meet Moses and is the one who reunites Moses with his wife and children. They converse with animation and in great detail, each one narrating his story to the other. Moses narrates the story of the Exodus, of the splitting of the sea, and of the war with Amalek.

Yitro too tells a story, but it is a very different one. He tells of his religious quest, of his search for a God he can believe in. He informs Moses that he has dabbled in every conceivable type of idol worship. He has seen it all and "now he knows" who the true God is.

Every son-in-law tells his father-in-law his story, although I suspect that often some of that story is suppressed. And every father-in-law, that is every father-in-law worth his salt, shares his narrative with the young man who requests his daughter's hand.

I remember telling my father-in-law some of my story. I remember some of the questions he asked me, and his disappointment when he discovered that I did not share his fascination with the game of chess.

But I can never forget the story he told me not once, but throughout the more than forty years that we knew each other. His was a story of pre-Holocaust Eastern Europe, of a culture that is no more, a culture that he never ceased to mourn.

It is no wonder that the Torah characterizes the dialogue between Moses and Yitro by the word *"vayesaper,"* which means to tell a story. Most relationships consist of stories told by one party to the other. In the case of the father-in-law and son-in-law relationship, these stories become essential and, at least in my case, were lifelong narratives.

Yitro models another essential aspect of this unique relationship: He offers counsel, he gives advice. Not that Moses asked for Yitro's opinion as to how he should conduct the judiciary system for his people. But Yitro assumed that it was his prerogative as a father-in-law to gently and constructively find fault in his son-in-law's approach to things and offer reasonable alternatives.

I number myself among those fortunate sons-in-law whose father-in-law did not hesitate to occasionally criticize him, but who did so lovingly. He offered wise and practical suggestions, which indeed were often drawn from his own past and sad, personal experiences.

It has been pointed out that the Hebrew word for a son-in-law is *ḥatan*, a bridegroom. I am convinced that this is because in the relationship between son-in-law and father-in-law, the former always remains the young bridegroom and the latter, the sage elder. In the end, Moses asks Yitro to remain with him, the ultimate tribute that a son-in-law can pay to his father-in-law.

I would like to close with an original thought, and if it is theologically daring or in some other way off the mark, I beg the reader to forgive me.

It is a truism that God is our Father, and we are his sons and daughters. It strikes me that, in a certain way, God is also our Father-in-Law. God, as Father, is the God with whom we began a relationship in our infancy. God, as Father-in-Law, is the God whom we freely choose, sometimes repeatedly, at later stages of our lives.

God is also our Father-in-Law because we have taken, so to speak, His daughter, as our bride. The Torah has been described, by prophets and rabbis, as God's daughter. And we, who have accepted the Torah, are betrothed to the daughter of God Himself. He entrusted His beloved princess to our inadequate and unreliable care.

But we asked for her hand. We accepted the Torah and committed ourselves to "doing and listening" to her words. If we are faithful to the Torah, we are demonstrating to our "Father-in-Law" that we deserve his daughter.

Only then we can claim a close relationship to Him, closer even than the relationship I had with my father-in-law, may he rest in peace.

Parashat Yitro

The Seeker

T his is the most shocking and astounding phrase in the entire Torah!" These were the words uttered in Hebrew by the aging and ailing rabbi who had come for medical treatment to Baltimore, where I was living at the time. The rabbi was from Israel where he was the revered and popular dean of a rather famous yeshiva. The treatment he needed was unavailable in Israel at the time, so he journeyed to the community where I was a young pulpit rabbi.

I had developed the habit of taking advantage of the opportunity to meet visitors of this sort. He was too frail to give a formal lecture, but he found it invigorating to sit with a few of us and engage in conversation about various religious subjects, his favorite one being the weekly Torah portion. I felt especially privileged to be a part of that small group. The Torah portion that week was *Parashat Yitro* (Ex. 18:1–20:23).

Before identifying the shocking phrase that he wished to discuss, he asked us to participate in the following thought experiment:

Imagine that you are asked to write a brief biographical sketch of some saintly rabbinic figure, such as Rabbi Yisrael Meyer HaKohen, known as the Ḥafetz Ḥaim, and you happened to know that this man's father-in-law was some rogue who had a disreputable past. Would you share the nature of the father-in-law's past in a biography for all to see? Would it not be embarrassing for both the Ḥafetz Ḥaim and his father-in-law to publicize the latter's past misdeeds, especially if he had long repented of them?

He then launched into a very eloquent and forceful discourse about the ethical prohibitions against publicly disclosing a person's past, or even reminding him of it in private. To bolster his argument, he quoted the following passage from Maimonides' *Mishneh Torah*:

> It is a serious sin to say to a penitent, "Remember what you once did," or even to mention those past actions in his presence, thus embarrassing him.... We are admonished by the Torah not to abuse others verbally. (*Hilkhot Teshuva* 7:8)

He then drew our attention to the opening verse in our *parasha*, "And Yitro, the High Priest of Midian and the father-in-law of Moses, heard about all that the Almighty had done for Moses and Israel his nation" (Ex. 18:1).

"In the same breath," he exclaimed, "he is referred to as a pagan priest and as the father-in-law of Moses! What a combination of titles! Yes, he was an idolater and the "Zaide" of Moses' children. This is as unlikely as the witch doctor of some primitive tribe who is also the very close personal advisor of the saintly Ḥafetz Ḥaim, or the Archbishop of Canterbury as the mentor of some hasidic sage! Are not those juxtapositions jarring, astonishing, irreconcilable?"

Now that you have some sense of how graphic and dramatic this honored guest to our community could be, I will identify him by name. His name was Rabbi Simha Zissel Broida, and he was the dean of the Ḥevron Yeshiva in Jerusalem.

Rabbi Broida went on to offer a suggestion as to why Yitro is introduced to us again in our *parasha* in terms of his old title, High Priest of Midian. After all, at this point in time he had renounced his idolatrous past, and indeed according to rabbinic tradition, was about to convert to Judaism.

"You see," taught Rabbi Broida, "our tradition respects the seeker, the person who searches for the truth and never tires of that search, no matter how many blind alleys he encounters and no matter how much frustration he experiences. Yitro is described as an individual who worshiped every idol in the world in search of the truth. As he became disappointed with each faith that he explored and with each religion that he practiced, he rejected that path and renewed his search. He retains the title High Priest of Midian because that title represents the heights he could achieve in the religious hierarchy within which he sought truth. That title is symbolic of the degree to which Yitro was a seeker of truth."

The old man at this point began to show signs of fatigue and we begged him to stop his discourse and rest. But he told us that he refused to rest until he was convinced that we had learned the lesson he was trying to teach. "That lesson," he whispered hoarsely, "is best conveyed in the words of Talmud in Tractate Gittin 43a: 'No man truly achieves Torah knowledge without first experiencing error.'"

When a person's errors in life culminate in his finally making proper choices and correct decisions, then those errors are to be publicized and respected, because they are indicators of the degree to which that person was a seeker.

As far as I can recall, Rabbi Broida did not share with us on that occasion the following *gematria*. As you may know, every Hebrew word has a numeric equivalent, also known as a *gematria*, and often very diverse terms have identical numerical equivalents, suggesting otherwise unpredictable connections. The proper name, Yitro, has the numeric equivalent of 416. Two contradictory Hebrew terms have the exact same numeric equivalent. Those terms are "he was an idolatrous priest (*komer haya lavoda zara*)" and "The Torah (*HaTorah*)," indicating that this one individual combined within himself two diametrically opposed tendencies. One of those tendencies, *HaTorah*, prevailed, but only because of the lessons learned from his experiences with idolatry.

For those of you who are intrigued by *gematria*, I suggest you consult the commentary of the Baal HaTurim to corroborate this one.

Every year since I was privileged to first learn Rabbi Broida's lesson, I look forward to the opening verse of *Parashat Yitro*. Not only must we learn from our mistakes, but it is only by virtue of making those mistakes that we ultimately learn. That is a powerful and practical lesson indeed.

Parashat Yitro

Redemption

She was the daughter of Holocaust survivors, but she was not Jewish. Her parents were Polish citizens who heroically, and at the risk of their own lives, rescued Jews from certain death. Her parents are no longer alive, but their memories are enshrined in Yad VaShem, the Holocaust memorial museum in Israel, in the pavilion reserved for righteous gentiles.

She was a psychotherapy patient of mine about thirty years ago. I learned many things from her, including an answer to a question that arises in *Parashat Yitro* (Ex. 18:1–20:23).

The question appears in the commentary of Rabbi Avraham ibn Ezra on the very first verse of the Ten Commandments. The verse begins, "I am the Lord thy God who brought you out of the land of Egypt, the house of bondage: you shall have no other gods besides Me."

In his commentary, Ibn Ezra cites as the source of this question his famous predecessor, Rabbi Yehuda Halevi, perhaps the greatest poet in all of Hebrew literature, and the author of one of the most indispensable works of philosophy in our tradition, the *Kuzari*.

The question is simply this, "Why would God, about to reveal the very basis of the Torah, introduce Himself to those assembled at the foot of Mount Sinai as the one who 'brought you out of the land of Egypt'? Wouldn't it be more appropriate and more awe inspiring for Him to proclaim, 'I am the Lord thy God who created heaven and earth'?"

Does not the creation of the entire universe precede the Exodus from Egypt chronologically, and does it not supersede the Exodus as a wondrous and marvelous event? Would not people be more moved to obey the commandments of a God who created the entire world than they would be motivated to obey the commandments of He who merely freed a group of slaves?

There have been several attempts to answer this question. Traditional Jewish commentators have struggled with it, and Christian students of the Bible have been hard put to justify the relevance of the Ten Commandments to all humanity when it was addressed by God only to those whom He delivered from the land of Egypt.

Whatever forms these many answers take, one thing is undeniable. Two aspects of God pervade the first two books of the Bible. One is the aspect of God as Creator and the other is the aspect of God as Redeemer. Genesis emphasizes that God is the Lord over Nature, while Exodus stresses His role as the Lord of History.

This is not the place to discuss the central dynamic of the world of nature, but it is the place to identify the central dynamic of human history: the concept of redemption (*geula*). But what is redemption? It is a common word in the religious lexicon not just of Judaism, but of its so-called daughter religions, Christianity and Islam. But what does it mean?

It was from my psychotherapy patient, let's call her Catherine, that I first fully understood the significance of the word redemption, and why it was in His role as Redeemer that God chose to begin the Ten Commandments, and not in His role as Creator.

It was during a particularly emotionally charged psychotherapy session. Catherine was recounting the tragedy of her father's life. He had been a prominent attorney in pre-war Poland. He had been interned in Auschwitz as a political prisoner because of his participation in the Polish resistance against the Nazis. After the war, he returned to his hometown, but instead of being given a hero's welcome, he was shunned as a traitor for saving Jews. He was unable to return to his former prestigious position and chose instead to emigrate to the United States. But here he found himself unable to master a new language and was compelled to earn his livelihood as a janitor. He lived the rest of his life vicariously through his children, whom he helped obtain advanced professional educations.

As she recounted the story with great sadness, I expressed my empathy for her and spoke of individuals within my family who had had similar stories to tell after the Holocaust – to which she retorted sharply, "For you Jews, it was different. You have had a redemptive experience. You have rebuilt your culture, your religious communities, your educational institutions. My father had no such redemptive experience. He regained nothing of his glorious past. He died unredeemed."

Ever since that conversation, the word redemption has been replete with meaning for me. It is a process by which a slave becomes free, individuals become a nation, and those who were condemned to lives of emptiness become enabled to live lives of immense significance. If God the Creator brought forth something from nothing (*yesh me'ayin*), then God the Redeemer brought forth a people from the depths of the forty-ninth level of degradation to the exalted summit of freedom and faith.

Hence, my personal response to Yehuda Halevi's question. The Almighty prefaced the Ten Commandments with the assurance that personal redemption is a real possibility – a possibility though only for those who absorb the ethical and moral lessons He was about to teach in those Ten Commandments. He redeemed us once from the land of bondage and He offered us the tools to redeem ourselves again and again throughout our lives.

Parashat Yitro

The Maternal Influence

When I was young, I was an avid reader of novels. As I've grown older, I have found myself more interested in good biographies. I especially appreciate those biographies of great men that try to focus on what exactly made them great. Particularly, I try to discover the roles played by father and mother in the formation of these personalities.

Until relatively recently, Jewish tradition did not have many biographies of our heroes and heroines. Bible and Talmud contain much material about the lives of prophets, kings, and sages, but only occasionally give us a glimpse of the role that parental influences played in making them great.

I recently came across a passage in a book by a man I admire. His name was Rabbi Yitzchak Yaakov Reines (1839–1915). He was the head of an innovative yeshiva in Lida, Lithuania, and was one of the founders of the Mizrachi Religious Zionist movement. He was a prolific writer, and one of his works is entitled *Nod Shel Dema'ot*, which translates as *A Flask of Tears*.

In this book, Rav Reines writes about the important role that mothers play in the development of their children – sons and daughters alike. He emphasizes the role of the mother in the development of the Torah scholar. He claims that it is not only the father's teaching that motivates and informs the budding Jewish leader, rather it is the mother's feminine intuition and maternal compassion that are, at the very least, equally formative.

The sources of his thesis include a verse from *Parashat Yitro* (Ex. 18:1–20:23), in which we read that the Lord called to Moses from the mountain and said, "Thus shall you say to the House of Jacob and declare to the Children of Israel…you shall be to Me a kingdom of priests and a holy nation" (19:3–6).

The Midrash explains that "the House of Jacob" refers to women and "the Children of Israel" to men. Both men and women must be involved if we are to become "a kingdom of priests and a holy nation." "Why the women?" asks the Midrash and answers, "Because they are the ones who can inspire their children to walk in the ways of Torah."

Rav Reines adduces another biblical verse to make his point. He refers to the words in the very first chapter of the Book of Proverbs in which King Solomon offers this good counsel, "My son, heed the discipline (*musar*) of your father, and do not forsake the instruction (*Torah*) of your mother" (Prov. 1:8). From this verse, it seems that the mother's message may be even more important for the child's guidance than that of his or her father. After all, father merely admonishes the child with words of "discipline," whereas mother imparts nothing less than the "instruction" of the Torah itself.

Then comes the *tour de force* of Rav Reines' essay: the biographical analysis of a great talmudic sage, Rabbi Yehoshua ben Ḥananya. The student of Ethics of the Fathers will recognize his name from a passage in chapter 2 of that work. There, we read of the five disciples of Rabban Yoḥanan ben Zakkai. They are enumerated and the praises of each of them are recounted. Of Rabbi Yehoshua ben Ḥananya, we learn, "*Ashrei yoladeto*, happy is she who gave birth to him." Of all the outstanding disciples, only Rabbi Yehoshua's mother is brought into the picture. What special role did she play in his life that earned her honorable mention?

Rav Reines responds by relating an important story of which most of us are sadly ignorant. The story is recorded in Genesis Rabba 64:10.

It tells of a time, not long after the destruction of the Second Temple by Rome, when the Roman rulers decided to allow the Jewish people to rebuild the Temple. Preliminary preparations were already under way for that glorious opportunity when the *Kutim*, usually identified with the Samaritan sect, confounded those plans. They maligned the Jews to the Romans and accused them of disloyalty. The permission to rebuild was revoked.

Having come so close to realizing this impossible dream, the Jews gathered in the valley of Beit Rimon with violent rebellion in their hearts. They clamored to march forth and rebuild the Temple in defiance of the Romans' decree. However, the more responsible leaders knew that such a provocation would meet with disastrous consequences. They sought a respected figure, sufficiently wise and sufficiently persuasive, to calm the tempers of the masses and to quell the mutiny. They chose Rabbi Yehoshua ben Ḥananya for the task.

The Midrash quotes Rabbi Yehoshua's address in full detail. He used a fable as the basis of his argument: A lion had just devoured its prey, but a bone of his victim was stuck in his throat. The lion offered a reward to anyone who would volunteer to insert his hand into his mouth to remove the bone. The stork volunteered, and thrust its long neck into the lion's mouth and extracted the bone.

When the stork demanded his reward, the lion retorted, "Your reward is that you can forevermore boast that you had thrust your head into a lion's mouth and lived to tell the tale. Your survival is sufficient reward." So too argued Rabbi Yehoshua, our survival is our reward. We must surrender the hope of rebuilding our Temple in the interests of our national continuity. There are times when grandiose dreams must be foresworn so that survival can be assured.

Rav Reines argues that this combination of cleverness and insight into the minds of men was the result of his mother's upbringing. The ability to calm explosive tempers and sooth raging emotions is something that Rabbi Yehoshua learned from his mother. He was chosen for this vital role in Jewish history because the other leaders knew of his talents, and perhaps even knew that their source was to be traced back to his mother, of whom none other than Rabban Yoḥanan ben Zakkai had exclaimed, "Happy is she who gave birth to him."

This wonderful insight of Rav Reines is important for all of us to remember, particularly those of us who are raising children. Psychologists have long stressed the vital roles that mothers play in child development. In our religion, we put much stress on the father's role in teaching Torah to his children, but we often underestimate, and indeed sometimes even forget, the role of the mother. Our tradition urges us to embrace the role of the mother not just in the child's physical and emotional development, but in his or her spiritual and religious growth as well.

We would do well to remember that Rav Reines is simply expanding upon God's own edict to Moses at the very inception of our history, "Speak to the house of Jacob! Speak to the women as well as to the men."

Mothers, at least as much as fathers, are essential if we are to create a "kingdom of priests and a holy nation."

Parashat Mishpatim

Responsibility

I have to thank my dear parents, may they rest in peace, for many things. I must especially thank them for having chosen to provide me with a yeshiva day school education. This was not an obvious choice back in the 1940s, for few parents chose the day school option. Indeed, many of their friends advised them against depriving me of a public school education, and the cost of tuition was a great strain on my father's meager income. But I remember my mother insisting that I should learn "responsibility," and her belief was that I would learn it best in a Jewish school.

Looking back on my early school years, I certainly cannot recall any lessons specifically devoted to "responsibility." Learning the Hebrew alphabet and then going on to study the fascinating stories of Genesis were certainly interesting and exciting to me. But in those early grades, the concept of responsibility never came up, at least not explicitly.

In the school I attended, Talmud study began in the fifth or sixth grade. It was then that I first heard the word "responsibility" in the classroom and began to learn what it really meant.

We were introduced to Talmud study with selected passages in Tractates Bava Kamma and Bava Metzia. The passages we studied were almost exclusively based upon verses found in *Parashat Mishpatim*. And the single dominant theme of *Parashat Mishpatim* is unarguably responsibility.

I look back on my first exposure to Talmud, and to *Parashat Mishpatim* as studied through its lenses, and remember the teacher admonishing us, "A person is responsible for all of his actions, deliberate or unintentional, purposeful or accidental, awake or asleep." It was a direct quote from the Talmud, but he emphatically conveyed to us that it was also a formula for life.

And furthermore, it is a lesson derived from *Parashat Mishpatim*. Read it even superficially and you will learn that we all are not only responsible for our own actions, but also for the actions of the animals we own. We are responsible for damage caused by our possessions, if we leave them in a place where someone might trip over them and harm himself. We are responsible not only to compensate those whom we have harmed for the damages they suffered, but are also responsible to compensate them for lost employment or for the healthcare costs that were incurred by whatever harm we caused them.

What a revelation to a ten-year-old! How many ten-year-olds in other educational settings were exposed to these high ethical standards? Certainly not the boys in the park with whom I played stickball – boys whose parents had not opted for a day school education for them.

Even today, many criticize the curriculum of the type of education that I experienced. They point to the many verses in our *parasha* that speak of one ox goring another, and question the contemporary relevance of such arcane legalities. But when I studied about my responsibility for my oxen – and the consequences that applied if my ox gored you, or your slave, or your ox – I was living in Brooklyn, where I had certainly seen neither oxen nor slaves. But I do not at all recall being troubled by that, nor were any of my classmates.

Rather, we easily internalized the underlying principles of those passages. We understood that all the laws of oxen were relevant even for us Brooklyn Dodger fans. We got the message: Each of us is responsible for the well-being of the other, be he a free man or the slave of old. We are not only to take care that we avoid harming another, but we are to take care that our possessions, be they farm animals, pets, or mislaid baseball bats, do not endanger those around us.

There was so much more that we learned about responsibility from those elementary, yet strikingly related Talmud passages. For example, we learned that a priest guilty of a crime was to be held responsible and brought to justice, even if that meant "taking him down from the sacrificial altar." No sacrificial altars in Brooklyn then or now, but plenty of people in leadership positions try to use their status to avoid responsibility for their actions.

We learned that it was perfectly permissible to borrow objects from our friends and neighbors, but that we were totally responsible to care for those objects. We learned that if those objects were somehow damaged, even if that damage was not due to our negligence, we had to compensate the object's owner. Yes, we learned to borrow responsibly, but we also learned the importance of lending our possessions to others, especially others less fortunate than ourselves.

We learned that we were responsible to help others and that that obligation extended even to strangers in our midst; indeed, it extended all the more to those strangers. And we learned to be responsible for our very words and to distance ourselves from lies and falsehoods.

All this from a grade school introductory course in Talmud. How valuable our Torah is as a guide to a truly ethical life and how fortunate are those of us who learned these lessons early in life or who discover them at a later age. What an opportunity we all have to awaken ourselves to these vital ethical teachings found in *Parashat Mishpatim*.

And how fortunate I was to have parents who sensed that it was essential for their son to learn responsibility and that enrollment in a school that taught Torah and Talmud would help him learn it well!

The Many Lessons of Half

I was never very good at math. It all goes back to the fourth grade. I came down with a case of some ordinary childhood disease, probably chicken pox, at just the time that Mrs. Levine was teaching the class about the concept of percentages. I must have missed about a week of school, and when I returned to class, it seemed as if everyone was speaking Greek. Phrases like "fifty per cent" and "seventy-five per cent" and "a half" and "three-quarters" cut the air, and I simply did not know what these strange words meant. Mrs. Levine probably tried to catch me up with the rest of the class, but all I remember are feelings of frustration.

It was my rebbe, the man who taught us religious studies in the mornings, who came to the rescue. He realized that I was beginning to think of myself as dumb and he was concerned about my damaged self-esteem.

"You are far from the first person to be puzzled by percentages," he said comfortingly. "*Moshe Rabbenu*, Moses our teacher, also had his difficulties with math, and it was the Master of the Universe Himself, the *Ribbono shel Olam*, who helped him out."

As a mere fourth-grader, I was in no position to question the good rabbi and I was ashamed to ask him where he found a biblical allusion to Moses' incompetency in mathematics. But he soon filled in the gap.

"This week," he told me, "we do not only read *Parashat Mishpatim* (Ex. 21:1–24:18). This Sabbath is special because it is the last one before the month of Adar. It is *Shabbat Shekalim*. We will read a short additional paragraph (Ex.13:11–16), in which we will learn how Moses was instructed to ask each Jew to donate a half-shekel toward the maintenance of the Tabernacle. This donation was required throughout the history of the Holy Temple in Jerusalem. The funds were collected during the month of Adar. Now that the Temple has been destroyed, we commemorate the collection of the half-shekel by reading about it in the synagogue on the last Sabbath before Adar."

I told him that I remembered learning all about this mitzva last year, but failed to see any evidence of Moses' mathematical handicap in that passage. It was then that he shared with me the fascinating anecdote originating in the collection of homilies known as the Midrash Tanḥuma, and quoted in abbreviated form by Rashi in his remarks on verse 13. As an outstanding pedagogue, my rebbe did not read the quotation to me verbatim, but elaborated upon it in a way he knew I would find interesting and relevant to my personal quandary.

"Moses had great difficulty with this commandment. There was something about the half-shekel that he simply couldn't understand. We do not know precisely what he found so puzzling, but we are told that the Almighty sympathized with Moses and vividly demonstrated what the half-shekel was to look like by miraculously making a coin of fire appear in the heavens. So you are not the only one who finds the concept of 'half' challenging. Moses, too, needed a little help with it."

The rebbe's attempt at restoring my self-esteem was quite helpful. I did not get a visual demonstration from the Almighty, but I did get the courage to approach Mrs. Levine and asked her for an afterschool tutorial.

Ever since this little episode, which happened more years ago than I care to mention, I have sought out explanations of the significance of the half. Why were we not required to give a whole shekel, a complete coin, as our contribution? Was it simply because that would have been too great an expense to require of each individual? I somehow don't think so.

And so, over the years, I have amassed a collection of dozens of explanations on the symbolic meaning of half a coin. I can't possibly share them all with you, dear reader, in this brief chapter, but I'll give you some samples instead.

One explanation, which makes for excellent sermonic material, is that none of us is a complete entity. No one is spiritually self-sufficient. We are all only half of the picture and we all need each other. Hence, we contribute only half a shekel, to impress upon ourselves that we can't go it alone, but need another person in order to be complete.

Another approach is based upon that famous saying of Rabbi Tarfon in Ethics of the Fathers (*Pirkei Avot*). "It is not incumbent upon you to complete the task, but nevertheless you are not permitted to exempt yourself from it entirely." Being required to give only half a shekel drives home the point that total completion of the task is not expected of us. All we can each do is try our best and do our share.

Yet another approach is advanced by one of the classics of Jewish mysticism. The Zohar emphasizes that this world is a diminished one in which there are broken vessels that need to be restored. We live in an imperfect world, and its imperfection is symbolized by a broken shekel.

Parashat Mishpatim

Careers

What do you want to be when you grow up?" That was once the standard question to ask an eight- or nine-year-old when trying to make conversation with him or her. Somehow, every child had an answer, which ranged from "fireman" to "football player" to "nurse."

It seems to me that we don't ask that question of children these days, at least not as frequently as we used to. Perhaps we are afraid to put pressure upon them. Or perhaps ambition is no longer viewed as a positive value, as it once was. The fact is that our tradition does value ambition if it leads to some positive goal. A career that helps a person support himself and his family is one such goal. A career that serves the community is another.

Which careers are especially valued by the Torah? *Parashat Mishpatim* (Ex. 21:1–25:18) provides us with an occasion to reflect upon one highly valued career: serving on a court of law as a judge.

Our *parasha* begins with the verse, "These are the rules that you shall set before them." Rashi understands the phrase "before them" to mean questions regarding these rules must be adjudicated by Jewish judges familiar with the rules outlined in the ensuing several chapters of the *parasha*. Already, in *Parashat Yitro*, we learned that Moses saw the role of judge as being one of his leadership responsibilities. Only at the advice of his father-in-law did he assign the role of judge to a hierarchy of others. Judgeship is thus one of the first careers prescribed by the Torah.

The Talmud has something to say about just how noble a career judgeship is, and in the process, recommends several other excellent career paths for "nice Jewish boys." I am referring to the following passage in Tractate Bava Batra 8b, which in turn interprets two biblical verses:

> "The knowledgeable will be radiant like the bright expanse of sky, and those who lead the many to righteousness will be like the stars forever and ever" (Dan. 12:3).
>
> "The knowledgeable" are the judges who adjudicate the law with absolute truthfulness, as well as those who serve the community as trustees who distribute charity (*gabba'ei tzedaka*). "Those who lead the many" are the schoolteachers of young children.
>
> And as for Torah scholars? To them, the following verse applies, "May His beloved be as the sun rising in might" (Judges 5:31)!

There we have it. Four admirable careers are set forth by the Talmud: the judiciary, involvement in the distribution of charity, primary education, and Torah scholarship.

Tosafot, the collection of commentary in the margin of every page of Talmud, suggests that there is a rank order to these "careers." Starlight is less bright than "the bright expanse of sky." This implies that school teaching is less praiseworthy than acting as a judge or *gabbai tzedaka*, whereas the Talmud scholar, who is compared to the sun, ranks highest.

Other commentaries interpret the talmudic text differently. One interesting approach is taken by the nineteenth-century rabbi of Lyssa, Rabbi Yaakov Loberbaum, who is known for his masterwork on civil law, *Netivot HaMishpat*. He objects to the approach taken by *Tosafot*. After all, he asks, "Our eyes can see that the stars are brighter than the 'expanse of the sky,' and what connection is there between judges and *gabba'ei tzedaka* that allows us to compare both of them to the celestial expanse?"

His answer is most instructive:

> There are materials that are colorless, but that reflect whatever color shines upon them. An example is glass. It has no color of its own. Shine a red light upon it, and the color red is reflected. Shine a green light, and green is reflected. The expanse of the sky is itself colorless like glass. This is what a judge has in common with a trustee of charity. They both must be absolutely neutral, with no color of their own. The judge must be totally unbiased, and so must be the person who determines how charity is to be distributed. He must not favor one needy person over another but must distribute the community funds "without color." But schoolteachers are compared to the stars, which glow equally upon all. Whereas judges and *gabba'ei tzedaka* must discriminate between one party and the other, the schoolteacher must "shine" upon all of his pupils equally, without discrimination.

Although the Lyssa Rav does not comment on Torah scholars and their likeness to the sun, we can speculate on that connection for ourselves. The sun is the ultimate source of light and heat, and so too, the Torah is the ultimate source of intellectual light and spiritual warmth. Torah study, our tradition teaches us, outweighs all other values in its importance.

Truth to tell, each one of us individually must strive to incorporate into our behavior all four of these career roles. We are all judges, even if not clothed in judicial robes or sitting in judicial chambers. We are constantly called upon to judge others in all sorts of ways and we must always attempt to honestly judge ourselves. We all must decide how to distribute our charitable resources: the time we give to the community, and the money we contribute to the needy. We are all teachers – if not in the classroom, then in the family, and synagogue, and shopping mall.

And we certainly must all, according to our intellectual limitations and the restrictions that time places upon us, be diligent in our Torah study and become as knowledgeable in Torah as we possibly can.

From this perspective, each and every one of us is called upon to discharge the duties of our "careers": judge others without bias, distribute our resources compassionately and fairly, teach little children in some appropriate manner, and above all, study Torah.

If we do, then we are all worthy of being called luminaries as bright as the bright expanse of the sky, shining like the stars at night, and lighting up the world like the sun by day.

Parashat Teruma

The Missing Tzedaka Box

I t was a cold winter all over the world. It was the year 1991 and it was the time of the great Gulf War. Scud missiles were falling upon towns and cities throughout the State of Israel. To say that times were tense would indeed be an understatement.

The city of Baltimore had a sister city relationship with Odessa in the former Soviet Union. The communist regime had just fallen and travel to places like Odessa was becoming more practical. The Jewish community of Baltimore had begun to send representatives to assist the Jews of Odessa in various ways. Every six months or so, they would assign a different rabbi to travel to Odessa to ascertain the needs of the Jewish community there. That winter, it was my turn as a local Baltimore congregational rabbi to visit Odessa. It was a tense time for such a visit, and my family and friends urged me not to go.

However, I did go and had one of the most adventurous experiences in my life. My companion and I were stranded in the Moscow airport and could not continue on to Odessa because the Russian Navy was on maneuvers in anticipation of the spreading of the Gulf War – and we were considered potential spies. We spent a frigid Shabbat in

Moscow, eventually obtained the credentials to gain access to Odessa, and spent about ten days there.

I had a busy and rewarding time there, especially because of my visit to the one synagogue that was permitted to function throughout the communist era. I remember the synagogue well and I recall the fact that the prayer services were held in a basement room and not in the still beautiful and quite large sanctuary, because the community could not afford to heat the larger facility.

About twenty men and three or four women gathered in that basement synagogue every morning. They had Torah scrolls and read from them. Many individuals came by for a moment or two to light memorial candles. There were even *siddurim* and *Ḥumashim*. But something was missing, and for a while I couldn't quite put my finger on what it was.

Suddenly, it dawned upon me that there were no *pushkas* and no collection of *tzedaka* (charity) whatsoever. *Tzedaka* is an integral part of the Jewish prayer service, and no synagogue that I am familiar with, whatever its orientation, lacks a *tzedeka* box in which to at least put in a few pennies.

It was at that moment that I began to fully comprehend the effects of seventy years of communist domination upon the religious psyche of the Jews who lived under Soviet regime and tyranny. The deep-rooted custom of giving charity daily had been uprooted. The profound compassion, which has characterized the Jewish people throughout the ages, had been purged from the very souls of the victims of communism.

I reflect on this important personal observation when *Parashat Teruma* comes around. For although we have examples of charity and benevolence earlier in the Torah, in *Parashat Teruma* we read for the first time about the entire Jewish community and its response to a call, an appeal, for contributions.

In *Parashat Teruma*, the Jewish people begin to construct the *Mishkan*, the Tabernacle. In a sense, it is the first synagogue in our history. This is certainly the first time that we are summoned to contribute, each and every one of us, to a community-wide project. The Jewish people do respond, and respond generously, with all their hearts, and with whatever they have available, to the call for contributions to the Tabernacle. There is no record of anyone shirking this responsibility.

Our *parasha* begins with the command of the Almighty to Moses that he speak to the Jewish people and "have them take for Me a gift from every person whose heart moves him to give" (Ex. 25:2). Commentaries throughout the ages find it remarkable that we are asked to *take*, not *give*, a gift, establishing the basic teaching that he who gives takes a great deal in the process, that giving is a reward and not a deprivation. That fundamental lesson was expunged from the minds and hearts of the Jews of Odessa under the duress of a mere seventy years of communist oppression.

I have been reading a great deal about the science of genetics and its fascinating recent discoveries. Among these discoveries is the finding that many traits we ordinarily think are products of our education and experience are ultimately rooted in heredity, in our genes. One of those traits is altruism, the tendency to care about others and to act benevolently toward them.

This scientific finding is, in a sense, consistent with the talmudic teaching that three personality traits are part of the definition of the Jew, hardwired into our very nature: compassion, the capacity to feel shame, and generosity.

The Jews I met during those wintry days on the shores of the Black Sea have the same genetic composition as the alms-giving Jews I see every morning in New York, Baltimore, and Jerusalem. They share a common heritage and heredity with all other Jews. They too possessed the gene for altruism, if in fact such a gene exists.

But I am convinced that the power of our social experiences is sufficient to overwhelm the innate power of our inherited traits. Seventy years of indoctrination by a culture – which taught that one has no private property, no ownership, no say over giving or taking, but that everything belongs to the commune – was sufficient to undermine centuries of teachings and practices of an entirely different ethic. For the Jewish ethic of charity teaches that we are entitled to private property that we come by through honest effort and legitimate toil. The Jewish ethic of charity teaches, however, that we are accountable to take some of that legitimately earned private property and give it on to those less fortunate than we are or toward the needs of the larger collective, the *tzibbur*.

There are many ways to understand Jewish history and many perspectives from which to view our origins and our ability to have survived the vicissitudes we have encountered over hundreds of years. We can understand our history in terms of our persecutions, in terms of our heroic leaders, and in terms of our migrations to every part of the globe.

But I maintain that the way to understand Jewish history is through the recognition of the power of the mitzva of *tzedaka*, a mitzva that we have all faithfully kept whether we observed other mitzvot or not. We have had the amazing ability to recognize our obligation as individuals to the greater community. We have always demonstrated our compassion for the welfare of the poor, the sick, and the elderly. Jewish history can be understood in terms of our successes in the area of charity.

The old synagogue of Odessa, as I am told by those who have visited there more recently, now has a *tzedaka* box. Indeed, it has more than one. The Jews there are more than generous in their giving. The lessons of communism have been undone. The Jewish tradition of "taking gifts" has been restored.

That is the way I choose to understand the major theme of Jewish history: compassion for each other, generosity, charity, and altruism. Sometimes, for brief periods, we may lose our focus. But we are quick to regain it.

Parashat Teruma

Charity

Scholars have long disagreed about what distinguishes human beings from the rest of the animal world. Some have argued that it is man's intelligence and use of language that distinguishes him, hence the term *Homo Sapiens*. Others have maintained that it is the fact that he uses tools that makes man distinct from other living creatures, hence the term *Homo Faber*. There have even been those who have put forward the opinion that man alone of all the rest of the animal species engages in play, hence the term *Homo Ludens*.

This disagreement is the basis for my personal practice of stimulating debate by asking groups with whom I interact the question, "What distinguishes the Jewish people? What makes us unique and different from other human groups?"

Here, too, opinions abound. There are those who will instinctively respond, "We are the people of the Book." By this, many mean that we are the people who follow the ultimate book, the Bible. Others simply mean that we are a bookish people, tending to be intellectually oriented, and certainly read a lot more than most other cultures.

Another response is that we alone among other faith communities think of ourselves as a family, as a *mishpaḥa*. I always find this response especially gratifying because it recognizes a feature of our people of which we can all be proud.

Another answer I sometimes encounter is that the Jewish people are a giving people, that it is our generosity that distinguishes us from others, that *tzedaka* is our highest value. This point of view is emphatically expressed, with a degree of irony, in a passage in Tractate Shekalim of the Jerusalem Talmud, which reads:

> Rabbi Abba ben Aḥa said: One can never fully understand the character of this nation. When they are asked to contribute to the Golden Calf, they give. When they are asked to contribute to the Holy Tabernacle, they give.

This can be seen as an indication of indiscriminate giving, and the Talmud emphasizes that it reflects a deeper tendency to be responsive to all appeals for help, often without paying sufficient attention to the merits of the cause.

The first indication of the charitable instincts of our people is found in *Parashat Teruma* (Ex. 25:1–27:19). In the very first verses of our *parasha*, the Almighty instructs Moses to gather gifts from the people in order to construct the Sanctuary in which He is to dwell. He goes so far as to itemize the materials that will be necessary. The list begins with gold and silver and extends to spices, incense, and precious gems.

The people respond willingly and generously, and establish a precedent of charitable giving for all future Jewish generations. Indeed, the Talmud, in the passage just referenced, insists that the gifts of gold donated to the Holy Tabernacle were intended to atone for the gifts of gold, which were molten into what became the Golden Calf.

In most calendar years, the Torah portion of *Teruma* is read about a week prior to the holiday of Purim. This holiday too is all about giving. The very celebration of this joyous day consists, as we read in the Book of Esther, of "sending gifts to one another and presents to the poor" (Est. 9:22).

There is an interesting contrast, however, between the practice of giving on the holiday of Purim and the proper strategy for giving during the rest of the year. On Purim we must not prioritize our gifts. We give to "whomever extends his hand." We are permitted to be indiscriminate in our giving, without judging as to who is more needy and who is less so.

But when it comes to the distribution of charity during the rest of the year, we are instructed to be far more careful about our practices of giving. It might indeed be our ethnic tendency, as the passage in the Jerusalem Talmud above suggests, to give to idolatrous causes as freely as we give to sacred ones. But we must realize that that tendency is typically based on impulse, on the emotions of the moment, whereas proper charitable giving requires planning and intelligent thought.

These days, there are numerous causes that beg for our resources. I hasten to add that few, if any of them, are "idolatrous." Quite the contrary, most of them are legitimate and even important. But charitable giving, according to our rabbis, requires triage, that is, careful determination of which causes have priority. The rabbis have even set down rules for how to make that determination.

The importance of realizing that not all charitable causes are of equal merit is well illustrated by a homiletic insight that I found in a book written by my respected colleague, Rabbi Daniel Feldman. The book is entitled *Divine Footsteps: Ḥesed and the Jewish Soul.* I quote:

> The Vilna Gaon...homiletically understood the verse, "thou shall not...close your hand against your destitute brother" (Deut. 15:7), as an instruction about the evaluative responsibility contained within the *tzedaka* imperative. When our hand is closed in a fist, all fingers appear to be the same size. However, when the hand is open, it becomes clear that the fingers are all of different length.... Appropriate giving will always require a judgment call.

We are often moved by appeals that tug at our heartstrings and that prompt us to what some have called "emotional giving." But all of us, no matter how wealthy we are as individuals, and no matter how strong are our finances as organizations, have limited resources. We must attempt, although we can never be absolutely certain that our judgments are correct, to discern the priorities of the moment, and to distinguish between urgent overriding needs and causes, which, despite their great merit, must be lower down on our list of priorities, and indeed which may, because of the paucity of our resources, have to be eliminated from that list entirely.

These are difficult decisions, no doubt, but necessary ones. Proper charity must be given with an open hand and with an open heart. But it must also be given with an open mind.

Parashat Teruma

A Tale of Two Grandfathers

T hose who knew him used many different words to describe him. Some called him stubborn. Others called him staunch. Still others used the word steadfast. I am his grandson and I prefer to think of him as having been unbending in his commitment to the truths he believed in.

I often refer to my paternal grandfather in my writing. But I don't think I've ever yet introduced you, dear reader, to my maternal grandfather, Mr. Max Hartman. The nature of his relationship with all his many grandchildren is conveyed by the fact that none of us referred to him as "Grandpa" or "Zaide." To all of us, he was "Dad," a loving father figure who refused to acknowledge the many decades that separated us from him.

My grandfather was one of those now legendary Jews who came to America at the turn of the twentieth century, but remained totally observant of all Jewish religious practices. One indication of his "stubbornness" was his reaction to the difficulties he initially faced in observing the Sabbath as an employee of others. He eventually started his own business and scrupulously kept it closed on the Sabbath and

Jewish festivals throughout the difficult years of the Great Depression and the World War II.

He was one of the founders of a synagogue – one of the few in pre-war United States that required of its members total adherence to Sabbath observance. That synagogue remains well attended to this very day and carries the name *Shomer Shabbat Shtiebel,* the Sabbath observant chapel.

He passed away more than forty years ago. His Hebrew name was Mordekhai, and in my eulogy for him, I compared him to the biblical Mordekhai. I applied to him a verse in the Book of Esther, read in the synagogue on the holiday of Purim. The verse reads, "All the King's courtiers in the palace gate knelt and bowed down to Haman, for such was the king's order concerning him; but Mordekhai would not kneel or bow low" (Est. 3:2). Like Mordekhai, my grandfather "would not kneel or bow low" to the pressures and influences of the secular society.

It was not until long after my grandfather's demise that I found an apt metaphor for my grandfather's firm dedication to our tradition in *Parashat Teruma* (Ex. 25:1–27:21). In *Parashat Teruma,* we read of the construction of the Tabernacle. We learn about its various contents, its coverings, and its walls. Of the latter, we read, "You shall make the planks for the Tabernacle of acacia wood, upright."

Many commentators interpret every component of the Tabernacle in terms of its symbolic significance. Using this approach, the planks of the Tabernacle represent the quality of standing upright and firm, with unbending commitment to a cause.

The Hebrew word for the planks is *kerashim,* for which the singular is *keresh.* The letters of the word *keresh,* when transposed, spell out the word *sheker,* falsehood or untruth. Each plank, each *keresh,* represents truth, which in our tradition is permanent, in contrast to falsehood (*sheker*), which does not last.

In that sense, my "Dad" was a *keresh,* firm and unbending in his belief in eternal verities, and a bastion against the transient fashions of faithlessness.

We also read in *Parashat Teruma* of another component of the Tabernacle, and it too has symbolic significance. I refer to the *briaḥ hatikhon,* the center bar, which is to be inserted "halfway up the planks and shall run from end to end" (Ex. 26:28). This center bar was what held all the planks together. What does this center bar represent metaphorically?

For this, I draw upon the homiletic insight of a different "grandfather," namely Rabbi Shaul Taub, the hasidic rebbe of Modzitz, who was my wife's paternal grandfather. Although he was as firmly committed to religious tradition as was my own grandfather, he is remembered best by his followers for his compassionate and comforting hasidic melodies.

In his posthumously published work, *Yisa Berakha*, he seeks to elucidate the cryptic statement in the ancient Aramaic *Targum Yonatan*, which reads, "The source of the wood for the center bar was the tree that Abraham planted in Beersheba." "What can this possibly mean?" he asks. "What connection can there be between Abraham's tree and this component of the Tabernacle?"

To answer this, the rebbe of Modzitz reminds us of the account in the Midrash of the consultation between the Almighty and two angels, the Angel of Truth and the Angel of Loving-kindness. The former opposed the Almighty's plan to create man, insisting that man was full of falsehood. The latter consented to man's creation, arguing that man was capable of great loving-kindness. Thankfully for us, the Angel of Loving-kindness prevailed.

The rebbe expands upon the argument of the Angel of Truth. It was not man's propensity for falsehood that troubled him as much as it was his deceitful tendency to have falsehood masquerade in the guise of truth. The Angel of Loving-kindness was able to counter the argument of the Angel of Truth by suggesting a test by which authentic truth would be distinguished from hypocrisy, that is, from falsehood disguised as truth. That test was whether or not the truth in question led to cruelty or led to loving-kindness. If it led to cruelty, it was not truth. Authentic truth leads only to loving-kindness.

The tree that Abraham planted in Beersheba is understood by our sages to have been either an inn that offered hospitality to wayfarers or an orchard that fed them and slaked their thirst. That tree was the ultimate expression of loving-kindness.

The central bar that held the planks together is, from the rebbe's perspective, a metaphor for loving-kindness, for the force that assures that the unbending truths do not stand in the way of gentleness, sympathy, and compassion.

The essence of a Jew, whether famous like my wife's grandfather, or a layman like my grandfather, is the ability to insert the "central bar" into the "planks." It is the rare quality of being able to infuse unbending truths with loving-kindness. It takes a skilled spiritual artisan to place the *briah hatikhon betokh hakerashim*, the central bar halfway up the *kerashim*, and running through them from end to end.

Judaism today faces this challenge: Can we refuse to compromise the timeless truth of our tradition and still retain the traits of our forefather, Abraham? The "central bar," flexibly bending its way through the "upright plank," symbolically assures us that the challenge can be met.

One of the Angels

My grandmother was one of the angels. Like every Jewish grandmother, she loved each and every one of her grandchildren. As her oldest grandchild, I believed that I was surely her favorite. But I eventually discovered that my siblings and cousins were all equally convinced that they were her favorites.

She had a way of making us each feel special. I remember distinctly how, even as a very young boy, I knew that in her eyes I could do no wrong. She was a typical grandmother in almost every way.

I say "almost" because in some ways she was very different from her peers. She was one of the first women in New York State to receive a driver's license. I vividly remember the newspaper clipping on the bulletin board in her kitchen. It showed her receiving a certificate from some public official under the headline, "Brooklyn Grandma is in the Driver's Seat." It didn't mention that said driver's seat was in a huge Packard, one of the most glamorous cars then on the road.

Something else was unique about Grandmother. She was devoted to synagogue life. She spoke perfect English and rarely spoke to us in Yiddish, but she never used the word "synagogue." Instead, she called every Jewish house of worship "*ah heilige sheel*, a holy *shul.*" She prayed privately twice a day and only attended *sheel* on the Sabbath and festivals. But those were the most glorious moments of her week.

When *Parashat Teruma* (Ex. 25:1–27:19) is read, I am reminded of Grandmother's dedication to the synagogue. *Parashat Teruma* enumerates the components of the Tabernacle that the Jews built in the wilderness and describes what can be termed the first fundraising campaign in synagogue history.

Grandmother spearheaded synagogue building campaigns wherever she lived: the Lower East Side of Manhattan, Harlem, and finally Brooklyn. But it was not as a community activist that she conveyed her spiritual fervor to me. Rather, it was when she drove me and my cousin in the shiny black Packard to purchase kosher groceries in the "old neighborhood" every Sunday morning. She would drive over the Manhattan Bridge, and just as we crossed the river, she would point to a large gray stone building just under the bridge. Her eyes would tear and her voice would choke every time we passed that building. In a very subdued voice, she would deliver this message, "That building was once a *sheel*, built by angels. Now it is no longer a *sheel*. It is a *kloyster*. Non-Jews worship there."

When we asked her why "we" lost it and whether it was really built by angels, she would respond evasively, in typical grandmotherly fashion, "You are too young for me to answer you. One day, when you are older, you will understand."

Grandmother passed away more than fifty years ago. Gradually, after her passing, I began to understand who the angels were who built the *shul* (synagogue) and why "we" lost it. I discovered the angels when perusing the Midrash Rabba on the Book of Ecclesiastes one Sukkot afternoon. I came across this passage:

> Rabbi Ḥanina ben Dosa observed the people of his city bringing materials for the reconstruction of the Holy Temple. He wished to follow their example. He found a large boulder that would serve well as part of the Temple's new wall. He sculpted the stone and polished it. But it was far too heavy for him to carry up to Jerusalem. He asked passersby to help him, but they would only

do so for a fee, which he could not afford. Finally, he beheld five strangers approaching him. They agreed to carry the stone, but only on the condition that he would place his hand on the stone. He did so and suddenly found himself, and the stone, miraculously transported to Jerusalem. The five men were nowhere to be found. He entered the Temple chamber in which the Sanhedrin sat and inquired after them. The sages told him that they were not men, but angels.

That passage in the Midrash taught me that those who simply lend a hand to a holy project are granted the assistance of the angels. Angels build synagogues.

That's the good news. The sad news is that only angels can sustain synagogues once they are built. Only when those who attend synagogue behave like angels, in a decorous and reverent manner, do synagogues endure. Improper behavior in a house of prayer results in its ultimate destruction. More than one of our great sages has identified irreverence in the synagogue as the reason that many former Jewish houses of worship are now churches or mosques, theaters or museums, and often entirely destroyed.

I can hear Grandmother speaking to me today, "Synagogues are built by angels, but we must behave in them as angels would. If we don't, we lose them." She recognized that the old gray building in Lower Manhattan may have been built by angels, but it wasn't maintained by angels. It was maintained by those who came to synagogue to chatter idly, gossip maliciously, and cynically mock the rabbi and the cantor. Achieving proper synagogue decorum has been a perennial problem for the Jewish community. When a community gathers to build a new synagogue, it does so as a group of angels with noble motives. But as we grow accustomed to the synagogue, as it becomes too familiar to us, we lose our "angelic" enthusiasm.

The holy Zohar, the magnum opus of Jewish mysticism, devotes much of its commentary on our *parasha* to this very problem. It is excited by the Torah's description of a successful building campaign, of men and women generously donating gold and silver to the new Tabernacle. But then the Zohar offers these words of caution:

Woe to the person who engages in mundane conversation in the synagogue. He causes a cosmic schism, a degradation of faith. Woe to him, for he has no portion in the God of Israel. He demonstrates by his levity that God does not exist, and that He certainly is not be found in the synagogue. He asserts that he has no relationship with Him, that he does not fear Him, and that he is indifferent to the disgrace of the Upper Celestial Realm.

With these words, the holy Zohar expresses in mystical terms what my Grandmother knew with her ample common sense. How well she taught me the lesson of our need to remain "angels" in the synagogue. I can still hear her tearfully grieving for that *heilige sheel*, and all too numerous other sacred spaces, which "we" lost because of our callous indifference to the Almighty's presence.

Mrs. Gussie Hartman, Gitel bat Tzvi Hersh HaLevi, rest in peace knowing that I am older, and that I understand, and that many others have just read your heartfelt message.

The Stigma of Fame

P eople are motivated by many things. The search for pleasure is certainly one of the great motivators of human beings. So are the search for power and the search for riches. There are also those among us who seek to be liked by others, to the extent that the search for adulation is their primary motivation in life.

Others, and this is particularly true with religious people, hope for a place in the World to Come. For them, a vision of eternity is a major motivation. Still others devote their lives to the search for meaning, wisdom, or spiritual enlightenment.

For me, while all of the motivations listed above are interesting and deserve study, there is yet another human motivation that is more noteworthy: the search for fame.

We all know individuals who are devoted, sometimes even obsessed, by their urge to become famous. For them, just to be mentioned in a newspaper article or to be glimpsed on television for a fraction of a minute, is a powerful reward.

This particular motivation is hard to understand. Fame does not necessarily bring material rewards. Not every famous person is rich, nor is he powerful. Famous people are often not popular people; indeed, they are often disliked. And there are certainly no spiritual or intellectual achievements that come with fame. Furthermore, fame is notoriously fleeting. Yesterday's famous person often dwells in oblivion today.

Since the beginning of the Book of Exodus, we have been reading about Moses. Surely he is the most famous person in the Jewish Bible. Yet for him, fame was of no consequence whatsoever. He was not motivated by a need to make headlines, to be immortalized for all eternity, or even to be popular and well-known. He would be the last to be concerned if a weekly Torah portion did not even contain his name.

Parashat Tetzaveh is the only *parasha* since we were introduced to the newborn Moses in which he is not mentioned by name. *Tetzaveh*, a Torah portion rich in all sorts of particulars and details, fails to mention Moses.

Long ago, some keen Torah scholar noted this fact and attributed it to a verse in the following *parasha, Parashat Ki Tissa*. There, we read of how Moses pleads to God to forgive the Israelites who worshipped the Golden Calf. He says, "If You will forgive their sin [well and good]; but if not, erase me from the book that You have written." "Erase me from the book!" I have no need for fame. Insightfully, this keen scholar found *Tetzaveh* to be the book from which Moses was indeed erased.

I suggest that Moses learned how unimportant fame is from his personal experiences with stigma. For you see, just as fame is no indication at all of the genuine worth of the famous person, so, too, stigma does not reflect the genuine worth of the stigmatized individual.

One of the most perceptive observers of human relations was a writer named Erving Goffman. Almost fifty years ago, he authored a classic work entitled *Stigma: Notes on the Management of Spoiled Identity*. There, he describes the psychology of stigma and of how society assigns negative labels to people, spoiling or ruining their identities as valuable members of that society.

A person who has suffered from being stigmatized learns how meaningless the opinions are that other people have of him. Should he shed these stigmas and gain the positive opinions of others, he would know full well how meaningless those opinions are.

Moses was a stigmatized individual earlier in his life. Goffman distinguishes three different varieties of stigma, and all three were experienced by the young Moses.

The first of these conditions, Goffman termed "abominations of the body." Physical deformities result in such a stigma. Moses had such a physical deformity; he stammered and stuttered. The second condition, Goffman called "blemishes of individual character." In the eyes of the world, Moses was a fugitive, a criminal on the run, who was wanted by Pharaoh for the murder of an Egyptian citizen. Finally, the third source of stigma: "tribal identities." Moses was a Hebrew, a member of an ostracized minority.

In contemplating what the life of Moses was like in the many decades he spent as a refugee before returning to Egypt as a redeemer, it's clear that he suffered from a triple stigma: stutterer, fugitive, and Jew.

I suggest that one of the greatest achievements of Moses our teacher was his ability to retain a sense of his true identity, of his authentic self-worth, in the face of the odious epithets that were hurled at him.

This is how, in his later life, when fame and prestige became his lot, he was able to retain his self-knowledge and eschew fame. This is what enabled him to say, "Erase me from the book." This is why he was able to not only tolerate but to value this *parasha*, where his name is not mentioned.

"The man Moses was humbler than all other humans" (Num. 12:3). The deeper meaning of Moses' humility was his ability to understand himself enough to remain invulnerable to the trials of stigma and insult, and to remain equally unaffected by the temptations of glory and fame.

When we refer to Moses as *Rabbenu*, our teacher, it is not just because he taught us the law. It is also because he showed us how to remain impervious to the opinions of others and to value our own integrity and character. Would that we could be his disciples in this teaching.

Parashat Tetzaveh

Appearances

Whenever I think of people I knew who dressed impeccably, I recall three of my favorite people. One was my maternal grandfather, a businessman who was firmly dedicated to religious observance, but who chose his clothing carefully and was proud of his collection of cufflinks, tie clips, and colorful suspenders.

The other was my predecessor in the pulpit of the synagogue I served in Baltimore. He was known for his elegant demeanor and dress, and I will always treasure the image of him entering the synagogue on the eve of the major Jewish festivals. He wore a gray rabbinic frock, a gray Homburg hat, and a gray tie with a splash of red in it.

I can never forget the ninety-year-old woman philanthropist, who single-handedly financed a summer camp for those who were then called "the underprivileged," where I served for several years as head counselor. She visited the camp daily, and walked from table to table making sure that the children she loved were well fed and happy. She always wore a dark blue or purple outfit, appropriate to her advanced age, with a fresh flower pinned to her blouse. The fact that it was an ordinary weekday, and that she was sure to have the dress soiled during her visit to the camp kitchen, did not prevent her from always looking her best.

It has been said that "clothes make the man," and in these politically correct times, we must hasten to add, "and clothes make the woman." Our clothing makes a statement about us, and in the case of my grandfather, my predecessor, and the elderly philanthropist, that statement was all about dignity, a sense of self-worth, and yes, respect for all those with whom they came into contact.

You may wonder, "What does Judaism have to say about clothing? Is there any spiritual significance to what a person wears?"

In *Parashat Tetzaveh* (Ex. 27:20–30:10), we discover that Judaism has a lot to say about clothing and that there is indeed great spiritual significance to what a person wears. It is in this *parasha* that we learn about the special garments that the priests were to wear during their service in the Temple, and the very special garments assigned to Aaron, the brother of Moses, and to all subsequent High Priests throughout the history of the Holy Temple.

These are the instructions Moses received from the Almighty:

> Make sacral vestments for your brother Aaron, for dignity and adornment.... These are the vestments they are to make: a breast piece, an *ephod*, a robe, a fringed tunic, a headdress, and a sash." (Ex. 28:2–4)

The design, the colors, and the materials for these vestments are described in exquisite detail, and that long description concludes with the verse, "They shall be worn by Aaron and his sons when they enter the Tent of Meeting.... It shall be a law for all time for him and for his offspring to come" (Ex. 28:43).

The message here is unambiguous: when one is engaged in the service of the Lord, he or she must be dressed in a manner that befits that role, and that projects, if not the image of majesty, then surely the image of pride and dignity. To the extent that all of us are engaged in the service of the Lord in one way or another in much of what we do, we must be mindful of our physical appearance, and we must dress in a dignified manner that reinforces our sense of the important tasks that we are about, and impresses upon others that we take their opinion of us into consideration and care about the impression we make upon them.

It is no wonder, then, that the Talmud (Shabbat 114a) severely condemns individuals in religious public positions who dress sloppily and who thus project a lack of dignity. The "*talmid ḥakham* (rabbi or yeshiva student) upon whose clothing a greasy stain is found" is castigated in extreme terms by our sages.

The Sabbath during which we read *Parashat Tetzaveh* is soon followed by the joyous festival of Purim, when we read the Book of Esther (*Megillat Ester*). Interestingly, we find additional support for the importance of clothing in that very book.

The hero and heroine of the Megilla are of course Mordekhai and Esther, and whereas we imagine that Esther as a Queen was certainly bedecked with the finest clothing, it is the clothing worn by Mordekhai that is highlighted by the Megilla. We learn that Mordekhai wore two starkly contrasting sets of clothing.

In the early chapters of the narrative, which describe the dire straits in which the Jews found themselves because of the wicked Haman's genocidal decree, we read:

> When Mordekhai learned all that had happened, Mordekhai tore his clothes and put on sackcloth and ashes, until he came in front of the palace gate; for one could not enter the palace gate wearing sackcloth. (Est. 4:1–2)

How significant it is that Mordekhai expressed his grief and concern by changing his clothing. If it is true that "clothes make the man," then it is equally true that the clothing we wear gives voice to the emotions we feel and to the circumstances in which we find ourselves. Mordekhai's clothing gave voice to his people's pain.

Our sages suggest that it is precisely because he empathized so strongly with his brothers and sisters that he was ultimately privileged to don a different sort of clothing altogether. Hence, toward the end of the Megilla, when the evil decree is revoked and a new decree proclaimed, we read:

> Mordekhai left the king's presence in royal robes of blue and white, with a magnificent crown of gold and a mantle of fine linen and purple wool. The city of Shushan rang with joyous cries. (Est. 8:15)

When the Jewish people suffer, the very clothing our leaders wear expresses our suffering. When the Jewish people celebrate their redemption, that redemption is embodied in the garments those leaders choose to wear.

The Book of Esther is but one of the five books of the Bible to which the name Megilla applies. The word Megilla means a scroll, and there are five such scrolls within our Holy Scriptures. Besides the Book of Esther, they are: The Song of Songs, Ruth, Lamentations, and Ecclesiastes. In this latter work, we find the following mitzva, "Go, eat your bread in gladness, and drink your wine in joy.... Let your clothes always be freshly washed, and your head never lack ointment." (Eccl. 9:7–8)

This verse is especially apt as we celebrate the joyous festival of Purim. We feast, eat our bread, and drink our wine in gladness. But our clothes, the external manifestation of our human dignity, must always be "freshly washed," or, to translate the Hebrew literally, "always white."

We must never sully our behavior, even in moments of great joy, by celebrating in an excessive and unbecoming manner. We are entitled, in celebration of the victories of the Jews in ancient Persia, to wear "royal robes of blue and white," but we must wear them with the same dignity and humility with which Aaron and his offspring wore their sacred garments.

Yes, clothes make the man and the woman, but it is they who must make their clothes, and their demeanor, appropriate expressions of propriety and modesty. A lesson for Purim, certainly, but a lesson as well for the rest of the year.

Clothes Make the Man

My interest in the relationship between a person and his or her clothing goes back to my early days in graduate school. I was taking a course on human personality under the tutelage of a remarkably insightful and erudite woman, Dr. Mary Henle. I was so enthusiastic about the courses that I took with her that I asked her to supervise my master's degree thesis.

I remember the morning I shared my proposed topic with her. I thought that one of the ways to assess personality was to take note of the kind of clothing that a person wore. I further postulated that not only does a person's clothing tell us a lot about him or her, but the clothing that we wear actually has an impact upon us. Our clothing helps make us who we are.

Dr. Henle tactfully deflated my ego that morning. She said, "That's just an old wives' tale. Our personalities are very profound, subtle, and complex. At most, our clothing reflects just a superficial aspect of our identity. You give too much credit to the saying, 'Clothes make the man.' It is really only a wisecrack attributed to Mark Twain. There is nothing more to it than that." I subsequently chose another topic for my master's degree thesis.

Many years have passed since that disappointing encounter, and Dr. Henle has long since passed away, although I remember her respectfully. During those years, I have learned that she was mistaken on many grounds. For one thing, the saying, "Clothes make the man," did not originate with Mark Twain. Centuries before the American humorist, the sixteenth-century Catholic theologian Desiderius Erasmus wrote, "*Vestis virum facit,*" which translates as, "Clothes make the man." Not long afterwards, none other than William Shakespeare put these words into the mouth of the character Polonius in his famous play *Hamlet*: "The apparel oft proclaims the man."

Truth to tell, statements about the relationship between a person and his clothing go back much further than a mere several centuries. Such statements originate in the Bible, and a passage in *Parashat Tetzaveh* (Ex. 27:20–30:10) is a case in point. We read:

> You shall bring forward your brother, Aaron, with his sons, from among the Israelites, to serve Me as priests.... Make sacral vestments for your brother Aaron, for dignity and adornment. Next you shall instruct all who are wise of heart...to make Aaron's vestments, for consecrating him to serve Me as priest.

Maimonides, codifying the concepts that emerge from the biblical text, writes:

> A High Priest who serves in the Temple with less than his eight vestments, or an ordinary priest who serves with less than his four required vestments...invalidates the service performed and is subject to punishment by death at the hands of Heaven, as if he were an alien who served in the Temple.... When their vestments are upon them, their priestly status is upon them, but without their vestments their priestly status is removed from them. (*Hilkhot Klei HaMikdash*, 10:4)

We are left with the clear impression that these vestments are external manifestations of the royalty and majesty of the priestly role. The clothing literally makes the man. Without the clothing, each priest is "ordinary," one of God's subjects for sure, but without any regal status. With the clothing, he is not only bedecked with "dignity and adornment," but has become a prince, and can play a royal role.

Nahmanides makes this even more explicit. He writes, "These are royal garments. These cloaks and robes, tunics and turbans, are even today [he lived in thirteenth-century Spain] the apparel of nobility...and no one would dare to wear the crown...or the *tekhelet* (blue yarn) except for royalty."

From this perspective, clothes make the man. With them, he is imbued with the spirit of royalty and can carry himself with regal bearing.

Others interpret the function of the sacred garments differently, but all agree that garments influence the wearer in some fashion. For example, Rashi, commenting on the verse, "Put these on your brother Aaron, and on his sons as well; anoint them, and fill their hands" (Ex. 28:41), points out that in the Old French language, with which he was familiar, when a person received a new official position, the nobleman would put gloves upon him, indicating that he now had the authority of a new position. Rashi uses the Old French word, *gant*, which the reference books that I consulted translate as a "decorative glove." This would indicate that the garments were a type of official uniform, not necessarily regal, but symbolic of a specialized responsibility. With the donning of the *gant,* the person himself gained the self-assurance of authority and power.

The late fifteenth-century commentator Rabbi Isaac Arama, in his classic *Akedat Yitzḥak,* provides even stronger support for our contention that clothes make the man. He identifies a similarity between the Hebrew word for the Kohen's uniform and the Hebrew word for ethical character. The Hebrew word for uniform is *mad* (plural *madim*), and the Hebrew word for a character trait is *midda* (plural *middot*).

Rabbi Arama notes that in Latin, too, the word *habitus* refers to both a special garment (e.g., a nun's habit) and a character trait (e.g., a good habit). He persuasively argues that "just as it can be determined from a person's external appearance as to whether he is a merchant, or a soldier, or a monk, so too the discovery of our hidden inner personality begins with our external behaviors."

For Rabbi Arama, that our clothing is metaphor for our moral standing is evident in this biblical verse, "Now Joshua was clothed in filthy garments when he stood before the angel. The latter stood up and spoke to his attendants, 'Take the filthy garments off him!' And he said to him, 'See, I have removed your guilt from you'" (Zech. 3:3-4).

Finally, there is another biblical verse that demonstrates the central role of clothing in "making the man." And here we go back even further in history than our *parasha*. Indeed, we go all the way back to the first *parasha* in the Torah, *Parashat Bereshit*, "And the Lord God made garments of skins for Adam and his wife, and clothed them" (Gen. 3:21).

Nehama Leibowitz comments:

Everything in the way of culture and civilization was given to man to discover and develop on his own, with his own capacities. Nothing in the way of repairing the world and settling it was given to him by God. Neither the discovery of fire nor farming nor building houses was revealed to man by God. Rather, he was required to invent all these procedures on his own. Only clothing was given to him from Above. "And the Lord…made garments." God made clothing for man. And clothing makes the man.

Ah, do I now wish that I had not abandoned my original idea for a master's degree thesis. What a fascinating thesis it would have been!

Don't Take Down the Sign

Times were very different then. When one of our books was torn, we didn't junk it. We took it to a little shop where a bookbinder rebound it. When our briefcase (we didn't have backpacks then) was falling apart, we didn't discard it. Instead, we took it to that same shop where the proprietor stitched it and fixed it.

The proprietor of the shop that my friends and I frequented, down on the Lower East Side of Manhattan, was an old man named Yossel. Looking back, I now realize that Yossel, who was arthritic physically and far from genial emotionally, was a Holocaust survivor who eked out a meager livelihood by binding books, fixing broken zippers, and repairing all sorts of every day tools and trinkets.

I remember once bringing some books to Yossel for rebinding and finding that the shop was closed. There was no sign on the door indicating that he was out to lunch, or that he had gone to pray, or when he would return.

So I came back to Yossel's shop several times that week, and then occasionally for the next two or three months. His sign, advertising his services, was still suspended over his doorway. I had every reason to assume that he would eventually reopen.

Finally, one day I approached his shop, and saw that the sign over his door was taken down. Now I knew that Yossel was out of business.

This experience, hardly significant in its own right, took on a very profound meaning for me when I first heard an explanation, given by the great sage known as the Ḥafetz Ḥaim, of why the Torah calls the Sabbath a sign in *Parashat Ki Tissa*. "The people of Israel shall keep the Sabbath…. It shall be a sign for all time between Me and the people of Israel" (Ex. 31:16–17).

The Ḥafetz Ḥaim explained that the Sabbath is like a sign on a shopkeeper's door. However far a Jew might stray, he is still connected to the Jewish people as long as he keeps the Sabbath in some manner. As long as there is a sign on the shopkeeper's door, he may one day return and reopen for business. But once the sign is removed, once Sabbath observance is totally abandoned, then even that tenuous connection is severed.

It occurs to me that just as there are all sorts of signs, and Yossel's makeshift shabby sign was certainly very different from signs on more luxurious stores, so too do Jews differ in the way in which they observe the Sabbath.

There are those who focus on every halakha involved in Sabbath observance. They are punctilious in following every rule contained in our code of laws. There are others whose observance is a more spiritual one. They may keep the basic Sabbath laws in some fashion, but find the joy of the Sabbath more personally rewarding. They enjoy the festive meals and they heartily sing the Sabbath songs. Still others take delight in intellectual indulgences in celebration of the Sabbath. They study, they read, they converse, and they teach. Then there are those of a more mystical bent who use the Sabbath for introspection, meditation, and contemplation, and maybe even as an occasion to delve into the classics of Jewish mysticism. For some, the Sabbath is something entirely different. It is merely a day of rest, a physical respite from the toil and stress of a busy week.

Whatever your Sabbath is like, dear reader, as long as it is a special day for you in some way, the sign of Sabbath is suspended over your door. You are, at least potentially, a Sabbath observer, and that is a sign of your connection to God and to the Jewish people.

But there is a lesson here for all of us: None of us can say that our Sabbath observance is a perfect one. None of us is innocent of some minor halakhic infraction. Certainly, none of us can say that our Sabbath is one of pure and untainted spirituality. We all have "a way to go." Yet, the vast majority of Jews whom I know, of whatever level of observance or denominational persuasion, have the sign of Sabbath on their shop door, in some manner or another.

As long as that sign hangs suspended over our doorway, we can confidently look forward to that day when each of us will celebrate a Sabbath worthy of the ultimate redemption of which our sages assure us. For they have said the *geula*, the final redemption of our people, will come about when we fully observe two Sabbaths in succession. Don't take down the sign!

Parashat Ki Tissa

The Hindu Princess
and the Golden Calf

She was a Hindu princess. She was one of the brightest students in my graduate school class. We studied psychology and she went on to return to her country and become a psychotherapist of world renown. For our purposes, I shall refer to her as Streena.

We were a class of twelve, and except for one lapsed Catholic, she and I were the only ones who had a serious interest in religion. And we were the only ones who actively practiced our faith.

This was back in the days when religion was far from a popular subject in psychology departments. Religion was seen as foolish at best and as quite possibly a sign of neurotic pathology. So neither of us was very public about our religious practices.

In the early afternoons, when the time for the afternoon prayer service (Minḥa) rolled around, I would usually find an excuse to absent myself from the psychology department library where our group hung out. There was a small synagogue not far from the campus, and I would make my way there and unobtrusively return to the library when Minḥa was over.

But there were times when it was impossible for me to leave the building. During those times, I would make use of a small side room and pray in private. It was during one of those times that I discovered I was not the only one to use that side room for prayers. Streena was there too.

I remember the first time I noticed her there. I had just taken the customary three steps back after concluding my *Amida* (*Shemoneh Esreh*). She was in the far corner of the room, doing her utmost not to disturb me. She was deep in prayer herself, but what was most striking was that she had a small object in her hand.

When it was apparent to me that she, too, had concluded her prayers, I approached her and inquired about that object. She showed me what looked like a small doll, only she referred to it by a Hindu name that meant that it was her deity, her God. Plainly and simply, it was an idol.

Over our years in graduate school, we had numerous conversations about religion, the nature of prayer, and of course the nature of the divinity. I stressed that when I, as a Jew, prayed, I did not pray to any image, statue, or portrait. I prayed to an invisible and unknowable God. She found that impossible to accept. "When I pray," she insisted, "I must have some concrete visual image before me. I know that this little doll is not the deity. But it is what I call a concretization of the higher power that I worship."

The stark contrast between Streena's mode of prayer and my Jewish conception of the way in which we are to conceive the Almighty is one of the lessons of an exceedingly provocative episode in *Parashat Ki Tissa* (Ex. 30:11–34:35). I refer to the story of the Golden Calf.

Moses ascends the mountain to receive the holy tablets. He is delayed in his return, and in their impatience, the Jewish people collect gold, fashion an idol out of it in the shape of a calf, and worship it with sacrifices and an orgiastic feast.

Every reader of the Torah has been puzzled by the sudden descent of the people from a state of lofty spiritual anticipation to the degrading scene of dancing worshipfully before a graven image.

One such reader, himself a pagan, was the king of the Khazars, a nation in central Asia, whose search for religious truth is the theme of one of the most intriguing books of Jewish philosophy, Rabbi Yehuda Halevi's the *Kuzari*.

In that king's dialogue with the Jewish sage, who is his spiritual mentor, he condemns this behavior and challenges the sage to justify the apparent idolatry of the Jewish people. The sage, who is actually the voice of the author of the *Kuzari*, responds, in part:

> In those days, every people worshiped images.... This is because they would focus their attention upon the image, and profess to the masses that divinity attaches itself to the image.... We do something like this today when we treat certain places with special reverence – we will even consider the soil and rocks of these places as sources of blessing.... The objective was to have some tangible item that they could focus upon.... Their intent was not to deny the God who took them out of Egypt; rather, it was to have something in front of them upon which they could concentrate when recounting God's wonders.... We do the same thing when we ascribe divinity to the skies (for example, we call fear of God "fear of heaven").

This is but one explanation of the motivation for what is one of the greatest recorded sins of our people. But it is an especially instructive explanation, for it renders understandable, in our own terms, an act that is otherwise totally mystifying.

In our own inner experiences of prayer, we have all struggled with the difficulty of "knowing before whom we stand." It is frustrating to address an abstract, invisible, and unknowable deity. It is comforting to imagine that we stand before a mortal king, or a flesh and blood father figure, someone physical and real. I think that we can all confess to moments when we have, at least in our visualizations of the Almighty, resorted to the same process of concretization as Streena did.

Ideally, we know that we must resist the temptation to "humanize" God, to anthropomorphize Him. We believe in a deity who sees but is not seen, hears but is not heard, and who is as far from human ken as heaven is from earth. In this fundamental belief, we differ from other religions, and indeed not only from Hinduism but from certain forms of Christianity as well.

Nevertheless, we can sympathize with Streena's need to pray to her doll, and in the process, we can come to grips with what must have been going on in the minds of our ancestors when they stooped to idolatry and committed the sin, which the Almighty has never totally forgiven, the worship of the Golden Calf.

Parashat Ki Tissa

The Inevitable Comedown

I t was over forty years ago, but I remember the feelings very well. They were overwhelming, and were not dispelled easily. It was just after I had completed all of my course requirements and dissertation defense in the process of obtaining my doctorate in psychology. Like any graduate school experience, this was the culmination of several years of study and hard work. The ordeal was now over and a celebration was in order.

And celebrate I did, together with my wife, my young children, several other students, and assorted friends. But then, the celebration was suddenly over. I found myself inexplicably moody and depressed. A sense of emptiness enveloped me. At first, I thought it was just a result of a transition from a state of being busy to a state of boredom.

However, the feelings lingered for quite some time. I tried to rid myself of my moodiness in various ways, and it must have been difficult for those close to me to be around me. Luckily, the feelings were soon gone, as suddenly and as mysteriously as they had come.

Quite a while later, I learned that this curious phenomenon was very common. When people achieve great accomplishments, having put great effort and toil into them, they experience a sense of exhilaration and excitement, a "high." Soon afterwards, and often very soon afterwards, there is a "comedown" from that "high."

It is as if, now that the goal with which one had been long preoccupied has been reached, life has become meaningless. There is nothing further to do, no ongoing purpose. A pervasive sense of emptiness ensues.

The struggle to fill that emptiness is fraught with danger. In my own case, the emptiness thankfully passed in relatively short order, with no harm done and no unusual "acting out" on my part. But others in similar predicaments frequently attempt to fill that emptiness in ways that result in great, and sometimes tragic, difficulties.

The psychological mechanism I have just described helps to explain a most puzzling event in *Parashat Ki Tissa* (Ex. 30:11–34:35). I refer, of course, to the episode of the Golden Calf.

Just a few short weeks earlier, in *Parashat Yitro*, we read of how the Children of Israel experienced the most momentous occasion in human history. The Almighty revealed Himself to them at Mount Sinai in an awe-inspiring atmosphere of thunder and lightning. They heard the voice of God and they were spiritually elevated by His revelation. They were, almost literally, on a "high."

Moses then ascends Mount Sinai and remains there for forty days and forty nights. During that time, the people come down from their "high." His disappearance mystifies them and they become impatient and irritable. We can empathize with their sense of emptiness, although we are shocked by the manner in which they choose to deal with that emptiness:

> When the people saw that Moses delayed to come down from the mount, the people came together unto Aaron, and said unto him: "Up, make us a god." And all the people broke off all the golden earrings that were in their ears, and brought them unto Aaron…he…made it a molten calf and they said: "This is thy god, O Israel." He built an altar before it…. And the people sat down to eat and to drink, and rose up to make merry. (Ex. 32:1–6)

What a comedown! How can one explain a process of spiritual deterioration as drastic as this? Just weeks ago, the Jewish people were on the highest possible level of religiosity and commitment to the one God. Now they are dancing and prancing before a golden idol. Is this not inexplicable?

Yes, it is inexplicable, but it is a common human phenomenon. People are capable of attaining greatness, but they are not as capable of sustaining greatness. They can achieve "highs" of all kinds, but they cannot maintain those "highs." There is an inevitable "comedown."

This concept is well expressed in the following verse, "Who may ascend the mountain of the Lord? Who may stand in His holy place?" (Ps. 24:3) Homiletically, this has been interpreted to mean that even after the first question is answered and we learn "who may ascend the mountain," the question still remains, "Who can continue to stand there?" It is relatively easy to ascend to a high level; much more difficult is remaining at that high level and preserving it.

My revered colleague, one of the most insightful spiritual thinkers of our age, Rabbi Adin Steinsaltz, believes that the best example of deterioration following an exciting climax is the experience of childbirth itself. He points to the phenomenon known as "postpartum depression." A woman, a mother, has just experienced what is probably the highest of all "highs," the emergence of a child from her womb. But quite commonly, that experience is followed by a sense of depression, which is sometimes incapacitating, and sometimes even disastrous.

The physiological process of giving birth calls upon the utilization of every part of the mother's body, from her muscles and nervous system to her hormonal fluids. Her body has exerted itself to the maximum. In the process, she has achieved the greatest of all achievements, the production of another human being. But soon afterwards, when the body, as it were, has nothing left to do, she feels depleted and empty. She can easily sink into a depression, sometimes deep enough to merit a clinical diagnosis of "postpartum depression."

This is an important lesson in our personal spiritual lives. Often we experience moments of intense spirituality, of transcendence. But those moments are brief and transitory. When they are over, we feel "shortchanged," and we despair of ever returning to those precious experiences.

We must take hope in the knowledge that almost all intense human experiences are transitory and are followed by feelings of hollowness. We can ascend the mountain, but we cannot long stand there. We must humbly accept our descent, our frustrating failures and limitations, and persist in climbing the mountain. Ups and downs, peaks and valleys, are to be expected, in all aspects of our life. We will experience "highs," but we must expect the inevitable "comedown." And we must hang in there and try and try again to recapture those "highs."

This is the lesson of our *parasha*. Our people ascended a spiritual mountain. They then descended into an orgy of idolatry. But then they persisted, and with the assistance of God's bountiful mercy, as we read later in the *parasha*, they received this divine assurance:

> And he said, behold, I make a covenant: Before all Thy people I will do marvels, such as have not been done in all the earth.... And all the people...shall see the work of the Lord. (Ex. 34:10)

Little Did I Know

Birthdays are important, and the older one gets, the more important they become. As we age, birthdays begin to stimulate ambiguous feelings. On the one hand, every birthday is cause for celebration. Another year of life and accomplishment has gone by, and a new year full of hope and great possibilities is about to begin. There is much to be thankful for. On the other hand, one can no longer deny that he or she is getting older. Sadly, some of the people we celebrated with last year are no longer around to celebrate with us this year. Birthdays bring back memories of the past. The memories themselves are sometimes wonderful, but sometimes remind us of tragic experiences that we would rather forget.

My own birthday is coming up soon. My bar mitzva *parasha* was *Parashat Ki Tissa* (Ex. 30:11–34:35), and each year, the reading of this Torah portion is an occasion for reflection for me.

My memories center about the people who were there. My parents, of course, are among them, and three of my grandparents, all long gone. A great-uncle, already old then, who went on to live until he was 110-years-old, and who was one of the few people then who actually taught me something about my *parasha*. My sisters were there, although one was barely a year old.

I also remember fondly and with great respect, the man who taught me to read the Torah. His name was Mr. Sender Kolatch, and he was a world-class Torah reader (*baal koreh*) himself. I would walk to his home every Friday night for lessons, each of which was followed by tea and cookies. I still keep in touch with one of his children. He too is long gone.

But what I reflect on most is the discrepancy between what I knew about my *parasha* then and what I have learned about it in the many decades since my bar mitzva. I did learn to read it from the Torah scroll, and I'm told I did it well, but I had only a very superficial knowledge about this profound *parasha* and its very diverse contents.

I knew, for example, that it opened with the mitzva of *maḥatzit hashekel*, that every Jew was to contribute a half shekel to a central fund, out of which the costs of the Tabernacle services would be paid.

I knew that the opening two sections of the *parasha* were among the longest, if not the longest, in the entire Torah. This was one of my biggest obstacles to mastering the Torah reading. But I hadn't a clue as to the details of those two sections: about the special oils and fragrances that were an essential part of the Temple service. It was much later that the talmudic tractate that discusses these details and their significance, Tractate Keritot, became one of my favorite talmudic tractates.

I knew about the reference to Shabbat in the opening sections of the *parasha*, but it was not until much later that I began to appreciate the connection between sacred space – the Temple precincts, and sacred time – the Shabbat day.

I knew the story of the Golden Calf, but only as a story. I did not appreciate its contemporary relevance and rich symbolism until much later. I have since, for example, become enamored of Rabbi Yehuda Halevi's explanation of the attractiveness of a Golden Calf for the people. He maintains that the demand to worship an invisible god was just too much for the Children of Israel, so that they chose a tangible object through which to worship a God who could not be seen. How tempting it is to this very day to try to find tangible physical or ideological substitutes for the transcendent Almighty, a temptation that leads us to modes of worship that are more "sophisticated" than dancing around a Golden Calf, but no less idolatrous.

The courageous confrontation of Moses with God, as he intercedes for the sinful people and begs forgiveness for them, was "over my head." It made no impression upon me. And yet, now, for me, these verses have come to exemplify the essence of true leadership:

> Moses went back to the Lord and said: "Alas. This nation is guilty of a great sin in making for themselves a god of gold. Now, if You will forgive their sin [well and good]; but if not, erase me from the record that You have written." (Ex. 32: 31–32)

Nor did I in any way understand Moses' plea, "Now, if I have truly gained Your favor, pray let me know Your ways." What ways? What exactly was Moses asking for?

I now have learned that Moses was asking to understand God's inscrutable will. He needed to understand so much that we find difficult in our daily lives as we struggle to make sense of "why the righteous suffer." But for a thirteen-year-old, blessed with a relatively problem-free life, I was protected from such a "need to know."

Our *parasha* contains so much else that was not part of the agenda of a thirteen-year-old boy, brought up in the United States in those years. It was not that the period of history in which I was born and raised did not have its immense trials and tribulations. After all, I was born months after World War II began. When I was safe and secure in my baby bunting, my cousins in Poland were being shot and buried alive. My childhood years were concurrent with the State of Israel's struggle for independence. My bar mitzva took place during a time when our neighbors' sons were off in the distant land of Korea, from which one of them did not return.

Yet, there is much in the *parasha* that was relevant then: God's response to Moses' request that he know His ways: "You cannot see My face, for man may not see Me and live;" the mysterious "cleft in the rock" in which Moses hid; the symbolism of the Second Tablets that Moses was instructed to carve of stone; the Thirteen Attributes of God's mercy; the radiance that graced Moses' face, so that "the people shrank from coming near him"; and the mask, or veil, which Moses wore so as to frighten the people no longer.

All this rich content, and more, was not taught to me, and had it been taught to me, it wouldn't have meant very much.

There is a lesson in the ignorance of this particular bar mitzva boy and all that he has subsequently learned about the Torah and about this *parasha*. It is a lesson I have tried, albeit neither constantly nor consistently, to live by. The lesson is this: One cannot be complacently satisfied with the understanding of Torah that one attained as a schoolchild. As we mature, so must our knowledge of Torah mature. The Torah of a thirteen-year-old cannot slake the intellectual thirst of a thirty-year-old, nor can the Torah we learned when we were thirty satisfy our spiritual needs when we turn sixty.

Our Torah must be renewed as we grow older. Torah study must be a lifelong endeavor. Then, and only then, can it continue to inspire and instruct us as we struggle with the challenges of living and with the challenges that change as we age.

Parashat Vayak'hel

Three Dimensions

Since my childhood, I have been an avid reader. When I first discovered the joy of reading, I read everything I could get my hands on. Even today, my taste in reading is eclectic. However, there is at least one genre of literature that I seem to avoid.

I do not read science fiction. I trace my distaste for science fiction to one of its common themes: the possible existence of a fourth dimension. Somehow, the three dimensions of our ordinary reality are quite enough for me. The possibility of a mysterious fourth, of a "black hole" in the universe, is one that I have always dismissed as unimaginable.

The three dimensions of our existence are not only part of our physical reality. Forward and backward, horizontal left and right, and vertical up and down, all play a part in our religious experience as well.

For example, when the Jew shakes the lulav on Sukkot, he moves it from left to right, up and down, and forwards and backwards. In doing this, he mimics the ritual in the ancient Holy Temple of waving (*tenufa*), in which various sacred objects were lifted and rotated in all of the three dimensions.

When the *Shema* is recited and the Jew declares that the Lord is one (*eḥad*), he is instructed to imagine that God's dominion is over all the three dimensions of existence. He rules the horizontal plane, the vertical plane, and the dimension of inner/outer.

Our tradition knows, too, of an entirely different dimensional triad. Not merely three aspects of space, but three modes of human experience: time, space, and person. In Hebrew, this triad is known as *olam-shana-nefesh*, literally, "world-year-soul."

Part of our experience is temporal; we live in time. We also live spatially, bound by geographical parameters. And we have the inner experience of being, of consciousness, of personal awareness. Thus, three dimensions.

These three dimensions play a central role in *Parashat Vayak'hel*. Three themes are intertwined in the chapters of Exodus 35:1–38:20, which comprise our *parasha*. These three themes are the Sabbath, the *Mishkan*, and the individuals to whom the words of this *parasha* are addressed and who contribute, both materially and creatively, to the construction of the *Mishkan*.

The portion begins as Moses assembles the entire congregation of the Children of Israel. Moses and all the Jewish people constitute one dimension, one *nefesh*, one person.

He shares with them the message of the Sabbath, of working for six days and resting on the seventh. He enjoins them to kindle no fire in their homes on the Sabbath day. He thereby introduces them to the second dimension, that of time. He initiates the concept of sacred time, of a time that stands separate from the mundane and the ordinary.

The rest of the *parasha* describes the construction of what is to become a sacred place, a demarcated space set off from the rest of the spatial environment.

And throughout *Parashat Vayak'hel*, we read of those whose "hearts are stirred up and whose spirits are willing" (Ex. 35:21) to come forward with the gifts and contributions out of which this space will be constructed. We read of the "wise hearted women...whose hearts stirred them up in wisdom," (35:26) and whose hands crafted the beautifully embroidered cloths that decorated this haven in space.

We also read of two individuals, Betzalel and Oholiav, who are "filled with a Godly spirit, with wisdom, understanding, and knowledge in all manner of workmanship" (Ex. 35:31).

These three utterly different dimensions delineate the physical reality of horizontal and vertical space, but even more so accentuate the spiritual reality of man. The human condition is such that space can be sanctified, that time can be hallowed, and that humans have a transcendent spirit that distinguishes them from the rest of the animal world.

Parashat Vayak'hel is often considered to be an uninspiring, even boring, list of irrelevant details. In truth, however, the lessons inherent in these three dimensions are about as important as any in our Scripture.

First, there is the lesson of the year (*shana*), of time. We have the capability of setting aside special times for celebration, for introspection, and for memory. And this capability has kept the Jewish people in good stead throughout their history. As the nineteenth-century Jewish thinker Aḥad Haam expressed it so well, "More than the Jewish people have kept the Sabbath, the Sabbath has kept the Jewish people."

Then there is the lesson of the world around us (*olam*), of space. There are places in the world that are home and there are places that are exile. Indeed, "home is where the heart is," in the psychological sense. But in the national and religious sense, the Land of Israel is our place, and our synagogues and study halls are our sacred spaces in every corner of the world.

Finally, there is the lesson of the personal soul (*nefesh*). It is our spiritual potential that makes us able to sanctify time and place, and thereby lend meaning and purpose to our existence.

A fourth dimension? Perhaps there is one. But for me, the three dimensions of *olam*, *shana*, and *nefesh* are more than sufficient to provide an agenda for religious life. What a powerful framework! And all are encompassed in our *parasha*.

Culture, Counter-culture, and Creativity

I t was quite a few years ago that I spent almost every Sunday afternoon in one of the great museums of the city in which my family then lived. I no longer remember what first stimulated my interest in art, and specifically in the type of art known as Impressionism. But I know that I relished those Sunday afternoons, as did my youngest daughter, then no more than six or seven years old.

The museum we frequented possessed the most extensive collection in the world of the paintings of the French artist, Henri Matisse. My daughter became so familiar and so fond of the works of Matisse, particularly his colorful "cutouts," or paper cut collages, that when we once ventured into a new museum, she saw some Matisse works at a distance and gained the admiration of everyone in the crowded gallery by shouting excitedly, "Matisse, Matisse." I glowed with pride as the others present exclaimed, "What a precocious child!"

It was on that occasion that I first encountered a most fascinating gentleman. I'll call him Ernesto. Ernesto was a tall hulk of a man, who

I later learned was a brilliant Talmud student before the war, but who had given up all religious observance and indeed almost all connection with the Jewish people. He had totally lost his faith as a result of his horrible experiences during the Holocaust.

With my black velvet yarmulke, I was readily identifiable as an Orthodox Jew, so I was easy prey for Ernesto. "Jews know nothing about art," he bellowed. "Matisse! How can you glorify Matisse? His art is only decorative. All Jewish art is nothing but decoration."

I must confess that I had no clue as to what he was talking about. We soon sat down together at a nearby bench and he began to share his story with me. Over the subsequent years, I came to know him better and discovered that he had many "bones to pick" with Judaism and was in a perpetual rage against God. But that morning, he confined his remarks to his disappointment with what he saw as the absence of fine art in the Jewish culture.

Frankly, I had never given much thought to the subject of the place of art in Judaism. The best I could do was to refer to the person of Betzalel, mentioned in *Parashat Vayak'hel* (Ex. 35:1–38:20).

I quoted these verses to him, "See, the Lord has singled out by name Betzalel, son of Uri son of Hur... He has endowed him with a divine spirit of skill, ability, and knowledge in every kind of craft and has inspired him to make designs for work in gold, silver and copper."

"Surely," I argued. "The figure of Betzalel, so prominent at the very beginning of our history, is evidence that art has a central place in our tradition."

Not only was he unimpressed, but he responded with a rant that seemed as if it would go on forever. "Betzalel was no more than a Matisse," he insisted. For him, Matisse was the epitome of a bankrupt artist, one who could produce colorful designs but who had no message for the culture at large. He contrasted Matisse with Picasso, who had a lot to say in his art about the political world in which he lived. He concluded his tirade by shouting, "Besides pretty decorations for the Tabernacle, what did Betzalel have to teach us? What did he have to say to the human race?"

For the many years since that first encounter with Ernesto, who by the way, passed away sixty years to the day after his release from

Auschwitz in 1945, I have struggled with that challenging question, "What can we learn from Betzalel?"

I have since concluded that Betzalel had a lot to teach us all, especially about the creative process. He was able to do what so many others who are blessed with great creative talents have not been able to do.

Most creative geniuses throughout history, and I say this fully expecting some of my readers to object with examples to the contrary, have either been misfits in society, or have, in one way or another, rebelled against society. Creativity often sees itself as in opposition to conformity. The place of the artist is rarely in the contemporary culture; rather, it is in the counter-culture. The creative artist, whatever his medium, typically sees himself as the creator of a new culture, one that will replace the current culture and render it obsolete.

Betzalel's genius lay in his ability to channel his substantial artistic gifts to the cause of the culture that was being constructed around him. He was not rebellious and certainly not withdrawn. He participated in a national project as part of the nation and not as one whose role was to find fault. He was able to combine creativity with conformity and that is no mean feat.

One lesson that he taught all subsequent artists is that they need not limit their role to critical observation of society. Quite the contrary, they can cooperatively partner with society and bring their skills to bear in the service of what is going on around them.

This is the deeper meaning of the passage in the Talmud, which reads, "Betzalel knew how to combine the mystical primeval letters from which heaven and earth were created" (Berakhot 55a). Betzalel's art was an art that "combined" letters, joining them together harmoniously. His was not the art that tears asunder the constituent elements of the world that surrounds him. His was the art that blends those elements into a beautiful whole.

Betzalel's lesson is not just a lesson for artists. It is a lesson for all gifted and talented human beings. Somehow, the best and the brightest among us are the ones who are most cynical and most critical of the societies in which we live. We see this today in the harsh criticism that is directed at Israel precisely from the world of the academe, and sadly, especially from the Jewish intelligentsia. There is something pernicious about great intelligence that makes one unduly and unfairly critical of the world within which one resides.

Betzalel, on the other hand, was able to demonstrate that one can be highly gifted, indeed sublimely gifted, and use those gifts in a positive and constructive fashion, cooperating with others who are far less gifted, and participating in a joint venture with the rest of society.

This is a lesson in leadership that all who are blessed with special talents must learn. Special talents do not entitle one to separate oneself from the common cause. Quite the contrary: They equip one to participate in the common cause, and in the process, to elevate and inspire the rest of society.

Black Sabbath

We were walking down the long airport corridor on the way to the boarding gate. Somehow, it seems that whenever my wife and I have a flight to catch anywhere, our gate is always at the farthest end of the long hall. We had plenty of time until the airplane departed, but I somehow experience an urgent need to rush whenever I am in an airport, and so we were in a hurry.

There was a couple coming toward us, equally hurried. At first, they didn't even come into focus for me. They were just anonymous faces in a crowded hallway. As they came closer, there was something vaguely familiar about them. I turned to my wife and said, "Don't we know those people from somewhere?" "I don't think so," she responded, "but they resemble the Goldblatts."

As we came still closer, we realized that indeed they were the Goldblatts, but a twenty-year older version of the Goldblatts we knew. Of course, we were a twenty-year older version too, so it was no wonder that they didn't recognize us either.

But soon we were face-to-face, the intervening years vanished, and the good memories resurfaced. We all slowed down our rushed pace and took some time to reconnect with each other.

"We can never forget," exclaimed Mrs. Goldblatt, "the Friday night that you had us over for a Shabbat meal. What we remember most was the light – the candles, the chandelier, and the standing lamps in the corner. They made the entire dining room glow."

"Yes indeed," agreed her husband. "Real light and spiritual light; real warmth and the warmth of friendship."

I first met Mrs. Goldblatt in a professional context. She was the administrator of a large social services agency where I consulted. She was, to say the least, not a religiously observant Jew. But when her mother passed away, my wife and I paid her a condolence call. She did not "sit *shiva*" in any traditional sense, but let her friends and acquaintances know that she was home for the weekend and accepting condolences.

At that visit, we learned about her background. Her parents had been ardent communists, and in fact her father was the last editor of a once-famous Jewish communist newspaper. She made it clear that she shared her father's atheistic vision as well as his social ideals. Her husband's *weltanschauung* was not very different from hers.

As we left her house, my wife and I uttered the same words to each other, "We must have them over for a Shabbat meal!" And so we did.

Now, do not think for a moment that I am about to relate some wonderful story of a religious transformation. Quite the contrary. The Goldblatts came to our home one Friday night, we had a stimulating conversation, good food, and our kids behaved themselves. And then we went our separate ways, occasionally exchanging greeting cards over the years, but no more. As far as we knew, they remained religiously indifferent.

Until that encounter in the airport corridor. It was then that we learned how much of an impression that Shabbat dinner had made upon them, and how that one evening had changed their attitude toward Judaism. And of all the things they remembered, it was the light and warmth they remembered most.

When we were finally on our flight, I had time to think, and I found myself reflecting upon a verse in *Parashat Vayak'hel*. The verse occurs very near the beginning of the *parasha* and reads, "On the seventh day you shall have a Sabbath of complete rest, holy to the Lord.... You shall kindle no fire throughout your settlements on the Sabbath day" (Ex. 35:3).

Two classic Jewish thinkers speak about this verse and its interpretation by an ancient sect of the Jewish people, the Karaites. This group denied that there was any interpretation possible of the Bible except a literal one. They claim that there was no such thing as an Oral Law and rebelled against rabbinic tradition.

This sect persisted for many centuries and was persecuted, along with mainstream Jews, by our enemies throughout history. I have heard tell that there are still remnants of that sect in Israel and the Balkan countries.

But all I know about the Karaites is what I have read in the works of the great Jewish philosopher, Saadia Gaon, and in the biblical commentary of Avraham ibn Ezra. Both of these sages see our verse and its interpretation as one of the major differences between traditional rabbinic Jews and the Karaite sectarians.

The rabbis understood this verse to mean that one could not kindle fire on the Sabbath and that cooking was prohibited on that day. But they go into great detail about how to prepare in advance stoves and lamps that will heat and illuminate our homes and keep our Sabbath foods warm throughout the Sabbath day.

The Karaites understood the verse quite differently. "You shall kindle no fire" meant for them that all fires had to be extinguished before sunset on Friday and that the home had to remain dark and cold. They would partake of no warm food for the entire day.

Their Sabbath was darker still. They forbade intimate relations between husband and wife on the Sabbath, and they insisted that the biblical verse that enjoins us to remain in our places on the Sabbath was also to be taken literally. So they left their homes only to attend their houses of prayer, but not even to visit family and friends.

How different is the Sabbath prescribed by our rabbinical sages. They insist that our homes be well lit, and to this day, we are careful to include at least one hot portion of food in our Sabbath day meal as a statement against the Karaite heresy.

The Goldblatts (this of course is not their real name) remain to this day as ignorant of rabbinic Judaism as I am of the Karaite version of our faith. But their one visit to our Shabbat table was sufficient to dispel their previous notion of the Sabbath as a day of darkness and despondency. They learned that the Sabbath home is a home of warmth and light and that the Sabbath day is indeed a gift from the Almighty's special treasury.

My family and I are proud that we were able to create a Sabbath environment, on that Friday night long ago, that could teach that lesson to our dear and respected friends, the Goldblatts.

Would that each of us, less observant or more so, would create such a Sabbath environment every Friday night for the rest of our lives.

Words of Fire

Words, words, words," he shouted at me. He was a young man, raised as an observant Jew, but now in rebellion against his traditional upbringing. His parents had asked me to meet with him for several sessions to see if I could at least temper his rebellious spirit, and perhaps even convince him to return to the path they desired him to follow.

To put it mildly, he was reluctant to meet with me. But he agreed to do so, and in fact, was a bit more cooperative than other youngsters of a similar mind with whom I have had such discussions. He spoke, argued, debated, questioned, and expressed himself quite articulately. Occasionally, he even listened.

I well recall his major concern with traditional Judaism. He felt that our religion insisted that we limit our experience of the world to the verbal modality. "There is so much to see and hear, to touch and feel, to taste and smell, in this world. But all our religion tells us to do is to use words. Read, study, pray. Words, words, words. I want a richer life, a more robust experience!" he exclaimed.

The attitude expressed by my young friend is not at all limited to rebellious youth. Many of our adult co-religionists have similar objections, although they are often too ashamed to articulate them. But when they let their guard down, many Jews, including some who are regular participants in synagogue services, admit to finding our religion overly focused upon thought and language.

It is interesting to note in this regard that one of the most profound Jewish thinkers of the twentieth century characterized our religion as one of listening and hearing (*shemia*), and not as a religion of seeing (*re'iya*). I refer to Rabbi David Cohen, a close disciple of Rabbi Abraham Isaac Kook.

Rabbi Cohen's personal lifestyle was an extremely ascetic one, having committed himself to the role of a Nazirite and thus renouncing the pleasures of the products of the vine. It is thus no surprise that he wrote a book called *The Voice of Prophecy*, in which he maintained that our religion relies upon the ear, and not the eye, the auditory sense to the exclusion of the visual sense. Hence, the single most popular phrase in the Jewish religious language is, "*Shema Yisrael*, Hear O Israel."

As for me, I am quite confident that neither my young friend, nor those adults who find our religion excessively verbal, nor even the pious and philosophical Rabbi Cohen, are correct. For me, the Jewish religion is much more full-bodied and allows for the entire panoply of human senses: visual certainly, but also our senses of touch, taste, and smell.

Historically, in the days of the ancient Temple, there were many glorious examples of ceremonies and rituals that employed a wide range of activities besides the mere recitation of words. Granted, nowadays such examples are fewer, but they are readily and regularly accessible to every Jew.

The most powerful of these rituals has its source in the verse near the beginning of our *parasha*, which reads, "You shall kindle no fire throughout your habitations on the Sabbath day" (Ex. 35:3).

It is instructive that, although we are forbidden to kindle a fire during the Sabbath, it is fire that symbolically ushers in the Sabbath, and it is fire that accompanies it at its conclusion. Sabbath begins when, traditionally, the woman of the house lights the Sabbath candles. It ends when the family, and sometimes the entire congregation, gathers around a torch of fire and participates in the Havdala service.

The use of fire to bracket the Sabbath experience is a dramatic example of a non-verbal experience involving the sense of touch, with the experience of heat and warmth, as well as the visual experience of seeing.

The view of the modest candles heralding the approach of the Sabbath is what sets the tone of tranquility and serenity, which defines that holy day. The fiery image of the Havdala candle, which halakhically must be torch-like, symbolizes the return to the activity and productivity of the coming week.

But Havdala not only incorporates the senses of vision and touch, it also includes the sense of smell – the spices – and, of course, the sense of taste – the cup of wine. A multi-sensory experience if there ever was one.

The fire of Havdala is its dominant image and the one that contains such rich symbolic meaning. This meaning is best conveyed by the following passage in the Midrash, which describes Adam's emotions at the conclusion of the first Sabbath of creation:

> The sun set at the conclusion of the first Sabbath. Darkness began to descend. Adam was terrified.... What did the Holy One, blessed be He, do? He prepared for him two flint stones. Adam rubbed them together. A fire was ignited, and all was illuminated. Adam blessed the fire, and thus it is written "and the night will be light for me" (Ps. 139:11). What blessing did he recite? "Blessed are You, Lord our God...who creates the lights of fire." (Genesis Rabba 11:2)

The message here is clear. Fire was given to man. Man is to use it to continue the work of God's creation. Just as God worked during the first six days of creation, so too must man be productive during the six days of his work week. The Almighty gave Adam fire so that, after his restful Sabbath, he could return to the world of action.

How different is this midrash from the Greek myth of Prometheus. Prometheus stole fire from the gods of Mount Olympus, from Zeus.

In contrast to the Greek tradition in which the gods are protective of fire and wish to keep it from man, the Torah insists that it was God who enabled man to create fire so that he could continue the process of creation using his own resources.

We can readily conclude then that there is much more to our religion than words. There is a place, and a prominent one, for visual imagery, for delicious tastes, and for fragrant scents. And above all, there is a demand that we move from our essentially passive Sabbath stance to one of creative and constructive action.

Our faith contains much more than "words, words, words."

Parashat Pekudei

Count Me In

It was a cold and wintry day when I paid a visit to a small Jewish community in the Midwest. The rabbi of the local synagogue invited me to join him for Minḥa.

Because of the time of year, the day was short, and sunset was shortly after 4:00 pm. I told the rabbi that, even in the larger Jewish community in which I then lived, it was difficult to put together a *minyan* of ten adult men at that time of day. He assured me that there would be a *minyan*, and said, "Just come and see."

We both arrived in *shul* where there were six or seven elderly men, all retired so they had the leisure to gather in *shul* so early in the afternoon. I told the rabbi that I still feared we would not reach the required quorum of ten. He motioned to the rear door of the synagogue, and said, "Just watch."

With about thirty seconds to go until the announced time for Minḥa, I could see two bicycles pull up to the rear of the *shul* with two young boys dashing into the small beit midrash. It seems that the rabbi had an arrangement with the local day school that they would send several students of bar mitzva age each day to guarantee the *minyan*.

I will never forget the enthusiastic welcome those two boys received. I will especially never forget the look on their faces when they realized how much they were appreciated and how much they really counted.

One of the benefits of being a member of a small Jewish community is that each person counts. And on that winter day, those two boys literally counted. Throughout the year as well, each of their parents counted; one was responsible for the local burial society (*ḥevra kaddisha*), and the other gave a daily class for those who knew no Hebrew.

This is a common experience of Jews who live in small towns. No one is taken for granted and everyone has a significant role to play. In short, everyone counts.

In *Parashat Pekudei*, we learn many lessons about counting and accounting. The very word means "accounts of," and the entire *parasha* is one long accounting of every single gift to the Tabernacle. One way of looking at this *parasha* is as a lesson in the importance of accountability.

But as each Tabernacle item is carefully counted, we learn a deeper lesson as well. We learn that each item that is counted is blessed.

That each counted item is blessed may seem obvious, but it contradicts an interesting dictum in the Talmud (Taanit 8b):

> Blessing is not bestowed upon things that are weighed, nor upon things that are measured, nor upon things that are counted. Blessing is bestowed only upon things that are hidden from the eye.

This talmudic adage reflects the negative attitude of our tradition toward the procedure of counting. King David, for example, was sorely punished for undertaking a census of the Jewish people. Indeed, as we read in *Parashat Ki Tissa* just two weeks earlier, when a census of the people was necessary, each person was asked to contribute a half shekel so that the coins could be counted, but not the people themselves.

I have often thought that this aversion to counting reflects a reluctance to reduce a person to a number. It is dehumanizing to be a statistic. The ultimate reduction of a person to a number was the tattooed number, which we have all seen on the arms of Holocaust survivors.

The Nazis knew how thoroughly demeaning it is to count a person as if he or she were an object.

Aware of this negative attitude toward counting, the great hasidic master, Rabbi Levi Yitzhak of Berditchev, finds the counting that pervades our *parasha* very troubling. He finds the description of the public counting of each and every Tabernacle item to be inconsistent with the statement that blessings are not bestowed upon things that are counted.

His answer, found in his commentary *Kedushat Levi*, is based upon a verse in Song of Songs, "Your eyes are as the pools of Ḥeshbon" (Song. 7:8). Creatively, Rabbi Levi Yitzhak points out that the Hebrew word for "pools" can also mean "blessings," and that the place name "Ḥeshbon" can mean "counting." Thus, the verse then reads, "Your eyes bring blessings even upon that which is counted."

The lesson here is that whether counting is negative or positive depends very much upon one's perspective, upon one's "eyes." If you are counting people as numbers, or even physical things in a materialistic manner, then counting is negative. However, if the things you count are seen from a spiritual perspective, then counting is undeniably a positive process. The items of the Tabernacle are counted in this *parasha* from a spiritual perspective. They are consecrated objects, used only to express religious devotion. Therefore, counting them designates them as special and unique.

On that winter day, in the small synagogue in the American Midwest, two young boys were counted. But they were counted from the perspective of their importance to a group of men who wanted to pray. They were counted in recognition of the role each and every individual plays in the broader community. They were counted because they mattered very much.

When I extract the experience I had that day from the recesses of my memory, I recall what the boys exclaimed as they enthusiastically bounced into that small beit midrash. They each shouted, "Count me in, count me in!"

Parashat Pekudei

Above Suspicion

I have written and lectured extensively on the topic of Jewish leadership. I have frequently indicated that I consider Moses, our teacher, *Moshe Rabbenu,* a role model for those who would be leaders.

Once, after a lecture on just this topic, I opened the floor to a question-and-answer session. I have always found such sessions useful and instructive. The questions that are raised by the audience are often quite provocative, raising unanticipated issues.

On this particular occasion, a gentleman in the audience raised a question that encouraged me to think long and hard. He asked, "Rabbi, can you recall a moment in your own career when Moses' example influenced your leadership behavior? What specific lesson did you learn from Moses?"

At first, a number of possibilities came to mind. After all, Moses was a teacher, an advocate for the people, a person who came to the aid of the oppressed, a selfless person. Surely there are many aspects of Moses' life that I have tried, however inadequately, to emulate.

But after some introspection, I recalled one specific incident and shared it with the audience. I told them that the one time I most consciously followed Moses' example was the time when I was entrusted with some Ḥanukka *gelt*.

When I was a child, I remember fondly how my grandfather would gather all of his grandchildren around the Ḥanukka menora, have us line up in order of our ages, and distribute to each of us a silver dollar, Ḥanukka *gelt*. Many still practice this custom, although I suspect that nowadays far more than a silver dollar is distributed.

One year, back when I was the rabbi of my former synagogue, I received a phone call from a gentleman just a few days before Ḥanukka. This gentleman was one of the influential trustees of a major charitable foundation. I had interacted with him many times with regard to proposals I submitted to the foundation for grants to community institutions. He typically studied these proposals very assiduously and asked very demanding questions of me about these proposals. He would say, "There is much that I find worthwhile in your proposal. My tendency to be generous inclines me to grant you the funds you request, but I cannot be generous with someone else's money."

He voted against almost every proposal that I submitted.

One year, just a few days before Ḥanukka, he called. At that point, none of my proposals for charity was even under consideration. I was surprised by his call and even more surprised when he asked me to lunch that very day. We met at a local restaurant and chatted about all sorts of things for the better part of an hour. Finally, he asked me if I knew what Ḥanukka *gelt* was. He himself had fond memories of the Jewish customs he had experienced in his childhood.

When I assured him that I knew very well what Ḥanukka *gelt* was, he withdrew an envelope from his pocket and said, "Here is a check for Ḥanukka *gelt*. I know that you control a discretionary charity fund and I'd like you to deposit this check in that fund for the use of truly needy families."

Of course, I thanked him profusely for the donation. I did not think it was proper to open the envelope in his presence, so I didn't open it until I returned to my car. I was astonished to find that the sum was easily equal to the yearly salary of most of the members of my congregation. When I looked at the check more carefully, I noted that he had made out the check to me personally, and not to my discretionary fund.

I cannot deny that I immediately heard the loud voice of temptation. But along with that voice, another voice was heard, and it uttered nothing other than the first verse of *Parashat Pekudei* (Ex. 38:21–40:38), "These are the records of the Tabernacle ... which were drawn up at Moses' bidding ... under the direction of Itamar son of Aaron the Priest."

The people had contributed vast amounts of silver and gold and other precious materials for the construction of the Tabernacle. Moses, and only Moses, was in charge. He was, in the words of the Midrash, a *gizbar*, the comptroller of those funds. Technically, he was accountable to no one. He did not have to make a reckoning and he certainly did not have to invite another person into the process. But our verse tells us that he not only initiated a reckoning, but he invited his nephew, Itamar, to hold him to account. He insisted upon full accountability for every bit of the material collected.

Midrash Rabba comments, making use of other biblical verses:

"A dependable man will receive many blessings, but one in a hurry to get rich will not go unpunished" (Prov. 28:20). Moses was a dependable man, as is written, "Not so with my servant Moses; he is trusted throughout my household" (Num. 12:7). He alone was the *gizbar*, yet he invited others to perform the accounting ... our verse does not read, "These are the records that were drawn up by Moses," but rather, "These are the records that were drawn up at Moses' bidding." Moses asked to be held accountable, and did what he could to be assured that he would be held accountable.

Getting back to that cold pre-Ḥanukka afternoon, I am proud to say that my conscience prevailed. It was in the days before cell phones, but I immediately went to the nearest phone booth and called my "Itamar," a respected member of my congregation. I told him that I held this magnanimous gift in my hands and wanted him to know about it. I asked him to form a small committee, which would decide exactly how to distribute the "Ḥanukka *gelt*" to those who needed it the most. Until today, we jokingly refer to that committee as "the Itamar committee."

The commentary known as *Torah Temima*, written by the early twentieth-century rabbi, Rabbi Baruch Epstein, opens his remarks on our *parasha* with a citation from an earlier halakhic authority known as the Bakh, "Although a trustee of charity who has proven himself trustworthy need not be scrutinized, it is, nevertheless, advisable that he give a full reckoning of his collections and distributions, as did Moses our teacher."

Long after the incident with the Ḥanukka *gelt*, I came upon this astute remark in the book *The Transparent Society* by David Brin, "When it comes to privacy and accountability, people always demand the former for themselves and the latter for everyone else." Not so with Moses. He demanded accountability for himself, and so should we all.

Parashat Pekudei

Endings and Beginnings

W hat is life all about? One answer to that question is that life is all about beginnings and endings. Birth and death, marriage and divorce, hopeful anticipation, and inglorious defeat.

Most commonly, beginnings are bright. Even the pessimists among us cherish new beginnings and find promise in them. A new leaf is exciting, encouraging, and full of possibilities. Yet, beginnings have downsides, too. They are often fraught with the handicap of inexperience and sometimes contain moments of anxiety and even foreboding.

Our sages recognized this well when they cautioned us, "*Kol hathalot kashot* (all beginnings are difficult)!"

Endings, on the other hand, are not always negative. Sometimes it is good to close the book on an unfortunate set of circumstances and to exclaim, as we do on Rosh HaShana Eve, "Let the past year and its curses be gone!"

Indeed, some endings are truly happy occasions that represent the successful conclusions of long processes of efficient effort and hard work. Those endings celebrate achievement and accomplishment.

Parashat Pekudei, and the supplemental reading of *Parashat HaHodesh,* exemplify celebratory endings and hopeful new beginnings.

The *parashot* of *Vayak'hel* and *Pekudei* are replete with technical details. They describe the completion of the construction of the Tabernacle, a significant accomplishment made even more significant because it was a process in which every Jew participated.

Additionally, with these readings, we conclude the Book of Exodus, in its own right an achievement worthy of celebration. What can be a more joyous ending than a *siyum,* the completion of one of the most basic and essential books of the Bible?

One of the most powerful educational tools in our tradition is the festive party known as the *siyum.* Even the very young Jewish student knows that when he or she finishes a chapter or a Book of Torah, at least a modest party will mark the occasion. The cupcakes, ice cream, or pizza of the *siyum* is the perfect reinforcement of the achievements of learning. Adults too celebrate *siyumim* and find them rewarding markers of adult learning. The grand *siyum* of the entire Talmud in which those who study *Daf Yomi,* a page of Talmud each day, has in our time become an event that fills large stadiums and in which tens of thousands participate.

We have, then, *two* happy endings: The completion of the first Jewish house of worship, so long ago in our history, and the completion of a formidable section of our Torah.

The supplemental Torah portion, *Parashat HaHodesh* (Ex. 12:1–20), heralds a new beginning in which we hear the Almighty proclaim the upcoming month of Nisan as the beginning of all the months on our calendar. A beginning of beginnings.

It is no coincidence that, although we call this month Nisan, it carries but one name in the Torah, *Hodesh Haaviv,* the month of spring. For springtime is the ultimate beginning, nature's herald of newness and hope. No wonder then that spring was the season chosen by God for the Exodus long ago, and for the festival of Passover.

Every one of us endures numerous endings and beginnings in our lives. As we welcome a new month, it is profoundly appropriate that we reflect on those life events, attempt to transcend the challenges of those that were difficult, and celebrate those that are worthy of celebration.

Leviticus

Courtesy and Confidentiality

There is no such thing as privacy anymore." "There are no secrets anymore." These are two complaints that are heard frequently nowadays. We live in a world of cell phones and e-mails, blogs, Facebook, and Twitter. We have no privacy, for almost anyone can reach us wherever we are, whatever we happen to be doing, at all times of the day. And we can have no secrets, because anyone who knows anything about us can spread it to the entire world in a matter of seconds.

How often have I sat down for a moment of private time, for study or contemplation, or just to "chill out," only to have the silence disrupted by some total stranger who managed to obtain my cell phone number? How many dozens of e-mails and blogs fill up the space of my inbox with communications that are, at best, of no interest to me and often are offensive and obnoxious? We once felt entitled to privacy and courtesy, but they no longer seem achievable.

Often, we write a confidential note to a trusted friend, sharing a message that we would rather others not know, only to discover that the note is now circulating in cyberspace, accessible to literally everyone. Sometimes, it is the friend's betrayal that has made our secret public. Often, it is simply misjudgment or carelessness on his part. But more frequently, it is an unwanted error, a mistaken pressing of "send" instead of "delete."

We once expected confidentiality and discretion, but they, too, no longer seem possible. Our contemporary society has lost what once was among its primary values. "A man's home is his castle" once meant that decent citizens respected the "fences" around another individual's personal space and would not casually trespass those boundaries. The value of trusting in the discretion of another, once a cornerstone of human interaction, is now in danger of being relegated, along with other once cherished values, to the oblivion of "old-fashionedness."

The right to privacy and the ability to assume confidentiality are universal human values. It is important to know that they are primary Jewish values as well. Sources for these values in our tradition include *Parashat Vayikra*. This might come as a surprise to you, dear reader, because you know that *Parashat Vayikra* is the introduction to Leviticus, the biblical book that focuses upon sacrifices and Temple ritual. This *parasha*, especially, seems limited to the comprehensive and complex details of sacrificial offerings. Where is there even a hint of these contemporary concerns, courtesy and confidentiality?

The first two verses in the first chapter of *Vayikra* say it all, albeit between the lines, "The Lord called to Moses and spoke to him from the Tent of Meeting, saying, 'Speak to the Israelite people and say to them.'"

The rabbis of the Talmud saw in these simple and direct phrases two subtle messages. First of all, the Lord called to Moses first and then spoke to him. He didn't surprise Moses. He didn't intrude on Moses' privacy and autonomy. First, He called to him. He knocked on Moses door, as it were, ringing the bell first, asking to be invited in. No unwanted intrusion, even from the Lord Almighty, to his favorite prophet!

This observation is made by the rabbis in Tractate Yoma. In a less well-known talmudic source, Tractate Derekh Eretz, the rabbis find that the Almighty's courteous concern for the privacy of his lowly creatures did not begin with Moses. It goes back to the way He treated the very first man, Adam. "The Lord God called to Adam and said to him, 'Where are you?'" (Gen. 3:9). Here, too, even when the Lord wishes to rebuke Adam, He first "calls to him," signaling the uncomfortable conversation that is about to ensue. God respects Adam's privacy, and He doesn't just "barge in" on Moses. Surely a lesson in human values.

On the same page in Tractate Yoma, the rabbis find another message in the deceptively simple opening verses of our *parasha*, "saying: 'Speak to the people and say to them.'" From the redundancy here – "say," and "speak," and "say" – the rabbis derive the lesson that when someone tells you something, you are forbidden to share it with another unless you are given explicit permission to do so.

Moses was not permitted to re-tell even the divine message that he heard until God Himself told him that it was okay to "say it over."

The medieval Rabbi Moses of Coucy actually enumerates this admonition for utter confidentiality as one of the prohibitions comprising the 613 commandments of the Torah.

As I have reflected upon these specific teachings over the years of my personal *parasha* study, I have come away with several conclusions. First, there is much that is implicit in the Torah, much that lies beneath the surface. The long and complicated ritual laws that confront us as we read *Parashat Vayikra* are contained in a context that teaches us more than the surface lessons. Our rabbis of old were particularly expert at digging out these unexpected but precious nuggets. Secondly, these nuggets are often of astounding relevance for our contemporary condition. What can be more relevant than a reminder about the values of courtesy and confidentiality? Finally, these lessons are not merely abstract teachings or bits of wisdom for us to ruminate upon as we relax in our armchairs. Rather, they are calls to arms. They are challenges.

It is difficult indeed to combat the value system that is foisted upon us by the technology that pervades the world in which we now live. Very difficult, but very necessary. If we lazily submit to the pernicious influence of modern convenience, we risk the ultimate loss of our very humanity. A culture devoid of courtesy can turn into a culture of callousness and cruelty. A world where one cannot trust his confidante is a world where authentic friendship is impossible.

Troubling thoughts? Yes, indeed. But they are thoughts that we ignore at our own peril. How fortunate are we that these thoughts are available to us, subtly embedded in the opening verses of our *parasha*.

Forgiving Fallibility

I was wrong. I am sorry. Please forgive me." These are rare words, indeed, but I heard them pronounced clearly by a woman I once worked for, and whom I still admire.

She was the superintendent of a small school district just outside of Washington, DC. Several of the school districts in that geographical area were under a federal court order to guarantee desegregation of the races in the public schools. Believe it or not, the court found that even as late as the early 1970s, proper integration of the races was still not achieved in many of these schools.

The superintendent, whom I will call Dr. Cassidy, had selected a group of school-system employees to serve as part of a specially trained team to deal with the tensions in the community that were caused by the implementation of this court order.

I was then working as a school psychologist in this school district and was one of those chosen to serve on this team. We had spent several weeks training for this sensitive human relations project. Dr. Cassidy had initially assured us that federal funding for our salaries was guaranteed, and that we could be confident that our jobs were secure once certain formalities were finalized.

One Monday morning, we were summoned to an urgent meeting. She informed us that the funds were not available, and that we would be denied not only our future salaries, but even remuneration for the time we had already spent. It was then that she uttered the words, "I was wrong. Please forgive me."

I have subsequently witnessed many situations in which a leader made a terrible mistake that affected the lives of others. But, almost invariably, those leaders shirked responsibility, blamed others, or concocted ludicrous excuses for their failures. Very few had Dr. Cassidy's courage.

Parashat Vayikra (Lev. 1:1–5:26) describes an individual who demonstrated just such courage, and who indeed was expected to do so.

Chapter 4 of our Torah portion lists a number of individuals who occupied special roles in the ancient Jewish community. They included the High Priest; the judges of the central court, or Sanhedrin; and the *nasi*, or chieftain. Of the latter, we read:

> In case it is a chieftain who incurs guilt by doing unwittingly any of the things that by the commandment of the Lord his God ought not to be done, and he realizes his guilt.... He shall bring as his sin offering a male goat without blemish.... Thus the priest shall make expiation on his behalf for his sin, and he shall be forgiven." (Lev. 4:22–26)

The Hebrew for the first phrase in the above quotation, "in case" is "*asher*." Rashi notes the similarity between the word "*asher*" and the word "*ashrei*," or "fortunate." Based on that similarity, he comments, "Fortunate is the generation whose leader is concerned about achieving forgiveness for his unintentional transgressions. How much more so will he demonstrate remorse for his intentional misdeeds."

Fortunate indeed is the community that is blessed with leadership that can acknowledge error unambiguously. Even more fortunate is the community whose leaders ask for forgiveness.

Our commentators note that it is to be expected that leaders will commit moral errors. Rabbi Ovadia Sforno, the medieval Italian physician and Torah scholar, comments that it is unavoidable that men in positions of power will sin. He quotes the phrase in Deuteronomy 32:15, which reads, "Jeshurun grew fat and kicked," indicating that when one becomes "fat" with power, he will "kick" sinfully. How similar is this insight to Lord Acton's famous quote, "Power corrupts. Absolute power corrupts absolutely."

If the Torah assumes that misdeeds by leaders are unavoidable, it also expects that those leaders will humbly acknowledge their misdeeds and beg forgiveness for them. That is the lesson of the passage in our *parasha*.

However, the process cannot end with the leader's apologies. His followers must accept his sincere regret, and, much more difficult, must bring themselves to forgive him. In the passage in our *parasha*, it would seem that it is the Almighty who forgives a leader, and not necessarily the people.

My personal experience has taught me that just as it is difficult for people, especially those in power, to confess their shortcomings and to appeal for forgiveness, so is it all the more difficult for people to grant forgiveness to those who have offended them.

Yet, our sages point out that the Almighty wants us to be as forgiving as He is. Thus, there is a verse in the book of the prophet Micah, which reads, "Who is a God like You, forgiving iniquity and remitting transgression?" Upon this verse, the Talmud comments, "Whose iniquities does God forgive? Those of he who remits the transgressions of others" (Rosh HaShana 17a).

So, let's return to the story. Dr. Cassidy proved herself to be capable of confessing that she was mistaken, and of asking us to forgive her. But I also remember our reaction – the reaction of the small group of hard workers who learned that not only had we lost our jobs, but we would not even be getting the paychecks we had earned.

Our reaction was one of great anger. I imagine that the feelings in the room were close to those of a lynch mob. We vented some of those feelings, but then moved on to feelings of frustration and impotence.

We asked Dr. Cassidy to leave the room so that we could plan our next step rationally, which she did.

I won't report on the details of the long discussion that ensued. Suffice it to say that we moved from anger and frustration to acknowledging Dr. Cassidy's good intentions, to empathizing with her dilemma, and finally, as a group, deciding to express to her our understanding and forgiveness. She re-entered the room, and was visibly touched by our compassionate response.

I must conclude by telling you, dear reader, that although happy endings are generally confined to fairy tales, this particular story did have a happy ending. Perhaps emboldened by the support she felt from our group, Dr. Cassidy renewed her efforts to obtain the grant from the federal agency, enlisted the assistance of several regional congressmen, and obtained the funds available for this training program.

The lessons of ordinary life often parallel the lessons of the Torah. For a society to advance, its leaders must be self-aware and courageous enough to recognize and confess their failures, and to seek forgiveness from those whom they have affronted. Equally important, those who have been affronted must find it in their hearts to sincerely forgive. Then, and only then, can problems be solved and greater goals be achieved.

Parashat Vayikra

The Victorious Victim

I always experience a sense of excitement when I begin a new book. I am convinced that most avid readers feel the same way.

The Book of Leviticus has historically had "mixed reviews." On the one hand, our tradition reveres this book, calling it *Torat Kohanim* (the Torah, or Teachings, of the Priests). The dominant theme of Leviticus is the role of the priests within the various rituals connected to worship in the Holy Temple, and their role in various rituals associated with purity and holiness.

So special a place does Leviticus have in our tradition that there was once a time when schoolchildren began their study of the Bible with this very holy book. "Let those who are pure and holy be involved in the study of purity and holiness."

In more recent times, however, Leviticus has become a "victim" of negative criticism. I remember participating in a protest against a publisher who planned an anthology of inspiring biblical texts but deliberately omitted Leviticus from the table of contents. He felt that most of the book was irrelevant and outdated. Only instead of using the term *outdated*, he called it *primitive*. Those of us who protested his omission adduced many passages in Leviticus that were not only relevant, but of great import to contemporary society – but to no avail. I realized how futile our protest was when he asserted that the verse, "Love your neighbor as yourself" couldn't have been part of the original text of Leviticus, but must have been inserted centuries after the book was first written.

Of course, the source of this publisher's bias traced back to the early school of biblical criticism, which assigned the "author" of Leviticus the title "P," standing for "Priestly Code." These critics maintain that the entire Book of Leviticus was written much later than the rest of the Bible. As a believing Jew, I disassociate myself entirely from this school and its theories.

During one of the public lectures of Rabbi Joseph B. Soloveitchik, he said that we have a standard by which to assess the sanctity and importance of those matters that we consider holy. "The more virulent the opposition to one of our beliefs, the more sacred and important we can consider that belief to be." He offered two examples of this phenomenon. One was the Book of Leviticus, which some so-called "Bible scholars" consider inferior to other books of the Bible. This antagonism, argued Rabbi Soloveitchik, is in and of itself sufficient to convince us that the Book of Leviticus, is especially important. As a second example, he pointed to the State of Israel, which already in his time, faced extreme hostility in the international arena. This very hostility, he insisted, demonstrates the State of Israel's essential importance.

Viewing the entire Book of Leviticus as a "victim" of misunderstanding and defamation provides an opportunity to consider the relevant lessons the book may actually have about the nature of victimhood. As I hope to demonstrate, our tradition has many lessons to teach us about the relationship between the perpetrator and the victim, between the pursuer and the one he pursues.

Many of those lessons are rooted in the overall Book of Leviticus, and in *Parashat Vayikra*, in particular. But first, let me share with you a verse from another biblical book that has had its share of detractors over the centuries, the Book of Ecclesiastes:

What is occurring now occurred long since,
And what is to occur occurred long since:
and God seeks the pursued. (Eccl. 3:15)

In this verse, King Solomon, the author of Ecclesiastes, maintains that history is cyclical. Today's events and future events have their precedents in the past. One aspect of this repetitive narrative is consistent and predictable: God seeks the pursued. God is on the side of history's victims, and ultimately, it is they who will prevail. Here is how the Midrash expands upon this concept:

> Rabbi Huna said in the name of Rabbi Yosef, "God always seeks the pursued. You will find that when one righteous person pursues another righteous person, God sides with the pursued. When a villain pursues a righteous person, God sides with the pursued. When one villain pursues another villain, God sides with the pursued. Even when a righteous person pursues a villain, God sides with the pursued! In every case, God sides with the pursued! (Leviticus Rabba 27:5)

This midrashic passage continues to offer examples throughout history of this principle: Abel was pursued by Cain, and God chose Abel. Noah was pursued by his society, and God favored Noah. Abraham was pursued by Nimrod, Isaac by the Philistines, Jacob by Esau, Joseph by his brothers, Moses by Pharaoh, David by Saul, Saul by the Philistines. In each and every instance, God favored the pursued and eventually vanquished the pursuer. So, too, the Midrash assures us, although the people of Israel have been pursued by enemy nations throughout their history, God will seek the pursued. He will favor the victim.

The Talmud takes this theme one step further, recommending that we consciously strive to be among the pursued and not join the pursuers:

> Rabbi Abahu preached that one should always include himself among the pursued, and never among the pursuers, for, after all, no species of fowl is more pursued than pigeons and turtle doves,

and yet these are the only species of fowl that are fit for the altar."
(Bava Kamma 93a)

Maimonides includes Rabbi Abahu's advice in his description
of the proper demeanor of the Torah scholar, the *talmid ḥakham*: "His
guiding principle should be to include himself among the pursued but
not among the pursuers. He should be one of those who forgives insult
but never insults others" (*Hilkhot De'ot* 5:13).

Do not be misled. Joining the pursued does not mean that one
should be a pushover, a "nebbish." The Torah encourages us to stand up
for ourselves and defend ourselves vigorously when necessary. Rather,
joining the pursued means that we do not always need to win, that we
give others credit and allow them the limelight. We join the pursued
when we are careful not to trample others competitively in order to get
ahead, but we work collaboratively with them. Those are the qualities
that are blessed by the God who seeks the pursued.

The nineteenth-century commentator and rabbinic authority,
Rabbi Jacob of Lyssa, offers a brief insight into the verse of our focus,
"God seeks the pursued." He points out that, in a certain sense, we are all
"pursued." Every human being is pursued by his or her passions, moral
failings, and selfish egos. Part of man's existential condition is that he
is pursued by evil urges. God seeks the pursued, offering succor to all
those who valiantly struggle to overcome their internal temptations and
strive to live an ethical and moral life.

As individuals, as a people, and as human beings, we often are
fated to be victims. Still, our sages see in this *parasha* the lesson that we
can be victorious victims.

Parashat Tzav

Increasing Gratitude

There are certain phrases or expressions that many of us find hard to say. "I love you" is one of them. Another such phrase is "thank you." Although these words are difficult for us to pronounce, they each reflect powerful emotions, and when finally uttered, have an unbelievable impact upon the person to whom they are addressed. It is wonderful to hear that one is loved, and it is also wonderful to learn that another person is grateful and appreciative of what one has done for him or her.

In our tradition, gratitude is a primary value. Baḥya ibn Pakuda, in his renowned medieval book *Duties of the Heart*, stresses the centrality of gratitude in the religious experience. For him, the worship of God begins with a sense of gratitude for being alive, for being healthy, and for having one's needs met.

It is no wonder, then, that as the Book of Leviticus enumerates the many types of sacrificial offerings that comprise the ancient Temple service, the thanksgiving offering (*korban toda*), is prominently included. In *Parashat Tzav* (Lev. 7:11–18), the sacrifice known as the peace offering (*korban shelamim*), is described in detail. Generally speaking, when a person makes a vow to offer such a sacrifice, whether in a time of distress or when remembering God's tender mercies, he must bring an animal offering. He brings it to the Temple, the priest (*kohen*) performs various ritual procedures, and then most of the meat can be consumed by the individual who donated the offering, as long as he finishes it all during the day he brings it and the following night and day. This provides the individual with much more than twenty-four hours within which to consume the meat.

But the passage dealing with this offering begins with a subtype of the *shelamim* – the *toda*. In this instance, besides bringing an animal sacrifice, the donor must also bring four types of bread, and ten breads of each type, totaling forty loaves. The meat and the accompanying loaves of bread must be consumed by daybreak after the night following the preparation of the sacrifice.

The late nineteenth-century commentator known as the Netziv suggests that the thanksgiving offering (*toda*) must be accompanied by a public celebration with many guests invited. Therefore, unlike the ordinary *shelamim*, the numerous loaves of bread are prescribed so that all the guests can partake of the meal. The time within which the meat and breads can be consumed is limited to much less than twenty-four hours, necessitating the invitation of numerous guests to share in the thanksgiving celebration. The Netziv teaches us here that expressions of gratitude should ideally not be kept private. Thankfulness is an emotion to share with others in a public celebration.

Not long ago, I came across an article in an academic journal of psychology. The article was entitled "Can Prayer Increase Gratitude?" The authors quote numerous research studies that correlate gratitude with mental health. They therefore seek ways to promote the feeling of gratitude to foster increased mental health. One way they tried to instill gratitude in their subjects was to encourage them to engage in prayer.

How consistent their findings were to the teachings of Judaism! They found that when people engaged in prayer they became more aware not of what they were lacking, but of the blessings they had to be thankful for. The very act of prayer inculcated an attitude of gratitude.

The sacrifices offered in our ancient Temple were forcibly discontinued two millennia ago. Our sages teach us that our prayers, although they are mere words, substitute for the sacrifices of old. Whereas once upon a time a Jew would express his gratitude by bringing a thanksgiving offering, today he recites a prayer instead.

The article in the psychology journal teaches us that the relationship between prayer and gratitude is a mutual one. Not only does gratitude lead to thankful prayer, but prayer leads to increased thankfulness. Thus, for those of us who come by our sense of gratitude naturally and with ease, these sacrificial offerings, or, these days, the appropriate prayers, can help us express that gratitude. But for those of us whose sense of gratitude is numbed, prayer is one way to free feelings of thankfulness that are otherwise locked up within us. It allows those feelings to well up and to be effectively expressed.

We often hear the admonition to "count our blessings." Many of us, either because of our inborn pessimism, or because of the difficulties of life that seem to overshadow our blessings, find it difficult to acknowledge the positives of our life. Without such acknowledgment, gratitude is impossible.

In *Parashat Tzav*, we learn not only that gratitude deserves celebration in the Holy Temple, but that temple worship can help us feel grateful for what we do have. And we also learn, following the Netziv, of how worthwhile it is to express gratitude in a circle of family and friends.

That gratitude is the most pleasant of human emotions is so well expressed in these lines from the poet Thomas Gray's "Ode for Music":

> Sweet is the breath of vernal shower,
> The bees collected treasures sweet,
> Sweet music's melting fall, but sweeter yet
> The still small voice of gratitude.

The sage advice we can derive from our *parasha* is: Express gratitude, and not in a "still small voice," but in a resounding and booming voice for others to hear so that they can share in the emotions of the grateful person, and so that the grateful person can feel those emotions in every fiber of his being.

Parashat Tzav

The Practical Mystic

The world did not know he was a mystic. He was an accomplished diplomat who knew how to deal with people in positions of great power. Some characterized him as a shrewd, and even manipulative, manager of men. His name was Dag Hammarskjold, and he was the second Secretary General of the United Nations.

He died in an airplane crash in September of 1961 and was posthumously awarded the Nobel Peace Prize. It was as an astute and successful politician that the world knew him.

It was only after his tragic and untimely death that his personal journal was discovered. It was subsequently published under the title *Markings*, and it revealed a rare depth of introspection, which some described as poetic, whereas others saw in it poignant expressions of mystical experiences.

For me, Hammarskjold was a twentieth-century example of my own favorite type of hero, the person who combines worldly skills with a private spiritual essence. He was a man who lived in the world of action, dealing with the obstinate problems of international relations, but he drew his inspiration from sources within his innermost being.

The Jewish biblical tradition knows of quite a few heroes of this type – men who were engaged in the affairs of the world, but also in touch with the deep wellsprings of their souls. Surely, the Patriarch Abraham was one such person, and King David was clearly another.

Another twentieth-century example of an individual who could harmonize his profound inner inspiration with the demands of life as a public figure was Rabbi Abraham Isaac Kook. He, too, was characterized by many as a mystic, and indeed his written works testify to his mystical bent. But he was engaged in public affairs in an era of history that demanded political acumen, diplomatic skill, and the courage to act upon religious and nationalistic convictions.

Rav Kook's commentary on a passage in *Parashat Tzav* (Lev. 6:1–8:36), offers a creative analysis of the symbolism of the Temple sacrifices, which illustrates the combination of inner inspiration and outer action, which I find so fascinating, so rare, and so very necessary.

At the beginning of the *parasha*, we read of the *ola* offering, the *ola* being that sacrifice that was totally consumed by the fire upon the altar. As we read the details of this offering, we learn that its service involved three different locations with descending sanctity:

- Upon the altar, of which we read, "It is burned upon the altar all night until morning, while the fire on the altar is kept going on it" (Lev. 6:2);
- Next to the altar, of which we read, "The priest ... shall take up the ashes to which the fire has reduced the burnt offering on the altar, and place them beside the altar" (Lev. 6:3);
- Outside the camp, of which we read, "He shall then take off his vestments and put on other vestments, and carry the ashes outside the camp" (Lev. 6:4).

We then read that "the fire on the altar shall be kept burning, not to go out" and that "every morning the priest shall feed wood to it" (Lev. 6:5).

Rav Kook sees the three different locations as metaphors for three necessary stages in what he calls the prophetic life, but which we can readily apply to the life of every human leader.

The first stage is "a blaze of sacred flames inside the human soul, corresponding to the fire on the altar. This is the deep inner experience, which can be superficially described as introspective insight, but which is in truth a mystical moment.

The prophet, or genuine leader, must not allow that experience to remain buried internally. He must raise it to the surface of his being and integrate these "flames" into his external character and unique personality. This integration is the second stage.

But he cannot stop there. He must now take the person whom he has become (by virtue of incorporating the profound spiritual experiences into his very human self) and connect to the outside world, far away from the mystical cocoon, which he has heretofore enjoyed.

In this third stage, when he engages the real world with all its imperfections, he must be ready to change his vestments. He must put on not only new clothing but a new persona. In the words of the Talmud (Shabbat 114a), "The clothes worn by a servant while cooking for his master should not be used when serving his master wine."

Yet, even during this third stage of interaction with the mundane affairs of the world, the fires on the altar continue to burn. The sources of warmth, illumination, and inspiration are ever present, even if they are in some manner far removed.

And the prophet, or leader, must ever seek to renew himself by returning each and every morning to the altar's hearth, to place new kindling wood there, and to rejuvenate his soul.

This brilliant application of the detailed laws of the Temple sacrifices to the psyche of the prophet/leader can be found in the first volume of Rav Kook's commentary on the siddur, or daily prayer book, *Olat Re'iya*. It is masterfully summarized in Rabbi Chanan Morrison's *Gold from the Land of Israel*.

Some readers might find it odd, and others might even find it improper, for me to compare the saintly Rabbi Kook to the worldly Dag Hammarskjold. But I have long followed Maimonides' advice to accept the truth from every source, and I find much spiritual truth in the words of this Swedish diplomat.

This was a man wise enough to say, "The longest journey is the journey inwards."

This was a man sufficiently spiritual to say, "God does not die on the day when we cease to believe in Him, but we die on the day when our lives cease to be illumined by the steady radiance, renewed daily, of a wonder, the source of which is beyond all reason."

This was a man who could offer us this sage advice, "In our age, the road to holiness necessarily passes through the world of action."

Rav Kook, using the ritualistic terminology of the ancient Temple sacrifices to be found in our *parasha*, delivered a similar message and offered us the identical sage advice, "The road to holiness passes through the world of action." But he would add, "And back again!"

Gratitude, Not Solitude

Loyal readers of mine know that I am addicted to books. Not just "holy" books, and not just Jewish books. All books. Included in my addiction is my fondness for browsing bookstores. It took me a while, but I've even mastered the self-discipline required to enter a book store, browse for a long while, even finger a few books, and then walk out without buying any.

These days, many bookstores, particularly ones that are part of large national chains, often feature an author speaking about his or her book. I find those talks irresistible and have not ever been able to leave the bookstore once the author starts speaking. I generally just sit there and listen to the author, although many writers of interesting written works make quite boring speakers.

One evening, I heard the author of a rather famous work of nonfiction brag that her book was different from most of the others of its genre. "I dedicated my book to no one," she said. "I thanked no one, and you will find no page, indeed not even a paragraph, of acknowledgments to those who helped me in the long and arduous process of writing the book."

There was something about that statement that made me feel quite sad. I figured that it would be futile for me to say what I had in mind, but I did consider telling her how wrong I thought she was. She missed an opportunity to publicly, and for posterity, express her gratitude to others. She had an occasion to give voice to a profoundly human response, and she blew it.

Gratitude is a primary religious value. Many early Jewish philosophers, Baḥya ibn Pakuda foremost among them, consider gratitude to be the basis of our entire religion. They define the root of all worship as the articulation of thanks to the Creator for our very existence and for the many benefits we receive from Him constantly. Recognizing God's blessings and acknowledging them is the foundation of religious devotion.

As important as gratitude expressed to God in moments of devotion is, our tradition further insists that we express gratitude to others in our lives who have helped us, even in modest ways. The rabbis point out that even inanimate objects that have "been there" for us deserve our gratitude, and thus explain Moses' reluctance to even symbolically strike the Nile or the sand of the desert. After all, they provided protection to Moses at an earlier stage of his life.

But there is an aspect of gratitude that is less commonly recognized and that is what particularly bothered me that evening in the bookstore. It is the power of public expression of expressing gratitude, of doing so in a social forum, thereby inviting others to share in one's personal feelings of thankfulness.

The importance of public statements of gratitude – nay, public celebrations of gratitude – has its roots in a number of biblical sources, one of which is found in *Parashat Tzav* (Lev. 6:1–8:25). There, we read of the thanksgiving offering:

> If he offers it for thanksgiving, he shall offer together with the sacrifice unleavened cakes with oil mixed in, unleavened wafers spread with oil, and cakes of choice flour with oil mixed in, well soaked. This offering, with cakes of leavened bread added, he shall offer along with his thanksgiving sacrifice of well-being. Out of this he shall offer one of each kind ... to the priest .... And

the flesh ... shall be eaten on the day that it is offered; none of it shall be set aside until morning." (Lev. 7:12–15)

The rabbis explain that this sacrifice, which combines an animal offering with no fewer than four species of breads, is to be given by a person who has successfully emerged from a great trial: an illness, an imprisonment, or a sea voyage or desert journey. As an expression of gratitude, he is to bring the animal offering together with a total of forty breads, ten from each species, and donate one of each species to the priest. That leaves him with the meat of an entire animal plus a total of thirty-six breads, all of which must be consumed before dawn of the next day. Can he possibly consume all that food himself?

To this, Don Isaac Abrabanel – who, as personal advisor to Ferdinand and Isabella, no less, had an eminently practical side to him, besides his skills of biblical exegesis – comments:

> There was no way he could consume all this himself in such a short time. Obviously, the Torah encouraged him to invite his family, friends, and acquaintances to join him in feasting and in rejoicing. In this assembly, they would ask him to tell his story and question him about what prompted his thanksgiving feast. Thus, he would relate to them the miracles and wonders that God had bestowed upon him, and together all would join in praise of God, in a communal expression of thanksgiving and song.

One of my personal rabbinic role models was a man named Rabbi Elimelech Bar Shaul. He was the chief rabbi of Rehovot in Israel, and was a pioneer in the field of religious outreach. He was especially adept at teaching Torah on the university campus, and many of his lectures have been published in a volume called *Min HaBe'er* (*From the Well*). He passed away at a young age, under tragic circumstances, in 1965.

Rabbi Bar Shaul elaborates eloquently upon the benefits for the grateful person to share his experiences with others. "Narration of one's story changes the story," he writes. "It helps one integrate it into his behavior, it helps one remember it longer, and it helps one more fully appreciate his good fortune."

He proceeds to elaborate upon the great benefits that accrue to those who share in the celebration. "It enables them to learn skills of empathy, to see beyond themselves, and to gain the special joy that can only come in the company of other people."

Rabbi Bar Shaul concludes his inspiring essay on the subject of gratitude by quoting a prophetic midrash, "In the future-to-come, all the animal sacrifices will be discontinued. But the thanksgiving sacrifice will not be discontinued. All prayers will no longer be necessary, but prayers of thanksgiving will endure."

He then quotes a collection of comments on the Midrash, *Asifat Maamarim*, in which these words appear, "In that distant future, no one will sin; hence, sacrifices will become irrelevant. Prayer will not be necessary because there will be no illness and no woe. Not that mitzvot will be obsolete, but if one has no roof, there is no mitzva to build a protective fence around the roof. So too: no sin, no sacrifice; no woes, no prayers. But gratitude, that will be eternally necessary, and even more so in a more perfect world."

There are certainly religious occasions that warrant solitude. But occasions for gratitude are not times for solitude. They are occasions for a party.

The Open Curtain

As a pulpit rabbi, I maintained that mine was the busiest profession. Eventually, I conceded that other professions were equally busy, but I continued to insist that the rabbi's busy days are unique, for he is constantly faced with conflicting emotions.

The average rabbi may begin his day attending a happy event – a circumcision (*brit*). There, he shares in the special joy of welcoming a new child. There is a feeling of warmth between him and the parents of the newborn, and he glows with pride along with the grandparents. But he takes his leave before the ceremonial meal begins. He must be off to his next appointment.

Often he must shift from joy to grief. The next family he meets has just lost a loved one, perhaps under especially tragic circumstances. He must assist with the details of arranging the funeral and burial, but he dare not allow his preoccupation with those details to detract from the sensitive task of consoling the inconsolable and showing compassion to the bereaved.

The rabbi's day alternates from one extreme emotion to another, from one set of demands to a contrasting set of responsibilities.

Sometimes, he must deal with ideologies diametrically opposed to his own. Let me tell you about one such day in my own experience.

I had scheduled a meeting that I knew would be uncomfortable for me. I had often met with clergy of other faiths, although I have always been guided by the teachings of those of my mentors who discouraged interfaith dialogue on theological matters. But I have sought to work cooperatively with spiritual leaders of other faiths on matters of social welfare. I learned, though, that it is hard to draw a firm boundary between theological matters and social concerns.

That morning, during my prayers, I asked the Almighty to somehow spare me the trials of theological confrontations at the meeting. My "backup" prayer was that He help me tackle whatever theological discussions did arise with wisdom and tact.

My anxieties soon proved to be justified. The announced agenda was to plan opposition to municipal legislation that would permit gambling in our community. However, the conversation soon turned to the Bible. My discomfort increased when the focus narrowed to one specific biblical narrative: the story of the Binding of Isaac. I knew the differences between the manner in which Jewish tradition and Christian teachings each interpret the story. But the discussion was unavoidable, and I did my best to present the Jewish point of view.

Eventually, the conversation returned to the agenda, and we did commit to jointly oppose the proposed municipal legislation. But I left the meeting recommitted to my profound belief that Judaism and Christianity differ profoundly and fundamentally from each other.

After that morning's discomfort, I looked forward to my afternoon, during which I planned to prepare the daily page of Talmud for a group of my constituents dedicated to a program known as *Daf Yomi*, which aims to complete the voluminous corpus of Jewish law known as the Talmud in seven-and-a-half years, by unfailingly studying one folio page every day. Little did I know that the discussion stimulated by that day's page would bear upon the differences between the Jewish faith and other religious perspectives.

That day we were to study page fifty-five in the Tractate Zevaḥim. This tome deals with laws pertaining to the ritual sacrifices in the Holy Temple. The biblical basis of these laws is found in *Parashat Tzav*

(Lev. 6:1–8:36). There, we learn about a variety of voluntary sacrifices that individuals can offer: a burnt offering (*ola*), totally consumed by fire upon the altar; a meal offering (*minha*), composed of flour and oil and frankincense; and the *shelamim*, in which some sections of the sacrificial animal are placed upon the altar, but other portions are distributed to the priests and to the donors of the sacrifice to be eaten by them.

We had already been studying this particular tractate for almost two months when we reached page fifty-five. We were familiar with the many differences between the aforementioned sacrifices, including the fascinating fact that the *ola* and *minha* could be offered by non-Jews, whereas the *shelamim* could not. Many reasons are offered for this distinction. I had shared with the class a reason that I personally favored, based upon the thinking of early twentieth-century rabbi and mystic, Rabbi Abraham Isaac Kook.

Rabbi Kook wrote, "The world's many cultures cannot comprehend how matters of the flesh can be considered sacred. They struggle with the concept that physical tasks can be intrinsically spiritual."

Other cultures can readily accept that a sacrifice that is totally consumed upon the altar can be an act of worship. But they cannot accept that ordinary people, the donors of a particular sacrificial offering, can sit down to a festive meal, eat and enjoy the food and in the process perform a sacred act of worship – that is totally alien and unacceptable to them. Only one who identifies with the teachings of the Jewish tradition, in which all physical activities, no matter how mundane, are infused with holiness, can appreciate that partaking in a delicious meal in the company of one's family and friends is sublimely spiritual.

Part of that day's lecture dealt with the requirement that the magnificent doors separating the area of the altar from the central Temple chamber (*heikhal*), must be opened before the *shelamim* sacrifice can commence. While preparing for that day's lecture, I encountered an interesting dispute between the two major commentators on the talmudic page: Rashi and *Tosafot*. Rashi maintains that only for the *shelamim* must these doors remain open. They did not have to remain open for other sacrifices. *Tosafot* disagree and maintain that this requirement was true for all sacrifices. Interestingly, Maimonides sides with Rashi.

I suggested to the class that the approach of Rashi and Maimonides was consistent with Rabbi Kook's thinking. The open doors of the *heikhal* were symbolic of the connection that exists in Judaism, and arguably only in Judaism, between that most sacred inner chamber of the Temple in which the Divine Presence was centered, and the outer world in which ordinary humans share sacrificial flesh. The open doors symbolize the absence of barriers between the sacred and the profane.

When I began to deliver my lecture that afternoon, I was struck by the contrast between my early morning theological discussions with Catholic priests and my talmudic musings later that day. But as I continued to teach, I realized that these two experiences were but two sides of the same coin. In the morning and in the afternoon, I was actually making the same point, albeit to two very different audiences. I was doing my job as a rabbi, teaching that Judaism is unique in its understanding of biblical passages, and also unique in its insistence that one did not have to abstain from physical pleasure in order to reach spiritual heights.

The one lesson that distinguishes Judaism from other religions is this: Holiness and daily affairs may occupy separate compartments, but the doors between them must remain open.

And Aaron Was Silent

He was an old man and in many ways came from a very different world than I. And yet, he taught me more than anyone else ever did. One of the things he taught me was that no one suffers as much as a parent who loses a child.

He delivered this lesson to me on a wintry day more than fifty years ago. He was my grandfather, my father's father, and the family had just broken the news to him that his youngest grandchild, my baby cousin, had died. It was a sudden death, totally unexpected, and everyone was distraught. Also Grandpa took the news very hard.

He then did something that surprised everyone present. He rose to leave the room, beckoning to me – his oldest grandchild, then fourteen – to accompany him. We both entered a small adjoining room in which there were a few sacred books, including a siddur. He opened the siddur, read from it for several moments, and then looked up to me, and tearfully whispered: "There is nothing worse in the world than the death of one's own child. A parent never recovers from such a blow. May the merciful God protect us all from such a fate."

I will never forget those words. I remember them verbatim even today. And a lifetime of experience in the vocation of counseling has confirmed the truth of these words over and over again.

In *Parashat Shemini*, we read of just such a tragedy. On a bright and sunny spring day, somewhere in the Sinai wilderness, the Tabernacle is being inaugurated. It is an awesome spiritual experience in which "a divine fire descends from on high, in which all the people sing in unison, and fall upon their faces." It is the moment of a peak experience for all the people, but especially for Aaron, the High Priest.

At that very moment, his two elder sons, Nadav and Avihu, step forward and commit a sacrilegious act, which dispels the mood and ruins the entire experience. Commentators differ widely as to exactly what was the sin of these two sons of Aaron. Scripture just says that "they offered God a strange fire, something He did not command of them."

God's wrath was expressed instantly. "A fire descended from before Him and consumed them, and they died in the presence of God."

A parent, a father, lost a child. Not just one, but two. Not through a long and debilitating illness, but suddenly, unexpectedly. And not in any ordinary set of circumstances, but in the context of an act of sacred worship.

What is Aaron's reaction? Does he moan and groan and rend his clothing? Does he scream out in grief? Or does he vent his anger against the God who took his boys from him?

None of the above. "*Vayidom Aharon*." Aaron is silent. The silence of shock? Perhaps. The silence of acceptance of fate? Perhaps. Or, perhaps, the silence that results when the range and depth of one's emotions are too overwhelming to express in words. But silence.

If the sage words that my grandfather shared with me in my early adolescence are true, and I have every reason to believe that they are, Aaron remained silent about his grief for the rest of his life. Had he used the words of his ancestor Jacob, he could have said, "I will go down to the grave in my agony."

Soon after this episode in which my grandfather shared his wisdom with me, I had the occasion to read a book, which taught me a bit more about a grieving parent. It is quite possible that it was precisely during the winter of my cousin's death that I was assigned the book *Death Be Not Proud* by John Gunther in my English literature class.

I somehow doubt that this book is still on the required reading lists of many tenth graders today. But if it is not on those lists, I certainly recommend that it be read, and particularly by teenagers who are learning their first lessons about life and its tragic disappointments.

In the book, the author describes his own son, who was taken from him by a vicious disease. He describes his son positively, but realistically. And he rages against the disease, and in some way, the Divine Being who took his son from him. He insists to Death itself that it be not proud about its victory over its victim, his dear child.

It has been decades since I have read Gunther's book, and it could very well be that I do not remember it with complete accuracy, but I do recall the poignancy and the power with which the author conveyed the full range of his painful emotions. And I will never forget those passages in which he insists that he will never recover from his loss, that the wounds of a parent's grief for his child can never heal.

Many are the lessons that students of Bible and Talmud have derived from the sad narrative contained in our *parasha*. But there is at least one lesson that every empathic reader will surely learn as he or she attends to the opening verses of Leviticus 10.

It is the lesson contained in the mystery of Aaron's reaction when his sons are consumed by a heavenly fire. For within the deafening silence of "*Vayidom Aharon*" are the depths of the terror, which every parent dreads and some parents have suffered – the dread of bereavement, of the loss of one's child.

As always, in contemplating darkness, light stands out in contrast. Reflection upon death leads to an appreciation of life. The story of the death of Aaron's children should, if nothing else, enable us to appreciate all the more those of our children who are alive and well.

Parashat Shemini

The Stork and the Heron

I don't think that parents tell this one to their children anymore, but they used to when I was a boy. When children once inquired about where babies come from, they were told that the stork brought them.

The stork is a migratory bird that was very familiar to people living in central Europe. The stork would suddenly, almost mysteriously, appear in the spring after a long absence during the cold winter. The stork would nest on rooftops, adjacent to and often right on top of the chimneys of the house.

Since every child was witness to the absence and ultimate return of these large white birds with long beaks, it was only natural that parents would avoid telling their children the "facts of life" for as long as they could get away with, attributing the appearance of new babies to the stork.

Interestingly, the stork makes its appearance in *Parashat Shemini*. The Bible, however, does not stoop to the once-common myth that the stork was responsible for the delivery, if not production, of new babies. Indeed in the following *parasha, Parashat Tazria*, the opening verses contain a fairly explicit account of the biology of conception and childbirth.

But the Bible does enumerate the stork as one of the numerous "unclean" birds; that is, as one of the species of birds that a Jew is forbidden to eat.

The Hebrew term for the stork is *ḥasida*, upon which Rashi has a fascinating commentary. He begins by identifying the *ḥasida* as "a large white fowl" and applies the old French name *tzikonia* to it. A quick consultation with a children's book on zoology informed me that the European white stork, which nests on rooftops and in trees and is a symbol of childbirth, is technically classified in Latin as *ciconia ciconia*.

Rashi was apparently very familiar with this bird. He continues to suggest the reason why the *ciconia ciconia*, or stork, is called *ḥasida* in Hebrew. After all, that Hebrew term means "the kindly one," the one who does acts of loving-kindness (*ḥesed*). The reason already offered in the Talmud is that the stork "is kind to her friends"; that is, generous and protective of other members of its own species.

Keen students of the *parasha* long ago began to wonder why a bird that was so kind and passionate should be listed among the unclean fowl. After all, it is commonly assumed that those animals that are prohibited to be eaten are each representative of some undesirable character trait. Here is a bird that deserves to be called *ḥasida*, pious one. Why should it be considered unclean?

One such keen student, and it is difficult to ascertain his identity, long ago suggested that the problem with the *ḥasida* is that, although she is kind, she is kind only to her friends. She shows compassion only for other members of her own species. To those who are not her friends, but belong to a different species, she is indifferent and often even cruel. Being kind in a discriminatory fashion is a negative character trait. Hence, the stork is *treif*, forbidden.

What a powerful and relevant lesson for each of us! From time to time, we learn about natural disasters, hurricanes, and tsunamis that occur across the world, often in distant and exotic countries, to people who are ethnically and culturally very different from us. Nevertheless, it is only right that we pay attention to people other than our own kind who are faced with horrible, tragic disasters. We cannot be concerned only with ourselves.

But who among us can deny not having at least had a fleeting temptation to look away from that human suffering because it occurred so far away from us, to people who are unrelated to us? It is only natural that our response would be, "Charity begins at home," and that we would turn to the needs of our own friends and close ones, blotting out the cries and tears of those of an "alien species."

The message that Rashi gives us is clear. Such a reaction is *treif.* It is utterly wrong to ignore the suffering of human beings just because they are different or distant from us. The *ḥasida* is sympathetic and charitable, but only to its own kind. We are not allowed to emulate the *ḥasida.*

Just after the *ḥasida* is listed in our *parasha* (Lev.11:19), we find mentioned another bird, the *anafa.* Rashi describes the *anafa* as an ill-tempered large fowl, an angry bird, and hazards a guess that it is the heron, with which he was personally familiar, living in north central Europe.

If the stork symbolizes the evil of discriminatory generosity, the heron symbolizes the evils of anger. Anger is judged very negatively by the Jewish tradition. Our sages tell us that it is by the manner in which a person controls his anger that his true character can be assessed. The Talmud tells us that a person who becomes angry is susceptible to grievous errors, so that even the wisest of men can make mistakes if he permits himself to become angry.

Our sages offer an example of a wise man who fell prey to anger and then erred. That wise man was none other than Moses himself, and the incident is described in our very Torah portion, *Shemini.* "And Moses diligently inquired for the goat of the sin offering, and, behold, it was burnt; and he was angry with Elazar and Itamar" (Lev. 10:16). In the immediate subsequent verses, it became clear, as Aaron, Moses's brother, pointed out, that Moses "rushed to judgment" and was mistaken. To his credit, Moses was not too embarrassed to admit his mistake.

Malbim, a brilliant and often creatively insightful nineteenth-century commentator, suggests with regard to these verses that there is a reciprocal relationship between anger and error. Yes, when one is in a state of anger, his judgment is clouded and he is prone to error, but it is also true, he argues, that when one is blinded by error, he is prone to anger. Often, seeing the facts clearly precludes the angry response.

Once again, we have seen the great wisdom that can be accessed by merely "scratching the surface" of the biblical text. On the surface, our *parasha* offers us the names of two species of fowl that are ritually excluded from the Jewish menu. But beneath the surface, these two birds, the stork and the heron, open up two vast chapters in the comprehensive book of Jewish ethics. From the stork, we learn how important it is that our charity be inclusive and extend even to populations far-removed, geographically, ethnically, or religiously, from us.

And from the heron, we learn about the dangers of anger and about the dynamic relationship between our intellectual powers and our emotional passions. Sometimes, intellectual faults lead to sinful emotions. More frequently, unbridled emotions compromise our intellect in ways that can be disastrous.

Two lessons from two birds: Be sensitive to the needs of all human beings, whether they resemble you or not, and control your anger, lest you fall into the snares of errors and mistakes.

Aging Grace

W e all applaud when an old man runs in the marathon. We expect that his physical powers diminished long ago, and when he proves otherwise we celebrate for him. We are impressed when an old woman professor can still give an extemporaneous lecture, drawing upon her memory of things she learned long ago. We expect that her mental powers have considerably weakened and are pleasantly surprised when she proves otherwise.

We all know something about the natural course of aging and the toll it takes upon our bodies and minds, but we are much less familiar with the social impact of the process of aging. We know less about the effects upon the older person of the reaction he or she evokes from other people. What others think of us is important at every stage of life, and older persons are no different from the rest of us in their need for respect, admiration, and approval from others in their social circle.

I was a long way from old age myself when a revered mentor explained to me how he realized that, at least in the eyes of others, he was getting old. "I find that people give me honor and respect, but not power. They seem to be listening carefully to what I say, but they do not really hear my words, and they never heed them."

It is no wonder that the great novelist Hermann Hesse wrote the following in a letter to a friend:

> Growing old is not just a winding down and withering – like every phase of life it has its own values, its own magic, its own wisdom, its own grief, and in times of a fairly flourishing culture, people have rightly shown age a certain respect, which nowadays is somewhat lacking in youth. We shall not hold that against youth. But we shall not let them talk us into thinking that age is worth nothing.

The most that Hesse experienced from others as he grew old was "a certain respect." He insistently protested against the all-too-common belief that "age is worth nothing."

There is a phrase in *Parashat Shemini* (Lev. 9:1–11:17) that the rabbis of the Midrash refuse to pass by without comment. The very first verse of this *parasha* reads, "And it came to pass on the eighth day that Moses called out to Aaron and to his sons and to the elders of Israel."

Rabbi Shimon bar Yohai, a second-century talmudic sage who was famed and revered for his mystical insights, is impressed by the role that the elders of the community, men of great age, play, not only in this verse, but throughout the Torah. He comments:

> We find that the Holy One, blessed be He, bestowed the honor upon the elderly very frequently. At the burning bush: "Go and gather the elders of Israel"; in Egypt: "And you and the elders of Israel shall approach"; at Sinai: "Go up to the Lord, you… and seventy of the elders of Israel"; in the desert: "Gather unto me seventy men from among the elders of Israel"; at the tent of meeting: "Moses called upon…the elders of Israel"; and in the messianic future, the Holy One will again bestow honor upon the elderly, as it is written (Is. 24:23), "The moon will be embarrassed and the sun ashamed, for the Lord of Hosts will Himself

reign upon Mount Zion and Jerusalem, and His elders will be granted honor." (Leviticus Rabba 11:8)

Rabbi Shimon bar Yoḥai is emphasizing something that is fundamental to Judaism. Not only are the elderly granted respect (*kavod*), they also must be taken seriously. They represent an indispensable resource for the community and its leadership.

The important role of age in our history has its roots in the very beginning. The Talmud (Bava Metzia 87a) makes a remark that many have found strange: "Before Abraham, age did not exist." This does not mean that there were no old people before Abraham, nor does it mean that people got older but did not show signs of age.

One of my revered teachers, Rabbi Nisan Telushkin, of blessed memory, whom I knew in his advanced old age, explains this passage as follows. Until Abraham, the world was materialistic and the primary activities were the practical ones that allowed for physical survival. At that time, age was no advantage at all. Quite the contrary, what was necessary was the vigor and energy of youth.

When Abraham came on the scene, things changed. He successfully introduced the spiritual dimension to mankind. In this realm, the skills of youth were no longer the only skills necessary. To the extent that mankind became more spiritual, the skills of age became more and more important. Thus, of course age existed before Abraham, but with his arrival on the scene, the advantages of age began to become recognized as crucial. Before Abraham, age was simply not a vital and necessary part of the human community. He was the first "old man," because he was the first person of age to be revered as an integral and essential part of the leadership of the human community.

It has been said that contemporary Western civilization can be characterized as a youth culture. Judaism objects to such a culture. It insists that there is a role for the elders and it is not just a marginal role. This lesson is so basic to our faith that it can be traced back to our very beginnings in the life of Abraham.

It is so basic that the elderly are placed front and center in the Torah's account of our national beginnings, as Rabbi Shimon bar Yoḥai pointed out in the midrashic passage cited above.

It is so basic that it deserves to be reiterated again and again, particularly in the spring season. If in spring, a young man's fancy turns to love, then in spring, an older man's fancy turns to wisdom and accomplishment.

Parashat Shemini

Religion Versus Spirituality

It was a brief but powerful lesson and I learned it from a recovering drug addict. He was telling his story to an audience of rabbis who were there to learn about substance abuse. Treatment for addictions involves being in a process of recovery for quite some time. This fellow maintained, and many experts agree, that an addict seeking cure must commit to being "in recovery" as a life-long process.

He had a lot to say about religion. He was especially interested in the distinction between religion and spirituality. Here is how he expressed that difference, "Religion is for people who are afraid to go to hell. Spirituality is for people who have been there."

His message struck a chord within me. I had long pondered the concepts of religion and spirituality. I once believed that the two terms were virtually synonymous. After all, weren't all religious people also spiritual? And where else besides religion could one find spirituality?

But I have long since become disabused of that naïve belief. On the one hand, over the years, I have seen many Jews go through the motions of religious observance with neither emotion nor conviction.

On the other hand, I have come to see individuals of no particular religious faith – and indeed some who are confirmed atheists – who, nonetheless, have profound spiritual sensitivities.

It was because of my personal confusion about the relationship between religion and spirituality that the ex-addict's remark struck me as worthy of further contemplation. That was why I invited him to join me in my own addictive substance, coffee, after his talk.

My new friend's distinction between religion and spirituality was based upon his theory of human nature. He had not come by this theory in a book he read or a course he took. He formulated it on the basis of his traumatic real life experiences.

"People," he said, "require a feeling of connectedness to a Higher Being. That's 'spirituality.' But it is just a feeling. A good feeling to be sure – a high. For me, drugs helped achieve that feeling, but I needed to learn to achieve it elsewhere."

He quickly went on to explain the other half of his theory: "But just feeling is not enough. There needs to be some structure, some framework, and some guidelines. It can't all be just good feelings. That's where religion comes in. It provides the context within which the feelings can be contained, nurtured, and expanded."

I told him that I had to put his idea into my own private context. I immediately found myself drawing from a biblical source. The source that came to mind was a passage in *Parashat Shemini* (Lev. 9:1–11:47).

There, we find the following passage:

And the glory of the Lord appeared to all the people. And there came a fire out from before the Lord, and consumed the burnt-offering and the fat upon the altar; which, when all the people saw, they shouted, and fell on their faces. And Nadav and Avihu, the sons of Aaron, took each of them his censer, and put fire in it, and put incense in it, and offered strange fire before the Lord, which He commanded them not. And a fire went out from the Lord, and devoured them, and they died before the Lord.

I shared this brief biblical narrative with my new friend, and I used his terminology to explain it:

The procedure prescribed by God for sacrificial offerings is what you are calling "religion." There are ways to do it, and ways not to do it. Nadav and Avihu were caught up in what you call "spirituality," the ecstasy of the moment. They wanted to draw close to God. But they wanted to do it their way, with their own fire. But that was "a strange fire." He, God, had not commanded it, and that rendered it illegitimate – fatally illegitimate.

"I remember the story, but never quite understood it," he admitted. "Now I can relate it very well to a drug-induced 'high.' You see, when you're on a high, you want it as your own. There is a powerful drive in you that seeks autonomy, which, when uncontrolled, can be fatal. At some point, that drive has to be reined in. It needs discipline. That's where religion comes in."

I asked my new friend if he was ready for some more "religion," some words from the rabbis. When he consented, I informed him that the rabbis suggest quite a few reasons for the horrible punishment suffered by Nadav and Avihu. Although the Torah clearly identifies their sin as doing something that God had not commanded, the rabbis find other factors that caused them to act the way they did.

He was curious and asked, "What are some of those factors?"

"For one thing," I explained, "the rabbis accused Nadav and Avihu of entering the sacred precincts of the Tabernacle having excessively indulged in wine. They were inebriated. This suggested that their 'spirituality' was artificially induced and thus inauthentic."

"Others maintain," I continued, "that they were disrespectful toward Moses by not consulting with him regarding the proper sacrificial procedure. Some rabbis even suggest that they envied Moses' and Aaron's lofty positions and secretly prayed for the time when they would inherit those positions of power and glory."

"Wow," he exclaimed. "That fits with the anti-authoritarian sentiments of so many who are hooked on pure spirituality. Their motto is, 'Down with authority. Let us take over!' Tell me, do the rabbis have any other suggestions about what might lie behind this raw, unbridled 'spirituality?'"

"Indeed, they do," I responded. "they suggest that Nadav and Avihu weren't wearing the proper priestly garments when they performed their incense offering."

He looked puzzled. He couldn't connect this particular flaw to his own experience. So I gave him my take on the significance of their failure to don the proper "uniform."

"The priestly robes are described as 'garments of honor and glory.' You cannot just approach God in your jeans and sweatshirt. Doing so demonstrates a feeling of familiarity with Him, which is inappropriate. God is not your pal. Approaching Him calls for reverence, and the priestly clothing attests to that reverence. With them, your actions are sacred and inspired, truly spiritual. Without them, you're on a 'trip' with a buddy; you're not in the presence of the Higher Being with whom you strongly desire a deep connection."

The discussion that evening ended with a disagreement.

"Rabbi, you taught me so much tonight. You encouraged me to connect the dots between my admittedly unhealthy experience and Jewish teachings. I owe you a debt of gratitude," he said.

I disagreed. "No, I owe *you* a debt of gratitude. You forced me to realize that spirituality and religion are not one and the same. They are both essential for a fully religious experience."

Parashat Tazria

My Earliest Memory

Have you ever been asked the question, "What is your earliest memory?" I have been asked that question many times. There was a time, long ago, when I was a graduate student in psychology, when that question was posed. The answer was considered very revealing of the respondent's deeper psyche.

Such exceptionally early memories were known in psychoanalytic circles as "screen memories" and were considered quite significant diagnostically. The scientific significance of such memories is now considered to have no basis, but they are certainly interesting and make for great conversation.

Considering the question posed, I had a clear image of my first memory. I was standing outside a brick building, looking up at my father, may he rest in peace, surrounded by a small crowd of other men. Everyone was looking at the moon.

This may have been my first experience, at age three or four, of *kiddush levana*, the monthly ceremony during which the congregation exits the synagogue and acknowledges the first appearance of the new moon.

I have another memory of the religious significance of this ceremony. I remember being told that the Hebrew word for "month" is *ḥodesh* and the Hebrew word for "new" is *ḥadash*. It was then that I learned of the significance of the new moon, which commences a new month, and became aware for the first time that the Jewish people follow the lunar, not solar, calendar.

When it is the last Sabbath before the new moon of the month of Nisan, the month of Passover, spring time, and the beginning of the new calendar year, in addition to reading *Parashat Tazria*, we also read a portion from Exodus 12:1–20, known as *Parashat HaḤodesh*. Famously, according to Rashi, these verses are the true beginning of the Torah.

The theme of newness and the constant potentiality for renewal is the central theme on this Shabbat. It is also the central theme in the Jewish calendar – and, one might say, in Jewish tradition in general. The symbolism of the moon constantly renewing itself is coupled with the symbolism of springtime and nature's renewal.

We herald the approaching holiday of Passover, but not as a holiday of freedom and redemption. Not just yet. We recognize that Passover is the festival of springtime (*ḥag haaviv*). Passover has myriad symbolic meanings, one of which is the perennial opportunity for personal and national rejuvenation.

When I focus on my earliest memory with extra effort, I remember what the men who surrounded me under that moon so long ago were saying to each other. Each man addressed three others with the traditional Jewish greeting, "*Shalom aleikhem.*" I remember being puzzled that Daddy was greeting friends he saw daily with this special welcome, generally reserved for those whom one hadn't seen in a while.

I didn't ask him about it then; after all, it was still the era when "children were to be seen and not heard." But I have since answered the question for myself, and have explained it to my children and to my students as follows, "The new moon is a symbol for renewal. It is a time for each of us personally to begin again, to forget past mistakes, to 'turn over a new leaf.' It is also a time for us to renew and recharge our relationship with others. It is a time to begin a new slate, to forgive each other, and to appreciate each other anew. Hence, we greet at least three friends, even old friends, with a '*Shalom aleikhem*,' as if they were newcomers in our lives."

And so, the supplemental reading teaches us about newness, and about, to borrow Lincoln's famous phrase, "a new nation, conceived in liberty." Is there any connection between the supplemental *Parashat HaHodesh* and the main Torah portion of *Tazria*?

I would say so, for the *parasha* begins, "Speak to the Children of Israel, saying, 'If a woman conceives and bears a male child, she shall be unclean seven days...and on the eighth day, the flesh of his foreskin shall be circumcised.'" (Lev. 12:1–3) The opening theme is also one of a new beginning, of a birth of a new baby. It is a time for the celebration of the entry of a new member into the Jewish people. Hence, there is surely a connection between *Tazria* and *Parashat HaHodesh*. They both adumbrate the centrality of the new in our tradition.

It is at this point that you, dear reader, might well ask, "If we are celebrating not just newness in general, but the arrival of a new human being into this world and of a new member of the Jewish faith, then why does the mother enter the realm of ritual uncleanness (*tuma*)? Should she not rather enter the realm of sanctity and cleanness (*kedusha vetahara*)?"

I found a most thought-provoking answer to this oft-asked question recorded in the name of that most profound of the hasidic masters, Rabbi Mendel of Kotzk. He cites the passage in the Talmud, which states that the "keys of childbirth" are kept by the Almighty Himself. It is He who presides, as it were, over "labor and delivery." Once the baby is born, His Presence departs as well. Just as when the soul of man departs, *tuma* descends, so too when the Divine Spirit departs, *tuma* ensues.

The Kotzker once again teaches a very deep, albeit existentially pessimistic, lesson. Perhaps one must be Rabbi Mendel of Kotzk to truly understand why he forces us to face darkness even at the moment of joyous celebration of birth.

For most of us, on the other hand, the lesson of our *parasha* is of light, and not of darkness. It is an occasion to contemplate all that is new in our natural and interpersonal environments, especially in the spring season. It is an opportunity to seize the moment by taking advantage of the constantly available potential for renewal of ourselves and of our friendships and relationships.

Is this just a Jewish message? Of course not. It is a message for all of humanity. And it is so well expressed by the famous adventurer and explorer of the sea, Jacques-Yves Cousteau, in his book *The Silent World*, when he writes:

> Sometimes we are lucky enough to know that our lives have been changed, to discard the old, embrace the new, and run headlong down an immutable course. It happened to me at Le Mourillon on that summer's day, when my eyes were opened to the sea.

In reading *Parashat Tazria*, our eyes open to a different kind of sea. May we embrace the new and run, headlong and happy, down a different and better course.

Going at it Alone

"N o man is an island." "It takes a village." These are just some
of the clichés that are used to convey the importance of social groups, of
the realization that people cannot "go at it alone." But just as it is vital for
each of us to learn that we are ultimately limited in what we can accomplish by ourselves, it is equally vital to learn of the benefits of occasional
solitude and of the need to sometimes just be alone.

In *Parashat Tazria* (and *Parashat Metzora*), we read at length and
in great detail about an individual who is afflicted by a condition known
as *tzaraat*, often translated as leprosy. It is a condition characterized by
specific discolorations of the skin, and it is understood by our sages to
be the consequence of immoral behavior, particularly malicious gossip.

The Torah prescribes that such an individual rend his clothes and
let his hair grow. He is considered ritually unclean, and "he shall dwell
apart; his dwelling shall be outside the camp" (Lev. 13:46).

Opinions vary as to why he must be removed from society. Some
say simply that he is quarantined because his condition is contagious.
Others insist that since his misdeeds caused harm to others, he must be
punished by living apart from others.

I prefer, however, the view that a period of solitude is imposed upon this individual to afford him an opportunity to think, to reconsider his actions, and to resolve to live a new moral lifestyle. He is afforded the social isolation necessary for thorough-going introspection, a chance to think for himself.

There is a lesson here about the benefits of solitude that is of renewed relevance in our day and age.

The American Scholar (Spring 2010) carries an essay by William Deresiewicz, which he delivered to the plebe class at the United States Military Academy at West Point in October of that year, entitled "Solitude and Leadership."

Mr. Deresiewicz eloquently conveys the message to these future military leaders that leadership demands a mindset that can only come about with frequent and sustained periods of solitude. He emphasizes the importance of thinking, and he writes, "Thinking means concentrating on one thing long enough to develop an idea about it." He further emphasizes the importance of concentrating and writes that it means "gathering yourself together into a single point rather than letting yourself be dispersed everywhere into a cloud of electronic and social input."

Ralph Waldo Emerson made Mr. Deresiewicz's point long ago when he said, "He who should inspire and lead his race must be defended from traveling with the souls of other men, from living, breathing, reading, and writing in the daily, time-worn yoke of their opinions."

These opinions of a famous nineteenth-century essayist and one of his contemporary counterparts stress and amplify a message implicit in our Torah portion. The message is that time by oneself, reflecting and engaging in serious introspection, is an essential component of self-improvement and a prerequisite not only for membership in society, but for leadership of society.

Jewish sources go much further than Emerson and Deresiewicz. The latter restrict their insightful comments to the importance of solitude in everyday, mundane affairs. Our tradition goes beyond that and teaches that solitude is necessary for spiritual growth and for religious leadership.

The sages of the Talmud insist upon the necessity of self-reckoning (*ḥeshbon hanefesh*). The Jewish ethical treatises of medieval times recommend that one regularly withdraw from society to engage in such self-reckoning. Hasidim, and most particularly the followers of Rabbi Nahman of Breslov, daily engage in periods of solitary contemplation (*hitbodedut*).

The secular writers quoted above are helpful in that they make it clear that solitude need not entail mystical practices or spiritual techniques. Rather, solitude provides an opportunity for thinking on one's own and for concentrating deeply without the undue influences of one's social surround. I personally am convinced that occasional solitude would be a healthy antidote to the blind conformity imposed upon all of us by our contemporary world.

Once again, the Torah, in the midst of a passage that seems most out of tune with modernity, gives us a lesson essential for coping with modernity.

Parashat Metzora

A Time for Silence, A Time for Speech

He did most of his writing and public speaking almost exactly one hundred years ago. He had no secular education and it is doubtful that he even read the newspapers of his day. Nevertheless, he had insights into the problems of his era that were astounding, even prophetic.

His diagnosis of the ills of the early twentieth century holds true even now, a century later. He understood the power of words. He knew how written and spoken language could be used as weapons to destroy humanity. How incredibly relevant his words are in our age when words can be communicated electronically!

He based his teachings and preaching upon the verse in Psalms, which reads:

> Who is the man who desires life,
> Who desires years of good fortune?
> Guard your tongue from evil,
> Your lips from deceitful speech. (Ps. 34:13–14)

321

He took this biblical advice seriously and urged all who would listen to guard their tongues and speak no malice and no falsehood.

His name was Yisrael Meir HaKohen, and he named his first major work *Ḥafetz Ḥaim* (*Desirous of Life*), after the above verse in Psalms. He is now part of Jewish history and forever known as the Ḥafetz Ḥaim.

His teachings have a special connection to *Parashat Metzora* (Lev. 14 and 15), and to its *haftara* (II Kings 7:3–20). Note that there is no explicit reference in the text of our *parasha* to the theme of the negative powers of language, nor is there any such reference in the *haftara*.

Our text deals, rather, with the detailed laws of the *metzora*, usually translated as "leper," and the selection from II Kings tells the story of the four lepers who dwelled outside the gates of Samaria, who were the first to discover the abandoned camp of the Aramean army that had laid siege to the city.

Rabbinic tradition, however, looks to understand why the *metzora* has been afflicted with his disease. The Talmud in Tractate Arakhin understands the word *metzora* as a contraction of the phrase "*motzi shem ra*," one who spreads a bad name about his fellow. And so, the *metzora* has come to symbolize the person who is guilty of malicious gossip (*lashon hara*), or other abuse of words – deception, profanity, and verbal assassination.

Interestingly, another early twentieth-century rabbinic sage, Rabbi Baruch Epstein, author of *Torah Temima*, points out that the talmudic rabbis had the license to thus interpret the word *metzora*. This is because the usual term for the leper is *tzarua*, not *metzora*. The use of the unusual term suggests another, in this case, homiletic, meaning – he who speaks evil.

When the Ḥafetz Ḥaim urged us all to "guard our tongues" and "speak no evil," was he suggesting that we adopt silence as a guide to our behavior, avoiding speech and self-expression entirely?

The answer to this is a resounding "no," and this is illustrated in a fascinating story about Rabbi Yisrael Meir and his son-in-law, Rabbi Hershel Levinson. I found this story in a Yiddish-language biography of the Ḥafetz Ḥaim, written by Moshe Mayer Yashar. An excerpted edition of this book is available in English, but without some of the more interesting and personal anecdotes.

Rabbi Hershel, the son-in-law, was a very pious man who spent his days in the study hall, and who seldom spoke at all. Many believed that he was even more saintly than his revered father-in-law. After all, his father-in-law spoke all over the place and taught and preached, and even joked, at every opportunity.

However, the Ḥafetz Ḥaim did not entirely approve of his son-in-law's avoidance of speech and devotion to almost complete silence about worldly matters. Rather, he insisted that one must use his gifts of speech, and use them widely and frequently, yet wisely and carefully. Silence, for the Ḥafetz Ḥaim, was not the preferred way of life. Speech that carefully avoided gossip, insults, and profanity was the preferred behavior.

Today, there are groups of very well-intentioned individuals who emphasize the evils of *lashon hara*. Sometimes, I am afraid, they do so by avoiding to speak negatively when such speech is necessary. They sometimes refrain from protesting criminal behavior out of fear that in doing so they are maliciously gossiping about a criminal.

This was not the Ḥafetz Ḥaim's way. In the book mentioned above, by the title of which he is known, he emphasizes that there are opportunities when one *must* use speech to warn against sinful or dangerous individuals, or to protest breaches of Torah, or of universal moral law. When negative talk has a beneficial objective, it is no longer to be considered negative, but actually becomes a mitzva.

The four lepers who are described in the narrative contained in the *haftara* of our *parasha* were stationed outside the gates of Samaria because such was what the Torah required of lepers. They were to have no contact with the residents of the city, perhaps because of the fear that their condition was contagious.

They were thus doomed in a sense to silence. They could not communicate with their friends and family within the city's gates. And so it is no wonder that when they found that the Aramean besieging of Jerusalem had been abandoned overnight, their first inclination was to keep that secret to themselves. But then, in II Kings 7:9, they came to their senses, and their sound consciences prevailed:

Then they said to one another,
"We are not doing right.
This is a day of good news,
And we are keeping silent!
If we wait until the light of morning,
We shall incur guilt.
Come, let us go and inform the king's palace.
They went and called out to the gate keepers of the city
And told them.

Words can harm, but they can also heal. This was the teaching of Rabbi Yisrael Meir HaKohen. It is perhaps best encapsulated in the words of Kohelet:

There is a time for all things...
A time for silence
And a time for speaking. (Eccl. 3:7)

Parashat Metzora

Pinkus the Peddler

He was a character straight out of the novels of Charles Dickens. Scholars have long found Dickens' attitude toward Jews problematic. The character Fagin in the novel *Oliver Twist* is certainly a negative stereotype, but many are unaware of the character named Riah in Dickens' last completed novel, *Our Mutual Friend*. Riah is portrayed as a proud Jew, honest, wise, compassionate, and courageous.

Pinkus always reminded me of Riah. He was a Holocaust survivor with no family, who eked out a livelihood by peddling his wares from door to door in Jewish neighborhoods. Such street peddlers were commonplace several generations ago and he was among the last of them. He occasionally visited the Brooklyn neighborhood in which I grew up, but I knew him best from the Lower East Side where I went to yeshiva.

I no longer recall his real name, but we called him Pinkus because of a then-popular but now long-forgotten Yiddish song about Pinkus the Peddler. We would buy our school supplies and other amenities from him, mostly out of sympathy. But those of us who had the patience to listen to his tales were more intrigued by his conversation than by the quality or price of his wares. Like Riah, the Dickens character, he was proud, honest, wise, compassionate, and courageous. He discussed neither his Holocaust experiences nor his ultimate rescue. Rather, he plied us with riddles about the Bible and Talmud and was a treasure trove of anecdotes about the people he knew from what he called "my world which is no more."

Much later, I discovered another peddler in our own tradition, so that I no longer needed to identify just Pinkus with Riah. This peddler of old was one from whom not I, but none other than the talmudic sage Rabbi Yannai, learned a great deal. And that brings us to *Parashat Metzora.*

We read in comprehensive detail about the *metzora,* the person inflicted with blemishes of the skin, often translated as leprosy. In the Bible, and even more so in the Talmud and Midrash, these blemishes are seen as divine punishment for sins of speech: malicious gossip, slander, and defamations of character – so much so that the very word *metzora* is said to be a contraction of the words *motzi ra,* he who spreads evil.

Hence the anecdote described in the Midrash Rabba associated with this Torah portion:

> It once happened that a certain peddler was wandering from town to town and crying out, "Who wishes to buy a life-giving potion?" Rabbi Yannai heard this man's shouting and called upon him for an explanation. The peddler took out the Book of Psalms and showed Rabbi Yannai the verse: "Who is the person who desires life, loving each day to see good? Then guard your tongue from evil and your lips from speaking deceit. Turn from evil and do good; seek peace and pursue it."

Rabbi Yannai exclaimed:

> All my life I have been reading this verse and never quite understood what it meant, until this peddler came and explained it.... Therefore, Moses admonished the Jewish people and said to them these are the statutes of the *metzora,* the statutes of the *motzi shem ra,* the bearer of malicious gossip.

From time immemorial, commentators have struggled with the question, "What did the peddler say that Rabbi Yannai did not already know?" Rabbi Yannai, by his own testimony, had read the Book of Psalms many times. The meaning of the verses quoted seems to be self-evident. What could this peddler have added to Rabbi Yannai's understanding?

Permit me to share with you one approach to demystifying this passage in the Midrash. It is drawn from a work by Rabbi Shlomo Yosef Zevin, a very insightful twentieth-century rabbi who lived and wrote in Israel. He reminds us of a teaching by Maimonides to the effect that there are similarities between physical health and illness and moral health and illness.

Taking that analogy further, Rabbi Zevin reminds us that there are foods for healthy people that those who are ailing can simply not digest. They need to first ingest medicine, healing foods, before they are ready for a proper diet.

Similarly, before one can embark upon the proper moral life, he or she often needs to first be healed from a prior tainted moral status. Thus, before one can live a life of "turning from evil and doing good, seeking peace and pursuing it," which is a normal healthy moral life, it is often necessary to first wean oneself from habitual immoral practices that are typically very resistant to change.

Hence, the ingenious insight of the peddler Rabbi Yannai heard. "Do you want to know the secret of a long life? Of a properly lived life of doing good and pursuing peace? Then first you must guard your tongue from evil. That is the secret potion, the healing medicine, which will enable you to go on to the next step, moral health."

In this analysis, correcting one's patterns of speech is a therapeutic process, a life-giving potion, not a food, not the bread of life. Only after this pernicious but pervasive fault is corrected, only after this moral disease is cured, can a person actively engage in the next verse in Psalms, "Turn from evil and do good."

Rabbi Yannai was accustomed to reading these verses differently. He understood the question, "Who desires life?" But he thought that there was one compound answer: guard your tongue, turn from evil, and do good.

The peddler taught something much more profound. The answer to, "Who desires life?" is a complex one. It consists of stages, the first of which is a healing process acquired by ingesting the potion of good speech. Then one can move up to the next stage, living a full and healthy moral life.

Pinkus the Peddler taught me a lot when I was but a teenager. What I did not realize then was that he was following a long and honored tradition of itinerant peddlers who peddled not just trivial commodities, but words and wares of wisdom.

Parashat Aḥarei Mot

No Exit

T here is much that the Torah leaves to our imagination. Regular students of the weekly *parasha* soon become convinced that the narratives they read each week are deliberately abbreviated, as if to encourage us to fill in the missing links on our own.

One outstanding example of such an incomplete narrative is the story of the death of Nadav and Avihu, the sons of Aaron the High Priest. Just a few short weeks before, in *Parashat Shemini* (Lev. 10:1–7), we read of their tragic sudden deaths. In their eager enthusiasm to draw closer to the Almighty, they brought an "alien fire" to the altar, a ritual procedure that they invented on their own and were never commanded to perform. For that, they were instantly struck down and consumed by a heavenly fire.

This terrifying event occurred on a day of momentous importance during the inauguration of the holy Tabernacle. It happened in the presence of a throng of celebrants. We can assume that there were at least some eyewitnesses to the events, and we can be certain that many individuals heard about it within mere minutes. But we know almost nothing about the reactions of those who were apprised of the tragic news that two princes in Israel, two young men who were next in line for the High Priesthood, potential leaders of the Jewish nation, were executed, cremated, by an act of God.

It is natural for most of us to empathize immediately with the father and mother of these ill-fated young men. We wonder what they felt when they first learned of their unspeakable loss. But we are left to our own devices by the text and can only imagine their reaction. All we are told is, "And Aaron was silent." Aaron's silence leaves us silent, lost in introspection, asking ourselves how we would react to such nightmarish news.

In *Parashat Aḥarei Mot* (Lev. 16:1–18:30), we read a bit more of the story. The opening paragraph of our *parasha* begins, "And it came to pass after the death of Aaron's two sons ...." Those words encourage us to believe that the suspense has been lifted and that we are about to learn the rest of the story. We are teased into supposing that we are about to discover the nature of the emotions that lay buried in Aaron's silence.

Alas, we are disappointed. Instead of a glimpse into Aaron's tormented soul, we are taught in elaborate detail of his newly prescribed ritual role. We read of the Temple procedures that he is to conduct on the holy Day of Atonement, Yom Kippur. We soon discover, to our surprise and dismay, that Aaron is to be required to replicate his sons' behavior, the very behavior for which they were frightfully punished. They lost their lives because they sought to draw too close to the Divine, and now Aaron their father is commanded to draw close to the Almighty. Indeed, he is summoned to enter a sector so sacred that his sons dared not set foot there.

Granted, he is to enter that sacred space at one specific moment in the entire year, and only after many preparatory procedures. But, nevertheless, the objective of Aaron's great mitzva and privilege, approaching the Almighty as closely as possible, is the identical objective that his sons desperately strived for, and for which they were catastrophically punished.

We can easily suppose that we are being called upon to imagine how Aaron, in the very act of entering the Holy of Holies, would be overwhelmed by heartbreak, haunted by the image of his children who were cut down in the prime of their lives while performing the very act that he was now commanded to perform!

In what way, however, was Aaron's entrance into the innermost sanctum fundamentally different from the attempt of Nadav and Avihu to approach the Most Sacred One? The answer lies in a careful reading of the rest of the opening chapter of the *parasha*. For there we learn that Aaron was not only instructed to enter the Holy of Holies; he was also instructed to leave that sacred space. To use contemporary jargon, he was given an exit strategy.

Attaching an exit strategy to an intense and sublime religious experience is one of the secrets of authentic spirituality. More specifically, the exit strategy is intrinsic to the Yom Kippur experience. Aaron was instructed to enter the inner sanctum, yes. But he was also directed to depart from it and return to the far less sacred world at large. Usually, we enter Yom Kippur with an attitude of remorse and solemnity. But we exit Yom Kippur with the confidence that our sins have been forgiven and that we can now embark upon the forthcoming joyous Sukkot days.

Nadav and Avihu, on the other hand, entered a "no exit" situation. The lesson is clear: spiritual ecstasy is wonderful, but it can never be an end in itself. It must be only a means to an end, an opportunity to become inspired with the purpose of bringing inspiration back to a mundane and imperfect world.

This was the example that Moses taught when he entered a realm even more sacred than the Holy of Holies. He ascended to the peak of Mount Sinai, and even farther upwards to the very heavens on high, to the realm of the angels and the site of the divine throne of glory. But he never lost sight of his goal of returning to his people with the message he received from on high. His intent was always to descend, to ultimately reunite with the people who sought to cope with the problems of ordinary existence.

This is also the central message of Yom Kippur. It is a day of atonement and repentance, of introspection and awe. Our spirituality that day is akin to that of the angels, removed from the human body's physical requirements of food and drink. But the climax of Yom Kippur must be the image left to us by Aaron and all the subsequent high priests. That image is described by our sages as "the holiday of festivities that the High

Priest celebrated when he exited safely from the Holy of Holies." The exit strategy from Yom Kippur is a festive and joyous meal, a return to reality, a reconnection to the ordinary, to the vulnerable, to the human.

Our religion has its serious, even somber, occasions; we know well days of self-examination and of longer periods of time dedicated to remorse and self-criticism. We know well days, months, and even years of grief and mourning. But for all these, our religion prescribes exit strategies: forgiveness for the sinner, return for the wayward child, and consolation for the mourner.

Nadav and Avihu were guilty of a truly fateful error. They wished to enter the spiritual state of no return. Our religion teaches us that spirituality must never be a condition of "no exit." Authentic spiritual experience must be designed to culminate with a return to the real world with song for those formerly sad, and speech for those once crippled by silence.

Parashat Kedoshim

I Get No Respect

I love visiting residences for senior citizens. For one thing, being around truly older people invariably helps me feel young by comparison. Recently, I was a weekend guest scholar at such a residence. I dispensed with my prepared lectures and instead tried to engage the residents of the facility, not one of whom was less than ninety years old, in a group discussion. This proved to be a very wise move on my part, because I learned a great deal about the experience of getting old. Or as one wise man insisted, "You don't get old – you get older."

The question that I raised to provoke discussion was this, "What made you first realize that you were getting older?" I was taken aback by the reactions of the group, because there were clearly two very different sets of responses.

One member of the group responded, "I knew I was getting older when people started to ignore me. I was no more than a piece of furniture to them. Worse, they no longer noticed me at all."

About half of the group expressed their agreement with this person's experience. They proceeded to describe various experiences that they had in being ignored. Some of those stories were quite poignant and powerful. One woman even described how she was present at the outbreak of a fire in a hotel lobby and the rescue workers "simply did not see me sitting there. That is, until I started to scream!"

But then some of the others spoke up expressing quite different experiences. One gentleman said it for the rest of this second group, "I knew that I was getting older when passengers on the subway or bus stood up for me and gave me their seat." That basic gesture of respect conveyed to the members of this group of senior citizens that they had indeed reached the age when they were not ignored, but rather the beneficiaries of acts of deference.

The discussion then entered another phase as both groups agreed that, while they certainly did not want to be ignored, they also were resentful of these gestures of respect. The group unanimously supported the position articulated by the oldest person there, who said, "We don't want gestures of respect. We want genuine respect."

It seems that the entire group, although appreciative of those who relinquished seats on the subway for them, wanted something more. They wanted their opinions to be heard, their life experience to be appreciated, and their accumulated wisdom to be acknowledged. Symbolic gestures were insufficient and sometimes were even experienced as demeaning.

Parashat Kedoshim (Lev. 19:1–20:27) contains the basic biblical commandment regarding treatment of the elderly: "You shall rise before the aged and show deference to the old; you shall fear your God: I am the Lord" (19:32).

Rashi's comments on this verse indicate how sensitive he was to the subtle reactions expressed by the members of my little group. Here is what he says, paraphrasing the talmudic sages, "What is deference? It is refraining from sitting in his place, and not interrupting his words. Whereas one might think to simply close his eyes and pretend not to even see the old person, the verse cautions us to fear your God, for after all, he knows what is in the heart of man."

Interestingly, not sitting in *his* seat means much more than just giving him a seat on the bus. It means recognizing that the elderly person has his own seat, his own well-earned place in society, which you, the younger person, dare not usurp. It is more than just a gesture. It is an acknowledgement of the valued place the elder has in society, a place that is his and his alone.

Similarly, not interrupting the older person's conversation is much more than an act of courtesy. It is awareness that this older person has something valuable to say, a message to which one must listen attentively.

How well our Torah knows the deviousness of which we are all capable. We can easily pretend not to notice the older person, but He who reads our minds and knows what is in our hearts will be the judge of that. We must fear Him and not resort to self-justification and excuses. We must deal with the older person as a real person whose presence cannot be ignored, but must be taken into full account in our conversation.

Rabbi Naftali Tzvi Yehuda Berlin, known as the Netziv, in his commentary on this verse, refers us to a passage in the Midrash Rabba on the weekly portion of *Behaalotekha* in the Book of Numbers, which understands the phrase "you shall fear your God" as being the consequence of your showing deference to the elderly. Thus, if you treat the elderly well, you will attain the spiritual level of the God-fearing person, but if you refrain from showing the elderly that deference, you can never aspire to the title "God-fearing person," no matter how pious you are in other respects.

There is another entirely different perspective on our verse, which provides a practical motive for honoring the elderly. It is to be found in the commentary of Avraham ibn Ezra, who explains the phrase, "You shall fear your God," in the following way:

> The time will come when you will be old and frail and lonely. You will long for proper treatment at the hands of the young. But if you showed disrespect for the elderly when you were young, and did not "fear God," God will not reward you with the treatment you desire in your own old age.

As each of us strives to show genuine respect to our elders, we help construct a society in which the elderly have their proper place.

That society will hopefully still be there when we become older, and then we will reap the benefits of our own youthful behavior.

Our *parasha* is entitled *Kedoshim*, which means "holy." One of the major components of the holy society is the treatment it accords to every one of its members, especially those who are vulnerable. Treating the elderly with genuine respect, truly listening to them, and valuing their contributions, is an essential part of what it means to be a "holy people."

It's All Commentary

I am proud of my large library of Jewish books. My collection, which my wife half-jokingly refers to as my addiction, began on my eleventh birthday with a gift from my maternal grandparents, may they rest in peace. They bought me the then recently published Shulzinger edition of the Five Books of Moses surrounded by numerous traditional commentaries. Those volumes became the cornerstone of my personal library of many hundreds of Judaic works on the Bible, the Talmud, philosophy, history, and codes of law. These books line the walls of my private study from floor to ceiling.

Over the years, I have had many visitors who were struck by the overwhelming number of books and who reacted with awe and curiosity. Some, particularly non-Jews, would ask, "Have you read all of these?" When I confessed that I hadn't read more than very few of them, they often proceeded with yet another question, "What are they all about? Why are so many books necessary just to explain one religion?" They could not fathom why so much commentary was written on just a few basic biblical texts.

Often, as I responded to their inquiries, I found myself resorting to an old story of one of our greatest sages, Hillel. To most of you, this story is probably well-known, perhaps even trite. But for many of my visitors, the story was novel, instructive, and almost revelatory.

In this story, Hillel, known for his scholarship and commitment to Torah study, but particularly famous for his patience, is provocatively challenged by a heathen who demands that Hillel teach him the entire Torah while standing on one foot. Hillel accepts the challenge and says, "What is hateful to you, do not do unto others. That is the entire Torah, the rest is but commentary. Now go out and study the commentary."

I would then explain to my inquisitive visitors that Hillel's remark was based upon a verse in *Parashat Kedoshim*, "And thou shalt love thy neighbor as thyself" (Lev. 19:18).

Now, I would continue, loving one's neighbor as oneself is no easy task. We are likely to have numerous and diverse neighbors in the course of a lifetime and myriad circumstances arise that pose great barriers to our love for them. And so, Jewish scholars throughout the ages have recorded their advice, suggestions, and guidelines for just how to love one's neighbor in every conceivable context and condition. That's what all these books are about and that's why we need so many of them.

Note that Hillel himself does not choose to use the Torah's original phrase to explain the essence of Judaism to the heathen. He does not say, "Love your neighbor," rather, he says, "Do not harm your neighbor." Perhaps this is because, as the medieval commentator Nahmanides suggests, loving one's neighbor as oneself is an exaggerated expectation, just too tall an order, and the most Hillel could do was to urge the heathen to do no harm.

Whether one uses the biblical formulation commanding us to love our neighbor, or chooses Hillel's version, which asks us to refrain from harming him or her in a way in which we ourselves would not want to be harmed, the essence of our Torah is this ethical imperative. And the many hundreds of volumes in my personal library, and the hundreds of thousands of similar tomes written throughout the centuries, can all be understood as the constant and perpetual struggle of our sages to develop a "database" sufficient to enable us to realize this ethical imperative.

One such commentary deserves mention, particularly in our age and culture, which has been diagnosed as narcissistic, as overly self-loving. This commentary takes the form of a story about a disciple of Rabbi Mendel of Kotzk who eavesdropped upon his master as the latter was reviewing our *parasha* aloud. Rabbi Mendel read, "And thou shalt love thy neighbor…as yourself?! Yes, as yourself!" First as a question, and then as a forceful declaration.

The disciple was puzzled by the manner in which his master read the passage. He asked the master's chief disciple, Reb Hershel, for an explanation. This was his answer:

> The master first asked a question. Can it be that we are asked to love our neighbor as ourselves? Are we to understand that it is permissible to love oneself? Is it not a basic teaching here in Kotzk that one dare not love oneself, lest he thereby become blind to his own faults?

In our terminology, Rabbi Mendel could not accept the slightest suggestion that narcissism was acceptable.

> Then the master realized a deeper meaning of the verse. Namely, we ought to love our neighbor to the same extent that we are critical of ourselves. The mitzva is that we put in as much effort loving our neighbor as the effort that we should be investing in our own personal spiritual and moral perfection.

In an age of "me first," it is even more important that we direct our love outward toward the other and not inward toward ourselves. We must at all costs avoid self-adulation and self-worship.

That is just one small sample of the vast treasure of commentary that is in our Jewish library. No wonder that our sages refer to the "ocean of the Talmud," and to our Torah, as deeper than the sea.

Holiness: A Definition

He never returned phone calls. He certainly never returned e-mails. He rarely smiled. He had very sophisticated tastes in wine and fine liquor. A seven-course gourmet dinner with a wine pairing at each course was almost an everyday occurrence for him. He had the vocabulary of a sailor and seemed to be acquainted with the obscenities and profanities of every known language.

Don't get me wrong. He had many fine qualities and considered himself to be religious, even pious.

"After all," he would say, "I am careful that the meals that I order are always absolutely kosher. The Torah doesn't prohibit wine, nor does it require us to refrain from delicious food, and it places no limits on the quantity of food that we eat."

He would expound upon the fact that he found nothing in the Torah requiring one to return phone calls or e-mails. He even insisted that, at least in the Written Torah, he found no objection to the use of vulgar language.

I knew this person, let's call him Reuben, for nearly fifty years. I was associated with him in various capacities and often worked with him on charity projects. Although he scrupulously investigated every cause that approached him for contributions, and he was very careful as to the causes to which he made contributions, I cannot deny that he was generous by almost all standards.

I must admit that I often wondered about his relationship with his wife. Obviously, I was not privy to the intimate details about their relationship. I did meet Reuben's wife several times, and she always appeared to be quite sad, even defeated. She certainly did not share his *joie de vivre*, dressed quite modestly compared to his lavish wardrobe, and she certainly never resorted to his foul language.

When Reuben died, one of his close business associates who knew him as a religious Jew, eulogized him as a person who exhibited holiness. "He was no saint," proclaimed this associate, "but from my perspective as an irreligious person, Reuben was a holy man."] *heuly*

Now it is common, and even to some extent permissible, to exaggerate the merits of the deceased during a eulogy for him, but there was something about the adjective "holy" that I simply could not accept, and felt compelled to protest. It was certainly inappropriate for me to protest in public at the funeral and I felt it was pointless to protest to the well-meaning person who delivered the eulogy. So I decided to use my writing as a venue for that protest.

What does it mean to be holy? For the answer to that, we need to examine a verse at the beginning of *Parashat Kedoshim* (Ex.16:1–20:27). The verse reads, "You shall be holy; for I the Lord your God am holy."

The two greatest commentators on the Bible in the Jewish tradition, Rashi and Nahmanides, enunciate definitions of "holiness." Rashi insists that to be holy means to be separate, distant, from various sinful exploits, especially sexual promiscuity. He says that the Hebrew words, "you shall be holy (*kedoshim tihyu*)," are best understood as, "you shall keep a distance (*perushim tihyu*)."

Nahmanides, however, takes issue with Rashi, although he characteristically does so with great courtesy and even reverence for his predecessor. Nahmanides' definition of holiness expresses one of his most basic teachings, and in my opinion, one of the perspectives of Judaism that is often forgotten and needs to be re-emphasized from time to time.

Nahmanides writes that there is more to being holy then merely abiding by the rules and regulations of the Torah. Yes, he writes, the Torah does not forbid gluttony and it is quite possible to be a glutton yet not violate any of the laws of *kashrut*. True, he continues, one can use all manner of vulgar language yet violate no explicit biblical command. A man can observe every detail of the Torah's laws about family purity, yet not be a loving husband.

Nahmanides coins a phrase, "*naval bireshut haTorah*," which can be translated either as, "a knave within the bounds of Torah," or alternatively, "a knave with the Torah's permission." Holiness, for Nahmanides, consists of all those behaviors that are to be expected from a decent human being, even if those behaviors are not explicitly prescribed by the Torah.

Reuben was a man whom I knew all of my life. Although he was not perfect, he had his positive qualities, and I certainly cannot take it upon myself to condemn him. But he was not holy. Indeed, he missed the point about what the Jewish religion is all about.

Our religion is indeed about obedience and compliance to a set of laws – some ordained by God and some instituted by wise and holy men – but that is not *all* that it is about. It is about attitudes and it is about relationships. It is about ethical behaviors that need not be prescribed in the form of rules, but are to be expected of every reasonable human being.

Some would explain Nahmanides' thesis in terms of the age-old distinction between the letter of the law and the spirit of the law. That is certainly one way of understanding it. Reuben is a prime example of someone who did not see beyond the letter of the law.

Our daily prayer book contains the following verse in Isaiah 59:21:

> This is my covenant with them says the Lord: My spirit, which is upon you, and the words I have placed in your mouth, shall not depart from you or your children or your children's children.

Clearly, the Almighty's covenant has two components: His spirit and His words. Reuben kept the latter, but ignored the former. Holiness consists of adherence to them both. Nahmanides teaches us that holiness is about that spirit. The Torah itself, by addressing the commandment "be holy" to all of us, is teaching us that we are all capable of achieving that spirit. We are expected to be a *goy kadosh*, a holy people.

The Unburied Corpse

Dead. Unburied. Abandoned. Forgotten. What can be a worse fate?

I recently finished a very moving novel about the events immediately preceding World War I and the fate of those who were caught up in the chaos of the opening days of that war. The author of the book, a Jew, was Joseph Roth, and the name of the book is *The Radetzky March*.

I was drawn to this book because it deals, in part, with the Jews of Galicia and the effect that World War I had upon them. Both my paternal and maternal great-grandparents were caught up in the events of those times and I wished to learn more about those events, if only from a fictional account.

I found the book informative and troubling, but the single event recorded in it that had the most impact on me was a description of the novel's hero, a combatant in the initial outbreak of the battle and gunfire. At one point, as he was fleeing for safety, he encountered the corpse of one of his fellows. Rather than pass this corpse by in his flight, he chose to drag the corpse to a nearby graveyard, dig a shallow grave with his bayonet, and bury the poor man.

Although the hero of this story was not a Jew, he was acting in accordance with a supreme Jewish value. At great personal risk, he buried a *met mitzva*, an abandoned corpse, with no one else present to bury it. Our Torah insists that giving such a corpse the dignity of a proper burial is a mitzva, one that takes priority over almost any other good deed.

The source for this great mitzva is in *Parashat Emor*, where we read of the strict prohibition upon *kohanim*, members of the priestly caste, to come into contact with the dead. Exceptions are made for the *kohen's* parents, children, siblings, and spouse. And an exception is made for the *met mitzva*. Should the *kohen* encounter an abandoned corpse, and no one else is available to bury it, he is commanded to ignore the prohibition against contact with the dead, and he must bury that corpse himself.

This is the meaning of the phrase in the very first verse of our *parasha*, "He shall not defile himself for any dead person among his people" (Lev. 21:1). Paraphrasing Rashi's words here, "When the dead man is among his people, the *kohen* cannot defile himself, but when the dead man is not among his people, that is, there is no one else to bury him, then the prohibition does not apply."

Our tradition is unusually sensitive to the sanctity of the human body, in life certainly, but even in death. A proper Jewish burial is the last "kindness of truth (*ḥesed shel emet*)" that one can perform for another.

It is this important Jewish value that has led Jewish communities throughout the ages to do all that they could to recover the bodies of those of our brethren who perished in prisons, on battlefields, or in tragic natural disasters.

During one Passover, a good friend reminded me of a long-forgotten incident in our history, an incident that culminated in the recovery of two *metei mitzva*.

Part of the story of these two heroes is recounted in the book *The Deed* by Gerold Frank. It is the story of two boys who gave their lives to assassinate a high British official, based in Egypt, whose policies threatened to block Jewish immigration into what was then Palestine. Their names were Eliahu Bet Zouri and Eliahu Hakim. They acted under the orders of the high command of the "Stern Group." They succeeded in assassinating the official, but were tried and hanged for their efforts. They were buried near Cairo in 1945, but they were never forgotten. In 1975, the State of Israel exchanged twenty Arab prisoners for the bodies of these two young men and reburied them in hero's graves on Mount Herzl.

In recovering these bodies and eventually affording them an appropriate Jewish burial, the Israeli government was adhering to the teaching of our *parasha*. They saw to it that these *metei mitzva* were buried properly.

And more recently, the contingents of Israeli rescue workers who dug beneath the rubble of the horrific earthquake in Haiti, in search not only of survivors but of dead bodies, were acting in accordance with this great mitzva. They were exemplifying a major Torah value.

And so, as so often in our study of the *parasha*, we discovered a value of paramount importance, a priority mitzva, buried between the lines, nay between the words, of a simple phrase. That phrase is in the very first verse of *Parashat Emor*.

Parashat Emor

Becoming a Kohen

I n every group, there is one person who stands out as special. In childhood, it is often the kid with the greatest athletic prowess. Later in life, different attributes begin to qualify a person to become the group's star.

In my post-high school peer group, many years ago on Manhattan's Lower East Side, we had one such towering figure. I use the word "towering" literally because he was well over six feet tall. He had jet-black hair, which turned the heads of all the young ladies who passed him by. He had an outstanding academic record and seemed to earn his grades effortlessly.

After high school, our group began to disperse as each of us went off to different colleges and yeshivas, and he announced that he was accepted into a very prestigious university across the country. He was so distinctive and distinguished that, although he was not born into the priestly tribe, we called him "the *Kohen*."

In *Parashat Emor*, we learn about the priests (*kohanim*), and their special role in the Jewish nation. This is certainly not the first time that we have encountered them in our Torah readings. We already know that they stem from the tribe of Levi and descend from Aaron, brother of Moses. We have learned that they were charged with the performance of the sacrificial rites and other Temple practices. But for the first time in our *parasha*, we learn about the restrictions that are imposed upon them, especially with regard to their permission to come into contact with the dead.

We also learn that the rest of us, not born into the priests' tribe, are required to "sanctify" them, and to treat them deferentially. "And you must treat them as holy" (Lev. 21:8). "To be first in every way and to offer the first blessing at the meal," explains Rashi. They are to receive the honor of being first in many activities, especially in the ceremonies of leading Grace after Meals (*Birkat HaMazon*), and being called to the Torah.

Sociologists distinguish between two kinds of roles in society: those ascribed to us by others, and those we achieve ourselves by virtue of our own efforts and accomplishments. The *kohen's* role is clearly an ascribed one. Once a *kohen*, always a *kohen*, and unless he is guilty of truly egregious behaviors, he does not lose his status or forfeit his privileges.

One of the most remarkable features of our people is that we still have *kohanim*. So proud were the *kohanim* over all the generations that the "kohanic" identity has been passed from father to son for millennia. Indeed, genetic evidence seems to confirm the validity of this verbal communication down the ages by isolating a "*kohen* gene."

But Judaism also recognizes other paths to privileged status that depend upon personal achievements and hard work that are not ascribed at birth. These are statuses that must be earned and are not determined by one's genetic endowment. Indeed, the Talmud recognizes the equality, if not superiority, of the *talmid ḥakham* to the *kohen gadol*. Greater respect is shown for the person whose piety and erudition earned him his status than to one who gained the role of High Priest by virtue of his genealogy.

Many of us have been transfixed by the events surrounding the wedding of a member of the British royal family; a perfect example of how prominence, grandeur, and glory redound to an individual whose position is ascribed by his lineage and not achieved by his accomplishments. It would seem that even in our day and age, we are captivated by those who are born to their positions. But how much more deserving of our reverence and respect is the "low-born" person who has achieved his prominence by virtue of his hard work. In this sense, all of us are potentially *kohanim*, even if our genealogy is not comprised of ancestors from the tribe of Levi and who are not descendent from Moses or Aaron.

As is often the case, it was Maimonides who said it best, "Not just the tribe of Levi, but every inhabitant of the world whose inspiration and intellect guide him to stand before the Almighty, to serve Him and to know Him...is elevated to sanctity and holiness...and deserves the same material privileges as the *kohanim*" (*Mishneh Torah, Hilkhot Shemitta VeYovel* 13:13).

Introvert/Extrovert

Although many of his adherents deny it, he definitely had an anti-Semitic streak and was at least for a time sympathetic to the Nazi cause. Yet he was one of the major psychological theorists of the twentieth century and I personally have found his insights into the human mind both fascinating and practical.

His name was Carl Jung, and he introduced two terms into the field of psychology that eventually became so well known that they are part of our everyday language. It was he who distinguished between the "introvert" and the "extrovert."

I confess that I have always been so troubled by Jung's anti-Semitism that it has been difficult for me to make use of the concepts of introversion and extroversion without feeling that I was somehow betraying my people. But his ideas make such great sense to me that I have admittedly come to utilize and apply his teachings, setting aside his anti-Jewish sentiments.

Over the years, I have developed the somewhat ornery habit of "cleansing" Jung's dichotomy by applying it to Jewish texts, heroes, and institutions. What follows is an example of this habit.

The popular mind stereotypes the introvert as a shy, withdrawn, and even antisocial individual whose difficulties with others make it hard for him to adjust to society. On the other hand, the extrovert is stereotyped as a gregarious, friendly, and outgoing person, who gets along with all his fellows.

However, Jung's understanding of the two contrasting terms was far more nuanced and complex than those stereotypes. As Jung explains it, there are two fundamentally human attitudes. The first, introversion, is characterized by a hesitant, reflective, retiring nature that keeps to itself, remains somewhat distant from others, and is autonomous in a very profound way. The second attitude, extroversion, is characterized by an outgoing and accommodating nature that adapts easily to a given situation and that quickly forms attachments to others. Furthermore, Jung insists that there is neither a pure introvert nor a pure extrovert. Rather, each of us contains a combination of introversion and extroversion in varying proportions.

In *Parashat Emor* (Lev. 23), the Sabbath and all the major Jewish festivals are described in rich detail. Indeed, this *parasha* constitutes the Torah readings for many of these holidays. What is remarkable is that the chapter opens with the phrase, "These are My festivals," but then first lists the Sabbath, as if the Sabbath, too, were a festival. Only afterwards does this *parasha* go on to Passover and the rest of the holidays on the calendar. It seems the Sabbath, too, though it occurs every week, is a festival.

Yet we know that there are important basic differences between the Sabbath and the other festivals. For starters, the Sabbath was ordained as a special day at the very beginning of creation and was ordained as such by the Almighty Himself. The festivals, on the other hand, did not begin until Jewish history began, millennia after the creation; and their sanctification, at least in ancient times, depended upon the declaration of a human court.

There are further distinctions between the Sabbath and the festivals, between Shabbat and Yom Tov. On the Sabbath, objects may not be carried from private to public domains. On festivals, with the exception of Yom Kippur, there are no restrictions upon transporting objects from one domain to the other. On the Sabbath, all manner of creative work is forbidden, even the cooking and baking of Sabbath food. During the festivals, again Yom Kippur excluded, cooking and baking fresh food for the holiday is not only permitted, but encouraged.

The twentieth-century sage and rabbi of Dvinsk in Latvia, Rabbi Meir Simha, was intrigued by these and other contrasts between the Sabbath and festivals. He saw the Sabbath as being primarily a private time, a time for the individual to be alone and engaged in spiritual introspection. After all, the Sabbath did not depend upon other humans, but was initially proclaimed by God to Himself, for Himself. The Sabbath did not allow for easy commerce from private to public places and did not encourage cooking meals for guests.

In psychological language, the Sabbath caters to the introvert within us. It is consistent with the attitude of introversion, which prefers silence and solitude over socialization and interpersonal interaction.

The festivals, on the other hand, depend upon other human beings for their very existence. Absent the proclamation of the human Jewish court, there is no festival. The barriers between private and public domains, which are so characteristic of the Sabbath, disappear during the festival. Entertaining guests during the festival is so important that it is the factor that permits cooking and baking even late on the festival day. In psychological language, Yom Tov is designed for the extrovert within us. Festivals are the time when our attitudes of extroversion have their opportunity to be fully expressed.

Given the origin of the concept of introversion/extroversion in the mind of a person who failed to honor the Jewish tradition, it gives me a special pleasure to utilize it as a way of elaborating upon the deep insights of a proud and pious Jew, Rabbi Meir Simha.

I would conclude with yet another example of the introversion of the Sabbath and the extroversion of festivals. The key emotions of Shabbat are dignity (*kavod*) and personal delight (*oneg*). Both of these typify the introvert's experience. Yom Tov is characterized by a different emotion entirely, the emotion of joy, an emotion best experienced, and arguably only possible, in the company of others.

It is because the human being is a complex combination of the attitudes of introversion and extroversion that we can understand why there is both a weekly Sabbath and a yearlong series of festivals. We need times to nurture our autonomous selves, and we need the opportunities for contemplation and reflection that the Sabbath offers, but we also need times to connect to others in the context of joy and celebration, opportunities that the festivals amply provide.

No wonder then that our *parasha* insists upon including the Sabbath, the introvert, among the extroverted festivals. It is the complex combination of the two attitudes that brings about the spiritual harmony, which our Torah advocates and which is the essence of the complete person.

Like All Other Boys

The custom is fairly prevalent nowadays, but it was not a common practice thirty years ago when my friend raised his sons. He would seek out especially pious rabbis, generally quite elderly ones, to request that they bless his children.

In keeping with tradition, these rabbis would place a hand upon the head of the little boy, perhaps quote a biblical verse or two expressing blessing, and then say something like, "May he grow up to be a *talmid ḥakham*, an excellent Torah student." Sometimes, they would say, "May he grow up to be an *ehrliche yid*, a righteous Jew."

But I will never forget the day that my friend and his young son encountered Rabbi Israel Gustman, of blessed memory, and requested a blessing from him. I will remember that day because my friend came to me just moments after he received the blessing and asked me what I thought the old rabbi meant by it.

For you see, the rabbi gave a blessing that was unprecedented and unexpected. He did place his hand upon my friend's son's head and did utter an appropriate biblical verse. But then he said something quite puzzling, "May he grow up to be a boy like all other boys."

I don't know why my friend considered me an expert on rabbinic blessings and I must confess to you, dear reader, as I confessed to him, that I hadn't a clue as to what the old revered rabbi meant and why he would deliver such an unusual blessing instead of a more traditional one. I also must admit that it took me quite a while until I became convinced that I understood the meaning of the rabbi's mysterious message.

Understanding that message required the knowledge of a verse in *Parashat Emor* (Lev. 21:1–24:23). It also required knowing something about Rabbi Gustman's tragic life.

The verse to which I refer reads, "You shall not profane My holy name, that I may be sanctified in the midst of the Israelite people" (Lev. 22:32). This verse is the source text for two opposing concepts that lie at the core of Jewish belief. One concept, the negative one, is the profanation of God's name (*ḥillul Hashem*), behavior that disgraces the divine reputation. The opposite concept is *kiddush Hashem*, behavior that sanctifies God's name and thus brings prestige and honor to Him.

Before providing illustrations of the types of behavior that might either profane or sanctify God, let me give you a brief sketch of Rabbi Gustman's biography. He was a brilliant Talmud student in the yeshiva he attended. As a very young man, he was betrothed to the daughter of the rabbi of one of the small suburbs of the great pre-war Jewish metropolis of Vilna. Soon after his marriage, his father-in-law died, leaving the position of rabbi of that community to his son-in-law, Rabbi Israel.

The towering rabbinic figure in Vilna in those immediate pre-war years was Rabbi Chaim Ozer Grodzenski. Rabbi Chaim Ozer was so impressed by this young man that, despite his age, he included him in his rabbinic court. Soon afterwards, the War broke out. Rabbi Gustman managed to survive by hiding in an array of unimaginable circumstances – in the forest, in a cave, in a pig pen, and in the abandoned ghetto of Vilna. In the course of his flight and evasion of the Nazis, his little son was murdered in front of his eyes. He would recount the story of how he witnessed his son's murder and of how he was forced to take his dead son's shoes and sell them for food.

Rabbi Gustman survived the Holocaust, emigrated to the United States, and eventually settled in Israel. There, he lived and taught in a small yeshiva in Jerusalem and experienced the various wars of those years. He carefully and compassionately made it his business to comfort the bereaved parents of fallen soldiers by sharing with them his grief over his own fallen son.

He was overheard telling a particular bereaved father that, in a certain sense, his soldier son was superior to the rabbi's own son. "Both your boy and mine," he said, "sanctified God's name by their death. They were both killed because they were Jews. But in the synagogue in heaven where they both reside now, my son is sitting in the pews. Your son is the prayer leader (*shaliaḥ tzibbur*). This is because my son died as a passive victim, whereas your son died as a hero, leading a group of soldiers in defense of our land and our people."

These two boys performed the mitzva of *kiddush Hashem* by virtue of their deaths, but that is only one way to perform the mitzva. There is another way to perform the mitzva of *kiddush Hashem* and that is by sanctifying God's name not in death, but in life, by living one's daily life in a meritorious fashion.

The Talmud, for example, tells us of one great sage who felt that had he purchased meat in a butcher store on credit, without paying immediately, he would be guilty of profaning God's name. By simply paying his bills immediately, not allowing anyone to suspect that he was taking advantage of his rabbinical position, he was performing the mitzva of *kiddush Hashem*.

The Mishna in Tractate Megilla teaches us that when a Jew simply attends the synagogue and participates in the recitation of the sacred passages of our liturgy (*devarim shebekedusha*), he is fulfilling the mitzva referred to in our verse, sanctifying God through his prayers.

Thus, there are ways to sanctify God not by suffering a martyr's death, but by living an ethical and spiritual life. The Talmud says that should others comment favorably on a person's behavior, complimenting his parents for having raised him in the path of the Torah, that person has sanctified and glorified God's name.

Now we are in a position to understand the seemingly strange blessing that Rabbi Gustman gave my friend's little boy. "I bless you," he was saying, "that you just be like other boys, like boys in peaceful times. I bless you that you not suffer times of persecution and that you never need to experience the battlefield. I bless you that you sanctify God in your ordinary life, in life and not, God forbid, in tragic death."

In his blessing, he envisioned a time when little boys would not have to grow up to be soldiers and would not be hunted down and shot, as his son was. He foresaw a time when this boy could be like other boys, living an ordinary life, full of living acts of *kiddush Hashem.*

Jewish people commemorate the *kiddush Hashem* of Rabbi Gustman's son, a Holocaust victim, by observing Yom HaShoa. We also commemorate the *kiddush Hashem* of the young soldier whose bereaved father Rabbi Gustman so poignantly consoled by observing Yom HaZikaron.

We all pray for the time when boys will not be forced to perform the mitzva of *kiddush Hashem* by giving up their lives, but will be able to do so by living their lives; a time when "boys will just be like other boys," allowed to emerge from their childhood alive and well, entering adulthood in a world at peace, able to sanctify God in their faith and in their noble accomplishments.

Parashat Behar

The Time of Your Life

I
t is a lesson I first learned long ago in a course I took on the skills of interviewing. The instructor taught us that the way to really size up a candidate for a job is to determine how he uses his time. He taught us that one question designed to assist the interviewer to make that determination is, "Where do you see yourself in five years?"

I have since had decades of interviewing experience in many diverse settings and have developed a set of other questions, all intended for the same objective. They include: "What do you in your spare time?" "How would you spend your time if you won the lottery and no longer had to work for a living?" And, in academic or rabbinic interviewing, "How would you use your time if you were given a sabbatical leave from your position?"

It is this last question that brings us to *Parashat Behar*. In the very beginning, we read of the mitzva of letting the land lie fallow (unsown) every seven years, which is the sabbatical year; also known as *Shemitta*. "But in the seventh year the land shall have a Sabbath of complete rest, a Sabbath of the Lord: you shall not sow your field or prune your vineyard" (Lev. 25:4).

The Torah spells out quite clearly what can and cannot be done in the way of tilling the soil. Indeed, there is an entire Tractate of Mishna and Jerusalem Talmud, which gives specific and detailed guidelines relating to the land and the produce of the *Shemitta* year. I have always been intrigued and even a bit mystified, however, by the fact that, to my knowledge, nothing is said about what the farmer is supposed to do with his spare time that year. Imagine a farmer who has been working industriously, 24/6, for six years. Then, as Rosh HaShana of year seven approaches, very little work is permitted to him and he becomes a gentleman of leisure. How does he use his time?

It is inspiring to note that there are pious farmers in Israel nowadays who scrupulously observe *Shemitta*. And it is interesting that they indeed create structured programs for their "leisure" time that year. They study Torah, particularly the sections related to agriculture. They travel to farms across the country teaching less knowledgeable farmers halakhot pertaining to farming. They even spend time updating their own technical agricultural skills.

There is a lesson to be learned here. The Torah legislates that the land needs a sabbatical year in order to renew itself. We must come to the realization ourselves that we too need a sabbatical year, but for us, staying fallow is not a mission. Rather, it is to use such a time for physical, intellectual, and spiritual reinvigoration.

The Torah continues to prescribe yet another "leisure" year, a sabbatical year after seven sabbatical years, called the Jubilee year:

> And you shall hallow the fiftieth year. You shall proclaim release throughout the land for all its inhabitants. It shall be a Jubilee for you: each of you shall return to his holding and each of you shall return to his family." (Lev. 25:10)

The personal, spiritual meaning of the fiftieth year of life was brought home to me recently. I have been re-visiting the writings of Hillel Zeitlin, a victim of the Holocaust. Zeitlin was a journalist, philosopher, and mystic who wrote a number of poems in the form of prayers, or perhaps prayers in the form of poems. One is entitled "On the Threshold of My *Erev Shabbat*."

He writes in anticipation of his fiftieth birthday when he is about to enter the sixth decade of his life:

> Life is like the days of the week, each decade a day. The seventh decade/day is our soul's Sabbath, and we are granted but seven days. I am at the brink of Friday, *erev Shabbat*, for my tired spirit. I pray that my Friday be a proper preparation, that I can use it for personal repair. For five days I have wandered, nay strayed. This day I hope to re-discover the path, and return before Sabbath Eve's suns sets.

The journey of Zeitlin's life was a tortuous one and its theme was perpetual search. He wandered from *shtetl* and *ḥeder* to Western European philosophy, from secular Zionism to Hasidism, from Warsaw's literary circles to its *shtieblakh,* and ultimately to Treblinka. But his poetry, especially the poem I translated above, displays an exquisite time-consciousness, an awareness of how fleeting our lives are, and how we must work hard to fill them with meaning.

Every seventh year is a sabbatical for the soul, and every fiftieth year, a time to recognize that we are past the zenith of our arc of life.

Fortunately, we have an even more frequent gift of time, and it is our weekly Sabbatical, the Holy Sabbath (*Shabbat Kodesh*). In the cycles characterized by the number seven, we have seven years, seven sets of seven years, and the seven days of the week. Jewish mysticism offers us a multitude of meanings for the number seven, but this much is not mysterious: There is a rhythm to our lives and part of that rhythm calls for regular times for reflection and renewal. The intervals between such moments vary greatly in their duration. It is up to us to make the most of those moments, whether they last a day or a year.

I once heard a wise man, Rav Elya Lapian, say, "Modern man is convinced that time is money. Spiritual man knows that time is life."

Anniversary, Birthday, Jubilee

My father, may he rest in peace, worked for many years in the garment industry. He worked hard, and there were times when he was without a job. I remember how happy we were as children when he found secure employment in a company that manufactured ladies' apparel, known as the "Jubilee Blouse Company."

I was very young at the time and had no notion of what "Jubilee" meant. All it meant to me then was that Daddy had a regular paycheck, was happy with the company and working conditions, and respected his boss, a Mr. David Zeiger, as a "real gentleman." Jubilee was a good thing.

All that was a long time ago and I have since come across the word "Jubilee" countless times. But I remained a bit confused about the real meaning of the word until I read a penetrating address given not long before the Holocaust by one of its most distinguished victims. Let me begin by telling you about my confusion and then I'll introduce you to the teachings of a great man.

The word "Jubilee" appears repeatedly in *Parashat Behar* (Lev. 25:1–26:2). For example:

> You shall count off…a total of forty-nine years. Then you shall sound the horn loud…you shall have the horn sounded throughout your land. And you shall hallow the fiftieth year. You shall proclaim liberty throughout the land for all its inhabitants. It shall be a Jubilee for you: each of you shall return to his holding and each of you shall return to his family. That fiftieth year shall be a Jubilee for you. For it is a Jubilee. It shall be holy to you. (Lev. 25:8–12)

Even the casual reader of this biblical text "gets it:" There is a fifty-year cycle in Judaism; that fiftieth year is called "Jubilee;" it is a year in which various observances apply; it is a holy year; and it is a year that celebrates freedom and liberty.

What does the word "Jubilee" itself mean? Not an easy question to answer and even the earliest commentators disputed its definition.

For Rashi, the word means a shofar, a ram's horn. It is a year of great sanctity and major significance, but it is named for one ritual act: namely, sounding of the shofar on the Yom Kippur of its inception.

Ibn Ezra, with his characteristic brevity, and Nahmanides, at greater length and in exquisite detail, disagree with Rashi. They concede that in some contexts, the Hebrew word for "Jubilee," *Yovel*, indeed refers to the shofar. However, they insist that in our text the word means "release," as Ibn Ezra believes; or as Nahmanides asserts, it means "to lead," perhaps "to guide," or "to cause to return." During that year, all are released from bondage and all lands in Israel are returned to their original owners. For these latter commentators, the year is named "Jubilee" because of the theme of freedom and not because of the sound of the shofar that heralds its beginning.

But why then is the term "Jubilee" regularly applied to birthdays of individuals and to anniversaries of social institutions? We have all received many more than a few invitations to the "Jubilee" celebrations from friends, alma maters, local hospitals, and even the municipalities in which we live.

I was privileged to learn a deeper definition of the term when I recently read a collection of the public addresses of a most unusual man – rabbi of the early twentieth century, chief rabbi of Bessarabia, member of the Romanian Parliament, and a victim of the first German bombardment of his home city in July, 1941. His name was Rabbi Yehudah Laib Tsirelson.

Several of these addresses carried titles such as "Upon the Jubilee of the Local Hospital," or "The Jubilee of the Free Loan Society." One is entitled "Upon the Jubilee of the Yeshiva of Kishinev."

Rabbi Tsirelson begins this latter speech by insisting that such gatherings may have been appropriate for the hospital or free loan society celebrations, but are not entirely appropriate for the yeshiva. He argued thus:

> Why do we celebrate anniversaries? We do so when, some years in the past, a group of people undertook an endeavor that entailed great risks and for which ultimate success was dubious. For example, we started a hospital but were never quite sure that it would be viable. Could we find the proper personnel? Would it be accredited by the anti-Semitic authorities? Would patients feel comfortable enrolling there?
>
> Or, we started a free loan society, but we were never certain that we could raise the requisite funds to meet the needs of all the poor in our community. If, after ten years or twenty years, these institutions still function – and function well, that's cause for celebration. Hence, a Jubilee celebration.
>
> But when one inaugurates a Torah institution, a yeshiva, there can be no doubt that it will succeed. We have God's own promise that the Torah is eternal. If a Torah institution lasts ten years or twenty or fifty, it is no wonder and no occasion for amazement or astonishment. Why, then, a celebration?
>
> The answer is that, whereas in the case of the hospital or the free loan society, we were celebrating the fact that those institutions persisted and endured, in the case of this, the seventy-fifth anniversary of our yeshiva, we are not celebrating the fact that the Torah persisted and endured. It will always endure. Rather,

we are celebrating a Jubilee in the true meaning of the term. We are celebrating the freedom and liberty, which Torah brings to the Jewish people, and to mankind. "Only he is truly free who occupies himself with Torah."

We are adhering to Nahmanides' understanding of "Jubilee" as a term that means leading, guiding, and causing us to return. Success of our local hospital and our great institutions of charity deserve anniversaries. Only our yeshiva, and other similar projects, deserve the term Jubilee.

Rabbi Tsirelson's teaching is one well worth taking to heart. The term "Jubilee," like so many other grandiloquent terms, is often cheapened by being applied to important, but basically mundane, occasions. It is best reserved for occasions celebratory of those achievements that guide us ethically, lead us spiritually, and return us to the divine goals of freedom and liberty.

As I read *Parashat Behar*, the warm memories that I associate with the Jubilee Blouse Company will surely still be there. But after a moment's reflection, I will also recall the powerful message of a great rabbi who, despite his eighty-one years, died before his time.

Parashat Behar

Bullying

Ⅰt is an old word, and it describes a behavior that has been around since the very beginning of history. Yet, the word seems to me to be used more and more frequently these days and the behavior it describes has gotten out of control.

The word is bullying, and it refers to a behavior that victimizes others, that abuses them physically, or more typically, verbally. The old adage "sticks and stones may break my bones but words will never harm me" is simply not true. Words do inflict pain upon others and often cause long lasting damage to them. Lately, we have read of more than one suicide that was the result of bullying.

Whenever the media focuses on some supposedly new phenomenon, I am contacted, usually by a reporter, sometimes by a constituent, with the question, "What does Judaism have to say about this?" During the past few years, as the public has become more concerned about bullying, I have heard that question many times.

The answer is a simple one. Judaism has a lot to say about bullying. One especially relevant source is in *Parashat Behar*: "Do not wrong one another" (Lev. 25:17). Rashi quotes the Talmud, which states emphatically that this refers to verbal abuse.

Rashi, following the Midrash, provides two interesting examples of how words can be used to abuse another. "One should not," writes Rashi, "tease or taunt another person, and one should not give inappropriate advice to others." The former is an obvious example of bullying, but the latter is a much more subtle example of the damage that words can cause. Misleading a person by giving him advice that does not fit his personal situation is, in the eyes of our sages, a form of bullying as well.

The Mishna and Talmud in Tractate Bava Metzia give numerous examples of verbal abuse, all of which provide insights into the definition of bullying that was adopted by our rabbinic sages. By analyzing these examples, we learn of some forms that verbal abuse takes:

1. One must not say to a repentant sinner, "Remember your former deeds." The person who speaks to a repentant sinner this way is guilty of cynicism. He is facing a spiritually motivated individual who sincerely wishes to change. But by confronting him with his past deeds, the penitent becomes discouraged and his idealistic commitment is thereby diminished, if not entirely eliminated.

2. One must not say to a sick person that his illness must be a punishment for his misdeeds. He who addresses a sick person in this manner is guilty of both pretentiousness and sanctimony. He dares to presume that he knows the workings of the divine system of reward and punishment, and, in addition, arrogantly proclaims the message, "I am holier than thou."

3. One should always be heedful of wronging his wife, for because of her sensitivity she is frequently brought to tears.

How aware our sages were of the fact that the likeliest targets of bullying are precisely the people who are closest to us. Sensitivity to others must begin with sensitivity to our spouses and family members.

It is apparent just from these examples that our sages were very familiar with the phenomenon of bullying in all of its diverse forms.

They knew that bullying takes many forms, including cynicism, arrogance, condescension, and disdain.

They were even aware of the prevalence of abuse within the spousal relationship. This is noteworthy because when I was receiving my graduate education in psychology, the topic of domestic violence was absent from our curriculum. It was much more recently that the gap in my professional education was filled, and the reality of the cruelty that pervades many families became the focus of my clinical work.

In the Book of Genesis, there is an example of emotional abuse within the context of a loving relationship. It is so shocking an example that I hesitate to mention it. When the barren Rachel bitterly bemoans her fate to her husband Jacob, he becomes angry with her and says, "Am I in place of God, who has denied you the fruit of the womb?" (Gen. 30:2) The rabbis in the Midrash disclose the Almighty's reaction to Jacob's retort, "Is this how one responds to a person in distress?" The Midrash is teaching us that even the patriarch Jacob was once guilty of a callousness that bordered upon emotional abuse and was held accountable for it.

There is a lesson we all should take to heart whenever we read about flagrant bullying. It is a lesson that must be learned whenever we encounter any prohibition in the Torah. That lesson is that we are all capable of bullying, and in fact, unless we guard against it, may engage in this practice much more often than we realize and certainly much more frequently than we admit to ourselves. When the Torah tells us, as it does in our *parasha*, that we are not to wrong another person by abusing him or her verbally, we must not think that this is addressed to some villain or scoundrel. Rather, it is a lesson directed to each and every one of us, and it is a lesson we must learn.

The Process of Sin

I
t is a word that one hears frequently these days in many contexts. The word is "process." It is a word that reflects our growing recognition that there are very few things in this world that occur in an instant, something out of nothing.

When one faces a complex set of circumstances, he is well advised to assume that these circumstances did not arise out of nowhere, but on the contrary, are the results of many prior events, some going back many years. Hence, we speak of the processes of nature, the historical process, the process of aging, and even the process of disease.

The concept of life as a process may be traced back to the Greek philosopher, Heraclitus, who pointed out that one does not step into the same river twice. Life, like the river, does not stand still, and no two moments in life are identical.

From a Jewish perspective, everything is in the process of change. Everything, that is, except God Himself, who is unchanging and eternal.

I first became aware of the philosophical importance of the notion of process in a course I took in graduate school on the great American philosophers of the nineteenth and early twentieth centuries. In that course, I was introduced to the thought of Alfred North Whitehead, who wrote a book entitled *Process and Reality*. Although I remember finding that book very difficult to read, I can still recall the instructor's helpful analogy of life as a flowing river that continuously carves out new paths. As an example, she showed us old maps of the Mississippi River, which demonstrated that it changed course many times over the centuries, but always had the same destination, the sea.

Much more recently, I attended a seminar in which a very prominent physician distinguished between those diseases that are the products of long-term processes of deterioration versus those diseases that are the result of sudden trauma with no previous pathology evident at all.

As this doctor made his point, a participant in the seminar rose to protest. He identified himself as a "process philosopher" who believed that even sudden traumatic events are part of a subtle ongoing process, which preceded them, rendering the individual susceptible to what appeared to be sudden trauma, but what was in reality only the inevitable outcome of a prior ongoing process. He insisted that even traumatic events, seemingly coming out of nowhere, are the culmination of a process.

Whereas this philosopher's contention is surely debatable, what is not debatable is that sin is part of a process. Sins are not merely isolated events in a person's life. This point has its roots in *Parashat Behar*. At the beginning of chapter 26, which appears near the end of the *parasha*, we read:

> You shall not make idols for yourselves, or set up for yourselves carved images or pillars, or place figured stones in your land to worship upon, for I am the Lord your God. You shall keep My Sabbaths and venerate my Sanctuary.

Rashi is puzzled by the placement of this particular simple verse. It follows the long and complex chapter 25, which discusses a great diversity of subjects: the sabbatical year; the transfer of merchandise and the sale of real property; laws of usury; the conditions that apply to a person who becomes destitute, who, when he has no other alternative, may even sell himself into slavery to another Jew.

Rashi responds, following a passage in the Talmud (Kiddushin 20a), that what we have in chapter 25 is a detailed account of a fundamental process of human nature, the process of sin.

Rashi tells us that sin typically proceeds in incremental fashion, from minor to major, from incidental and almost trivial infractions to a point where a person becomes trapped in a web of sin from which it is very difficult to extricate himself.

Thus, chapter 25 begins with the laws of the sabbatical year, alluding to a person who, in the interest of monetary gain, ignores those laws and does commerce with the fruits of that year. As punishment for this, his commercial plans are frustrated and he must sell his merchandise to raise cash. If he then persists in his sins, he finds himself forced to sell off his fields and then, still failing to repent, will become so desperate that he has to sell his very home. This process continues to spiral downward if he does not change his ways and he finds himself so strapped financially that he must borrow money under usurious terms.

Two parallel processes inexorably move forward: the process of deepening entrenchment in sin and the process of ever worsening financial conditions. But then, chapter 25 continues with even more disastrous consequences for this obdurate sinner, and with no other alternative, he is forced to sell himself into slavery to a fellow Jew. But in this condition, he still has hope, because the Torah here implores other Jews to come forward and redeem this poor fellow from his enslavement. However, continues Rashi, if the sinner still does not get the message of his need to change his sinful ways, help will not come forth. Thus concludes chapter 25, "For it is to Me that the Israelites are servants: they are My servants, whom I freed from the land of Egypt, I the Lord your God." And the Talmud comments, "They are to be My servants, and not the servants of other, human servants."

If such is the case and that stubborn sinner still doesn't "get it," we have the opening statement of chapter 26, to which we've already referred, "You shall not make idols for yourselves."

These words are addressed, Rashi tells us, to our stubborn sinner who, even when sold to fellow Jews, remains unrepentant. He then finds it necessary to sell himself to non-Jews, to other nations. And he therefore needs to be reminded that, even in an alien environment, he must remain faithful to his God.

He cannot say, "My master is immoral, why can't I be? My master is idolatrous, why not me? My master violates the Sabbath, why shouldn't I?" Even at the nadir of his process, he is encouraged to repent and is admonished, "You shall not make idols for yourself."

Sin is a process. Egregious sins have a history and are long preceded by minor, even trivial, infractions. That's the bad news. The good news is that repentance is also a process. When one commits to change his ways, he need not be discouraged by the enormity of the task ahead. He need merely proceed, step by small step, in the right direction.

The process of return (*teshuva*), requires just a "re-turn," a small change in behavior. How encouraging are God's words, as phrased by our sages, "Open for Me an opening the size of the eye of a needle, and I will open for you an opening as large as the door of a great Temple."

Walking the Walk

It is good for the body and good for the soul. It helps one lose weight, provides time for contemplation, is a favorite leisure activity, it can be entertaining – even edifying – and it costs nothing. In fact, there is no down side to it at all. It is the act of walking, or more colloquially, "taking a walk."

Walking is a universal human activity. It is a means of getting from one place to another, obviously. But it is more than that. It is so much a part of the essence of the human that when the Mishna refers to the human species, it uses the phrase "those who walk on two legs (*mehalkhei shtayim*)." Humans are almost unique in that they walk on two legs so that walking is part of our core identity.

The value of walking was brought home to me once when my physician, who had been preaching the need for exercise to me for years, finally gave up on formal exercise routines and the use of various gadgets and machines for physical fitness, and just prescribed two daily walks, at any pace, each at least twenty minutes in duration.

I have experienced further value in walking as the best means to really get to know a new city. In our travels, my wife and I have become familiar with cities as disparate as Paris and Prague and Montreal and Moscow by purchasing guidebooks of walking tours and ambling along main roads and side streets. When we returned to New York City after many years living elsewhere, we renewed our acquaintance and our love for the city by taking frequent walks all over town. And of course, walking the streets of Jerusalem is not only a profoundly emotional experience, but we are told that every four cubits that one walks there is equivalent to one mitzva.

I know of many examples of famous walks and walkers in mythology, world literature, and history. Jewish tradition knows of many examples of great sages who were fond of walking, and they range from Rabbi Akiva and his colleagues who walked among the ruins of the Temple in Jerusalem, to the Hazon Ish (Rabbi Avraham Yeshaya Karelitz, the twentieth-century rabbinic scholar), who took daily walks around the sand dunes outside of Benei Brak for health-related reasons and also to experience moments of solitude and inspiration.

I vividly remember being transfixed by Rabbi Joseph B. Soloveitchik's description of the walks he took during his one visit to the Land of Israel, when he walked about at night and gazed at the star-filled heavens above the Holy Land.

It is fascinating to note that even the Almighty Himself is described as enjoying a daily walk, so to speak. "They [Adam and Eve] heard the sound of the Lord God walking about in the garden at the breezy time of day" (Gen. 3:8).

It is no wonder then that *Parashat Behukkotai* begins with the phrase, "If you walk with My statutes and observe My commandments" (Lev. 26:3). Granted, many translations have it written otherwise, "If you follow My statutes," or, "If you obey My statutes." But the literal meaning of the Hebrew text is definitely, "If you *walk* with My statutes." Clearly, the Torah prefers the verb "walk" because of all of its implications. Walking is an exquisitely spiritual activity and walking in God's ways is the ultimate way to serve Him.

The body of commentary known as Midrash is a vast compilation of rabbinic exegesis of the Bible over many centuries. The largest single collection of such exegesis is known as Midrash Rabba. For much of my life, I have tried to at least sample a bit of that work every week, ever since my grandfather gave me a small pocket-size version of that work for my bar mitzva. Thus, I discovered the opening passage of this week's midrashic commentary long ago, and I reflect upon it frequently.

It reads, "If you walk in My statutes." This bears on the text, "I have considered my ways, and have turned my steps to Your decrees." (Ps. 119:59). King David said, "Sovereign of the universe! Every day I would plan and decide upon taking a walk to a particular place or dwelling-house, but my feet always brought me to synagogues and houses of study.... Hence it is written, 'and have turned my steps to Your decrees.'"

King David too was fond of walking. At the simplest level, this midrash means that although David often set out for other destinations, somehow he always ended up in sacred places. Others see deeper meanings in this passage. My own way of looking at it is that even when David set out for mundane and ordinary places, he somehow found God's spirit wherever he went. He realized that even ordinary places and plain dwellings can be as charged with the Divine Presence as the synagogue and study hall.

In our own journeys, be they brief strolls around the neighborhood or journeys of life, we have our preconceived destinations. But it is amazing how often we reach unanticipated final destinations. Fortunate are those who set out for worldly objectives and discover themselves, unintentionally and often against their will, in synagogues and study halls. Even more fortunate are those who reach secular or even profane destinations and are able to bestow upon them a spiritual significance equal to the synagogue and study hall.

Interestingly, it is not only in contrast to the animal world that we are called "*mehalkhei shtayim*," but our ability to walk is what distinguishes us from the angels as well. "And I have given to you the ability to walk among those that merely stand" (Zech. 3:7). Angels only stand. They do not walk. They neither change nor grow. Humans are walkers. They never stay still, but are constantly moving – hopefully ever higher, ever nobler, and ever holier.

The Walking Tour

I am the type of person who has always believed that the only way to learn about something important is to buy a book about it. For example, it has been my good fortune to have traveled widely in my life and to have visited many interesting cities. Invariably, I bought guidebooks before each such visit with detailed itineraries describing the "not to be missed" sites in those cities.

Eventually, I learned that there is a much better way to come to know a new city than to read a book about it. It is more interesting, more entertaining, and more inspiring to simply walk aimlessly around the city. I have even stopped buying those books that provide maps of walking tours around the city. Instead I just wander, and have never been disappointed in the process.

The list of cities I have aimlessly explored has grown quite long over the years. It includes my own native New York, the holy city of Jerusalem, numerous cities in the United States, and several in Europe, such as London, Rome, and Prague.

Despite the diversity of these cities, I inevitably end up in one of two destinations: either a used bookstore or a small park, usually one in which children are playing.

The last time I had this experience, I was quite taken aback and muttered to myself, "I guess my feet take me where my heart wants me to go."

As soon as those words occurred to me, I realized that they were not my own words at all. Rather, I was preceded in that reaction by two very glorious figures in Jewish history: the great sage Hillel and no one less than King David. That brings us to *Parashat Beḥukkotai* (Lev. 26:3–27:34).

The *parasha* begins, "If you follow My laws and faithfully observe My commandments, I will grant your rains in their season." That is the standard translation of this opening verse. But a more literal translation would begin not, "If you follow My laws," but rather, "If you walk with My statutes." Most translators understandably choose the word "follow" over the literal "walk" in this context.

But the Midrash takes a different approach. It retains the literal "walk," and links it to the phrase in Psalms 119:59, which reads, "I have considered my ways, and have turned my steps to Your decrees." After linking the verse in our *parasha* with this verse from Psalms, the Midrash continues, putting these words into the mouth of King David:

> Master of the universe, each and every day I would decide to go to such and such a place, or to such and such a dwelling, but my feet would bring me to synagogues and study halls, as it is written: "I have turned my steps to Your decrees."

Long before this midrash was composed, but long after the life of King David, the rabbinic sage Hillel is recorded by the Talmud to have said, "To the place I love, that is where my feet guide me" (Sukka 53a).

The lesson is clear. Our unconscious knows our authentic inner preferences very well, so much so that no matter what our conscious plans are, our feet take us to where we really want to be. To take myself as an example, I may have told myself when I visited some new city that

I wanted to see its ancient ruins, its museums, its palaces, and Houses of Parliament. But my inner self knew better and instructed my feet to direct me to the musty old bookstores where I could browse to my heart's content, or to off-the-beaten-paths, leafy parks where I could observe children at play.

This midrash understands the opening phrase of our *parasha*, "If you walk with My statutes," as indicating the Torah's desire that we internalize God's laws thoroughly so that they become our major purpose in life. Even if we initially define our life's journey in terms of very different goals, God's laws will hopefully become our ultimate destination.

There are numerous other ways suggested by commentaries throughout the ages to understand the literal phrase, "If you walk in my ways." Indeed, Rabbi Chaim ibn Atar, the great eighteenth-century author of *Ohr HaHaim*, enumerates no fewer than forty-two explanations of the phrase.

Several of his explanations, while not identical to that of our midrash, are consistent with it and help us understand it more deeply. For example, he suggests that by using the verb "walk," the Torah is suggesting to us that it is sometimes important in religious life to leave one's familiar environment. One must "walk," embark on a journey to some distant place, in order to fully realize his or her religious mission. It is hard to be innovative, it is hard to change, in the presence of people who have known us all of our lives.

Ohr HaHaim also leaves us with the following profound insight, which the author bases upon a passage in the sourcebook of the Kabbala, the Zohar:

> Animals do not change their nature. They are not "walkers." But humans are "walkers." We are always changing our habits, "walking away" from base conduct to noble conduct, and from lower levels of behavior to higher ones. "Walking," progressing, is our very essence. "Walking" distinguishes us from the rest of God's creatures.

The phrase "to walk" is thus a powerful metaphor for who we are. No wonder then that this final portion of the Book of Leviticus begins with such a choice of words. All of life is a journey, and despite our intentions, we somehow arrive at *Beḥukkotai*, "My laws," so that we end our journey through this third book of the Bible with these words, "These are the commandments that the Lord gave Moses for the people of Israel on Mount Sinai."

Parashat Beḥukkotai

The Work-Study Program

Ithas been quite a long time now since I first heard the term "work-study program." This was a special federal program designed to assist young adults with limited financial means to achieve a professional education. Recipients of this grant were encouraged to continue with their jobs, to work, but were also paid to enroll in college-level training courses, to study. Hence the term "work-study program."

There was something about this term that struck me as odd. It seemed to make a distinction between work and study. It conveyed, to me at least, the notion that study was not work. To someone who had been trained in the yeshiva system, this notion was unacceptable. Study is work!

In *Parashat Beḥukkotai*, we come across the following phrase, "If you walk with My statutes" (Lev. 26:3). Rashi explains what it means to "walk" in the ways of God's statutes. He suggests that "walking" here means that we must "toil in the Torah (*shetihyu ameilim baTorah*)."

The concept of "toiling in the Torah" is a basic one to anyone familiar with Torah study, but those less familiar with the subject can legitimately be puzzled by the phrase. They surely can understand learning Torah, or studying Torah, or comprehending Torah. But what does it mean to "toil" in the Torah?

My life-long interest in educational psychology has prompted me to analyze the process of "Torah-toil" and break it down into several components, or stages.

The first stage consists of diligence, or what is known in Hebrew as *hatmada*. This is a requirement of putting in time. Torah study cannot be done on a piecemeal basis, in small segments of five or ten minutes. It requires sustained concentration and long hours of simply sitting and poring over the text. The ideal Torah student is constantly studying. His is the image portrayed by the great poet Hayim Nahman Bialik in his masterpiece, *HaMatmid*. There he describes the night and day devotion of the young man to his studying task in moving and inspiring terms. For Bialik, himself once a yeshiva student, the *matmid* is the true hero of Jewish history.

The second stage is that of struggle, of encountering the text and figuring out its basic meaning. This is difficult even to the student whose first language is Hebrew, and is even more challenging to those of us who grew up speaking English or another language, and who come to the texts at a disadvantage.

There are skills that must be mastered in order to decipher the give and take of the Talmud and its commentaries. Simple meaning, punctuation, knowing where questions end and answers begin, understanding implicit assumptions, appreciating nuance – these are all aspects of this second stage, of wrestling with the text.

In recent times, aids to Torah study have proliferated. Translations, elucidations, and abbreviations make the process much more user-friendly. Sometimes, however, in my opinion, these valuable tools come at the cost of the kind of mastery, which can only emerge from intense efforts and cannot be achieved through shortcuts.

And here we come to a third stage of Torah study: learning from one's mistakes. The Talmud itself maintains that "a person can only study Torah successfully if he makes errors in the process (*ela im ken nikhshal ba*)." All Torah students make mistakes in the initial phases of study sessions. They, or their study partners, soon detect these errors and correct them. Then real learning occurs.

In the fourth stage of this toil, the student probes and questions. He searches his memory for passages that might contradict the text at hand. He wonders about the underlying assumptions of what he has just read and how they fit with principles from other sections of the Torah with which he is familiar. He consults the numerous supercommentaries to see whether his questions were anticipated by previous Torah students, perhaps centuries ago. This is stage four.

A fifth stage, omitted by some, but essential in my personal opinion, is the search for relevance. "What personal meaning," the student must ask, "can I find in the text I have just mastered? How can it be applied to current events, to contemporary problems, or maybe even to my own life experience and personal dilemmas?"

And finally, we come to a sixth stage: teaching others. Maimonides, in his *Treatise on the Mitzvot*, asserts that one has not fulfilled the mitzva of Torah study unless he shares his learning with others: *Lilmod*, to study, *ulelamed*, to teach.

How well I recall the process demanded of us by my favorite teacher, Reb Shmuel Dovid, who had each of us explain aloud every passage we learned to the rest of the class until our peers felt that we had explained it well. "If you can't explain something," he insisted, "then you don't understand it."

I have shared with you my own personal analysis of the many ingredients of effortful Torah study. Others have offered different analyses to be sure. But I hope that my highly personal perspective has helped clarify the idea of "toiling in the Torah" to you. The fact that the Torah involves so much effort, such intense and diverse tasks, helps us understand why true Torah greatness (*gadlut*) is so rare and so appreciated.

We also understand why the reward for such toil is "rain in its season, a land of bountiful crops, and trees of the field that yield their fruit" (Lev. 26:4).

Numbers

You Too Can Be a Levite

T he world is indeed a stage and we all play many roles in our lives. Some of these roles are assigned to us, leaving us with little choice but to fill them. Other roles, however, are freely chosen.

For example, we are all born as children to parents. As such, we have ethical and religious responsibilities toward them. We are in the roles of children, often for much of our lives, whether we like that role or not. On the other hand, there are other roles that we seek out intentionally and often with great effort. For example, our professional roles as doctors or lawyers or teachers are roles we chose freely and that we work toward diligently.

Sociologists thus distinguish between ascribed roles and achieved roles. The former are those assigned to us by society or circumstance. The latter are the ones we choose and for which we hope to qualify.

In *Parashat Bemidbar*, we read of the roles ascribed to the Levite. Persons born to the tribe of Levi were assigned certain privileges and certain responsibilities at birth. There were no special qualifications to be met and no titles or certificates to be earned.

One who was not born into the tribe of Levi could not attain any of those privileges no matter how hard he tried. Nor could he assume the responsibilities of the Levite even if he sought to do so with commitment and fervor.

The Torah outlines the special duties of the Levites at length and in great detail in our *parasha* (Num. 3, 4). Later on in the Book of Numbers, particularly in chapter 18, we read of the benefits due to them.

The twelve other tribes of Israel are not neglected in this *parasha*. Quite the contrary; they are listed, and their stations in the wilderness encampment and march are delineated very specifically. But the roles of the tens of thousands of members of these tribes are not specified at all. It is almost as if the Torah was telling us that, unlike the Levites, they had no ascribed roles, but were to pursue and achieve roles according to their individual motivations, ambitions, and personal predilections.

Thus, the community of Israelites in the wilderness was one in which one tribe had predetermined tasks, which it did not choose and could not shirk, whereas the great majority of people had great freedom of choice as to which roles in life to choose. This situation continued for many centuries, at least until the destruction of the second Temple. Even today, specialized roles for the descendants of Levi persist, albeit in a reduced and limited way.

Maimonides, however, offers an entirely different vision of the matter. He offers us an innovative idea, which opens up the ascribed and predetermined roles of the Levite to everyone.

In his masterwork *Mishneh Torah* (*Hilkhot Shemitta VeYovel* chapter 13), Maimonides describes the lot of the Levite in rich and graphic detail. He stresses that although the Levites had no equal portion in the Land of Israel, they did have their own towns and villages there. He even offers his personal opinion that, should the Jewish people come to possess land outside the perimeters of biblical Israel, the Levites will share equally in those lands.

He explains to us that the Levite is ascribed a limited social and economic role in order that he be freed to assume a greater spiritual role. It is incumbent upon him to serve God in the Temple service and to teach God's laws to the greater community.

Maimonides then makes an original, dramatic, and often quoted statement, which challenges the entire distinction of ascribed versus achieved roles. He writes:

> It is not only the tribe of Levi, but rather every individual in the entire world, who, if the spirit moves him to have achieved understanding, and who wishes to separate himself from others and to stand before God and worship Him, to shed from his neck the yoke of everyday concerns, and to become imbued with extreme sanctity so that God becomes his lot and inheritance forever and ever.

Maimonides, as it were, opens up the closed society of the Levites. He offers a vision, and notes that it is a vision for all humanity, of the possibility to transcend the limits defined in our *parasha*. He suggests that each of us can potentially become a Levite, even if we are born to parents of other tribes.

What is strictly speaking an ascribed role becomes for Maimonides a role that can be achieved by anyone. This is a drastic, almost revolutionary, statement, but it is one that challenges every one of us and offers each of us an opportunity. It is not only the biblical Levite who can attain closeness to God and spiritual sublimity. We all can. But to do so, we need the motivation to assume greater responsibility, to suffer solitude, to be absolutely just and righteous, and to teach others who might not wish to be taught. Then we all can achieve the benefits that were the due of the ancient tribe of Levi.

We can then each say, as Maimonides concludes, quoting King David in Psalms, "God, You are my portion and cup. You uphold my destiny!"

Parashat Bemidbar

My Teacher, My Father

I t was November, 1938. Dark clouds were gathering over all of Europe and particularly over the Jewish communities in countries like Poland and Lithuania. Although few foresaw the horrific extent of the Holocaust that lay ahead, everyone knew that those communities were in very grave danger.

One man, a teacher and leader of those communities, found himself in the United States at that auspicious moment. He was preparing to return to his responsibilities back home in Eastern Europe, particularly to return to his students at the yeshiva he led there.

His friends and supporters in the United States pleaded with him not to return. I personally was privileged to know one of those friends, Mr. Charles Fogel, who implored this leader to remain in the safety of the US. He steadfastly refused. "I belong with my *talmidim*, with my disciples in the yeshiva," he insisted.

This leader's name was Rabbi Elchonon Wasserman, himself the foremost disciple of the Ḥafetz Ḥaim, the great sage of pre-World War II Europe. Rav Elchonon, as he was known to his many followers, already had many accomplishments to his credit, including several major published works and commentaries on the Talmud. But Rav Elchonon's core pride and joy was the yeshiva he created for early teenage youngsters, preparatory to their going on to higher institutes of Jewish learning. The yeshiva was known by the name of the town in which it was located, Baranovitch.

Rav Elchonon insisted upon leaving the safe haven in which he then found himself in order to return to that yeshiva and to those youngsters. He said, "I am their father, and they are my children. A father does not abandon his children."

What was the source of Rav Elchonon's strong feelings? He had children of his own, some of whom were lost in the Holocaust, and some of whom survived to become teachers and leaders of a future generation. Why was he convinced that the students of his yeshiva were no less children of his than the ones who were his real offspring?

The answer to these questions is to be found in *Parashat Bemidbar*. "These are the offspring of Aaron and Moses at the time that the Lord spoke to Moses on Mount Sinai" (Num. 3:1). A simple verse indeed – so much so that you, my careful reader, might wonder what homiletic spin can be given to so straightforward a verse.

It is here where the words of an even more vigilant reader are so insightful. That reader, of course, is none other than Rashi, who notes that although our verse promises to list the offspring of both Aaron and Moses, only Aaron's offspring are enumerated. Peruse the rest of the chapter as scrupulously as you wish and you will find no mention of the descendants of Moses.

Rashi's answer is deep and powerful: Moses taught Torah to the descendants of Aaron. That made them his descendants, no less than the descendants of their biological ancestor, Aaron. In Rashi's own words, "He who teaches Torah to his friend's child is considered by Scripture to be a parent of that child."

Rav Elchonon took those words to heart and he felt for his distant students, threatened by Hitler's clutches, what a father would feel for his children. Remaining behind in a secure sanctuary while his children were in mortal danger was inconceivable to him and completely out of the question. And so, he returned to Europe and met his ultimate fate in the Kovno ghetto at the hands of the Nazi murderers.

As powerful as this story is, there is a footnote that I was personally privileged to hear from one of those students, my own special teacher, my rebbe, who survived the Holocaust and eventually did make his way to the United States. His name was Rav Shmuel Dovid Warshavshik, of blessed memory.

When the story of Rav Elchonon's heroism was told, my rebbe would tell us that as magnificent as that heroism was, it was only part of the story. The rest of the story, Rav Shmuel Dovid would say, was that "we, teenage boys who were stuck alone in Baranovitch, knew that he would return. We were absolutely certain that he would not abandon us and that he would risk his life to rejoin us. We knew he considered himself a father and we felt that way toward him. We were his children."

This is the secret of a great teacher. This is the root of all authentic pedagogy: the ability to instill in one's students the sense that they are cared for by the teacher no less than children are cared for by their parents. Students who are confident in their teacher's concern for their well-being are capable of the kind of learning that typified the students of those yeshivas of old.

It is a rare teacher who has that gift. Rav Elchonon was one of them. But Rashi assures us that, at least to some extent, "all who teach another person's child Torah" have the gift of becoming a teacher-parent.

I close this story, and this teaching from our *parasha*, with a reflection on what might seem to be a different topic entirely, the topic of resilience. There is much being written in the contemporary psychological literature about what makes for resilience in people. Why is it that some individuals can endure great trauma, while others fall apart under less severe stress?

One of the surprising findings is that individuals who grow up to be resilient persons were childhood beneficiaries of people in their lives who were not necessarily their parents or close relatives, but rather, mentors or random acquaintances who, even for brief periods, showed them sincere concern and gave them well-intentioned encouragement.

The students of men like Rav Elchonon, and I speak of those who survived the Holocaust, were men of great resilience. The ones whom I have been able to interview attribute that resilience to their master and to the sense of his making them feel special.

Few of us, perhaps none of us, are capable of the heroism and sensitivity of Rav Elchonon. But all of us are capable of occasionally approaching a young person in our synagogue or community and giving him or her words of sincere encouragement. You never know. You may be contributing to that young person's eventual resilience to the challenges of his or her future.

Parents must be teachers. Teachers can be parents. We all can be teachers.

The Wilderness First

My first exposure to the study of the Bible was in the Yiddish language. We spoke only English at home, but almost all the teachers we had in the yeshiva I attended were Holocaust survivors who had escaped to the safety of these shores only a few years prior.

I must admit that we learned to translate into Yiddish by rote and had little conception about what the words meant in English. Thus, we translated the very first verse of the Torah as "*In der anfang hatte der Oibeshter bashaffen*," not having a clue that "*In der anfang*" meant "in the beginning," that the "*Oibeshter*" was "the One Above," and that "*bashaffen*" meant "created."

When we reached the Book of Numbers (*Sefer Bemidbar*), we finally had a teacher who, although he continued to provide the Yiddish translation, told us in his broken English what the words meant in the language we understood. And he would even provide visual aids, photographs, and drawings, which would help us truly grasp the meaning of what we were studying.

I'll never forget his opening lesson. He told us that we were beginning a new book of the Torah, and a new weekly Torah portion, and that both went by the name *Bemidbar*. "In Yiddish," he said, "the word means '*in der veesternisht.*'" We were all about nine years old, and the word "*veesternisht*" triggered a giggle, which soon morphed into hilarious laughter. There is something about the sound of the word that is comical to me to this very day.

He waited for our laughter to subside, and then said that "*veesternisht*" in English meant "a desert," and he showed us a picture of the Saharan desert. "The Jewish people were wandering through such a desert," he explained, "and the entire book that we are beginning to study took place there."

He then asked us if we remembered coming across the word "*veesternisht*" earlier in our studies, in a slightly abbreviated form. It was my dear friend Michael, who passed away some years ago, who remembered that first verse in Genesis that contains the phrase "*tohu vavohu,*" which is generally translated as "unformed and void." In Yiddish, the phrase is rendered as "*poost und vest* (empty and desolate)."

Parashat Bemidbar (Num. 1:1–4:20) is the Torah portion that is always read on the Shabbat before Shavuot. I researched about a dozen biblical translations, including some non-Jewish ones, and found that only a few translated "*Bemidbar*" as "in the desert." The vast majority preferred the word "wilderness" to "desert," so that the key phrase in the first verse of our *parasha* reads, "The Lord spoke to Moses in the wilderness of Sinai."

Although the dictionaries I consulted did not distinguish sharply between "desert" and "wilderness," it is the latter that rings true as the English equivalent of the Yiddish "*veesternisht,*" an empty, confusing, and frightening wasteland. It was in that wasteland that our ancestors wandered for forty years and it was in that wasteland that we received the Torah.

Why? Why was the Torah given in this wild and chaotic terrain? Like most questions of this sort, numerous answers have been given over the ages. I would like to share with you an answer that makes great sense to me.

If one reads further than just the first verse of our *parasha*, one discovers that, although the image we have of the wilderness is one of disorder and confusion, the narrative theme of these several opening chapters is one of order and systematic organization. The tribes are divided into twelve distinct units, each one is assigned its own unique flag or banner, and its place in the procession through the wilderness is precisely specified. The entire *parasha* can be summarized as "making order in the midst of chaos."

It strikes me that the ability to organize one's environment in a beneficial and orderly manner is a basic human skill that every society must first possess before it can proceed toward greater cultural achievement. Understanding this, we can appreciate that, before the Torah could be given to the Jewish people, there was a necessary prerequisite: the establishment of a functional society in which people could get along with each other in a peaceful and productive manner. Only in such a context could the Torah be properly absorbed.

There is an ancient saying that states this idea unequivocally: "*Derekh eretz kadma laTorah*," literally translated as, "The way of the world precedes Torah" (Leviticus Rabba 9:3). More generally, it means, first one must have an ethical, just, and humane society. Only then can one proceed to Torah.

We can classify this *parasha* as the *parasha* of *derekh eretz*, because in it a nation successfully copes with the trials and tribulations of its environment. It tamed a wilderness by creating a civilization. It dealt with a wasteland by establishing a functioning and equitable society.

That is why it is precisely this *parasha* that precedes Shavuot. Shavuot is the anniversary of *Matan Torah*, of the divine revelation, the giving of the Torah. The Almighty does not reveal Himself to a people who cannot get along with each other in an orderly and civilized manner. He does not express His will to individuals, communities, or nations who, in today's jargon, "can't get their act together."

He does not give His Torah in a wilderness, in a wasteland, in a "*veesternisht.*" He expects us to first act toward each other with *derekh eretz*, respectfully and courteously. He demands that we first tame that wilderness and cultivate that wasteland. Only then are we deserving of His great gift.

Derekh eretz kadma laTorah. Humane behavior first and only afterwards the Torah. That's how it was that very first time in the wilderness of Sinai and that's how it must be when *Parashat Bemidbar* immediately precedes the festival of *Matan Torah*.

Sanctity and Sanctimony

W e are all full of contradictions. There is a part of us that is noble, kind, and generous, but there is another part that is selfish and stingy, and which can even be cruel.

That is the way we were created. We have the potential for good, yet it is matched with our potential for evil. At different times in our lives and in different circumstances throughout our lives, one part or the other dominates.

What is especially fascinating is that often, we are both good and evil, kind and cruel, at the same time. It is no wonder then that we know so many people who can best be described in paradoxical terms: the wounded healer, the generous miser, the sinful saint, the foolish sage, and the righteous knave.

In *Parashat Naso*, we meet an individual who displays both negative and positive qualities in the very same role. I speak of the Nazirite (*Nazir*), the man or woman who vows to adopt an ascetic lifestyle, a lifestyle of abstention from wine and anything connected to wine, and who commits to never shaving or taking a haircut, or to coming into contact with the dead, even at the funerals of his or her own parents or siblings.

The very word *nazir* means to withdraw, to remove oneself from others and from worldly pleasures. The Torah describes such a person, over and over again, as holy. "He shall be holy.... He is holy unto the Lord" (Num. 6:5, 6:8).

Yet, should the Nazirite inadvertently come into contact with the dead, then he is to offer a specified set of sacrifices. And these sacrifices are to "make atonement for him, for he sinned *al hanefesh*, by reason of the soul" (Num. 6:11).

What does it mean to "sin by reason of the soul"? The simple meaning is that the "soul" here refers to the soul of the dead body with whom he accidentally came into contact. So he needs atonement for his chance exposure to a corpse.

There is another opinion in the Talmud that says that "soul" here refers to the Nazirite's own soul, and that somehow, in renouncing the pleasures of life, he has sinned against his very own soul. In the words of Dr. Joseph H. Hertz, whose commentary on the Bible has become, regrettably in my opinion, less popular than it once was, "he was ordered to make atonement for his vow to abstain from drinking wine, an unnecessary self-denial in regard to one of the permitted pleasures of life."

The Torah recognizes the inner contradiction of the Nazirite's lifestyle. On the one hand, it is a lifestyle of holiness, and that is to be commended. But on the other hand, it is an act of renunciation of the pleasures of God's world, and as such it expresses ingratitude, perhaps unacceptably extreme piety.

I find myself frequently reflecting upon this talmudic view and its implications. For we often encounter in our religious worlds individuals who are in many ways paragons of spiritual virtue, but who at the same time radiate an attitude of condescension to others of lesser spiritual attainments. We have all met people who are outwardly very religious, and perhaps even inwardly and sincerely so, but who seemed to be saying to us, "I am holier than thou." And we have all felt belittled, sometimes insulted, but invariably put off by such individuals.

There is a word in English, although I have never been able to find a precise Hebrew equivalent, which describes such behavior. That word is "sanctimonious." Webster's dictionary defines "sanctimonious" as "pretending to be very holy or pious; affecting righteousness."

Whereas this dictionary definition seems to stress the fraudulent or insincere quality of the sanctimonious individual, I have often found that these individuals are quite sincere in their own inner conscience, but along with their righteousness is an attitude of "holier than thou."

I do not want to end this chapter by simply pointing out the self-righteous behavior that we experience in others. I think that we are all sometimes guilty of sanctimony and need to be on guard against it.

Religious people need to be very careful not to send the message, "I am holier than thou." We have to be careful that our acts of piety are sincere, that's for certain. But we also have to be cautious that those acts are not viewed by others as statements of spiritual superiority. The religious person must always be on guard against hypocrisy and must always be sensitive to the reactions he or she provokes in others. If those reactions are of respect and admiration, then we have made a *kiddush Hashem*, thereby advancing the cause of our faith. But if others are made to feel inferior by our airs of religious observance, then not only have we lost them to our faith, but we have fostered a *hillul Hashem*, causing others to look negatively upon the religion they represent.

I encourage the reader to find a Hebrew equivalent for the word "sanctimony." But even if such a word cannot be found, I urge all observant Jews to avoid sanctimonious behavior.

Parashat Naso

Can *Ḥen* Mean Charisma?

I once loved the word. I first heard it when I was introduced to the thought of German sociologist Max Weber. He differentiated between several types of leaders, one of whom had neither specialized expertise nor royal birth, but whose authority rested on the devotion instilled in his followers by the force of his personality. He termed that force of personality "charisma," and he wrote eloquently of the power of charisma and of the great danger charismatic leaders posed to society.

Ever since then, I have been fascinated by this quality of charisma and have studied the lives of charismatic leaders. In the Bible, Abraham and King David clearly had charisma; Isaac and King Saul, much less so. Closer to our day, both Churchill and Hitler had it, proving that it can equally be used for good and for evil. Harry Truman and Hubert Humphrey, two politicians I admired back in high school, did not have it. And Jack Kennedy had it in spades!

What is charisma? Dictionary definitions include "a rare personal quality attributed to leaders who arouse popular devotion," or more simply, "personal magnetism or charm." The word also has a religious connotation, because it stems from the Greek word *kharisma* (divine favor), so that in Christianity, it specifically refers to the "ability to perform miracles, granted by the Holy Spirit."

In *Parashat Naso*, we come across a word that, I will argue, can well be translated as "charisma." That word is *ḥen*, spelled *ḥet-nun*, and it appears in the second verse of the well-known Priestly Blessing, which reads, "May the Lord make His face shine upon you, and be gracious to you" (Num. 6:25).

That last phrase, which is the typical translation of *viḥuneka*, is not favored by Rashi. Rather, he renders it, "and He shall grant you *ḥen*" – the quality of grace, of charm, and as I maintain, of charisma.

Charisma, in the sense of grace, is mentioned elsewhere in the Torah as a divine gift. In Exodus 33:19, we come across a somewhat mysterious passage in which God says, "I will bestow *ḥen* upon whomever I bestow *ḥen*." It is almost as if He, somewhat arbitrarily from our human perspective, gives the gift of grace, charm, or charisma to whomever He chooses to give it. This is certainly the implication of the verse, "And Noah found *ḥen* in the eyes of the Lord" (Gen. 6:8).

We have all encountered individuals in our own lives who seem to have been blessed with the gift of *ḥen*/charisma. In every high school class, and certainly in my own, there was one fellow who had it. He was the most popular among his peers, excelled academically, and usually had great athletic prowess as well. He was the one chosen by his classmates as "most likely to succeed."

But is *ḥen* always a blessing? Is charisma always a virtue? Apparently not, for already in Scripture, we find it referred to in negative terms. "*Ḥen* is deceptive (*sheker haḥen*), and beauty is illusory," reads the verse in Proverbs 31:30, a verse we melodiously recite at the Sabbath table every Friday evening.

When I think back to the charismatic youngsters of my high school class and the one preceding it, I cannot help but reflect on their ultimate destinies. One struggled with alcoholism all of his adult life, constantly frustrated because he felt he was not living up to his potential. He died the premature death of a derelict on a New York City skid row. The other settled into a mediocre bureaucratic career, neurotically fearful to use his very real talents lest he be outshone by others.

What is more, the gift of charisma is often abused. Tyrants too numerous to mention have used their charisma for supreme evil. Adolf Hitler is but the most obvious case in point.

Religious leaders as well have all too frequently used their charismatic qualities for fiendish ends. The list of gurus and clergymen who have been guilty of perverse treatment of their followers, or even their own children, is a shamefully long one. Sadly, it includes spiritual leaders in our own community who have abused their devotees and disciples in vile manners.

The Talmud knows of a different kind of charisma entirely, one that is more common and may even be considered the force that makes for cohesive relationships and societies. Substitute the word "charisma" or "charm" for the word "*ḥen*" in this talmudic passage:

> Rabbi Yoḥanan said:
> There are three kinds of *ḥen*:
> The *ḥen* a city has for those who dwell in it;
> The *ḥen* a wife has in the eyes of her husband;
> The *ḥen* an object holds for him who purchased it. (Sota 47a)

Although I was born and bred in Brooklyn, I have lived most of my life in the city of Baltimore. It has charisma, enough so that for me it merits its claim to be "Charm City." My wife radiates charisma to me – as I hope your spouse does to you, dear reader – in the sense of charm, dignity, and grace. And who does not recall fondly that old "lemon" of an automobile that he or she purchased way back when? We react to the image of that jalopy with nostalgic and sentimental memories of its charm and charisma.

So the next time you hear the blessing, "May the Lord shine His face upon you and grant you *ḥen*," think of the kind of charisma you personally hope for, and make sure that if you get it, you use it for a blessed purpose.

The Mood of the Priestly Blessing

I am sure that you have a most favorite activity. I know that I do. I am also sure that you have a least favorite activity, as I do.

My most favorite activity is visiting Israel. One of the experiences I especially cherish during my visits to Israel is the opportunity to hear the Priestly Blessing every single day. Outside the Land of Israel, the custom has developed, at least in Ashkenazic communities, to dispense with the daily ritual of hearing the priests (*kohanim*) bless the people by reciting the verses contained in *Parashat Naso*:

> May the Lord bless you and protect you!
> May the Lord make His face shine upon you, and be gracious to you!
> May the Lord turn His face toward you and grant you peace!
> (Num. 6:24–26)

In Israel, however, everyone has the opportunity to hear those blessings from the mouths of the *kohanim* every day of the week, all year long. That experience is my favorite of favorites.

I also have a least favorite activity, and that is dealing with complaints on the telephone, or these days, via e-mail. Sympathetic friends are quick to tell me that dealing with complaints is a rabbi's job. That's probably true, because even Moses, the first rabbi, had to listen to more than his share of complaints. But there's one type of complaint that I have never been able to deal with without becoming angry. I refer to those occasions when the complainer is judgmental and finds fault in another.

Not long ago, I received such a call with reference to, of all things, the Priestly Blessing recited on the High Holidays in the fault finder's synagogue. She formulated her complaint as a question, "Were the blessings I heard valid? I happen to know that the *kohen* who announced the blessings is a sinner." And she proceeded to describe in detail the exact nature of the poor man's sins and how she came to know about them. Believe me, although he was far from perfect, he was guilty of neither murder nor idolatry, nor even adultery.

I assured her that the blessings she heard were perfectly valid despite the *kohen*'s alleged misdeeds. I was careful to explain that the *kohen* was merely an instrument through which the Almighty Himself blessed us and that the errant *kohen* was no more than His mouthpiece.

I quoted Maimonides who states emphatically that a *kohen*, even a wicked one, should never refrain from his mitzva to bless the people, and that the congregation should never be troubled by the lowly status of the *kohen*, because ultimately the Holy One, blessed be He, bestows His compassionate blessing on the Jewish people, in accordance with His will.

To be even more convincing, I closed my argument by quoting the *Shulḥan Arukh*, the authoritative *Code of Law*, which rules that no sin should stand in the way of a *kohen* blessing the people. Even for truly egregious crimes such as murder and idolatry, there are those who opine that if the *kohen* repents of his sin, he may resume blessing the people.

My elaborate response fell upon deaf ears. The woman was horrified by what she termed my "liberal permissiveness." She insisted that her entire year was ruined because she had failed to hear a proper Priestly Blessing on the High Holidays.

When individuals complain to one rabbi and are dissatisfied with his response, they of course turn to other rabbis. This woman was so disgruntled by my answer that she dashed off an e-mail to no fewer than six other rabbis and was careful to make sure that I received a copy of her appeal to higher authorities.

This incident occurred some time ago and I have since had numerous occasions to contemplate my interchange with her. I have come to the conclusion that the Priestly Blessing she heard was indeed invalid, not because of the *kohen's* sins, but rather it was her own sin that rendered them invalid.

This is because prior to blessing the congregation, the *kohanim* themselves utter a blessing to the Lord, "Blessed are You, Lord our God, King of the Universe, who...has commanded us to bless His people Israel with love."

Our sages understood that last phrase, "with love," to define the mood that must prevail in the synagogue if the blessings are to be effective. The mood must be one of love. The *kohen* must not even bear the slightest grudge toward any member of the congregation and the congregation must reciprocate with an attitude of acceptance and forgiveness toward the *kohen*. Absent the context of love, or at least tolerance, and the blessings are indeed invalid.

By virtue of her presuming to judge this *kohen*, and by her sanctimonious condemnation of his behavior, the woman who called me excluded herself from the *kohen's* blessing.

Armed with our understanding that the atmosphere of the Priestly Blessing must be one of brotherly love, we are in the position to more fully appreciate the insightful comments of Rabbi Yaakov ben Asher, the Baal HaTurim. His remarks are not found in our *parasha*, but rather in a verse in Leviticus, which tells us about the very first *kohen* and the blessing he bestowed upon the people.

That verse reads, "Aaron lifted his hands toward the people and blessed them; and he stepped down after offering the sin offering, the burnt offering, and the offering of well-being" (Lev. 9:22).

The Baal HaTurim believes that these three sacrificial offerings correspond to three fundamental human moods: the sin offering is a result of guilt feelings and remorse; the burnt offering is an expression of the exhilaration of success; and the offering of well-being derives from emotions of exuberance and joy.

The power of the Priestly Blessing is that it strengthens, enables, and encourages people to cope with and thrive under all manner of spiritual circumstances; it allows the sinner to overcome despair; it protects the victorious hero from prideful arrogance; and it helps the joyous person subdue excessive exuberance.

There is a lesson here for all of us, whether we are the *kohanim* who convey the Almighty's blessings or whether we are sitting in the pews, recipients of those blessings. All of us must cultivate an atmosphere in the synagogue of brotherly love and mutual acceptance. Only when that atmosphere is achieved can the blessings address our diverse and complex moods and help us overcome the challenges of both success and failure, achievement and despair.

Parashat Naso

Distinctly Different

The term is one that I first heard back in high school. There are times that I find it helpful and there are times I find myself resistant to using it. The term is "Judeo-Christian."

I understand that this term was first used back in the early nineteenth century to refer to the fact that the roots of the religion of Christianity are to be found in the Jewish religion and culture. Much later, the term came to be used as it is commonly used nowadays, namely, as a way of referring to the mores, beliefs, and ethical norms that our religion has in common with Christianity.

Long before my career in the rabbinate, in fact even quite early in my childhood, I was acquainted with Christians and fascinated by both the differences and similarities between our faiths and our lifestyles. I may have shared with my readers my family's exposure to a devout Irish Catholic family. When my siblings and I were quite young, we spent our summers in a cottage in Rockaway Beach that was owned by an elderly Catholic couple. We became familiar with their entire family, and indeed, my mother maintained a lifelong correspondence with the couple's daughter, Mrs. Eleanor McElroy.

Much more recently, I have been representing the Orthodox Union in a regular forum in which leaders of the Jewish community meet with their counterparts in the Catholic community to work on various social issues in which we have common interests. Following the guidelines of Rabbi Joseph B. Soloveitchik regarding interreligious dialogue, we carefully avoid discussing theological matters and confine our discussions to ways in which we can cooperate in achieving various shared goals.

Often we encounter striking similarities in the problems that we face; for example, difficulties in funding our respective parochial schools. Then we speak the same language. But quite frequently, we discover that even when we use the same terminology, we are referring to very different experiences. Indeed, these differences frequently make it almost impossible for us to understand each other.

In a recent such forum, for example, the Catholic group, having read so much about the *Ḥaredim* and their involvement in Israeli politics, asked me to define for them just who the *Ḥaredim* are. I tried my best to do so, but they remained confounded as to how a group of fervently pious believers in the literal meaning of the Bible could be anti-Zionist in their politics.

Just as the Catholic group had difficulty understanding such Jewish phenomena, so the members of our Jewish group found some Christian religious concepts and practices alien and even unacceptable. Thus, in one of our conversations, one of the Catholic clergymen wished aloud that he could retreat from the pressures of contemporary society and spend the rest of his years in a monastery. I was just one of our group who immediately protested that for us Jews there were no monasteries and that we did not see the monastic life as a positive religious alternative.

The response of members of the Catholic group to that remark finally brings us to *Parashat Naso* (Num. 4:21–7:89). "How can you not view monasticism positively? After all, the practice has biblical roots, in the Hebrew Bible," they insisted.

They were referring to the following verses in our *parasha,*

The Lord spoke to Moses, saying…. If anyone, man or woman, explicitly utters a Nazirite's vow, to set himself apart for the Lord,

he shall abstain from wine…. He may not eat anyth
obtained from the grape vine…. No razor shall touch his ne.
He shall not go in where there is a dead person. (Num. 6:1–7)

Of course, any one of the Jewish members of the group could easily have referred to the numerous opinions, already recorded in the Talmud, as to the non-desirability of the practice of *nezirut*. There are certainly forceful statements against taking the Nazirite vow and even those who consider it a sin.

But I found myself taking a different tack in this discussion. "It is wrong to equate the Nazir with the monk," I said. "Granted, the Nazir must be guided by certain very stringent prohibitions. But he does not absent himself from society. He is neither a hermit, nor a member of some ascetic sect. This is very different from one who undertakes monastic vows, as I understand them."

One of my companions rallied to my side after reaching for a volume of the set of encyclopedias, which was in easy reach in the library where the meeting was taking place. He read out this definition of "monasticism."

It is an institutionalized religious practice whose members live by a rule that requires work that goes beyond those of the laity…. The monastic is commonly celibate and universally ascetic, and separates himself from society either by living as a hermit or by joining a community of others who profess similar intentions.

Another good friend simply consulted his pocket dictionary, which stated, "The word 'monasticism' is derived from the Greek *monachos*, which means 'living alone.'"

Our Jewish group, which consisted of several diverse individuals who regularly disagree vociferously with each other, were united in our response to the Catholic gentlemen on that day. The Nazirite was not a monk, certainly not in the common understanding of that term.

The interreligious group did not persist in this particular discussion. Afterwards, however, some of us from the Jewish group continued our discussion over coffee. We were struck by the fact that three individuals are understood by our tradition as having been Nazirites, or at least partial Nazirites. They include the heroic warrior Samson, the prophet Samuel, and Absalom, the son of David, who rebelled against his father. No question about it: these men were not celibate, not hermits, and not men who refrained from the legitimate pleasures of life. Quite the contrary, they played active roles in the life of the Jewish people, albeit each in very different ways.

The distinct difference between our Torah's concept of the Nazirite and the Christian concept of the monastic is perhaps best expressed in a passage in the third chapter of Maimonides' *Hilkhot De'ot*, which I will allow myself to paraphrase:

> Lest a person mislead himself into thinking that since envy, lust, and vainglory are such negatives, I will therefore separate myself from them; forcefully distance myself from them to the extreme; eat no meat and drink no wine; practice celibacy; shun a finely furnished home; desist from wearing attractive clothing, and instead don sackcloth and coarse wool, and similar such ascetic practices. Let him be aware that this is the manner of gentile priests!
>
> Let me make clear that a person who pursues such a path is a sinner. Even the Nazirite, who merely refrains from products of the vine, requires atonement. How much more so the one who deprives himself of the many pleasures of life, which are not prohibited by the Torah. He is simply misguided.

Almost nine hundred years ago, Maimonides recognized the distinct difference between the concept of holiness as practiced by the gentile priests whom he knew and the model of holiness that is held up to us by our Torah. The Nazirite, in Maimonides' view, is not the paradigm of holiness. The truly holy man must not refrain from living a normal family life, must share in the joys and woes of his friends and neighbors, and must exercise the leadership skills with which he has been uniquely blessed.

It is doubtful, given the sacrificial Temple rituals, which conclude the Nazirite's term and which are detailed in our *parasha*, that one can practically be a Nazirite nowadays. But the lessons of the *parasha* are clear: there are guidelines for those who wish to be holier than the rest of us. But those guidelines rule out separating oneself from family and community.

In this regard, we cannot speak of a common Judeo-Christian norm. The Jewish norm and the Christian norm are distinctly different.

Parashat Behaalotekha

A Candle of God is the Soul of Man

I no longer remember which Israeli artist colony I was visiting, perhaps Jaffa, but I will never forget the crude, almost primitive paintings, which were on exhibit. They were all very different in color, style, and size. They varied from somber dark browns and grays to tropical oranges, reds, and yellows. Some were very realistic, some impressionistic, and some totally abstract. One was a large mural. But in the corner, there were postcard-sized miniatures. In every painting, a candle predominated.

The artist was obsessed with the image of the candle. A tall, slim candle, wax dripping down its side, the wick erect, the flame flickering. Somehow, each candle evoked the picture of a person.

I made a note of the artist's name, hoping that one day I would be able to afford one of his works and would then find him, but I lost the scrap of paper with his name and address long ago.

The memory of the candles bedecking his workroom walls has remained with me. As long as I can remember, I have been fascinated by candles and by their human-like quality. In my early teens, I was taught to meditate in front of a burning candle and to associate my meditation with the biblical phrase, "A candle of God is the soul of man."

"What are some ways that human beings resemble candles?" This question was assigned to me by the old rabbi who was my first spiritual guide. In my early adolescence, I was part of a group of six or seven peers who met with this rabbi once a month in a dark and, you guessed it, candlelit room.

It was our task to gaze at a burning candle and imagine the affinities between candles and men. At the end of the month, we were to report on our findings. I never returned at the end of that month. Without that closure, it is no wonder that I still reflect, fifty years later, on the resemblances between people and candles.

Parashat Behaalotekha speaks of the candles that Aaron lit in the ancient Tabernacle. The Bible speaks not of the "lighting of" the candles, but of the "raising up" of the candles. The commentaries eagerly point out that it is not sufficient to kindle the candle; one must see to it that the flame will continue to burn on its own.

The candle thus becomes a metaphor for the process of teaching: parent to child or master to disciple. It is never sufficient to merely touch the child with the flame of knowledge. Rather, one must "raise up" the flame so that it will grow and will nurture the student for a long time. The task of the teacher is to ensure that the flame will continue to burn on its own, that knowledge will be a lifetime process.

There is another traditional Jewish saying that inspires me, "A little bit of light can dispel much darkness." The little candle teaches us how much good a single person, or even a single act, can accomplish. It is not necessary for one to try to ignite powerful floodlights. If all that one can do is light a match, that paltry act can achieve unforeseen illumination.

Finally, there is a talmudic dictum, "A candle for one is a candle for a hundred." There are certain things in life, an item of food for example, that can meet the needs of only one person. There are other things, certain tools for example, that can meet the needs of only one person at a time. But one candle can benefit the single individual who needs illumination, and it can shed equal illumination for many others in the room. A candle for one is a candle for a hundred.

And so it is in the human realm. There are things we can do that will benefit not only a single particular other, but an entire group, an entire community, an entire world. If we teach, for example, lessons that are useful practically and that are spiritually uplifting, those lessons are not limited to who hears them. Rather, they can benefit many unseen others. Intellectual accomplishments and religious achievements are candles not just for one, but for hundreds.

I have listed but three of the infinite number of ways in which the soul of man is the candle of God. Candle lighting symbolizes the teaching process; the single act can have massive consequences; and we can affect a much wider circle than we think.

The opening verses of our *parasha* render the candle image so central to the Tabernacle and Temple service because the Torah wishes us to think about the candle, to meditate on it, and to discover for ourselves the manifold analogies that lie embedded in the candle image.

"Behold the candle," the Torah exclaims. It is one of the oldest, and certainly one of the simplest, human tools. But it can be a metaphor for the power and the potential of the human soul, which is no less than the candle of God.

A Second Chance

I was in a total fog during my first year in high school. I am convinced that my experience then was not unique. I entered a strange school, much larger than the one I had attended previously, and was not given the benefit of any orientation to the new environment. I did not know what to expect and I was not informed about what was expected of me. I struggled academically and socially. But I knew one thing, and that was that I liked to write, and I sought to learn how to do so.

Toward the end of the year, I learned that there was a special track in the English department for those who were interested in writing. The track was called "Journalism for Sophomores" and was open to those who did well in their freshman English courses. But as I said, I was in a fog that freshman year and was merely passing freshman English.

Nevertheless, I applied for entry into the journalism class. I was turned down. But I persisted and made it my business to arrange for an interview with Mr. Joe Brown, the instructor for the journalism class and also the advisor for the student newspaper.

I will never forget Mr. Brown because he was impressed by my perseverance and gave me a second chance, explaining that many

413

freshmen often become overwhelmed by the novelty of their new environment and don't always excel to their full potential. He would allow me into the elite journalism class, on condition that I prove myself by doing extra essays, and doing them well, during the first six weeks of the semester.

I fulfilled his conditions and spent not one, but three years, in the special journalism section under his tutelage. I enjoyed it, learned a great deal, became one of the editors of the prize-winning student newspaper, and was elected editor-in-chief of the senior yearbook. To this day, every time I put a pencil to paper or fingers to a computer keyboard, I think of Joe Brown.

In *Parashat Behaalotekha*, we read of a group of people who, like me, were unable to fulfill their responsibilities the first time around. In their case, it was the mitzva of bringing the Passover offering on the fourteenth day of the month of Nisan, which they failed to do. For them, it was not the strangeness of a new school that prevented them from doing the mitzva properly. Rather it was because "they were unclean, having come into contact with a dead body, so that they could not keep the Passover on that day" (Num. 9:6).

They could easily have taken the approach of shrugging their shoulders and saying something like, "We tried our best, but circumstances were such that we were unable to perform the Passover sacrifice. We have a good excuse, so let's move on."

But that was not their reaction. Instead, "they came before Moses and before Aaron on that day." They wanted, nay demanded, a second chance.

"Unclean though we are by reason of a corpse, why must we be debarred from presenting the Lord's offering at its set time with the rest of the Israelites?" (Num. 9:7) They persisted and insisted upon having the same benefits as the rest of the people, those who did not suffer the set of circumstances that denied this particular group of men this type of privilege.

Most fascinating is the fact that Moses did not know what to tell them. As far as I can tell, this is the first time in the Bible, and quite possibly the first time in the history of the human race, that a group of people asked for a second chance. Moses was unaware of a precedent for

the privilege that this group was requesting. So Moses, havi
of access that none of us has today to the Divine, said to them
and let me hear what instructions the Lord gives about you" (1

The Lord gave them a second chance. He told Moses th̲ ̲ ̲ev-
ermore in the history of the Jewish people, when individuals are faced
with circumstances that prevent them from bringing the Passover offering in its proper time, "they shall offer it in the second month." God, in
His infinite mercy, gave a second chance, a kind of a do-over session,
to a group of people who could have easily given up, but who did not
want to be left out, and therefore persevered in their search for a spiritual privilege.

There is so much to be learned from this story. Although we cannot play God, we can certainly emulate Him and give others a second
chance. We need not strictly enforce all of our rules, but can recognize
that there are circumstances in the lives of men that prevent them from
doing the right thing the first time around and who therefore require
a little "slack."

But the great lesson for me in the story is the value of perseverance, of not taking no for an answer, but continuing to knock upon the
doors of opportunity. These men who were "unclean because of their
contact with a corpse" are among the heroes (in their case, unnamed
heroes) of the entire biblical narrative. Had they not persevered, we
would never have learned of the Almighty's provision of a *Pesaḥ Sheni*,
an opportunity to compensate for the excusable failure to do it right
the first time.

So I learned much from Mr. Joe Brown about how an empathic
teacher can bring out the best in a confused youngster. But I also learned,
very early in my own life, about the value of persistence.

> Tis a lesson you should heed,
> Try, try again.
> If at first you don't succeed,
> Try, try again.

I am tempted at this point to hold a contest and offer a prize to the
reader who can identify the source of that famous quote. But I will forego

that temptation and tell you that it was first published in *A Teacher's Manual*, by early nineteenth-century educator Thomas H. Palmer.

Or in the words of another relative unknown, William Ward:

Four steps to achievement:
plan purposefully, prepare prayerfully,
proceed positively, pursue persistently.

Or, finally, in the words of the famous Goethe:

In the realm of ideas everything depends on enthusiasm;
in the real world, all rests on perseverance.

Parashat Behaalotekha

Earning Self-Esteem

It was a lesson I learned long ago when I was a high school teacher. I was new at this line of work and found that my greatest challenge was to find ways to motivate the students. I tried various approaches, which all were basically attempts to motivate by giving. I tried giving special prizes and awards, granting extra privileges, and even resorting to outright bribery in order to get the students to pay attention, do their homework, and learn the subject matter.

It was a wise mentor who taught me that you can't motivate students by giving to them. Rather, you must find ways to encourage them to give to others. The student who gives to others feels important, and it is the consequent sense of self-esteem that is the most powerful motivator of all.

I'll never forget the first time I tried that strategy. I approached the most recalcitrant student in the entire class. He happened to be a very bright young man who was, in today's terminology, "totally turned off" to his studies. I asked him to assist two weaker students with their daily assignment. I caught him completely off guard, so that his reaction was one of utter surprise.

"Who, me?" he exclaimed. "Why should I help those two dunces? If they can't figure it out for themselves, let them flunk."

Although I was convinced that any appeal to his sense of altruism would be futile, I nevertheless gave it a try. I told him that for a society to function successfully, the haves must help the have-nots, the strong must aid the weak, and those who are blessed with talent must share their gifts with those who were less fortunate.

It was the phrase "blessed with talent" that did the trick, for he responded, "Do you really think I'm blessed with talent? I guess you're right. I am a talented dude and I'm going to try to teach those blockheads a thing or two. But if I don't succeed, it won't be my fault!"

He did succeed and very dramatically. And he recognized that if he was to succeed again at this tutorial task, he would have to be even better prepared next time. He went home that night, studied hard, and was indeed even more successful with his two "blockheads" the next day.

I won't go on to provide the details of my strategy of applying this technique to the rest of the class. Instead I want to demonstrate that this secret of human motivation is implicit in a brief passage in *Parashat Behaalotekha*. In this *parasha*, the Torah devotes all of the tenth chapter of Numbers to a detailed description of the sequence in which the tribes marched through the desert. About two-thirds of the way into this chapter, we unexpectedly encounter the following conversational interlude:

> And Moses said to Ḥovav, son of Reuel the Midianite, Moses' father-in-law, "We are setting out for the place of which the Lord has said, 'I will give it to you.' Come with us and we will be generous with you; for the Lord has promised to be generous to Israel."
>
> "I will not go," he replied to him, "but will return to my native land."
>
> "He said, 'Please do not leave us, inasmuch as you know where we should camp in the wilderness and can be our guide [literally read as 'eyes']. So if you come with us, we will extend to you the same bounty that the Lord grants us.'" (Num. 10:29–32)

That ends the dialogue and we are never explicitly told w
not Moses' second attempt at persuasion convinced Hovav to ac
the Children of Israel. His first attempt, promising to be genero
was rejected emphatically by Hovav with a resounding, "I will not go!"

What did Moses change in his second attempt? Quite simply, he
told Hovav that he would not be merely the passive recipient of another's
generosity. Rather, Moses assured Hovav that he had expertise that was
indispensable to the Jewish people. He could give them the guidance
through the wilderness that they desperately required. He would not
just be a taker, but a giver as well.

In short, Moses was appealing to Hovav's sense of self-esteem.
He was saying to him, "You are an important person. Your talents are
needed. You are an actor with a part to play in this drama."

What I was doing as a fledgling teacher so many years ago to that
turned-off student was essentially precisely what Moses was trying to
do with Hovav in his second attempt to convince him to accompany the
Children of Israel upon their journey through the desert.

When reading the text, one can easily assume that Moses learned
a great lesson, which caused him to abandon the strategy of promising to
be generous. Instead, he adopted an entirely different strategy, one that
conveyed the message to Hovav that he would not merely be a consumer
of favors. Rather, he would earn the Lord's generosity because of the
valuable contribution that he would make and that only he could make.

There is a lesson here not just for teachers and students, or leaders and followers. There is a lesson here for all of us in dealing with
other human beings. We must be sensitive to their needs for self-esteem.
We must recognize their talents and what they can bring to bear upon
whatever task lies at hand. When a person is convinced of his or her
own importance and value, he or she will be motivated and will act
accordingly.

Understanding the dialogue between Moses and Hovav in this
manner allows us to readily accept the conclusion of our sages. They
filled in the "rest of the story" and assured us that Hovav was finally
convinced by Moses' second argument and did indeed join his fate and
those of his descendants to the destiny of the Jewish people.

Humble, Not Meek

I don't usually disagree publicly with lecturers, particularly when they are expressing opinions that are mostly consistent with my own. But there was one time when I felt that I had to speak up and object to one of the speaker's expressions.

It was at a lecture on the subject of self-absorption. The speaker characterized the time we live in as "the age of narcissism." He argued that we live in an era when most people are totally self-centered and guilty of false pride and arrogance. He advanced many examples to bolster his position.

Although I found his hypothesis to be somewhat extreme, I could agree with much of what he was saying. I too have often felt that the phrase "the me generation" was an apt appellation for contemporary society. But then the gentleman at the podium made a statement that touched a raw nerve in me. He said something that I had heard expressed many times over the years and have invariably felt compelled to correct.

He said that, as a good Christian, he found the hubris that predominated contemporary society to be quite contrary to "the Christian values of forgiveness and humility." It was his description of these noble values as being of Christian origin, and the way in which he conveyed his conviction that his own faith tradition somehow "owned" them, that brought me to my feet.

"I must object," I asserted, "not to your major thesis about the faults of our generation, but to your insistence on identifying what you believe to be the desirable qualities for the human race with Christianity, and with Christianity alone."

I must confess that I was secretly hoping that my protest would cause him to at least modify his remarks, and perhaps speak, as so many do, of the "Judeo-Christian values of forgiveness and humility."

But that was not to be. Instead, he cited chapter and verse in the Christian Bible on the importance of forgiveness, and then raising his voice for emphasis, said, "Surely, the learned rabbi knows that it is in the Book of Matthew that we find the phrase, 'And the meek shall inherit the earth.'"

I will not report what I said to him about forgiveness as a Jewish virtue. I will save those remarks for another occasion, but because of the connection to *Parashat Behaalotekha* (Num. 8:1–12:16), I will share with you the essence of my retort with regard to the Jewish origin of the all-important virtue of humility.

"Yes, my dear sir," I replied, "this learned rabbi does indeed know that the phrase you translate as, 'And the meek shall inherit the earth,' appears in your Scriptures. But I also know that the identical phrase appears in the Book of Psalms, chapter 37, verse 11, written many centuries before Matthew. And I also know that translating the Hebrew word *anavim* as 'the meek' is not quite correct. We preferred to translate *anavim* as 'the humble' and not as 'the meek.'"

I continued to build my argument by quoting the verse near the end of our *parasha*, "Now Moses was a very humble man, more so than any other man on earth" (Num. 12:3). "There is no way," I insisted, "that the Torah would use the word *anav* to describe Moses if the word meant 'meek.' Moses was not meek. I think you will agree that the image evoked by the phrase 'a meek person' is that of a weak person or at least a mild-mannered one. Moses was most certainly neither weak nor mild-mannered. He was strong, in body and in spirit, and could be quite assertive when circumstances called for assertiveness."

While I do not delude myself into thinking that I changed my adversary's mind, I did get the audience thinking. This was proven when about a dozen of those present gathered around me after the lecture was concluded and asked me to expand upon the Jewish definition of humility.

I told them that a comprehensive discussion of the importance Judaism assigns to the character trait of humility (*anava*) would take a very long time. I agreed, however, to share with them but one thought upon the subject.

I quoted to them the following passage in the Talmud (Nedarim 38a):

> Rabbi Yoḥanan said: "The Holy One, blessed be He, allows the *Shekhina* to rest only upon someone who is strong, wealthy, wise, and humble. All of these traits were to be found in Moses. Humility, as it is written, "Now Moses was a very humble man."

It was not long before one member of the group asked the question that I was expecting, "Does the Almighty really favor people with the mundane virtues of strength and wealth? I would think that He would rather favor spiritual virtues."

"Your question," I responded, "was anticipated by a rabbi who wrote in the early twentieth century. His name was Rabbi Baruch Epstein, and whereas his *magnum opus* entitled *Torah Temima* was written in 1904, he lived to an advanced old age and witnessed the Holocaust. His answer is a most instructive one."

I then went on to describe that answer. I told the group that the test of humility can only be passed by one who is strong, wealthy, and wise. If someone who lacks those resources acts humbly, we cannot be sure that he in truth possesses a humble character. It could be that he acts humbly simply because he is weak, or poor, or of limited intelligence. God therefore chooses to have the *Shekhina* dwell with the person who, despite his many assets and talents, remains humble. He is the one who is genuinely an *anav*.

Thus, writes Rabbi Epstein, "It is precisely because Moses was powerful, wealthy, wise, and tall, and yet humble, that we can speak of him as the 'humblest of men.'"

There is much wisdom in this manner of understanding the virtue of *anava*. The *anav* is not a meek person. Quite the contrary. He has many talents and many skills. He is fully aware of his capacities and of his strengths. And yet he recognizes that these gifts are just that, gifts. Moreover, these gifts are divine blessings, and he has no right to be proud of them as if they were his personal achievements.

The humble man recognizes that his very advantage over others is a gift of God. That is what allows him to utilize his powers to help achieve God's purposes, not out of meekness, but out of humility.

Once again, Moses is a model for all of us. We are called upon to be humble, but that doesn't mean that we are to be weak, passive, or submissive. We can be strong, active, and assertive – and humble.

Caleb at the Crossroads

Imagine standing at a crossroads. We have all been there. We have all experienced moments in our life's journey when we had to make a crucial choice and decide whether to proceed along one road or along another. (Except for Yogi Berra, of course, who famously said, "When you come to a fork in the road, take it.")

We have all also experienced moments much further along in our journey, often many years later, when we reflected back upon our decision and wondered what would have been if we had pursued the alternative road.

Now imagine standing at a crossroads together with a close friend. Both of you face an identical choice, either this road or that. One of you chooses one road, and the other decides differently and selects the other road. Each would have an intriguing tale to tell if, after many years, they met and had the opportunity to compare the results of their different decisions.

Throughout my adult life, I have been fascinated by the experiences of survivors of the Holocaust. Whenever I have been fortunate enough to have the time to engage in conversation with one of them,

I listened eagerly to their stories. When they permit, and they do not always, I ask them questions not just about their experiences, but about their choices and decisions.

I especially remember the discussions I had with one of them – let us call him Mr. Silver. He often would tell me about the hellish years he spent fleeing and fighting the Nazis in the forests of Poland. He had a companion then – let us call him Simon. Mr. Silver and Simon were boyhood friends who together witnessed the murder of their parents and who together managed to escape and join the partisans. Eventually, they were both caught and incarcerated in prisons and concentration camps.

In his story, Mr. Silver compared his attitude throughout those horrific times with the attitude of his friend Simon. "You know me," he would say, "and you know how I've always seen the bright side of things, the hopefulness of every situation, however dire." Indeed, I assured him that I could vouch for his consistent optimism.

"As much as I was an idealist," he would continue, "so was Simon a hard-core realist. He saw things as they were and dealt with them accordingly. He had no illusions whatsoever of hope."

Many years after my conversation with Mr. Silver, I finally met Simon and, together with him, was able to compare the life he led subsequent to the Holocaust, and subsequent to his crossroad decisions, with the life of Mr. Silver. Simon, after the war, chose not to marry and chose to live in a rather remote American community with little contact with other Jews. Mr. Silver married, raised a large family with numerous grandchildren, was very much involved with Jewish causes, and eventually chose to live out his final years in the State of Israel.

They were two individuals at the same crossroads, making different decisions, with starkly different life outcomes.

Parashat Shelah gives us the opportunity to witness individuals at the crossroads; individuals who make radically different decisions and whose lives thereby play out very differently.

Let us focus, for example, on the personalities of Naḥbi ben Vofsi, prince of the tribe of Naphtali, and of Caleb ben Yefuneh, prince of the tribe of Judah. Up until the dramatic moment described in our *parasha*, they led almost identical lives. They both experienced the Exodus from

Egypt, the miraculous splitting of the Red Sea, the revelation at Mount Sinai, and opportunities for leadership of their respective tribes.

They were both assigned to spy out the land of Canaan, and they both crisscrossed the Promised Land and returned to give their reports. But then we read (Num. 13:30–31), "Caleb...said, 'Let us by all means go up, as we shall gain possession of the land, and we shall surely overcome.' But the men who had gone up with him [one of whom was Naḥbi] said, 'We cannot attack that people, for they are stronger than we.'"

Two individuals, at this very same crossroads in their lives: one full of hope and trust and confidence, and the other frightened, albeit very realistic. How differently their lives played out from this point forward. Naḥbi perished in ignominy in the desert, while Caleb remained a prince, enhanced his reputation, and was granted his reward, the city of Hebron.

We all face crossroads in our lives; some of great significance, and some seemingly trivial. Our choices can be Naḥbi-like – practical and safe, but ultimately cowardly; or they can be informed by hope, trust, and confidence, and ultimately be brave and heroic. The choice is ours and so are the consequences for the rest of our lives.

Parashat Shelaḥ

History Repeats Itself

History repeats itself. I don't know the origin of that cliché, but I do know that our sages held a similar point of view. "*Maase avot siman labanim.*" What happened with ancestors is often a pattern that their descendants are destined to follow.

The repetitive nature of historical processes seems to be true in the stories of all nations and cultures. This is why historians such as Arnold Toynbee believed that history is cyclical, and they have been able to demonstrate that certain central issues recur repetitively in the history of the human race.

I remember reading, for example, in one of Toynbee's books, of how the lives of many world leaders are characterized by patterns of "withdrawal and return." Thus, for example, Moses went through a period of withdrawal in the desert of Midian and then returned to Egypt to lead his people out of slavery. Similarly, great figures in the history of Greece, of Rome, of medieval Europe, and of modern Western civilization endured periods of their lives when they were in prison or in other forms of voluntary or forced solitude, and were thus in a stage of "withdrawal." They then reemerged on the stage of leadership of their people, thereby entering a stage of "return."

In *Parashat Shelaḥ*, a pattern is laid down that has been tragically repeated all too frequently in the history of our people. I speak of the pattern whereby a major portion of the Jewish leadership is opposed to entering the Land of Israel. Only a small and courageous minority says, "Let us by all means go up, as we shall gain possession of the land, and we shall surely overcome" (Num. 13:30).

In our *parasha*, we read of the episode of the spies (*meraglim*). These men were a select group of talented and presumably pious individuals. They conducted their risky mission as it was assigned to them. They were to explore the Promised Land and determine the nature of its inhabitants and the nature of the terrain. This was, simply put, a preparation for entering the land, conquering it, and settling it once and for all. But ten of the twelve returned totally discouraged. I would say, literally discouraged; that is, their courage was undone. They said, "We cannot attack that people, for they are stronger than we."

This was only the first, but definitely not the last time in Jewish history, that Jewish leadership was internally torn apart by discord. The event described in this *parasha* is but the first precedent of a recurring pattern in which a few heroic visionaries, Joshua and Caleb, can commit not only to enter the land themselves, but to inspire their followers to do so. But these visionaries, alas, are only part of the pattern. The other part involves those leaders who are too cowardly, too cautious, or too blind to lead their people to do all that is necessary to enter and to possess the Holy Land.

During the Babylonian Exile, only unique individuals like Ezra and Nehemiah were made of the same stuff as Joshua and Caleb. And only a small remnant of the Babylonian Exile followed them and returned to the land. The great majority of Jews, and the great majority of the Jewish leaders, remained ignominiously behind in Babylon.

So frequently over the ensuing centuries did history repeat itself. Every so often, a pitifully small group of Jews from Persia and Morocco, from France, from the bastions of Hasidism in the Ukraine, or at the prodding of the Gaon of Vilna, follow the path advocated by Joshua and Caleb. Against all odds, they do return to the land. But the vast majority of their brethren, sometimes for practical reasons and sometimes for ideological ones, choose to remain behind in the Diaspora. They follow the path of the other ten spies.

Every portion in the Torah has relevance to contemporary Jewish life, but *Parashat Shelah* is especially timely. We live in an age when the ideal of return to Zion, which after all is the ideal preached so inspiringly by Joshua and Caleb, is beset by challenges from all sides.

We live in an age when the liberal intellectual community, composed to a great extent of fellow Jews, no longer accepts the ideal of a Jewish homeland for the Jewish people. At the very least, that community is willing to see the Holy Land shared by another people. And there are those of that community who totally delegitimize the notion of a return to Zion.

More troubling to me, however, are those elements of the observant religious community who are antagonistic to the enterprise of the Jewish people living as a sovereign nation in the land promised to us by the Almighty himself. I know full well that there are legitimate ideological views for or against Religious Zionism, and I am certainly cognizant of the faults and flaws of the government of the State of Israel.

But I fail to see how anyone reading this *parasha* cannot be impressed by its central messages. We left Egypt with a promise to inherit a specific land flowing with milk and honey. We had the opportunity to enter that land very soon after the Exodus. We failed to appreciate the opportunity and we lost it. True, we didn't lose it entirely, and it was only postponed for forty years – the blink of an eye from the perspective of the millennia of Jewish history.

The tragedy of *Parashat Shelah* transcends the one incident described there. Rather, the narrative of *Parashat Shelah* establishes a pattern that is repeated too often during our subsequent history. The conflict between foresight and fear, between courage and cowardice, between true faith and weaker faith, becomes an eternal theme in our history down to this very day.

I challenge you, my dear reader, to pay close attention to the narrative of the spies. I am quite confident that you will see the message it sends to our generation. It is the message of Joshua and Caleb. It is the message that says to the entire congregation of the Children of Israel:

The land that we passed through to spy it out is an exceedingly good land. If the Lord delight in us, then He will bring us into this land and give it unto us – a land that flows with milk and honey. Only rebel not against the Lord, neither fear you the people of the land; for they are bread for us; their defense is removed from over them, and the Lord is with us; fear them not. (Num. 14:7–9)

Of Grasshoppers and Jewish Pride

J ust as there were six million victims, so were there at least six million stories.

One of those stories seems to have occurred many times, because I've heard it told by quite a few survivors. It is the story of two or more Jews, witnessing the sadistic and murderous scenes around them, but momentarily spared from being victims themselves.

In the midst of that horror, one Jew turns to the other and says, "Yankel, you are always urging us to be thankful to God for what we have. What do we have to thank Him for now? Our brothers and sisters and children are being tortured and butchered in front of our eyes, and in all likelihood, these Nazis will come after us next!"

To which Yankel replies, "We can be thankful that we are Jews and not Nazis. Not only can we be thankful, but we can be proud. We can be proud that we are Jews and have retained our humanity, and not become the beasts that these Nazis have become. We can be proud that we can still claim to have been created in the image of God (*betzelem Elokim*). Our tormentors have forever relinquished that claim."

There are numerous other stories told with similar motifs, indicating that Jews were able to retain their Jewish pride even in the unspeakably horrible conditions of the Holocaust.

Thankfully, Jewish pride has also been amply manifested in much happier circumstances. The encouraging cheers echoing across the world as Jews from behind the Iron Curtain heroically struggled for their freedom, and the celebratory cheers that resounded when they finally achieved that freedom, expressed that pride dramatically. "The Jewish nation lives (*Am Yisrael Ḥai*)," were the words chosen to express that pride.

Jewish pride is sometimes even evidenced in American culture, such as in the boasting one hears about the Hank Greenbergs and Sandy Koufaxes, whose Jewish identities were apparent even to the baseball fans of yesteryear.

In more significant areas of human accomplishment, have we not all occasionally gloated over the disproportionably numerous Jewish Nobel Prize winners in science and literature? Do not the lifesaving medical discoveries of generations of Jewish physicians stir Jewish pride in our hearts?

Most important, of course, are the contributions that Jewish leaders have made, from the times of Abraham to this very day, to human religious development and to the advancement of ethics and morality for all mankind.

It is sad, therefore, and some would say tragic, that Jewish pride seems to be on the decline in recent times. The consequences of such a decline are poignantly illustrated in *Parashat Shelaḥ* (Num. 13:1–15:41).

We read of the adventures, better misadventures, of the spies. They spent forty days scouting out the Promised Land and discovered much that was very good. But in their report back to "Moses and Aaron and the whole Israelite community," they chose to emphasize that "the people who inhabit the country are powerful and the cities are fortified and very large."

When Caleb, the very embodiment of Jewish pride, confidently assured the people that "we shall surely overcome it," they shouted words of rebuttal, culminating in this assertion, "We saw giants there, and we looked like grasshoppers to ourselves, and so we must have looked to them" (Num. 13:33).

Grasshoppers! No more, no less. An individual with such a puny self-image is doomed to a life of mediocrity, if not failure and frustration. A nation that perceives itself as grasshoppers, that lacks proper pride in itself, has already fallen victim to God's curse, "And I will break your proud glory" (Lev. 26:19). Such a nation cannot live up to its mission.

There are those who would object and insist that the Almighty wants us to be humble and that pride is a negative value. To those, we must object that just as there is a false pride, which is really nothing but arrogance, there is also false humility, which leads one to shirk responsibility and to eschew greatness.

I have previously referred to some of my classmates in high school, college, and yeshiva who were voted "most likely to succeed," but who by no means succeeded. Many of them suffered from this very false humility, and it resulted in their failure to use the talents and skills, with which they were blessed, in a properly prideful manner. That was their loss and a loss to the world.

The Jewish people, as a nation, can easily fall prey to this false humility. As a nation, despite our faults and shortcomings, we have much to be proud of. We have much to teach the world spiritually because of our rich biblical and rabbinic heritage. And we continue to contribute to mankind's material welfare in countless ways.

We would do well to heed the pithy counsel of an early twentieth-century hasidic sage, Rabbi Yosef Yitzchak of Lubavitch, who said, "Man must be proud, but he must grow higher and higher, and not wider and wider." What he meant to say is that if we use our pride to grow wider, we are bound to infringe upon another person's space. That is selfish arrogance and not proper pride.

But if our pride motivates us not to grow wider, but to grow ever higher and higher, we displace no one. Instead, we draw closer to the Almighty and do what He demands of us. Jewish pride takes us higher and higher. *Am Yisrael ḥai!*

Parashat Shelaḥ

Memory Loss

When one reaches a certain age, he does not have to be reminded that his memory is not what it used to be. These days, one receives e-mails, unsolicited of course, with such titles as "Eight Tips for Improving Memory," and "Preventing Memory Loss in the Aging Person." Undoubtedly, one of the consequences of the passage of the years is the fading of some, but certainly not all, memories.

But it is not only older people for whom memory is problematic. Younger people, as well, forget a lot. Moreover, even those memories that they retain are often modified, if not distorted.

Our ability to substantially change the memories we have of past experiences is brought home to me forcefully almost every week. I often share my recollections of events in my life as the background for my writings on the weekly Torah portion. Very frequently, I receive e-mails from old friends and classmates protesting that these recollections are inaccurate. Typically, it is my younger sister, Judy, who chastises me and declares, "That's not the way I remember it." Or, increasingly, lately, "You must have made up that one!"

What about memories of a group? Surely, when a group of friends, for example, gets together after many years and discusses their memories, they will all agree about what transpired. Yet, if you ever attended a class reunion, you came away impressed by how different people remember events very differently.

The Jewish nation specializes in memory. We remember the Sabbath, the Exodus from Egypt, and a host of other historical experiences. We even remember our enemy, Amalek. Sociologists have termed such memories "collective memories." One wonders whether collective memories remain intact over time or whether different groups of descendants remember their ancestors' experiences differently.

Parashat Shelaḥ (Numbers 13:1–15:41) contains a description of the beginning of the ordeal of spending forty years in the wilderness. The story is a familiar one. The spies returned from their mission and spoke words of despair and discouragement. The Almighty was angered by this and by the people's reaction to the spies' report. He expressed His anger harshly, "Not one shall enter the land in which I swore to settle you.... Your carcasses shall drop in this wilderness, while your children roam the wilderness for forty years, suffering for your faithlessness."

Forty years of wandering must have left an indelible impression upon the collective memories of the Jewish people. Yet, note how very discrepant versions of the wilderness experience developed over the course of the centuries.

On the one hand, there are those who look back upon the years in the desert as a time of opportunity for spiritual development. They see it as a time when the Jews could concentrate upon Torah study without concern for mundane matters. After all, their needs were taken care of by the Almighty. They were fed the manna, food from heaven, and their clothing showed neither wear nor tear. According to an ancient midrash, *Mekhilta DeRabbi Ishmael*, the Almighty knew that, had the people entered directly into the Land of Israel, they would have busied themselves with their fields and vineyards and would have ignored Torah. He therefore rerouted them through the desert, where they ate the manna and drank from the miraculous well and absorbed Torah into their very bodies.

Rabbi Yonatan Eybeshutz, in his collection of sermons known as *Yaarot Devash*, uses idyllic terminology to describe the *midbar* experience, "With all their physical needs cared for, their time was freed to be totally devoted to the Lord, with no impediments and no distractions."

Indeed, Rabbi Haim of Volozhin, the early nineteenth-century founder of the famed Yeshiva of Volozhin, wanted his institution of higher learning to replicate the *midbar* environment. He dreamed of creating an institution in which the students gave thought to neither career nor creature comforts, but were free to devote all their time, day and night, summer and winter, to pure Torah study, with nothing to deter them from that sacred goal. To a large degree, Rabbi Haim was successful in achieving his dream.

The collective memory of men such as Rabbi Yonatan Eybeshutz and Rabbi Haim of Volozhin was of forty pleasant years of life in a placid wilderness, a paradise of sorts, in which men were free to indulge in Torah study in its most spiritual sense.

But we also have evidence of a very different collective memory of the experience of forty years in the *midbar*. One articulate expression of this very different version is to be found in the commentary of Nahmanides on Exodus 12:42. He views the wilderness experience as the very opposite of a utopia. He sees it instead as a precursor to the lengthy and persistent exile (*galut*) of the Jewish people from its land, the torture and persecution it endured, and its dispersal throughout the world. He writes:

> All these forty years were a time of great suffering, as it is written: "Remember the long way that the Lord…Has made you travel in the wilderness…. That He tested you with hardships…. He subjected you to the hardship of hunger." You had a total exile in a land that was not yours, but was the realm of the snake, the serpent, and the scorpion.

These two very different collective memories force us to question which version is true. The answer is, as in so many other such disagreements, that there is a grain of truth in both versions. For some people, and for some of the time, the wilderness experience was an unsurpassed spiritual opportunity. For others, and at other times, challenges prevailed, and deprivation and frustration were familiar phenomena.

All of us live, to one extent or another, in a "wilderness." At times we feel that we are in paradise and at times we are convinced that we are in the opposite of that. At times we use our "wilderness" for its spiritual richness and at times we find the "wilderness" arid and barren.

Eventually we will tell the story of our years in the "wilderness" to our children and they will pass the story on to our grandchildren.

It should be no surprise to us that our grandchildren will then have differing versions of what our experience was like. Collective memories differ because our world is complex. It is a world in which, as the Midrash puts it near the beginning of the Book of Genesis, "light and darkness are intermingled."

Parashat Koraḥ

Can Everybody Be Somebody?

The Jewish community in the USA is pleased and proud to live in a democracy. What is a democracy? It is often described as a society in which all are equal. But this description falls short of the mark. Because obviously we all are not equal. Some of us are stronger, some wiser, some wealthier, than others. We are not equally endowed with talents at birth, nor do we all partake in equal sets of circumstances as we grow and develop.

A more precise and useful definition is this one from the Webster's dictionary: "Democracy is the principle of equality of rights, opportunity, and treatment, or the practice of this principle."

The dictionary makes it quite clear. We are not equal, but we are entitled to equal treatment and to equal opportunities. Whether we take advantage of these opportunities is a matter of personal will and not a reflection of the justice or injustice of the society at large.

The above definition helps us understand that while we are all equally entitled to be members of a democratic society, we are not all equally qualified to fill all of the roles necessary for that society to function. We are not all qualified to be leaders, we are not all qualified to be teachers, and we are not even all qualified to be soldiers.

In the previous several Torah portions, we have been observing a society in the making – not a democratic society in the contemporary sense, but one designed to be fair and equitable, and to allow for the fullest possible spiritual expression of every individual within it.

In *Parashat Korah*, we learn of the first challenge to this society in formation. Korah, a close relative of Moses and Aaron, challenges their roles as leader and high priest. He also advocates what might be mistaken for a democracy, if we are to understand democracy in the fashion outlined in the first few sentences of this chapter.

This is Korah's understanding of the nature of the Jewish community in the desert: "All of the congregation is holy, and God is in their midst." Korah is, in the eyes of some, the arch democrat. He sees all in the community as being holy. All are equal in holiness and all are equal in the eyes of God. He is thus protesting the hierarchy represented by a tribe of priests, a tribe of Levites, and a group of elders. He is calling for radical equality and for utter sameness.

There is a line from Gilbert and Sullivan's "The Gondoliers" that is never far from my mind. It reads, "When everyone is somebody, then no one's anybody!" Korah is advocating a society in which everybody is somebody. Can that work?

I will not even attempt to answer that question in terms of political philosophy. But I will venture to speculate about the possibility of a society in which all are equally spiritual, in which everyone is a spiritual somebody.

For you see, much earlier in the Torah, such a society was indeed foreseen. Back in the Torah portion of *Kedoshim* (Lev. 19:2), the entire nation was told, "You shall be holy, for I, the Lord your God, am holy." We were enjoined to be a "kingdom of priests." Is Korah so far off then with his claim that all of the congregation is holy?

It is as an answer to this question that the dictionary definition of democracy is so helpful. We are not all equal; we are certainly not all holy. But we all have the opportunity, the equal opportunity, to become holy through our actions and the way we live our lives.

The "kingdom of priests" ideal is to be the product of our spiritual endeavors, not a hereditary honor. No person, in this sense, is born spiritual. We are not equally holy from birth. But we all have the equal opportunity to dedicate our lives to the achievement of holiness and to the attainment of spirituality.

Korah is wrong when he proclaims that the entire community is holy. He would have been correct to say that we all can *achieve* holiness. Judaism teaches us that although we are all equally endowed with the capacity for holiness and with the potential for spirituality, the achievement of those objectives is not easy. Spirituality is not obtained by a moment on a mountaintop or by fleeting inspirational experiences. Jewish spirituality can only be attained by hard work and painful self-sacrifice.

The leadership positions of Moses and Aaron were earned by virtue of their life-long dedication to the Jewish people. Korah is indeed wrong when he says that we are all equally capable of supplanting Moses and Aaron. We are all potential leaders and we all have the opportunity to develop leadership skills, but we are not automatically leaders just because we are part of the community.

The mitzva back in *Parashat Kedoshim* does not imply, as Korah does, that we all are *kedoshim*. Rather, it calls upon us to do what we can to become *kedoshim*. And so, our *parasha* teaches us an important personal lesson; one of special relevance to those of us who have absorbed a deep belief in democracy. We are not all spiritually equal. There are those of us who are more spiritual, and those who are less so. But we all have equal opportunities and equal possibilities to develop the levels of spirituality that God himself foresaw when He asked us to become a "kingdom of priests."

Parashat Koraḥ

Better They Learn
From Me

Conflict resolution is one of the most important tasks in human relations at every level. Open up any newspaper and you will read of schoolchildren bullying each other, of married couples who are in bitter conflict, of political parties enmeshed in verbal warfare, and of nations literally at war. What are some of the strategies available to foster conflict resolution?

One of the most interesting strategies can be found in an ancient endeavor known by the generic term of martial arts. I once watched a brief film on the subject in which I observed a fascinating technique. The participant in the battle was instructed not to fight his opponent head-on, not to counter aggression with aggression. Rather, he was instructed to yield to the attack, to move paradoxically backwards as if to surrender, and not to move forward in the attack mode. In a sense, he was directed to surprise his opponent by reacting unpredictably. This strategy can be applied to many situations in life in which there is strife and discord.

In *Parashat Koraḥ*, we read of such discord. We study the story of the rebellion led by Korah and his cohorts against Moses. Among this band are Datan and Aviram, the sons of Eliav, who had long been thorns in Moses' side. They challenge his authority and threaten outright revolt against his leadership. A civil war looms.

Interestingly, Moses' initial response is not one of anger. He tries verbal persuasion, he calls for divine intervention, and only then does he eventually, indignantly, express his anger. But before he reaches that point, he tries something that goes almost unnoticed by most commentators.

He sends for them. He adopts a conciliatory attitude and invites them into dialogue. "And Moses sent to call Datan and Aviram" (Num. 16:12).

Moses does not "come out fighting," at least not until his invitation to discussion and perhaps even compromise is rebuffed. "And they said, 'We will not come up…. Do you need to make yourself a prince over us? Will you put out the eyes of these men? We will not come up!'"

Only after his attempt at conflict resolution does Moses become angry and appeal for divine intervention. But first, he signals his readiness to talk things over.

I have been reading a biography of a great hasidic leader in early twentieth-century Poland. His name was Rabbi Israel Danziger, known today by the title of his book of inspirational homilies, *Yismaḥ Yisrael*. He was the heir to the leadership of the second largest hasidic sect in pre-World War II Europe. That sect was known by the name of the town near Lodz where he, and his father before him, held court. His father's name was Rabbi Yehiel Danziger, and the name of the town was Alexandrow.

The biography contains documentation of several talks Rabbi Israel gave describing many of the lessons he learned from his sainted father. In one of those talks, he tells of the time that he was sent, along with several of his father's emissaries, to visit the court of another hasidic rebbe. He describes how that rebbe's personal secretary made the delegation wait their turn on a long line. He describes how, when they finally got into the rebbe's reception room, they were treated perfunctorily, if not coldly. And the request that they were instructed to make of this rebbe was callously rejected by him. They returned to

Alexandrow feeling chastised. Rabbi Israel, who led the d
reported back to his father and relayed to him every detail of th.
appointing experience.

About a year later, the other hasidic rebbe needed a great favor
of Rabbi Yehiel. He sent a delegation to Alexandrow, headed by his
own son. The delegation arrived and much to Rabbi Israel's surprise,
his father issued orders that they be welcomed warmly and be shown
gracious hospitality. Rabbi Yehiel further instructed that the delegation
be given an appointment during "prime time" and not be asked to wait
on line at all. Rabbi Yehiel himself waited at his door for them, ushered
them into his private chambers, seated them comfortably, and personally served them refreshments. He listened to their request for a favor of
him and granted it generously. Then, as Jewish tradition prescribes, he
bid them farewell only after first escorting them part of the way along
the route of their return journey.

In his narrative, as recorded in this fascinating biography, Rabbi
Israel expresses amazement at his father's conduct. He describes how he
approached his father and asked him directly, "Why did you treat them
so well? Did you not recall how that rebbe and his followers treated us
not so long ago? Did you have to give them such an effusive welcome
after they embarrassed us so much?"

I found Rabbi Yehiel's response, in Yiddish of course, so impressive that I committed it to memory verbatim. He said, "Better that they
learn from me how to be *gute yidden* and *menschen*, than I learn from
them how to be boors and brutes!"

The biography does not tell the rest of the story. But when I
related the story to an audience of Hasidim a short while ago, I found
out about part of the rest of the story. An elderly man in the audience
approached me and said, "I am a descendant of that other rebbe. And
our family tradition has it that when his delegation returned with news
of their special treatment and of the granted favor, the rebbe burst into
tears and cried, 'He is a better Jew than I am. We must learn a lesson in
ethics (*musar haskel*) from him.'"

This is a lesson we can all benefit from as we attempt to resolve
the conflicts we face, and as we strive to increase the numbers of *gute
yidden* in our ranks and create more *menschen* in the world.

The Secret of Remaining Correct

V ery often, we think that if a person is especially spiritual, he cannot possibly be very practical. It is as if religious devotion and good common sense just don't go together.

My own experience has taught me that, on the contrary, some of the soundest advice I have ever received came from people who spent most of their time in sacred practice and who seemed on the surface to be quite detached from everyday affairs. Indeed, it was an old pious Hasid who encouraged me to embark upon my career as a psychologist, and it was a hasidic rebbe who, much later in my life, advised me to make a mid-career change and assume a rabbinic pulpit.

In my study of Jewish sources, I have encountered individuals who devoted their lives to very lofty ideals, but who had sage counsel to offer those who were engaged in much more worldly matters.

One such person was Rabbi Yisrael Salanter (1810–1883). Reb Yisrael, as he was known by his many disciples, founded the Musar movement, which endeavored to inspire the public to be more conscious of the ethical components of our faith. Whereas his "curriculum" consisted of sacred writings, some of which bordered on the mystical, he used techniques that were extremely down-to-earth. Indeed, it seems clear that he was aware of the theories of psychology that were just beginning to be introduced during the latter half of the nineteenth century when he began to spread his teachings.

Reb Yisrael had much sound advice to give, even to those who were not members of his movement, and one such piece of advice always struck me as unusually insightful and very useful, even in quite mundane situations. This is what he said, with reference to someone who is involved in an argument with another, "If you are right, make sure that you remain right."

He meant that it is human nature for a person who is right, and utterly convinced that his cause is just, to resort to ridiculous extremes in order to justify his position – so much so that he goes on to say or do things that undermine his position. He says things he shouldn't have said, attacks his enemies in an unseemly fashion, and further conducts himself in a manner that eventually proves to be his own undoing.

It is much better, suggested Reb Yisrael, to state your case succinctly and cogently, and leave it at that. It is even advisable to yield a bit to your opponent, losing a small battle or two, but winning the bigger war. It is best to remain relatively silent after expressing the essentials of your case and to realize that, in the end, "Truth springs up from the earth, and justice looks down from heaven" (Ps. 85:12).

Knowing about his magisterial erudition, when I first came upon Reb Yisrael's helpful admonition, I knew that he must have had sources in sacred Jewish texts for all that he said. Over the years, I have collected quite a few citations in our literature that might have served as the basis for his words.

One such source occurs in *Parashat Koraḥ* (Num. 16:1–18:32). I am indebted to a precious little book of Torah commentary, *Zikhron Meyer*, by Rabbi Dov Meyer Rubman, of blessed memory, who was a pupil of Rabbi Salanter, and who helped establish a yeshiva in Haifa.

The story is a familiar one. Korah rebels against the authority of Moses and Aaron, and rallies 250 "chiefs of Sanhedrin" to his cause.

The opening words of the story, "And Korah took himself," imply that, rather than expressing his complaint privately and respectfully to Moses, Korah chose to incite a crowd of others to publicly and brazenly protest.

Rabbi Rubman quotes from the collection known as Midrash Tanḥuma:

> "And Korah took." This bears out the verse, "A brother offended is more formidable than a stronghold; such strife is like the bars of a fortress" (Prov. 18:19). It refers to Korah, who disputed with Moses and rebelled, and descended from the prestige he already had in hand.

Korah, explains Rabbi Rubman, had some valid and persuasive arguments – so much so that he was able to gain the allegiance of 250 "chiefs of Sanhedrin," each of whom was a qualified judge. He was a "formidable stronghold."

Had he addressed Moses and Aaron properly, those aspects of his complaint that had legitimacy would have been heard. They may have been able to find an appropriate leadership capacity in which he could serve. Was this not the case when others, such as those who were ritually unqualified to bring the paschal offering, or the daughters of Tzlofhad, approached Moses with their complaints? Did Moses, under divine guidance, not find an adequate solution to their complaints?

Initially, there was some merit to Korah's dissatisfaction. In some sense, he was "right." But he was not satisfied with that. He had to push forward, involve others, speak blasphemously, and enter into a full-fledged revolt. He thus "descended from the prestige he had in hand."

Had he heeded the very practical counsel of Rabbi Salanter, "If you are right make sure you remain right," his story would have turned out very differently. Instead of being one of the rogues of Jewish history, he may have become one of its heroes.

Here you have it. Rabbi Yisrael Salanter may have been considered a naïve *luftmensch* by his contemporaries, a man with his head in the clouds. However, here we have an example of but one of his sayings, and it is a useful statement even for the most practical of men.

When we are convinced that we are right, we tend to invest as much energy as we can to prove ourselves right. Reb Yisrael advises us to spare ourselves the effort and trust more in our convictions. If they are indeed warranted, they will speak for themselves.

Parashat Koraḥ

Two Jews, Three Opinions

W̶e all nod our heads in agreement when we hear the phrase, "Two Jews, three opinions." We similarly chuckle when we hear the anecdote about the Jew who was discovered after years of living alone on a desert island. His rescuers noticed that he had built two huts aside from the one he lived in. He told the puzzled people who saved him that they were *shuls*. When asked why he needed two *shuls*, he retorted, "One is the one in which I pray, and the other is the one into which I would never set foot."

We have no trouble believing that Jews tend to be contentious and have to express their disagreements with others, even when stranded alone on a desert island. The question that must be asked is whether or not this contentiousness is a good thing.

Long ago, one could find unanimity among wise men about certain values. Everyone consented that wisdom, diligence, and harmony were values worthy of acclaim. Then a great philosopher, Erasmus, came along and wrote a book entitled *In Praise of Folly*. No longer could proponents of wisdom pretend that everyone agreed with them.

More recently, the philosopher and mathematician Bertrand Russell wrote an essay entitled *In Praise of Idleness*. Gone from the list of universally held virtues were diligence and hard work.

What about concepts such as peace and harmony? Have they also suffered the fate of the aforementioned values? Have people begun to believe that contentiousness and argumentativeness, if not outright strife, are to be extolled?

Parashat Korah (Num. 16:1–18:32) provides the occasion to reflect on just such questions. Korah is the biblical paradigm of the contentious individual. He is, to say the least, dissatisfied with Moses' leadership style and calls into question the entire social hierarchy with which he was confronted. According to the rabbis, he was even skeptical of various rituals, not being able to accept that a house full of holy books required a mezuza, or that a tallit made entirely of blue colored wool required tzitzit with the blue colored fringe. He had no difficulty finding contentious companions and he eventually organized them into a band of rebels and fomented a full-fledged revolt against the authority of Moses and Aaron.

For the rabbis of the Talmud, Korah epitomizes the negative trait of strife and discord (*mahloket*). A famous passage in Ethics of the Fathers distinguishes between legitimate disputes, those "for the sake of heaven," and those that are not so motivated. They add, "What is an example of a dispute for the sake of heaven? The dispute between Hillel and Shammai. What is an example of one not for the sake of heaven? The dispute of Korah and all his company." The former type of dispute has enduring value. The latter does not.

From this passage, it is apparent that our sages do not categorically oppose dispute, debate, and argument. Rather, everything depends upon the motive. If the motive is a noble one, "for the sake of heaven," then debate is not only tolerated but it is considered valuable. If the motive is ignoble, and certainly if it is merely contentious, it is strongly condemned.

An example of such a harsh condemnation is to be found in the Midrash on this *parasha*. The Midrash points out how each of the letters comprising the word *mahloket* represents a different vile trait. Thus, the first letter, *mem*, stands for *makka*, wound. The letter *het* stands for *haron*, wrath. The letter *lamed* begins the word *lakui*, smitten. The letter *kuf* represents *klala*, curse. The final letter *tav* stands for *tahlit*, which is often translated as goal or objective, but in this context means a final tragic ending.

But just as much as our sages condemned improperly motivated disputes, so did they find value in disputes of constructive purpose. They particularly appreciated disputes motivated by the search for truth. Hence, hardly a page in the thousands of pages of the Talmud is bereft of strong differences of opinion among the rabbis.

It is noteworthy in this regard that every single chapter of the work known as the Mishna, which is the core around which the Talmud developed, contains a dispute between the rabbis on one point or another. The only exception to this is the fifth chapter of the Tractate Zevahim, "*Eyzehu mekoman*," which begins with the question, "What is the location for the Temple sacrifices?" No dispute at all is recorded in this unique chapter. Yet, this is the chapter chosen for inclusion in the daily prayer book. It has been argued that it is precisely this chapter, which is devoid of even a trace of contentiousness, that merited inclusion in our sacred liturgy.

An objection has been raised to the criterion "for the sake of heaven" as a legitimate motive for dispute. Surely men have been motivated to commit horrible evil because they believed they were acting "for the sake of heaven." One of the strongest arguments raised by freethinkers against religion is the fact that so much blood has been spilled over the millennia by people who were convinced that they were performing God's will.

It is to counter such an objection that the rabbis gave as an example of an appropriate dispute the *mahloket* between Hillel and Shammai. The disagreements between these two sages and their disciples down through the generations were characterized by tolerance and friendship. So much so that the Talmud records more than one incident when Hillel came around to Shammai's way of thinking, and when Shammai conceded to Hillel.

The disputes between Hillel and Shammai endure to this very day. Although we generally rule in accordance with the opinion of the former, we carefully attended to the arguments of the latter. I, for one, am convinced that we do so to perpetuate the attitudes of attentiveness and harmony, which both Hillel and Shammai advocated and enacted.

Students of Torah must not only study the content of these ancient disputes; they must also learn to re-create the atmosphere that prevailed among the disputants, an atmosphere of civility and mutual respect, and a willingness to concede one's original position in order to achieve the truth.

Discovering our Mortality

It was at a house of mourning and she was saying something that I had heard many times before. In fact, I had said it myself when I was sitting *shiva* for my own mother.

She is a friend of long-standing and a member of my former congregation. I hope that I am not being unchivalrous by describing her as late middle-aged. She had just lost her own mother, having lost her father several years earlier.

"It is not just that I feel orphaned," she said. "It is that I feel vulnerable. As long as even one of my parents was alive, it was as if there was a kind of buffer between me and death. Now that they are both gone, it begins to feel that it is my turn. No one to protect me. I face the angel of death (*malakh hamavet*) directly, face-to-face, head-on."

We all deny our mortality, and as long as the older generation is around, we feel that they, and not we, are the ones on death's front-lines. We are insulated from death's claws by them. It is their turn and not yet ours. But once we lose our own parents, we can no longer deny our mortality. It is our turn.

There is an excellent book by my esteemed colleague, Rabbi Marc Angel, entitled *The Orphaned Adult*. I often recommend this book to mourners, particularly those who are fortunate to have entered adulthood, even late middle age, with both parents alive, and experience their deaths only after having long ago reached adulthood. Their feelings are unique and very different from those who experienced the trauma of a parent's death at an earlier stage of life. Rabbi Angel also describes this sudden sense of mortality, of vulnerability. With the death of parents, these older people finally must surrender their comfortable denial of their own inevitable demise.

In *Parashat Ḥukkat*, we read of the death of two beloved leaders of the Jewish people, Miriam and Aaron. Both of them were parent figures, albeit not actual parents, of the Jews in the years of their wandering in the wilderness. Instructively, a period of vulnerability ensues immediately upon their respective deaths.

We read first of Miriam's death. "The Israelites arrived at the wilderness of Zin...Miriam died there and was buried there." And then, immediately, "The community was without water" (Num. 20:1–2).

As long as Miriam was alive, she was a source of water, a source of life. While she was alive, the well of Miriam (*be'er Miriam*) provided water for the people. With her death, the well immediately dried up, the water ceased, and the people were vulnerable. Without "Mother" Miriam, death by thirst threatened the people. Soon afterwards, we read, "and Aaron died there on the summit of the mountain." And then, this time not immediately, but after thirty days of mourning, "When the Canaanite king of Arad heard...he engaged Israel in battle and took some of them captive" (Num. 20:28–29 and 21:1). "Father" Aaron died, and peace and security were shattered. War and that worst of fates, captivity, reared their ugly heads.

It seems that it is more than mere psychological reality that, with the passing of its leaders, a nation faces calamity. With the death of one's parents, one's own well-being is threatened. No wonder that when the young sister-in-law of the eighteenth-century sage, Rabbi Yonatan Eybeshutz, lost her husband, the rabbi cautioned her, in a letter that has come down to us, to take special care of her own physical well-being and the health of her young children. As our sages put it in the Talmud, "When one member of a group perishes, the entire group needs to be anxious."

How apt are the words of the Psalmist, "When my father and mother abandon me, the Lord will take me in" (Ps. 27:10).

When our parents "abandon" us and leave this world, we are bereft in many ways, and our positions in life become precarious. We need God at those moments, and turn to Him, confident that He will "take us in."

The Many Songs
of Leadership

Everyone has his or her own voice. Some express it loudly and clearly, some just mumble or whisper. There are those who let their voices be heard only in their professional lives and are silent and withdrawn at home. Others use their voices only within their families and stifle their voices in the outside world.

Our voices can be expressed in a variety of ways: through speech, through the written word, and even by means of our postures and gestures. Our voices can also be expressed through song.

In a book he wrote for managers of organizations coping with the complex challenges of the twenty-first-century work environment, Stephen Covey makes the following statement, "There is a deep, innate, almost inexpressible yearning within each one of us to find our voice in life." That statement is the basis for his book, *The Eighth Habit: From Effectiveness to Greatness*, which is designed to help organizational leaders find their voices and inspire others to find theirs.

Each of the great leaders of the Jewish people, from biblical times down to the present, had his or her own distinctive voice. The voice of Abraham was heard throughout his world; the voice of Isaac was almost silent in comparison. Moses described his own voice as defective, yet he was capable of supreme eloquence. Joshua's voice is never described as wanting in any way, yet we have few examples of his personal unique voice.

Some of our great leaders, including Moses, expressed their voices in song. We have the Song of the Sea in which the voice of Moses dominates; his sister Miriam responds to Moses' song in her own voice; the prophetess Deborah and King David are exemplary in their ability to use the medium of song to express their unique and distinctive voices.

All of the above are examples of how individual Jewish heroes and heroines found and expressed their voices. *Parashat Ḥukkat* provides an example of an entirely different kind of a voice: not the voice of one person, but the voice of an entire group, indeed of an entire nation. It is the Song of the Well, of the *Be'er*:

> The well where the Lord said to Moses,
> "Assemble the people that I may give them water."
> Then Israel sang this song:
> "Spring up, O well – sing to it –
> The well that the chieftains dug,
> Which the nobles of the people started
> With the scepter, and with their own staffs.
> And from the wilderness to Matana,
> and from Matana to Nahaliel,
> and from Nahaliel to Bamot." (Num. 21:16–19)

This is a much briefer song than the song that Moses led when the people of Israel miraculously crossed the Sea. But part of this passage, too, at least in the synagogues with which I am familiar, is chanted melodically.

I have long been impressed by the fact that our *parasha*, in which the Song of the Well appears, describes a critical transition in the leadership of the Jewish people. From the time of the Exodus from Egypt, the Jewish people essentially have had three leaders: Moses, Aaron, and Miriam. In this *parasha*, Miriam dies and is buried, Aaron too is "gathered unto his people" and is mourned, and Moses learns that his leadership role will come to an end sooner than he had thought, before the Jewish people enter the Promised Land.

This is indeed a story of transition, of the end of an era, of the passing of the mantle of leadership to a new generation. No wonder then that the song sung in this *parasha* is so very different from the song sung by Moses at that triumphant moment near the beginning of his leadership career.

Our sages tell us in Tractate Sota that the Song of the Sea was sung by the people responsively. That is, Moses said the first phrase, which the people said after him. He proceeded then to the second phrase, and the people echoed him. Moses was an authoritative leader and the people were obedient followers. Moses was the active composer of the song, the choirmaster as it were, and the people were but the choir.

In our *parasha*, two of the leaders pass from the scene, and Moses learns that his leadership authority is waning. The Song of the Well is an entirely different leadership song from the Song of the Sea. In this song, the entire people sing as one. It begins not "Then Moses sang this song," but rather "Then Israel sang this song." The leadership passes from one divinely chosen charismatic leader to the people as a whole.

The people find their voice, and it is the voice of song. How beautifully this is expressed in the Midrash *Yalkut Shimoni* I:764:

> After forty years, the people finally matured and began to sing a song on their own accord, saying, "Master of the Universe, it is now incumbent upon You to do miracles for us and for us to sing, as it is written: "It has pleased the Lord to deliver us and that is why we sing our song all the days of our lives." (Is. 38:20)

Jewish history has known epochs in which there were clear leaders, gifted, and often charismatic individuals who, by virtue of their wisdom or heroism, seemed ordained by the Almighty Himself to lead our people. But we have also known times, such as the present, when such prominent leaders are not apparent.

It is at times such as these that we all must assume leadership responsibilities. It is at times such as these that we cannot afford to humbly refrain from acting as leaders in our own families and communities. It is at times such as these that we must, each of us, find our own voice and sing the songs of leadership.

Parashat Ḥukkat

Let Me Repeat

T he poem had a place of prominence on our kitchen bulletin board for many years. We had clipped it from a women's magazine, and although it was too sugary and sentimental for my personal literary taste, it was very encouraging to my wife and me as we raised our teenage daughters. The poem was written by an early middle-aged mother and described a visit she had with her daughter, now grown, over tea one fine afternoon.

We have long lost our copy of that poem, but its message remains as clear as day. The poem relates how, over tea that day, the younger woman thanked her mother for all the lessons she learned from her. She confessed that she once found her mother's repetitive teachings about proper behavior to be useless and annoying. But she now had come to appreciate just how useful and important those teachings were. She thanked her mother for what she learned and expressed special gratitude for her patient reiteration of those lessons. The mother ends her poem with an expression of pride in herself and in her daughter.

This poem and its lesson came to mind recently when I visited the synagogue where I served as rabbi some years ago. A young man whom I remembered as a teenager approached me and said that he felt he owed me an apology. He proceeded to tell me how sorry he was for not appreciating my tendency, in my sermons and lectures, to repeatedly emphasize the importance of the precise translation of Hebrew words and phrases.

"Each time that you would insist that the common translation of, for example, *kedusha* as 'holiness' was not quite accurate, we kids would roll our eyes in exasperation. You would sometimes do that three or four times in just one sermon." He then told me how he and his friends had come to understand the importance of nuance, especially in rendering biblical Hebrew into English.

I must confess that, even today, I preserve that tendency to repeat myself, and it is not always attributable to my increasingly frequent "senior moments." Quite the contrary; I consciously and intentionally repeat matters that I think are important, especially in my public speeches. I base my conviction that repetition is necessary and effective upon a comment by a great man on a passage in *Parashat Ḥukkat* (Num. 19:1–22:1).

The story is well-known. The Children of Israel complain to Moses and Aaron about the lack of water in the wilderness. They fall upon their faces in prayer, and the Almighty responds by telling Moses to take his staff, gather the people, and speak to the rock that is before their eyes. The Lord assures Moses that he will be able to draw forth sufficient water from the rock for the people and for their cattle.

Moses takes the staff, assembles the people, and castigates them angrily. He then lifts his hand and strikes the rock with his staff, not once but twice. Indeed, abundant water flows from the rock.

The Almighty then expresses his disappointment to Moses and Aaron. He tells them that, because they did not believe in him sufficiently to sanctify his Name before all the people, they would be denied the privilege of bringing the people into the Holy Land.

Throughout the ages, commentaries have found difficulty with this narrative. Rashi insists that Moses sinned by striking the rock and not just speaking to it. Others have objected to Rashi's approach because drawing water from the rock in the desert is equally miraculous whether it is accomplished by speaking to the rock or striking it. Water flowing from a rock when it is struck with a wooden staff is itself a wondrous miracle, certainly sufficient to impress the people with God's miraculous powers.

Rabbi Moshe Feinstein, the late twentieth-century sage whom I was privileged to meet personally, offers a simple and innovative response to this objection. He writes:

> The Almighty preferred that Moses speak to the rock because he wanted to teach the lesson that one must speak words of Torah and ethics even to those who seem not to comprehend. Repeating and reviewing ultimately results in understanding. A parent, for example, must never despair of educating his children just because they appear not to understand what he is telling them. One must constantly speak to others, over and over, until they understand and act accordingly, just like the rock could not understand but eventually fulfilled God's will. Certainly, human beings, although they seem now not to understand at all, will eventually reach understanding.

Rabbi Feinstein's insight is such an important one, especially to rabbis, parents, and teachers. Rarely does our audience seem to be attentive and receptive to our message. But if we earnestly attempt to present our message intelligently, and if we repeat it sufficiently, we will be heard, later if not sooner. This was the experience of the mother who wrote the poem, which graced our kitchen wall for many years, and this was the experience of the young man who came to appreciate the importance of precise translation after hearing me drone on and on about it in his youth.

Although Rabbi Feinstein does not quote any talmudic sources supporting the great value of repetition, he could easily have referred to the following passage in the Talmud:

> Rabbi Perada had a student whom he would teach each lesson four hundred times until the student finally understood. One day, Rabbi Perada received an invitation to attend a mitzva celebration. He first sat with the student and repeated the daily lesson

four hundred times, but this time to no avail. The student simply did not comprehend. Rabbi Perada asked him why he was having such difficulty on that day. The student responded that as soon as he heard that the master was invited to a mitzva event, he became distracted, thinking that at any moment the master would interrupt the lesson and not review it with him the four hundred times that he required. Rabbi Perada patiently instructed his disciple to be calm, pay attention, and be confident that he would deliver the lesson as many times as necessary. He reviewed it four hundred times, and the disciple finally understood." (Tractate Eruvin 54b)

The Talmud continues to describe the earthly and heavenly rewards that Rabbi Perada received for his most unusual commitment and forbearance. The Talmud is thus teaching us, and Rabbi Feinstein underscores it, that our sincerely spoken words are not wasted. The educational lessons that we try to impart are eventually heard. We must not give up in our attempts to inspire, instruct, and influence others. We can be assured, in the words of King Solomon, "Cast your bread upon the waters, for you shall find it after many days" (Eccl. 11:1).

The Almighty had good reason to tell Moses to speak to the rock. Even rocks eventually get the message.

Parashat Balak

Doing It My Way

Most of us have had occasions in our lives when we acted as supervisors over others. It might have been in our role as parents disciplining our children, it might have been as employers giving instructions to employees, or it might have been any number of other contexts in which we had to tell others what to do.

I sometimes reflect on the many times in my own personal and professional life when I suggested, counseled, or otherwise instructed others. And I often think of the diverse reactions I received to my attempts to influence or guide the behavior of others.

There were certainly those who rejected my instructions, sometimes passively, sometimes defiantly. My own children were quite creative in devising ways to ignore their father's commands. And I have had subordinates in various positions that I have held who sometimes stood up to me and simply said, "No!"

I have also experienced numerous occasions when my suggestions or commands were carried out to the letter. These were occasions when the individuals I supervised acted with commitment and with obedience to my wishes. I must admit to my great preference for these individuals. Every supervisor likes commitment.

But there is a middle category. Here, the subordinates neither defy their orders, nor perfectly conform to them. Rather, the subordinate's response is, "Yes, but!" "I will listen to what you say," they respond, "but I will do it my way!"

When I received responses in this middle category, I found myself in a quandary. On the one hand, I wanted my orders obeyed, but on the other hand, I didn't want to squelch the initiative and self-reliance of the person to whom I was assigning the task. I may have preferred total commitment, but I compromised. I allowed concession.

It is from these personal reflections that I can better understand the interaction between the major character of *Parashat Balak*, Balaam son of Beor, and the Almighty.

Read the opening paragraphs of our *parasha*. Balaam begins as a very pious individual who dares not make a move without the Lord's permission. He asks God whether he can accept the request he has received to curse the Israelites. God answers, "Do not go with them! You must not curse that people, for they are blessed." Balaam accepts this response with commitment. He tells Balak's dignitaries, "I cannot go with you."

But then Balak ups the ante and sends more numerous and more distinguished dignitaries to Balaam. Again, Balaam consults the Almighty. But this time, He responds, "You may go with them, but whatever I command you, you shall do." How do we understand this shift in the divine instructions?

Drawing upon our own personal human experiences in giving instructions to others, we can begin to understand this shift. At first, Balaam responds with commitment. In his second consultation with the Lord, that commitment has diminished. The second delegation of dignitaries has weakened Balaam's resolve. So God, so to speak, has to adapt to Balaam's "Yes, but!" And God offers a concession, "Obey me, but do it your way."

Our sages describe this concession with the following adage: "On the road man wishes to pursue, upon that road he is led." That is, God allows us to follow the paths we ourselves choose. Our free will is so important to Him that He concedes to our wishes, and allows us to "do it our way." Of course, He prefers commitment, but He grants concession, hoping that, even in doing it our way, we will ultimately obey Him and conform, albeit imperfectly, to His will.

This approach to understanding one of the ways in which the Almighty deals with human weakness allows us to understand many other biblical examples of God's concessions to human willfulness.

Just a few *parashot* earlier, for example, we read in Numbers 13 of God's command to Moses to send spies to scout out the Promised Land. The commentaries struggle with the account in Deuteronomy 1, in which it is clearly the people's idea, indeed demand, that spies be sent, and not God's command. The rabbis resolved the problem of the differing texts by suggesting that God Himself did not think spies were necessary. He originally depended upon the people's commitment to rely unquestioningly upon His promise of the land to them. But the people wanted to "do it their way" by sending spies. God relented, as it were. His command to send out spies was a concession He felt was necessary in the absence of commitment.

This insight also helps us understand the questions, which have been raised by students of the Bible for millennia, about the desirability of a king in Israel. Is appointing a king a divine imperative, as some texts suggest, or is it a concession by God to the will of the people? Here too our approach is helpful. If He could depend upon the people's total commitment to His divine sovereignty, then there would be no necessity for a king. But the people wanted it "their way," and so we have God's concession, the mitzva of appointing a king.

This concept is particularly useful to apply to our own lives. Ideally, we all should act out of perfect commitment. But human nature often insists that we do it our way. The compassionate Lord of the universe "cuts us a bit of slack" and gives us some flexibility, but relies upon us not to veer too far from His expectations.

Balaam and Dostoevsky

Frustration. Disillusionment. But also insight and a lifelong intellectual perspective. That is how I would describe the experience I am about to share with you, dear reader.

It all started with Dostoevsky. That's right, Fyodor Dostoevsky, the famous nineteenth-century Russian novelist, author of *Crime and Punishment, The Brothers Karamazov*, and much more. His works were strangely not part of the curriculum of the high school I attended. I came to his writing on my own.

How impressed I was! Here was a writer who really plumbed the depths of the human psyche. He grappled, not only with profound moral issues, but with questions of existential religious significance.

I vividly remember reading *Notes from the Underground*, astounded by the fact that a gentile author, living in Czarist Russia, had so much to say to a Brooklyn yeshiva boy.

And then I learned a bit about Dostoevsky's background. I was stunned to discover that this perceptive, sensitive, and gifted man was a vicious anti-Semite. I had great difficulty in reconciling the discrepancy between the art – sophisticated and empathic – and the author, full of primitive hatred, which I experienced as aimed at me. After all, my ancestors lived in the towns and villages he describes – and not long ago!

I experienced this disillusionment time and time again in subsequent years. In college, I became enamored with the philosophy of Martin Heidegger, who was often acclaimed as the greatest thinker of the twentieth century. Then I learned of his support for the Nazi regime, and I could no longer bring myself to even open his books.

This experience was repeated later in my education when I became familiar with the psychology of Carl Jung, only to discover his complicated relationship with Jews and Judaism, and his pro-Nazi sentiments. What an exhaustive list of gifted men who possessed such talent when it came to humanity, yet who were so absurdly tainted by their active aversion to our people. It extends back in time to Martin Luther, persists through the music of Wagner and the history of Toynbee, and is certainly not lacking for contemporary examples.

Truth be told, the list goes back even further – to *Parashat Balak* and the extraordinary and fascinating man named Balaam. If there is one lesson to learn from the narrative of Balaam and his encounter with the Jewish people, it is this: A man can be a universally acclaimed spiritual leader, and a gifted poet and orator with prophetic powers almost identical to those of Moses, and simultaneously be a vile anti-Semite, capable of genocidal schemes.

Read this *parasha* very carefully, for there is an essential message in it. The message is: we dare not assume that we need fear anti-Semitism only at the hands of maniacs, fanatics, or ignoramuses. Quite the contrary! Sophisticated, educated, and highly cultured individuals can also detest us and conspire to destroy us.

This is one of the lessons of the Holocaust. True, Hitler was hardly an intellectual or artistic giant. But his evil genius lay in his realization that the most advanced civilization in the history of the world would eagerly abide by his murderous vision. He knew that German art, literature, philosophy and, yes, religion, were just part of a veneer that masked dark, primitive forces with potential for great evil.

In terms of our *parasha*, he knew what Balak knew: there are individuals with:

- Strong religious commitments: "I cannot go beyond the word of the Lord my God to do anything small, or great." (Num. 22:18)
- A direct spiritual channel to the Divine: "And God came unto Balaam at night, and said unto him." (Num. verse 20)
- Inventive skills sufficient to create a phrase, which we ourselves adopted to preface our daily prayers: "How goodly are thy tents, O Jacob." (Num. 24:5)

But in actuality, they are no more than "hired guns," and beneath the façade of the "gentleman," lies the "agreement" to discriminate, persecute, murder, and exterminate an entire people.

It is a difficult lesson to accept. But our history has long established its deep-rooted veracity and its urgency, clearly based upon the story we read in *Parashat Balak*.

Parashat Balak

The Ancient Near East: Its Relevance Today

U garitic. Sumerian. Akkadian. Hittite. These are words that I never heard in all the years of my traditional Jewish education. They are the names of four important cultures and languages in the ancient Near East. All of these cultures were contemporaneous with the stories of the Bible, which most of us have been familiar with since our early childhood.

There are many serious students of the history of the Jewish people who insist that we cannot ignore cultures of the kind listed above if we are to really understand the Torah and its teachings. They find many parallels between our language and customs – and even our religion – and those of these ancient societies. Yet there is no doubt (at least in the yeshivas with which I am familiar) that these cultures have no place in the curriculum.

For me, there is at least one important reason to know a bit about these now-extinct societies. This is because, as I see it, one aspect of all of our Torah, from the Ten Commandments given at Sinai to the sermons of rabbis alive today, is that the Torah is a protest against many of the major tenets and practices of the cultures with which we co-exist.

For this reason, it is helpful to know what the Torah is saying in protest to ancient Ugarit and Sumer, just as it is important to know what the Torah is saying about faults of our own age of instant gratification, electronic communication, and globalization.

In *Parashat Balak* (Num. 22:2–25:9), the Torah itself provides us with information about two ancient Near East cultures with which our ancestors were confronted in the very opening stages of our history. I refer, of course, to Moab and Midian.

It also introduces us to a "culture hero," possibly the most prominent "public intellectual" of his time, "Balaam son of Beor in Pethor, which is by the Euphrates." I think that the Torah does this in order to impress upon us the fact that the Jewish people, even while still in the desert, lived in a cultural context and not in isolation. Moreover, the Torah teaches us a bit about the nature of those cultures, all to which its own teachings stand in stark contrast.

The Torah reserves a description of the nature of Moabite and Midianite cultures for the end of our *parasha*. There we see how those cultures incorporated sensual practices into their religious rites and used temptations of the flesh as their way of both overcoming the Israelites militarily and of undermining the Torah's spiritual teachings.

But by far, the larger section of our *parasha* is devoted to Balaam: to his personal character, his eloquence, and surprisingly, even to his theology.

That Balaam was a "major player" in the ancient Near East is attested to not only in the Torah text, but in the texts of the remnants of other ancient cultures. Hence, we read on a fragmentary inscription on wall plaster (dated to the late ninth- to-eighth-century BCE) from a temple at Deir Alla in what is Jordan today, which records the night vision of a certain Balaam! The seer described in this precious relic bears the same name and patronymic as the Balaam in our *parasha*. Pethor is identified by archeologists as a site on the Sajur River in Aram (today, Syria), some 400 miles from Moab. All of this is important context for the message of our *parasha*.

What is that message? It is that even in the ancient Near East, there were forces antagonistic to our people, our belief system, and our morality. Furthermore, these forces were, in many ways, amazingly similar to some of the forces we face this very day.

What are some aspects of Balaam's mindset that may typify a philosophy prevalent in the ancient Near East but which are equally common nowadays? Let's begin with his willingness to sell himself and his services for the right price.

Balaam, we have seen, lived hundreds of miles from Moab. He himself was not at all endangered by the Israelites as they marched toward the Promised Land and posed a threat to trespass Moab's territory. Indeed, his first response to Balak's emissaries was a negative one. But soon we see that he was really just playing "hard to get." I rephrase what he said so that it sounds more like the language of so many contemporary politicians, "I have principles that I will not compromise. That is, I will not compromise except for the right price." Once the client ups the ante, the principles are abandoned and off he marches hand-in-hand with his new client, ready to comply with the client's wishes.

Our sages in Ethics of the Fathers (5:23) impress us with their ability to reduce Balaam's entire character into three concise phrases, "Whoever possesses these three qualities is a disciple of the wicked Balaam: an evil eye, a haughty spirit, and mighty desires." In other words, Balaam's special "assets" were envy, arrogance and lust – certainly not an uncommon triad of attributes among the politicians of our time.

Even more insightful is the talmudic observation that reveals the secret of Balaam's ability to place a curse upon others. The Talmud tells us that Balaam was somehow able to calculate the one precise moment in the day when the Almighty, compassionate at all other times, was wrathful. I have often understood this to mean that Balaam was able to separate out the aspects of the Deity that, taken out of the context of God's mercy, looked very much like violent anger. Balaam was able to use religion as an excuse for violence.

In this regard, he could easily find company in modern times, when so many are able to ignore the abundant religious teachings of peace and tolerance, and instead use religion as an excuse for hatred and harmful acts. The correlation between religion and violence is one that critics of religion use well on behalf of their cause. That correlation, to the extent that it is true, is directly attributable to the ability of some religious extremists to "calculate the fleeting moment of God's wrath," to ignore the 99.9 percent of the Lord's day, and dwell upon the microsecond in which His anger flares.

To fully appreciate the Torah's important messages, one must come to know against whom and against what they are aimed. The Torah elaborates upon the figure of Balaam because he represents what was most objectionable in the ancient Near East. But the Torah is eternal and all that it teaches in opposition to the prevalent culture of ancient times is equally relevant in modern times. Man's dark side has not changed. Neither have the Torah's lessons of light.

Parashat Balak

No to Here and Now

In an attempt to gain some space in my crowded apartment, I was going through some old records and discarding many of them. Uncertain about whether or not to keep some of them, I found myself guided by my mother-in-law's advice, "When in doubt, throw it out."

And so, although with some hesitation, I tossed into the trash: folders containing my children's report cards from thirty or more years ago, letters of congratulations at various family milestones, and letters of condolences that I received while sitting *shiva* for my dear departed parents.

About an hour after consigning those precious mementos to oblivion, I began to have second thoughts. I realized that I had chosen to eliminate documents of exquisite personal meaning. I had succumbed to the modern temptation to live only in the present and to ignore, nay suppress, the important role of the past in our lives. Luckily, I was able to retrieve these records and restored them to their rightful place in my personal archives.

These days, we must vigilantly resist this growing and powerful tendency to live only in the moment and for the moment. We dare not

473

forget the importance of the past, and yes, the future, upon our contemporary existence. Today's culture has aptly been called "ahistoric," and the loss of a historical perspective has taken its toll upon our society and upon each of us as individuals.

An excellent example of this anti-historical attitude is expressed in a passage in the writings of the Hebrew author Haim Hazaz. I am indebted to Professor Yosef Yerushalmi's book, *Zakhor: Jewish History and Jewish Memory*, for introducing me to the writings of Hazaz, who puts the following words in the mouth of his character, Yudka:

> I want to state that I am opposed to Jewish history. I would simply forbid teaching our children Jewish history. I would just say to them, "Boys, from the day we were exiled from our land, we've been a people without a history. Class dismissed. Go out and play football."

This attitude is personified by the hero, or perhaps better, the anti-hero, of our *parasha*, Balaam. He is described as one who "knows the mind of the Almighty." The Talmud wonders about this and suggests that Balaam is able to determine the one brief instant of each day when the Almighty is angry. As the Psalmist has it, "His anger is for a moment, but His favor is for a lifetime (*Rega be'apo hayim birtzono*)."

In a typically brilliant and provocative insight, Rav Kook suggests that there are two modes in which the Divine operates. There is the constant goodness, peace, light, and life that comprise the mode "eternity (*netzah*)." And then there are the transient moments when God, as it were, displays His fury, permits evil to get the upper hand, and allows strife, pestilence and war. That is the mode of "the moment (*rega*)."

Fortunate are those human beings who can connect and draw from God's mode of *netzah*. Beware those human beings who relate only to God's *rega* mode. Balaam is the biblical archetype of the person who isolates the present as all-important and denies both the past and the future.

In Rav Kook's terms, this Torah episode describes a confrontation between a people rooted in history, conscious of its past and proud of it, aware of its future and inspired by it, versus the villain Balaam, who would excise past and future and condemn us only to the transience of fleeting time. It is the battle between "an eternal people (*netzaḥ Yisrael*)," and a people without tradition and without hope.

Jewish tradition teaches us that our past is very much a part of who we are in the "here and now." Our religion is nothing if not a historical religion. Our personal lives are trivialized to the extent that we do not connect to both our recent past and our millennia-long history.

Permit me to relate these reflections to a very contemporary concern, and to express criticism of President Barack Obama's address to the Muslim world. In describing the Jewish people's claim to the Land of Israel, he only mentioned the relationship between the horror of the Holocaust and the founding of the State of Israel. He neglected to put our claim to the Holy Land in proper historical perspective. For us, the Holocaust is part of our present moment – its survivors are still alive among us. What legitimizes our claim to the Land of Israel is our millennia-long bond with that land, one that goes back to Abraham, Isaac, and Jacob, and that has ancient biblical roots.

There is a lesson here for us as a people and for each of us as struggling mortals. The Jewish people cannot survive in this world if our legitimacy as a nation is limited to the here and now. We are an ancient people and must proudly assert the power of our past and not forget the promise of our future.

And as individual human beings coping with the ordinary and extraordinary challenges of daily existence, we are also lost if we limit our temporal perspectives to today. We must be informed and influenced by yesterday and we must enthusiastically anticipate tomorrow.

Parashat Pinḥas

I Act, Therefore I Am

Are you feeling depressed? Then dance!
Feeling lazy? Work!
Angry? Smile!
Hostile? Act friendly!

These are not merely glib bits of advice when there is nothing better to say. Rather, they reflect a deep common wisdom that teaches us that our behavior influences our emotions. When we feel down in the dumps, the best thing we can do is to pretend, however artificially, that we are happy. To smile, to dress well, to be active, and enthusiastic. Acting happy is one of the best antidotes for depression.

This insight into the mysterious workings of the human psyche turns out to be more than just common folk wisdom. In medieval rabbinic literature, it is the unknown author of the *Sefer HaḤinukh* who consistently uses the maxim, "After one's actions, one's feelings follow." For him, this psychological fact is the reason for many of the rituals of Judaism. They are designed to provide us with a pattern of activity that will implant in us a desired set of inner attitudes and feelings.

Thus, for example, all of the many and detailed rituals that comprise the Passover service serve the purpose of stimulating inner attitudes of freedom and gratitude.

Not only were medieval rabbis aware of this profound psycholo︱cal truth, but the much later thinkers also prescribe action and activity as a way of influencing one's inner emotional life. William James, in the late nineteenth century, noted in his *Principles of Psychology* that outer behavior has a powerful effect upon internal emotions. In the psychological jargon of that time, this was known as the James/Lange theory.

We all have witnessed this phenomenon in our everyday lives. We know kindergarten teachers whose baby talk and immature classroom conversational styles have influenced their out-of-school personalities, so that even in adult conversation, they demonstrate a peculiar childishness. And I know personally of several ritual slaughterers (*shoḥetim*) who have consciously fought the tendency toward cruelty to animals, which their profession has instilled in them. The fact that some of the wisest women I know are kindergarten teachers, and some of the gentlest fellows around are *shoḥetim*, is simply testimony to the efforts they have invested to undoing the powerful impact of the behaviors they perform every day.

What about the soldier, the person whose task involves violence and harming other people? Does his behavior, however necessary to defend his life and the lives of his dear ones, change him into a violent and cruel human being? I think that the answer is yes, and I have spoken to many soldiers who have corroborated this, and report feeling hardened and callous after their battlefield experiences.

It is no wonder then that Pinhas, the hero of our *parasha*, after he thrusts a spear through the viscera of a Jewish prince and a Midianite princess, is granted the "covenant of peace." He committed a bloody act of violence, warranted only in rare and extreme situations, and that single act posed the danger of his deep internal transformation from a priest of peace to a violent murderer. The Almighty found it necessary to bless him with a special gift, His own divine *brit shalom*.

It was none other than Golda Meir, whose womanly wisdom found expression in the remark, "We can perhaps someday forgive you for killing our children, but we cannot forgive you for making us kill your children."

In the context of recent battles in which the Israeli army was engaged, we must recognize that today's soldiers, to whom I have spoken, resent being forced to kill and are fully aware that violent behavior produces an inner streak of violence that must be expunged. I take this opportunity to stress what we all should know and tell the world: The Israeli army is uniquely careful to avoid unnecessary acts of violence and debriefs its soldiers after they emerge from the tests of battle in a manner designed to avoid the incubation of cruel psychological tendencies and to restore sensitivity toward the lives of others.

There are times when each of us must act sternly, in a tough and harsh manner. Sometimes we must discipline others and be quite strict with them. At those times, we must vigilantly avoid permitting those justified behaviors to affect who we are and how we really feel. We must struggle to retain our humanity, gentleness, and compassion, even when our outer behavior necessitates firmness and even severity.

It is also very helpful to remember: we can reverse feelings of violence that threaten to emerge in us by acting kindly and compassionately; we can reverse tendencies toward sloth by energetic productive activity; and we can reverse feelings of depression and emotional darkness by dancing exuberantly and singing joyously.

Lessons in Leadership

T oo often, leaders cling to power. They are so intoxicated by the privileges of their position that they become blinded to their own vulnerabilities and even oblivious of their own mortality.

Even our own Jewish history has many examples, some comparatively recent, of great leaders who failed to provide for their succession. Their deaths left a vacuum, since they failed to designate their choice of a successor in a clear and unambiguous fashion. In some cases, chaos and strife ensued.

Such was not the case with the greatest of all Jewish leaders, Moses. In fact, one of the defining factors of his greatness was his concern that a proper successor to him be named. And it is in *Parashat Pinḥas* that the story of Moses' search for an appropriate successor is narrated:

> Moses spoke to the Lord, saying, "Let the Lord, Source of the breath of all flesh, appoint someone over the community who shall go out before them and come in before them...so that the Lord's community may not be like sheep that have no shepherd." (Num. 27:15–17)

Rashi draws our attention to the peculiar way in which Moses addresses the Almighty, "Source of breath of all flesh." Whatever can that mean? Why does Moses not address Him as "God of the heavens and earth," or some similar familiar appellation?

Rashi's answer yields a very important insight into Moses' concept of the nature of leadership. A leader must be able to tolerate the great differences that exist among individuals. Every human being is different from every other, and a leader must be able to inspire diverse individuals, even individuals with contradictory ideologies and objectives. Only the Lord Almighty, "Source of the breath of all flesh," can identify a leader who has the capacity to relate to "each and every person according to his personality."

So Moses was not only exemplary in taking the responsibility to find and to name a successor, but he was also careful to ask for divine assistance in locating a new leader with the capacity to deal with human uniqueness and individual differences. Moses knew from his long experience that a leader who expected uniformity and conformity was doomed to failure.

But there is another aspect of leadership that Moses did not seem to ask for, but which God provided for. God not only responds to Moses' request by naming Joshua as his successor, He also insists that Joshua himself stand before and consult Elazar the Priest. The effective leader, nay the great leader, dare not think of himself as infallible, as the only source of intelligent leadership, but he, too, must bow to a higher authority.

Hence, "he shall present himself to Elazar the Priest, who shall, on his behalf, seek the decision of the Urim before the Lord. By such instruction, they shall go out, and by such instruction, they shall come in...Moses did as the Lord commanded him. He took Joshua and had him stand before Elazar the Priest" (Num. 27:21–22).

Joshua was to be the undisputed leader of the Jewish people. Indeed, our sages see him as fulfilling the role of king. And he was chosen not just because he was a faithful disciple to his master, Moses, but because of the amazing skill he possessed to deal with a people as diverse and as fractious as the Israelites. Yet, he too, from the very beginning, was made to realize that he had limitations, that he needed to depend upon others, and that ultimately, he had to bow before "the Source of the breath of all flesh."

Whenever I read these key passages of our *parasha*, I cannot help but apply their lessons to the very many leaders across a span of history who began their careers with talents equal or perhaps even superior to Joshua's, but who ultimately failed utterly because they tried to "go at it alone." They yielded in their hubris to their inner conviction that they knew best and that consultation with others was a waste of time.

Failed leaders, leaders who do not look to the Elazars of their own times, are not just historical figures. In each and every generation (*bekhol dor vador*), ours too, leaders arise with God-given personal gifts and with great promise, but to our disappointment, they fail dismally. And, almost without exception, their failures can be traced back to their attempts to be a Joshua without an Elazar, a king without a conscience, an expert without a consultant, a wise man without an Urim, a human without God.

Parashat Pinḥas

Avoiding a Hateful Heart

Love is an emotion. It is a feeling, often a very passionate one, that we have toward another person, creature, or object. Our Torah speaks of the love we are to have for each other, for the stranger in our midst, and for the Almighty. Scripture alludes to the love a man and woman have for each other as a feeling akin to a divine flame, a passion as powerful as death itself, an emotion that cannot even be quenched by many waters (see Song. 8:6–7).

Giving is an action. Sometimes it is prescribed action, such as charity to the poor. "Give, yes give to him, and let your heart not begrudge what you give to him" (Deut. 15:10). Often the giving is voluntary and takes many forms: giving of tangible gifts, or of time, of compassionate words, or of careful listening.

The question has been asked, "Do we give to those whom we love, or perhaps, do we love those to whom we give?" What comes first? The love for one another or the giving to him or her?

This question was asked by Rabbi Eliyahu Dessler in the first volume of his posthumously published writings, known as *Mikhtav MeEliyahu*. Rabbi Dessler was a prominent twentieth-century educator and thinker who was born in Eastern Europe, worked in England, and spent his last years in Israel.

The question is truly an ancient one, posed by many philosophers from both within and outside of the Jewish tradition. It is the question of whether feelings motivate actions or whether actions stimulate feelings.

The medieval author of the *Sefer HaHinukh* enunciated a similar belief centuries before William James. He asserted, "The heart follows one's actions (*aharei hape'ulot nimshakhim halevavot*)."

If it is true that feelings of love derive from loving and giving behaviors, then it must also be true that feelings of hatred derive from hateful and violent behaviors. Thus, we can understand an otherwise puzzling passage in *Parashat Pinhas*.

Pinhas, the grandson of Aaron, the peace-loving High Priest, commits an action of zealotry. A Jewish man named Zimri parades his Midianite paramour, Kozbi, before the "eyes of Moses and the eyes of all the congregation of the Children of Israel" (Num. 25:6). Pinhas swiftly, almost impulsively, grabs a spear and thrusts it through the two of them, killing them instantly. That episode is narrated at the very end of *Parashat Balak*.

In our *parasha*, we read of the Lord's response to Pinhas' action. He commends it, saying that Pinhas "has removed My wrath from upon the Children of Israel" (25:11). And the Almighty proceeds to reward Pinhas with "My covenant of peace" (25:12).

In his commentary on this phrase, Rabbi Naftali Tzvi Yehuda Berlin (1816–1893), dean of the famed Yeshiva of Volozhin, expresses surprise at this reward. After all, Pinhas acted violently, militantly. Shouldn't his reward be a medal of war, a prize for zealotry and courage? Why a covenant of peace?

Rabbi Berlin, who is known by the acronym formed by the first letters of his long name as the Netziv, answers eloquently, "Because it is the nature of actions such as those of Pinhas, who killed another person by his own hands, to permanently leave behind strong feelings of hatred upon the heart of the perpetrator, therefore was the blessing of peace bestowed upon him so that he should always remain gentle and peace-loving and not develop into a cruel character."

Violence contaminates the soul, regardless of whether or not the violent acts are justified. This is why soldiers, when they are debriefed after battle, need special counseling. They need to be able to put the actions that they performed, even for reasons of self-defense, behind them so that they do not develop permanent feelings of hatred and cruelty.

All of us may have been guilty, even unintentionally, at one time or another, of some sort of cruelty to others. We must be sure that those cruel actions do not result in cruel hearts. We must be sure that we do not let the influence of actions that we legitimately perform in extreme circumstances become a permanent part of our character.

Zealotry and Tolerance

J ewish people teach Jewish values to their children and to all who wish to be informed about their faith. If one is asked, "Should I or should I not?" we generally respond with clear and certain advice. "Yes, you should," if the value is a positive one; or, "No, you should not," when the value in question demands inaction.

Strangely, however, there is one positive value in our religion to which we are not to respond, "Yes, go and do it." I speak of the value of zealotry.

Zealous acts are noble acts in our tradition. This is illustrated in the story begun in *Parashat Balak* and concluded in our *parasha* named for the zealot Pinḥas (Num. 25:10–30:1).

Pinḥas confronted a Jewish prince named Zimri in an act of idolatrous promiscuity with a Midianite woman named Kozbi. He "took a spear in his hand.... And thrust both of them through, the man of Israel, and the woman through her belly." For this he is commended by the Almighty Himself, who says, "Pinḥas...was very zealous for My sake.... Therefore...I give unto him My covenant of peace.... Because he was zealous for his God, and made atonement for the Children of Israel."

Clearly, zealotry is a divinely approved positive value. Yet, I ask you, dear reader, suppose you had witnessed an immoral and defiant act about to take place and had come to ask me, your rabbi, whether or not you should take up a spear and thrust it through the two sinners. Would I be permitted to encourage you to emulate Pinḥas?

The Talmud, in a passage in Tractate Sanhedrin 82a, tells us that Moses himself was uncertain as to whether this act of taking human lives was permissible. Pinḥas acted on his own. Indeed, the Talmud clearly states that if someone comes to inquire as to whether or not to commit such an act of extreme zealotry, he should not be instructed to do so. I, as a rabbi, would have to discourage him from taking up the spear and taking the lives of even the most blatant of sinners.

Yet, elsewhere in the Bible and in post-biblical writings, we find others besides Pinḥas who performed similar acts of zealotry. One of them is the prophet Elijah whose story we read in the *haftara* (I Kings 18:46–19:21). Elijah, whom our sages equate with Pinḥas, says of himself, "I have been very zealous for the Lord…. The Children of Israel have forsaken thy covenant."

Yet another famous example is the High Priest Matityahu whom we all recall from the story of Ḥanukka. Of him we read, "Matityahu saw a Jewish man about to offer a sacrifice on an alien altar in the presence of the entire congregation, and he was zealous, and swiftly slaughtered the man … and smashed the altar to bits; thereby, he was zealous on behalf of the Torah just as Pinḥas had done to Zimri" (I Maccabees 1:45–50).

What a paradox! Three great heroes of the Jewish people, all praised highly for their zealotry. And yet, if any of us today were to inquire of a rabbi of the highest rank, or of a Jewish court, as to whether he could emulate them and zealously harm a sinner, he would not receive permission to do so.

It is apparent that such acts of zealotry are limited to those whose motives are of the purest order and who are moved by their sincere desires to restore the glory of God when it is publicly profaned. Zealotry is not for every man.

This is a most timely lesson. There are many members of the Jewish people today who are stirred by feelings of righteous indignation to protest actions and statements that to them seem blasphemous, immoral, or just plain wrong. But they dare not act, and certainly not act violently, against those actions or statements. They must first be certain that their motives are as pure and authentic as were the motives of Pinhas, Elijah, and Matityahu. And none among us can be so certain of our motives!

Our times call for a different approach entirely. Today, we must conform to an almost opposite Torah value, namely, tolerance. Tolerance is preferable to zealotry. This is a lesson that can be found in the very text that tells of Pinhas' zealotry. After he commits his violent act, the Almighty concludes His statement of approval with the gift of "My covenant of peace." Many of our commentaries, notably the Netziv, emphasize that this covenant was given to Pinhas as a kind of corrective, as a way of demonstrating that, although zealotry is sometimes warranted, the ultimate Jewish value is peace.

For individuals who are sincerely motivated to be zealous, there is a helpful perspective, which is recommended. That perspective encourages us to find holiness buried within heresy and sanctity somewhere in the midst of sin. When human faults can be seen as transient aberrations, which cloud so much that is good and noble, zealotry fades into the background and kindness and compassion prevail.

This perspective is expressed so eloquently in the poetic words of Rabbi Abraham Isaac Kook in his brief collection, *Middot HaRaya*, page 84. I am indebted to my good friend, Yaakov Dovid Schulman, himself an eloquent and poetic soul, for providing me with a translation of this passage about tolerance:

> When tolerance of points of view comes from a heart that is pure and cleansed of all evil, that tolerance is not liable to chill the flame of holy feelings containing simple faith – which is the source of all life. Instead, that tolerance broadens and magnifies the foundation of heaven-directed fervor.
>
> Tolerance is armed with a very great faith. Ultimately, it realizes the complete impossibility of a soul being emptied of all holy life. This is because the life of the living God fills all life. And so, even where actions come out in a destructive fashion, where points of view collide into heresy, there still must be – in

the midst of the heart, in the depth of the soul – the living light of hidden holiness. And this is apparent in the good aspects that we find in many corners, even on those ravaged avenues touched by heresy and corroded by doubt.

From the midst of this great, holy knowledge and faith comes tolerance, which encircles everything with a thread of kindness.

"I will assemble Jacob, all of you!" (Mic. 2:12)

Honesty and Integrity

Every so often I come across a sentence of another person's writing that expresses one of my own thoughts in a language far superior to my own. Over the years, I have contemplated and written about the concepts of honesty and integrity and the difference between the two.

But never was I able to articulate their precise definitions and the difference between them as cogently and as concisely as in the following passage from Stephen Covey's *The Seven Habits of Highly Effective People*:

> Integrity includes but goes beyond honesty. Honesty is...*conforming our words to reality*. Integrity is *conforming reality to our words* – in other words, keeping promises and fulfilling expectations. This requires an integrated character, a oneness, primarily with self but also with life.

Honesty for Covey, and I for one heartily agree, is the virtue describing reality exactly as it is, of telling the truth. In this day and age, when there is so much confusion as to whether or not there even *is* such a thing as truth, it is refreshing to see the place of honesty restored to the list of important human virtues.

For Judaism, truth is more than just a virtue. It is one of the three fundamental principles, along with justice and peace, upon which the world stands. In the words of the Talmud, "The signature of the Holy One, blessed be He, is truth."

So rare is the man of truth that legend has the aged Diogenes searching for him with lanterns. But as rare as the trait of honesty is, the trait of integrity is even more difficult to find.

Integrity is the ability not only to say what you mean, but to mean what you say. Following Covey, it is the quality of conforming one's actions to one's words, of reliably following through on one's commitment. It is more than the ability to make things happen. It is making your own promises happen!

Parashat Matot (Num. 30:1–32:42) opens with a lengthy and intricate discussion of the concepts of "the vow." Biblical teachings insist that the words we express must be taken very seriously; indeed we are taught that our words are sacred. Once a person, man or woman, young or old, simpleton or scholar, utters a commitment, he or she is duty-bound to honor that commitment. "That which your lips express must be honored and performed (*Motza sefatekha tishmor ve'asita*)."

As helpful as is Covey's succinct definition of integrity, it is also deceptively simple. There is so much more that we need to know about integrity. And about honesty for that matter. For one thing, honesty and integrity are not just descriptors of individual persons' characters. Rather, they are social values, which ideally should define the essence of human communities and entire societies. From a Jewish perspective, honesty and integrity cannot be restricted to individual paragons of virtue, saints and holy men, but must become universal cultural norms.

This is why the laws of vows, unlike all the other laws of the Torah, are explicitly given to the chieftains of the tribes (*rashei hamatot*). It is to emphasize that the sanctity of speech is not a goal for just a few spiritually gifted individuals. It must be enunciated as one of the essential mores of the entire tribe.

The Talmud relates the story of an immortal community, a legendary village that knew not death. This was because no one there ever lied.

This idyllic existence came to an abrupt end, however, when a young person, eager to protect the privacy of his parent, told an inquiring visitor that his parent was not home – a harmless and well-intentioned remark, common to us all, a white lie perhaps, but a lie nevertheless, and one that ruined forever the eternal life of that fabled village.

Yet another lesson about keeping our word is taught in the opening verses of *Parashat Matot* (Num. 30:1–17). Sometimes, we overextend ourselves and make promises that we cannot possibly keep. In moments of extreme urgency, or sublime inspiration, we are wont to express commitments that are beyond our capacity to fulfill.

Can a vow thus expressed be annulled? The Torah, ever practical, answers "yes," and describes some of the procedures designed to release a person from his or her vows. The Talmud, in an entire tractate devoted to this topic, specifies the circumstances and conditions under which such a release can be obtained.

Most well-known among the "ceremonies" releasing us from our personal vows and promises is the *Kol Nidrei* prayer, which ushers in our most hallowed day, Yom Kippur. Not really a prayer in the ordinary sense, *Kol Nidrei* is a statement in which we declare our past vows null and void. This custom is experienced by many as strange and as an offense to the value of integrity. But I personally have always found that it reinforces the role of integrity in my life and in the lives of all of us who live in the "real world."

During the entire year, you and I make many commitments and resolutions. With the noblest of motives, we promise things to our loved ones, verbally establish objectives to improve the world around us, or simply vow to lose weight, stop smoking, or start exercising.

As the year wears on, situations change, priorities shift, and we ourselves become different. At least one time each year, on Yom Kippur, we realize how unrealistic we were and that we erred in our assessment of what we could accomplish. And so, we ask that the Almighty release us from these impossible and often no longer relevant commitments, and begin – with divine help – a new slate, hoping that the next time we make a promise, it will be one that we will be able to keep.

Judaism teaches us the primary importance of keeping our word. But it does not lose sight of our human frailties and limitations and recognizes that often it is not moral failure that explains our lack of integrity, but simple human weakness, hopefully rare and surely forgiven by God.

Integrity is a cherished value for the society at large. The acknowledgement of human limitations in maintaining integrity must be accepted. These are two important and timely lessons.

Breaking Promises

I t was a typical park-bench conversation. I hadn't seen my friend for quite some time and we both were delighted when we ran into each other by chance that afternoon.

We shook hands and withdrew to a bench in the shade to spend a few minutes together, catching up with each other. As is often the case in such conversations, we found ourselves discussing mutual acquaintances with whom one or the other of us had lost touch. Pretty soon we were discussing Sam.

Sam was a person who had many fine qualities, indeed some outstanding ones. But the one that made the biggest impression upon my park-bench partner and me was Sam's impeccable honesty.

"Once Sam says something," my pal remarked, "he never backs out or changes his mind. You can count on him to keep his word."

Something deep inside of me, perhaps the ornery part of me, then spoke up. "Is it always a virtue to keep your word and never change your mind? Isn't that a sign of a certain rigidity, which is not always beneficial, and may even sometimes be morally wrong?"

My friend objected. "Surely," he said, "you don't mean to condone lying."

At this point, I realized that our idle conversation was taking a deeper turn. We were beginning to wax philosophical and would soon have to resort to a higher level of discourse than we had bargained for when we initially sat down together.

But before changing the topic of conversation, I was reminded of the opening passages of *Parashat Matot,* which discuss the binding nature of vows and promises and the circumstances under which those verbal commitments can be annulled: "When a man vows a vow...or swears an oath to bind his soul with a bond, he shall not break his word; he shall do according to all that proceeds out of his mouth" (Num. 30:3).

The binding quality of one's promises is emphasized by many non-biblical authors. The Roman sage Horace writes in his *Epistles,* "Once a word has been allowed to escape, it cannot be recalled." The Spanish novelist, Miguel de Cervantes, puts these words in the mouth of his hero Don Quixote, "An honest man's word is as good as his bond."

It is apparent that being true to one's words is a universal ethical standard. The Torah, however, while fully supporting the binding quality of one's promises, also recognizes that there are situations that call for the revocation of those promises. Times change, circumstances are altered, and a reassessment of past commitments is not only permitted, but is to be commended. Blind obedience to one's past vows can lead to disastrous consequences.

Whereas the Torah explicitly grants the authority to a father to annul the vows of his daughter, and under certain circumstances, allows a husband to abrogate his wife's vows, our sages recognize that every individual must have access to a wise man who can help him assess his verbal commitments, and when justified, release him from those commitments.

The classic case of misguided adherence to one's words is the story, narrated in the Book of Judges, chapter 11, of Yiftaḥ. He was a great military leader who, when he embarked upon a battle against the Ammonites, vowed that if God would grant him victory, he would offer "whatever comes out of the door of my house...as a burnt offering."

Tragically, it was his daughter, his only child, who came out to meet him. He felt bound by his words and "did to her as he vowed."

Our sages see his blind obedience to his own words as being a result of his ignorance and they do not commend his fidelity to his vow. Quite the contrary: Our rabbis recognize the complexities of life and understand full well that situations calling for morality can be most ambiguous.

In certain circumstances, a sense of being bound by one's promises is an example of integrity and honesty of the highest order. But even one's promises need to be assessed in the light of changing circumstances. When those circumstances demand a loosening of the bond of verbal commitment, our tradition provides procedures whereby one can be released even from his most fervent oaths and vows.

The opening passages of our *parasha* recognize this complexity. These passages teach that one must be careful never to profane or violate his words. But they also teach that one's words need to be revisited, re-examined, and reassessed. And they teach that, under the guidance of a wise and pious *hakham*, the bonds of words can be undone, and the chains of past commitments can be loosened.

There is an additional lesson here and that is the lesson of forgiveness. Sometimes human relationships necessitate certain reactions. My vow to have nothing to do with you may have been based upon the factual consideration that your behavior was undesirable and might have a negative effect upon me or my family. But I must be ready to say, "That was then and this is now." I must be ready to realize that you have changed and that now our relationship must change.

And when I realize that, I must re-examine my past promises and commitments and be ready to undo them. That is the underlying concept behind the procedure known as the undoing of the bonds of words (*hatarat nedarim*). That is among the messages of this *parasha*.

I am sharing these thoughts with you, dear reader, but didn't share them with my park-bench partner. Certain matters are much too important for a park bench. But I am sharing my thoughts with you and hope you find them meaningful.

Parashat Masei

Journeys

For many of us, traveling on a long journey is a vacation, especially here in the United States where we have come to glorify long family road trips. We consider them recreational, fun, and a time for parents and children to be together.

Even before the advent of the automobile and the superhighway, a journey was thought to be a pleasant and even edifying experience. Thus, the early nineteenth-century British essayist, William Hazlitt, included an essay entitled *On Going a Journey* in his delightful collection, *Table Talk*. Among the statements in this essay, Hazlitt avers, "One of the pleasantest things in the world is going a journey; but I like to go by myself."

Somehow, from the perspective of Jewish history, journeys are not at all pleasant. "Wandering Jew" is an epithet that has been applied to us, sometimes out of sympathy and sometimes out of scorn, but never as a compliment. Never in our tradition is wandering viewed as pleasant. For us wandering is exile.

Interestingly, the very act of travel is seen in our tradition as negative. Abram, when he set out to travel the long distance from his birthplace to the Holy Land, was given a special blessing to counteract the effects of the journey. "And I will make of you a great nation, and I will bless you, and make your name great" (Gen. 12:2). On this verse, Rashi comments that this tripartite blessing was necessary because "the road interferes with reproduction, diminishes financial success, and makes it difficult to achieve a name, a reputation."

The very title of *Parashat Masei* means journeys. The portion begins with a long and detailed description of the many way stations that punctuated the long and arduous journey that our ancestors traveled in the wilderness on their way to the Promised Land. There is something about the mere recitation of these verses that suggests a slow and arduous process. The travel through the wilderness was no pleasant interlude.

I have always found it somehow ironic that the custom is to chant the monotonous list of journeys and sojourns with a triumphant melody. Listen and you will hear as the Torah reader, almost joyfully, sings aloud, "And they journeyed from the wilderness of Zin, and pitched in Dophkah...and they journeyed from Dophkah, and pitched in Alush" (Num. 33:12–13).

Why do the stages of a tortuous forty-year-long trip through the desert deserve musical accompaniment? After all, this ordeal was a punishment for the Jewish people, as we read several *parashot* earlier in *Parashat Shelaḥ*. It was as a result of the sin of the spies that all of this traveling became necessary. Absent that, the journey would have been one of days and not one of long and hot and aimless wandering during which an entire generation slowly died out.

I think the reason for the singsong chanting of the stations along the journey (*masa'ot*) has to do with the rest of our *parasha*. Immediately after the long list of brief stops on the painful journey, at the conclusion of all that travail, God says to Moses, "Speak unto the Children of Israel, and say unto them: when you pass over the Jordan into the land of Canaan...you shall drive out the inhabitants of the land, and dwell therein; for unto you have I given the land to possess it...and you shall inherit the land by lots according to your families" (Num. 33:51–54).

Aimless wandering, with no end in sight, is torture; a journey with a clear destination, on the other hand, is a wondrous experience, despite its many obstacles. Without the promise of the inheritance, without the assurance of an eventual place for our families to take root, the many way stations would be chanted to a very solemn melody, perhaps even to the melody of Lamentations, which we read on the Ninth of Av (Tisha B'Av).

But with the vision promised to us, with the delineation of the exact borders and boundaries of our lands, all of the suffering along the way somehow becomes worthwhile. The lengthy list of way stations becomes transformed into the lyrics of a triumphant marching song.

It is not by coincidence that we read *Parashat Masei* during the three weeks prior to Tisha B'Av, *shlosha depurinita*. These three weeks are reserved for reflection upon the experience of exile, upon the trials and tribulations of the centuries-long journey through "the desert of the nations." Our *parasha* begins with the long passage that foreshadows that experience.

But during these three weeks, while we deprive ourselves of all manner of special celebrations, we are at least aware of the seven weeks that are to follow. These are the seven weeks of consolation, the *shiva deneḥemta*, during which we rejoice for the conclusion of exile and celebrate our ultimate return to the Promised Land.

The words of the opening chapter of *Masei* drive home the painstaking station-by-station journey through history. But the accompanying marching melody assures us that celebration and triumph lie ahead.

Parashat Masei

Zionism

Theremust be at least a thousand jokes that begin, "A Catholic priest, an Orthodox rabbi, and a Protestant minister enter a bar." I'll begin with a story about a Catholic priest, an Orthodox rabbi, and a fine Jewish layman. They won't be entering a bar together, that's for sure. They won't even be sitting face-to-face. But they will all be expressing their opinions about a very important, and unfortunately very controversial, concept: Zionism.

I made the acquaintance of the Catholic priest many years ago before he became a prominent bishop. We had a conversation recently in which he asked me to explain to him how certain very Orthodox Jews can espouse a doctrine of anti-Zionism. "After all," he said, "if they believe in the Hebrew prophets and believe that their prophecies are to be understood literally, how can they possibly be against Zionism? Almost all the prophets speak of the return of the Jewish people to their homeland and see the repossession of the Land of Israel by the Jewish people as the highest ideal."

For my friend the bishop, supporting the sovereign Jewish government in the Land of Israel is an imperative of the Jewish religion.

I found it very difficult to explain to him the reasons that some devout Jews do not even recognize the modern-day State of Israel.

Not long after this conversation with my Roman Catholic friend, I ran into another friend whom I first met many years ago. He is a follower of a hasidic sect that is antagonistic to the Jewish State and that frequently publicly protests Israel's political and even military actions. He is a great scholar and we have long ago learned to avoid discussing the topic of Zionism. He knows that my opinions are very different from his. Instead, we confine our conversations to his recent writings, which ironically are based upon the commentary on the Bible by Nahmanides.

During this recent encounter, we again avoided discussing the topic of Zionism. I know his position well. He believes that it is absolutely wrong for Jews nowadays to reclaim the Land of Israel, but that we must wait for the coming of the Messiah to do so. He sees the current State of Israel as the audacious embodiment of sinful hubris. He believes the State of Israel is nothing less than the work of the devil himself. My own view is quite different, and we have both been long reconciled to the fact that we would never convince the other to change his opinion.

The third "player" in my little story is, sadly, long deceased. He was a gentleman back in the community where I was a pulpit rabbi. He described himself as a Religious Zionist and indeed was very active in leadership capacities within organizations that were ardently Zionist. Yet, when his own children informed him that they were making *aliya* and moving to Israel, he was very upset and shared his disappointment with me.

My connections with these three individuals often motivate me to return to sources in our sacred tradition to buttress my own point of view. One such source is *Parashat Masei* (Num. 33:1–36:13). For me, this *parasha* is the basic enunciation of what some call Religious Zionism. In it, we read of the many, many wanderings of the Jewish people before they were privileged to possess the Land of Israel. We read of the commandment to conquer the land, to settle it, and to preserve it as an inheritance for our descendants. We learn in detail about the boundaries of the land and about the requirement of all Jews to assist in the process of its conquest. Is this not what the world has come to refer to as Zionism?

Nahmanides, second only to Rashi as author of the most widely studied Jewish commentary on the Bible, remarks that in this *parasha*, we find one of the 613 commandments, namely the mitzva to possess the Land of Israel. He furthermore insists that this positive commandment (*mitzvat asei*) applies throughout Jewish history, even today, and is not just of historical interest.

The biblical verse reads, "And you shall take possession of the land and settle in it, for I have assigned this land to you to possess" (Num. 33:53), upon which Nahmanides comments, "In my opinion, this is a positive commandment. God is telling us to dwell in the land and to possess it, and not to reject it in any way, nor to substitute any other geographical dwelling place for it. Based upon this verse are the numerous eloquent remarks of our sages on the importance of dwelling in the Land of Israel and never leaving – to the extent that a husband can force his wife, and a wife her husband, to dwell in the Land of Israel rather than elsewhere."

In another of his writings, *Hasagot LeSefer HaMitzvot* (Mitzva 4), in which he enumerates the 613 commandments, Nahmanides emphasizes that this verse is to be understood as a command and not merely a divine promise that one day we shall dwell there.

Nahmanides echoes this attitude toward the Land of Israel and its central role in our religion throughout his vast writings. Furthermore, he personally practiced what he preached and left his native Spain to live in the Land of Israel and indeed to die there.

For me, Nahmanides is but one proponent of the religious imperative that underlies the modern State of Israel. Here are the words of a much more recent proponent of this position, the words with which Rabbi Abraham Isaac Kook opens his classic work, *Orot*:

> The Land of Israel is not something external, not an external national asset, the means to the end of collective solidarity and the strengthening of the nation's existence.... The Land of Israel is an essential unit bound by the bond of life to the people.... The expectation of salvation is the force that preserves exilic Judaism; the Judaism of the Land of Israel is salvation itself.

The State of Israel and its inhabitants frequently face a most difficult challenge, the onslaught of rockets aimed at them by an enemy. More than ever before, we draw our strength and our hope from the knowledge that it is the divine will that we dwell in His land and that we serve Him by defending it. With His assistance, we will succeed, and the land will continue to prosper materially and to flourish spiritually to an even greater extent than ever before.

Deuteronomy

A Sublime Autobiography

T here is a biography and then there is an autobiography. Our biography is the way others see us. Our autobiography is the way we see ourselves. Typically, there are sharp differences between the two. Others see us from their own perspectives. Some biographers can be boldly objective, confronting us with facts about ourselves that we did not see and perhaps do not want to see. Other biographers have their own agendas and interpret our lives to fit their perceptions, frequently distorting the facts and the meaning of our lives in the process.

Similarly, in the accounts of our lives that we ourselves write, there are two broad possibilities. We can disclose all of our lives' details accurately, hiding nothing; or our autobiographies can be gross distortions of our life stories, intentionally falsified or unconsciously mistaken.

Whomever we think we are, we are well-advised to be aware of how others see us. Deuteronomy (*Devarim*), the fifth of the five Ḥumashim, differs fundamentally from the preceding four, so much so that the rabbis call it *Mishneh Torah*, a "Second" Torah, a review of much that came before.

For me, there has always been something else that distinguishes Deuteronomy and makes it astoundingly different, not only from the other Books of Moses, but from every other book in the entire Bible. It is an autobiography!

Whereas the other biblical books are invariably written in the third person, Deuteronomy is written, or more correctly spoken, by Moses, in the first person. Moses speaks to us in his own voice.

Repetitively, until now, we have read, "And the Lord spoke to Moses saying." Starting with *Parashat Devarim*, we will read again and again, "And the Lord spoke to *me*." We will not read, "And the Lord commanded," but, "And I commanded." The attentive reader of these texts cannot help being astonished by this remarkable shift.

This transition into the first person gives us the opportunity to relate to Moses directly and to hear his personal take on all that we have been reading about until this point.

In our *parasha*, we will hear Moses complain about the pressures of leadership in his own voice. We will overhear him exclaim, "How can I alone bear your bothersome, burdensome, and petty squabbles?" And we will eavesdrop upon him as he transcends his resentments and profusely blesses the people.

And in the next *parasha*, again in his very own words, Moses will tell us of his enthusiasm for the Land of Israel and of how desperately he petitions the Almighty to allow him entrance into the land. And he will intimately disclose to us his disappointment when his prayers are rebuffed. As we proceed through the parade of self-disclosures in this book, we will learn more and more about Moses the person. He will not hide his faults from us; he will tell us his versions of events; and he will select the mitzvot that he deems important to introduce or to review.

Deuteronomy is the window into the mind and heart of *Moshe Rabbenu*, Moses our teacher, the single most important personality in Jewish history. It contains the opening chapter of what may very well be the world's oldest autobiography. Like every good autobiography should, it instructs the student, interests the reader, and inspires us all.

It is instructive, for it teaches us how to be honest with ourselves. Moses is humble, but he knows who he is. His self-image does not change in response to the hostility of his detractors, nor does his head swell because of the flattery of those who adulate him. He never loses sight of his mission and task, no matter what is going on in his psyche.

Reading it is a privilege because it describes a rare example of a leader who allows us to peek into his inner life and who shares with us his doubts, fears, and hopes. But more than a privilege, it is a challenge and an inspiration. We are challenged by the awareness that, in many ways, we are no different from Moses. We too have our frustrations, limitations, and unanswered prayers, and we too have the ability to cope, to overcome, and to graciously accept failure and disappointment.

Finally, it is an inspiration to read of a leader who candidly and openly shares his innermost thoughts and emotions for all to know, and for all time. It is surely an inspiration for all who wish to learn, to strive, to hope, and to persevere.

Have I convinced you that I was correct in the title I selected for this essay, "A Sublime Autobiography"?

A Time and a Place

Le was in the wrong place at the wrong time." We have
all heard this phrase and many of us have used it. It is especially apt
when it is used to describe a person with many virtues and talents who
just can't use them because of the social or physical circumstances in
which he finds himself. Needless to say, such a person faces profound
frustration.

Many Jewish immigrants came to the United States blessed with
spiritual gifts and intellectual skills, but found themselves in the wrong
place at the wrong time. For, you see, America was viewed in two very
different ways by the Jews back in the *shtetl* of the old country. On the
one hand, it was seen as the *goldene medina*, the golden country, the
land of material opportunity. But on the other hand, it was also viewed
as the *treifene medina*, the non-kosher country, the land of insurmount-
able religious challenges.

The usual "success stories" of Jewish immigration to the United
States in the late nineteenth and early twentieth centuries are narratives of "making it" financially, but utterly "losing it" from the point of
view of traditional Jewish culture. American Jewish fiction, and even

American Jewish history, know these narratives well and relate them in graphic detail.

Largely missing from this body of literature are the stories of those who came to these shores imbued with religious fervor, committed to traditional observance. Lacking are the stories of men and women who found it difficult, if not impossible, to live out their faith convictions in this new place and time.

Particularly lacking are the narratives of the struggles that rabbinic leaders had in coping with the *treif*, albeit golden, American environment. One such rabbinic leader was Rabbi Jacob Joseph, the first and only chief rabbi in the history of New York City, who died in 1902 on the twenty-fourth of Tammuz. How ironic it is that his *yahrzeit* often falls near the ultimate American holiday, the Fourth of July.

Rabbi Jacob Joseph, a disciple of the master moralist, Rabbi Yisrael Salanter, was a rising star in the Lithuanian rabbinic constellation, a gifted orator, a noted pedagogue, and an ardent proponent of meticulous ethical behavior. He accepted a call to the New York Chief Rabbinate and he soon found himself "in the wrong place at the wrong time."

Rabbi Joseph was certainly not the first great man to find himself in a human context in which he was misunderstood and in which he was beset by deep disappointment, nay disillusionment. I have long insisted that the first such individual was Moses himself, which brings us to *Parashat Devarim*.

The Book of Deuteronomy can be read as a personal retrospective of Moses as he reviews the highlights of his life and particularly of his relationship with the Jewish people. Time and again he expresses the frustrations he experienced in trying to bring his followers to the ideas and practices that he espoused.

There can be no greater frustration than that experienced by one who has encountered God face-to-face, but who cannot convey His message to his audience. And hence we have verses such as, "I cannot bear the burden of you by myself" (Deut. 1:9). Or, and this the reader intones with the classic melody of lament, "How can I bear unaided the trouble of you, and the burden, and the bickering?" (Deut. 1:12)

Moses had a unique set of personal experiences, unprecedented visions of the divine, natural tendencies toward all that is just and right, and above all, unparalleled humility. And he was predestined to live in a specific time and place. But how often he must have felt that this was the "wrong time at the wrong place," and certainly, "the wrong people."

Millennia after Moses, came Rabbi Jacob Joseph. He was born in Eastern Europe, educated in its old-fashioned yet positively formative schools, and began a successful rabbinic career. He spoke widely and wrote prolifically. His themes were the importance of ethical behavior and the need to be considerate of other human beings. He was by nature meditative and would often take his young students into the fields and forests for their lessons. He was an expert in halakha and meticulous in its observance.

And then he was thrown into the American fray. He encountered fraud where he expected honesty and violence when he was accustomed to gentleness. He found a land where materialism and profit were primary values and where spirituality and charity were scoffed at and mocked.

He suffered a stroke at an early age, and he died in anonymity and neglect. His funeral was attended by thousands, but it became the scene of a vicious anti-Semitic riot, which made the front page of the newspapers of the time. He was indeed a great man in the "wrong place at the wrong time."

One can only speculate about what Rabbi Joseph's accomplishments would have been had he lived in a different place and a different time. For the United States of America is still a *goldene medina* for the Jewish people, a land of religious freedom unprecedented in our history. But it is no longer a *treifene medina*, for it has been transformed into a land of spiritual opportunity and religious accomplishment for our people.

Rabbi Jacob Joseph would have been proud of the "yeshiva constructed upon his grave." The Rabbi Jacob Joseph School was known as the mother of all yeshivas when it was situated on the Lower East Side of Manhattan and when I was a student there. It has since been transplanted to a new locale and continues to educate hundreds of Jewish children.

His writings have now been compiled and are available for all to see and study. And his biography is incorporated into numerous anthologies of American Jewish history and into the history of the

Musar movement, which tried so valiantly to emphasize the importance of ethical behavior in our religious tradition.

Like many others who experienced the frustration of being in "the wrong place at the wrong time," Rabbi Joseph left a lasting impact on our place and our time. And so did his predecessor, Moses our teacher, so very long ago.

Although in Moses' case, we can only conjecture about his inner feelings; in the case of Rabbi Joseph, we know from records of his final sermons that he indeed believed he "was in the wrong place at the wrong time."

Our tradition, however, teaches us a contrary lesson, namely that none of us is in the wrong place or the wrong time. Each of us has a mission in life and the Almighty Himself chooses the time in history and the place in the world where that mission is to be accomplished. Moses was the right man at the right time. That is apparent. And even Rabbi Joseph, although he could not realize it in his lifetime, served a specific purpose as a transitional figure in American Jewish history, helping to bridge the divide between the doomed *shtetls* of Eastern Europe and the *treif* but changing New World.

That we all ultimately are in the "right place at the right time" is the deeper meaning of the teaching of our sages, "Despise no one and disdain nothing, for there is no one who does not have his hour, and there is nothing that does not have its place" (Avot 4:3).

Parashat Devarim

The Path to Eloquence

It is an experience common to all freshmen. One comes to a new campus, knows no one, and tries to orient himself by identifying the senior students who seem to have prestige. Then he tries to connect with these campus big shots.

This was my experience precisely when, many years ago, I explored a new yeshiva at a transition point in my life. I was barely nineteen years old and I was trying to decide whether I would pursue an exclusively talmudic education or combine my Talmud studies with college courses. I decided to spend the spring semester in an elite institution devoted only to Talmud and to determine whether this approach suited me.

I quickly came to learn that the senior students were organized in a kind of hierarchy, which reflected their respective degrees of erudition and their relationships to the world-famous dean of the school. I was somewhat impressed by all of them, but one in particular stood out for me. I do not recall his name now, but I can close my eyes and easily conjure up an image of him.

He was about twenty-five years old, of medium height, thin and wiry. He had a precision to him, which resulted from his carefully measured movements. When he walked, he seemed to be taking each step intentionally. When he moved his hands, there was a precision to his movements. The words that came out of his mouth were few and deliberate, and his comments, short and to the point.

I remember being impressed by how he sat down before the texts he studied, first brushing the dust off of his desk and chair, then opening his book cautiously, and then taking from his pocket a plastic six-inch ruler. He placed the ruler under the line of text that was his focus, almost as if he intended to literally measure the words on the page.

I was fascinated by him and began to inquire about his background. I soon learned that he was the wunderkind of the school. His scholarly achievements impressed everyone. In early adolescence, he had found his studies extremely frustrating. Had this occurred but a decade or two later, he would probably have been diagnosed as learning disabled. He was not as bright as his peers, had great difficulties in following the give and take of talmudic passages, and couldn't handle the bilingual curriculum.

At the suggestion of his high school's guidance counselor, he made a trip to Israel to study there, something more uncommon in those days. While there, still frustrated, he sought the blessing and counsel of the famous sage, Rabbi Avraham Yeshaya Karelitz, more commonly known as the Hazon Ish.

This great man, then in his waning years, encouraged the young lad to persist in his studies, but to limit the scope of his daily efforts to small, "bite-sized chunks" of text. He concluded the interview with a blessing, quoting the passage in Psalms, which asserts that Torah study can make even a dullard wise.

I befriended the young man, easily five or six years my senior, and attempted to enlist him as my study partner. But I soon discovered that his keen intelligence and the broad scope of his knowledge were far too advanced for me. The advice and blessing of the Hazon Ish, coupled with the young man's years of toil and commitment, had the desired effect. He may indeed have once been a dullard, but he was one no longer. He was now an intellectual giant.

Although I did not learn much Talmud from this fellow, I did learn a most important life lesson from him. I learned that one can overcome his limitations if he persists in trying to overcome them. I learned that one could undo his natural challenges with a combination of heeding wise counsel, becoming inspired spiritually, and devoting himself with diligence and dedication to the task.

It was much later in life when I realized that I could have learned the same important life lesson from *Parashat Devarim* and from no less a personage than our teacher Moses himself. Almost all of the Book of Deuteronomy consists of the major address that Moses gave to the Jewish people before he took his final leave from them. "These are the words that Moses addressed to all of Israel" (Deut. 1:1).

When we first encountered Moses back in *Parashat Shemot*, we read of how he addressed the Almighty and expressed his inability to accept the divine mission. He said, "Please, O Lord, I have never been a man of words, either in times past or now that You have spoken to Your servant; I am slow of speech and slow of tongue" (Ex. 4:10). Moses stammered and stuttered and suffered from a genuine speech defect.

How surprising it is, then, that in this *parasha*, albeit forty years later, he is capable of delivering such a lengthy and eloquent address. How did he overcome his limitations? What are the secrets of his path to eloquence?

These questions are asked in the Midrash Tanḥuma. There, the rabbis speak of the astounding power of sincere and sustained Torah study. They speak too of the effects of years of practice. And they emphasize the healing that comes about from a connection with the One Above. The rabbis of the Midrash Tanḥuma could have cited the Lord's own response to Moses' initial complaint, "Who gives a man speech? Who makes him dumb or deaf, seeing or blind? Is it not I, the Lord?"

But those rabbis chose another proof text entirely to illustrate that Man, with God's help, can overcome his handicaps and challenges. They quote instead that beautiful passage in the Book of Isaiah, which reads:

> Then the eyes of the blind shall be opened,
> And the ears of the deaf shall be unstopped.
> Then the lame shall leap like a deer,

And the tongue of the dumb shall shout aloud;
For waters shall burst forth in the desert,
Streams in the wilderness. (Is. 35:5–6)

We seldom contemplate the development, nay transformation, of the man who was Moses. But it is important that we do so, because although we each have our unique challenges and personal handicaps, we are capable of coping with them and often of overcoming them. We all can develop and we all can potentially transform ourselves.

As we read Moses' masterful valedictory and are impressed with the beauty of his language, we must strive to remember that he was not always a skilled orator. Quite the contrary, he was once a man of impeded speech, who grew to achieve the divine blessing of shedding his impediments and addressing his people with the inspiring and eminent long speech that is the Book of Deuteronomy. He can be a role model for us all.

The Jewish Obsession

The popular media often accuses the Jewish people of an obsession. Some accuse us good-humoredly of an obsession with food. Others maliciously accuse us of being obsessed with money. I agree that there is a Jewish obsession. I maintain that it is justice with which we are obsessed.

I define an obsession as an idea that dominates our thinking, even when there are other important concerns that we need to address. Thus, the person who is truly obsessed with a particular idea cannot ignore that idea even when he is busy working, playing, or attending to other personal needs. Naturally, this can reach the stage in which the obsession is pathological and actually interferes with the necessary functions of life. But the Jewish obsession with justice is not at all pathological.

One example of a Jew obsessed with justice is Rabbi Moshe Rivkish, who lived in the late seventeenth century. His name is certainly not a "household name," even among individuals who are familiar with the heroes of Jewish history. Students of the codes of Jewish law may know the name of his major work because it adorns the margins of every edition of the *Shulḥan Arukh*. The name of his work is *Be'er HaGola*, but not everyone who consults his work regularly knows the author's identity. Many more are likely to be familiar with the name of his distinguished grandson, Rabbi Eliyahu, the Gaon of Vilna.

Be'er HaGola is not a commentary in the usual sense of the word. It is a reference tool, in which the author supplies the sources in the Talmud for the statements found in the code. Occasionally, but rarely, the author allows himself a phrase or brief sentence of commentary. Inevitably, these few comments express Rabbi Moshe's "obsession" with justice.

Here is one example of such a comment:

> I write this for all future generations, because I have seen people who have grown wealthy from monies they derived from cheating non-Jews in business. Ultimately, they were unsuccessful and their properties deteriorated so that they left no blessing behind. On the other hand, I have seen many who have sanctified God's name and returned profits derived from non-Jewish customers who mistakenly overpaid for merchandise. Ultimately, they were successful, became materially wealthy, and left a significant inheritance to their offspring.

What do we know about the personal concerns of this individual who was "obsessed" with justice for non-Jews? Based upon the preface to his work, we learn that he was driven, not once but several times, from his hometown of Vilna in Lithuania. Each time, he was a victim of fanatically anti-Semitic non-Jews, and each time, he left with just the clothes on his back and his personal diary, forced to abandon all of his possessions, including his painstakingly accumulated library of holy books.

His critical personal concerns did not interfere with his fundamental obsession: justice for all human beings, even those at the hands of whom he suffered greatly.

This late seventeenth-century Moshe learned to be obsessed with justice from the first Moshe, Moses our Teacher, and from the words he speaks in *Parashat Devarim* (Deut. 1:1–3:22). Moses begins his lengthy and eloquent valedictory to the Jewish people with his predominant concern. He is nearing the end of his life and his duty was to prepare the people to enter the Promised Land. But instead of instructing them about the methods to be used in entering the land, conquering it, and settling it, we find him addressing the people with these words:

> So I took ... wise and experienced men, and appointed them heads over you.... I charged your magistrates at that time as follows, "Hear out your fellow man, and decide justly between any man and a fellow Israelite or a stranger.... You shall not be partial in judgment: hear out low and high alike."

Moses too is obsessed with justice, to the extent that he interrupted his final instructions to the Jewish people and prefaced them with his plea that they establish a fair and equitable judiciary that would mete out justice to all, even the "stranger," the non-Jew.

On the Shabbat that precedes the major fast day of Tisha B'Av, the *haftara* is from the very first chapter of the Book of Isaiah. It is called *Shabbat Ḥazon*, or the Sabbath of the "prophetic vision" of Isaiah.

Here too the prophet Isaiah has numerous concerns, not the least of which is his critique of the sinfulness of the Jewish people. But he does not fail to express his obsession, which like the biblical Moses and the seventeenth century Moshe Rivkish, was the cause of justice. So he concludes his vision of what the final redemption will look like, "I will restore your magistrates as of old.... After that you shall be called City of Righteousness ... Zion shall be saved by justice."

I wrote these words in the midst of a great and challenging crisis for the Jewish people, during a war against a vicious and treacherous enemy. Yet, even in the midst of our valiant efforts to defend ourselves, we remained obsessed with the cause of justice, and we strove in every way possible to wage a just war, even risking our own lives as we attempted to spare the lives of innocent civilians.

We are confident that Zion will indeed be saved, imminently and gloriously, and that the justice we practice will be acknowledged by all mankind, thereby resulting in the universal blessing of the Almighty God of justice and mercy.

Parashat Va'ethanan

What To Pray For

I t is a question that every religious person has been confronted with and confounded by. Even those of us who are not theologically inclined have struggled with this question: Why are my prayers not answered? After all, we do believe in the efficacy of prayer. Why then is it so often a frustrating experience?

Every rabbi (myself included) has found himself challenged by very sincere individuals who ask him to explain the point of prayers if they are so seldom answered. I especially remember one such challenge.

It was on a Motza'ei Shabbat some years ago when I was still with my former synagogue in Baltimore. A group of women would meet every week after Shabbat to recite Psalms, and pray for the sick in that community. Over the months, they had accumulated a long list of individuals who were seriously ill and for whose recovery they fervently prayed.

One week, they asked me if I would join them, offer them some words of inspiration, and answer some of their questions. Of course I complied, delivered a short homily, and opened the floor for questions. Although the questions took a variety of forms, they were best expressed by the individual who said, "We cry our hearts out in prayer every week and we feel compassion for every person on our list. But hardly anyone becomes cured, and names come off the list only when the person has died. So what is the point of prayer?" I do not remember my exact response, but I do remember that it was inadequate.

Later that week, I received a hand-written note in my office mailbox. It began:

Dear Rabbi Weinreb,

In a recent talk, you said that many people complain to you about having said *Tehillim* for a friend who was ill, but that the prayers didn't help and the person died. They asked if you could explain the point of their prayers.

The woman who wrote the letter was a nurse in the intensive care unit of a local hospital. She obviously spoke from profound personal experience. She went on to say that the reason people find praying frustrating is that they expect a total cure, but they need to realize that there is much more to pray for with regard to a seriously ill individual than his or her complete recovery.

Here are some of the things she suggested people pray for: that the sick person not suffer too much pain, anxiety, depression, or loneliness; that the sick person be treated gently and with dignity by the medical staff; that the veins of the sick person be easy to find for intravenous injections; that the family have the strength to hold up under the strain and to not abandon the patient; and that the correct decisions, medical and ethical, be taken by the family, patient, doctor, and rabbi.

"If you pray for all of the above for a sick person, you will find that many of your prayers will be answered."

Words of wisdom for sure. And words that are especially timely in *Parashat Va'ethanan*, which contains the story of Moses' prayer and how that prayer was not heeded by the Almighty.

Moses asked that he be permitted to enter the Promised Land of Israel. His prayers were deep and numerous. Indeed, the sages suggest that he offered no fewer than 515 prayers. But, as Moses himself tells us, God did not regard his prayers. On the contrary, God told him not to bring the matter up again.

Were the prayers of Moses indeed not heard at all? If we pay careful attention to the text, dear reader, we come to realize that God did respond with at least two pieces of good news for Moses. Number one, He granted him the ability to see the land, which was not a total fulfillment of Moses' prayer, surely, but a gift nonetheless. And number two, and perhaps more important, He told him that his successor, Joshua, would lead the people into the land and would help them settle there. A leader who is assured of a competent and successful successor has surely had his prayers answered.

We have, then, an entirely new perspective on prayer. We must pray for a greater range of outcomes and not limit ourselves to total success. We must be satisfied in our prayers for what the Lord has chosen for us. The outcomes may be modest, or even insufficient, from our mortal points of view, but they are substantial if we could but open our minds to them.

A wise man once said, "Be careful what you pray for because you might just get it!" The truth of that humorous piece of advice is that we are ignorant as to what is good for us. We don't know what we should pray for. How consistent this message is with the lessons I learned from that scribbled note written by a wise congregant many years ago.

We must consider carefully what we pray for and expand our list of requests to cover the entire range of human needs. Only then will we discover that God does not simply listen to prayers or ignore them; rather, in His wisdom, He responds to them selectively. He says "no" to some of our entreaties, but He pronounces "yes" resoundingly to a great deal of what we ask for.

Unanswered Prayers

I have learned the hard way that some of the most important lessons in life come from unexpected sources. I have also learned that later, equally unexpected sources often force me to reconsider those important lessons. Let me tell you the history of one of those lessons that I learned and then had to re-learn.

It all started on the Saturday night that I agreed to address a group of women who had been praying for many weeks for the healing of the sick. This group recited Psalms for a list of people in the community who were suffering from life-threatening illnesses. From time to time, they asked one of the local rabbis to address them at the end of their prayer session. On this particular Saturday night, they asked me, and I agreed.

I tried to give an inspirational speech, stressing the importance of compassion and the power of prayers on behalf of others. I commended them for their sincerity and concern, and for their willingness to surrender an hour of their time each and every week to address prayers on behalf of individuals whom many of them did not even know.

Then I made a mistake. I told the group that I had another ten or fifteen minutes and would be glad to answer any questions they had about prayer. The questions were not long in coming and they came from everyone in the group. "Why is it," they asked, "that we pray profusely, yet the only time we remove someone sick from our list is when they pass away?" "Our prayers seem to never be answered," they said in chorus. "What is the point of uttering unanswered prayers?"

I responded by "talking the talk." Every rabbi with even a smattering of theological training knows all of the stock answers to such questions. "God surely listens to our prayers," I pontificated, "but He sometimes says no!"

The next morning, I found a handwritten note in the mail. It was from a woman, a registered nurse in the emergency room of the local hospital, who had attended the previous night's session.

She wrote, "I suggest a different kind of answer that could have been given to the questions that inundated you last night. You could have said that when we pray for a sick person to recover, we do not only pray for his or her total recovery. We also pray that the patient not suffer undue pain, that the family be able to bear the travail of witnessing the suffering of their loved one, that the doctors be able to execute their procedures effectively, and that, if so decreed, the patient leave this world surrounded by family and at peace."

The lesson I learned was that when we pray, we pray for an entire constellation of events. Even if we are not granted a complete recovery for the person we are praying for, a lot of what we pray for is granted.

In *Parashat Va'ethanan*, we read how Moses fervently prayed that he be granted the privilege of entering the Promised Land. His prayer was denied: "Oh Lord...let me go over, I pray You, and see the good land that is beyond the Jordan...but the Lord was wroth with me...and hearkened not unto me; and the Lord said unto me: 'Speak no more unto me of this matter'" (Deut. 3:24–26).

After learning the lesson that the good nurse told me, I began to wonder whether indeed the prayer of Moses was not heard. True, his major request, that he be permitted to enter the Holy Land, was not granted to him. But wasn't there so much more that he might have prayed for that was indeed granted? His disciple Joshua entered the land.

His children, the Children of Israel, entered the land. He was buried in close proximity to the land. He was permitted to at least see the land. Could he not take comfort in the fact that, although his major goal was not achieved, so much else was? This is a question that I have been asking myself for many years, whenever *Parashat Va'ethanan* comes around.

Recently, I discovered the answer to that question. I had the very rewarding, although poignantly painful, experience of leading a retreat for bereaved parents. They came from a variety of backgrounds and the circumstances of the death of their children ranged from terrorist murders, to accidental drownings, and to long-term illnesses.

They too were troubled by the question of the efficacy of prayer. They asked questions similar to those asked by the women of the Saturday night prayer group. "Why were our prayers for our dear children not heard by the Almighty?"

I thought I was being helpful when I shared with them the handwritten note from the emergency-room nurse. I was wrong. They did not find that note helpful at all. As one bereaved mother in the group told me, "I was praying for the most important thing in the world – the life of my poor baby. Can I take comfort in the relatively trivial aspects of my prayer? Can I be consoled by the fact that he was killed instantly by the terrorists' bullet and suffered no pain?"

I had to unlearn the lessons taught to me so many years before by that nurse. I learned a new lesson. I learned that when there is something that you value above all else, you can tolerate no compromises. Some goals are so important that the achievement of lesser goals means nothing.

This is how we can understand the fact that Moses was disconsolate when his prayer was rejected. To him, entry into the Holy Land was of paramount importance. Not that he sought to eat the fruits and gain the material pleasures of the land flowing with milk and honey, but because he knew that he could reach spiritual peaks in the Land of Israel that even he could never attain outside the land. He wanted to enter the Promised Land. No lesser promises could possibly have satisfied him.

Shabbat Nahamu celebrates the end of the three weeks of mourning for the Temple's destruction and inaugurates the seven weeks of consolation. The *haftara* for *Parashat Va'ethanan* is from the fortieth chapter of the Book of Isaiah, which begins, "Comfort you, comfort you my people."

The message is clear. Many of our prayers over the millennia have been denied. Our history is replete with unanswered prayers. It is difficult to take consolation when we have suffered so. But the message of Isaiah is clear. There is a time, and hopefully it is very near, when even the pain of the unanswered prayer can be assuaged.

In the words of the historian Graetz, as quoted in the Rabbi Joseph H. Hertz commentary, "These words of the prophets are like balm upon a wound, or like a soft breath upon a fevered brow."

Parashat Va'ethanan

What, Me? Worry?!

I am a worrier. My friends and family tease me about it. I sometimes worry about personal matters and sometimes about professional concerns. More often, I worry about things that are going on in the community or in the world. I worry about the economy and I worry about Iran's development of nuclear weapons.

Because of my background in psychology, I sometimes compare my worrying to the thoughts of patients who suffer from obsessive compulsive disorder. Like them, I sometimes have one worry on my mind and can think of nothing else. But I long ago decided that my worrying, though it may seem obsessive, is far from an indication of mental illness. Many people worry.

It is only very recently that I came to consider the possibility that, although my worrying was not a sign of a psychological disorder, it might be a sign of a theological disorder, a spiritual fault.

What prompted that consideration was a passage in the writings of Rabbi Naftali Tzvi Yehuda Berlin, the late nineteenth-century head of the Yeshiva of Volozhin in Eastern Europe. In the introduction to his commentary on Deuteronomy, Rabbi Berlin, or the Netziv as he is known, makes a remarkable statement:

> Reading carefully the words of instruction contained in this book, Deuteronomy, words that were divinely inspired and uttered by Moses our teacher, each person will find "milk and honey" in accordance with his spiritual level.... Therefore, each person should read it contemplatively, according to his ability, and he will find a straight path upon which to walk.... So let this book be a source of illumination for one's life journey.

I decided to heed the Netziv's counsel in reading *Parashat Va'ethanan* (Deut. 3:23–7:11), but I immediately found myself facing a dilemma. Among the many themes and topics in the *parasha* are some strong words prohibiting idolatry. "Do not act wickedly and make yourself a sculptured image in any likeness whatever.... You must not be lured into bowing down to them or serving them" (Deut. 4:15, 19).

How does this apply to me? What "milk and honey" can I find in proscriptions against idol worship? When was I last tempted to make for myself a graven image or to bow down to the sun or moon or stars? The only answer I can find to resolve this dilemma is to profoundly redefine the meaning of the prohibition against idolatry for our day and age.

Idolatry in ancient times was a process by which primitive men identified a single object to worship. They turned away from the vastness of the universe and its complexity and isolated either a heavenly body or some artifact of their own making, and came to believe that it, and only it, was worthy of their adulation. They became fixated upon a small fraction of reality. They became obsessed with one thing and that thing was far from representative of the whole picture.

In more modern times, the process of idolatry took a different turn. Instead of fixating upon an object, human beings fixated upon an ideology. They came to believe that the vastness of the universe could be reduced to a set of ideas. Those ideas included the Enlightenment, Nationalism, Scientism, Socialism, Fascism, and Communism. Those are but several of the idolatries of more recent history.

What they all have in common is a fixation or obsession with one set of ideas, as if that is all there is to life. That is where my nasty habit of worrying comes into play. The worrier becomes consumed with one fear, which may be trivial or may be monumental, but which is only a small part of the totality of existence.

When worrying is conceived of in this manner, it becomes apparent that worrying, itself, may be a form of idolatry. When one is consumed by worry, one is limiting his or her attention to one idea, or fear, or concern. Such individuals are ignoring the fact that there is a big world out there with a lot going on. They are certainly forgetting all the positive blessings that probably surround them. Admittedly, this is a novel interpretation of idolatry, but it is one that fits our modern circumstances much better than sun worship or offering animal sacrifices to a totem.

This redefinition allows for a deeper understanding of another passage in our *parasha*, the *Shema*. "Hear, O Israel, the Lord our God, the Lord is One." Only the Lord is One, because only He is all-encompassing. Nothing else is One in that sense – not the sun or moon, and not the currently popular ideology. They are all but parts of the greater whole.

Only of God is it said, "He is the place of the world, and the world is not His place." He contains the world; the world does not contain Him. This is the real meaning of monotheism; not that there is one God, but that God is One. Only He is big enough, complete enough, total enough, to be worshipped. Everything else is partial, fragmentary, and fractional. Everything else, including our worries, are mere idols that do not deserve the devotion we give them.

Perhaps the cynical Alfred E. Neumann of the comic books of my childhood was making a profound theological statement when he said, "What, me? Worry?!"

Religion Is Good for You

Religion is good for you." "A religious person is a mentally healthy person." Statements such as these could not have been made when I was a graduate student in psychology back in the 1960s. Quite the contrary. The prevalent belief in the mental health profession then was that religion was a neurosis and that religious people needed to abandon their irrational beliefs.

Things have changed since then. Scientific research has proven beyond a shadow of a doubt that religion can have a positive effect upon a person's mental attitude and that a person's religious beliefs can enhance not only his mental health, but even his physical well-being.

Books are now being published with titles such as *Handbook of Religion and Health* and *Faith and Health: Psychological Perspectives*. Mental health professionals are now being encouraged to assess the religiosity and spirituality of their patients and to use a patient's religious beliefs and behavior as part of the therapeutic process.

These findings are of great importance to practitioners of all the world's religions. They certainly have relevance for the Jewish people. Thus, one recent article in a professional journal asks in its very title,

"Are religious beliefs relevant to mental health among Jews?" The article concludes with this resoundingly affirmative declaration, "Beliefs about God's benevolence are related to mental health among Orthodox Jews; specifically, higher levels of belief predicted lower levels of depression and anxiety."

The part of me that is a licensed psychologist celebrates these findings. But the part of me that is an ordained rabbi questions whether the fact that religion can be a positive factor in one's mental health finds support in traditional Jewish sources, and furthermore, whether it is appropriate to practice religion just because of its beneficial effects upon one's health. I have long pondered these questions and have found a significant amount of material that helps answer them.

One example is found in *Parashat Va'ethanan* (Deut. 3:23–7:11). Close to the beginning of the *parasha*, we read, "And now, O Israel, give heed to the laws and rules that I am instructing you to observe, so that you may live to enter and occupy the land that the Lord, the God of your fathers, is giving you (Deut. 4:1)."

Classical Jewish commentators have been puzzled by the use of the phrase, "to live." Similar phrases emphasizing "to live" and to "choose life" abound in biblical texts. One commentator, Avraham ibn Ezra, puts it this way, "Surely our verse could have read 'so that you may enter and occupy the land' minus the phrase 'to live.'" His answer is a startling, indeed frightening, one. He suggests that those who do not "give heed to the laws and rules" are equivalent to idolaters, worshipers of the Pe'or, and they will not be allowed to live, but will be annihilated.

As far as I can tell, Ibn Ezra's explanation remained unchallenged for many centuries. In the late nineteenth century, however, it was forcefully challenged by none other than Rabbi Naftali Tzvi Yehuda Berlin, more popularly known as the Netziv, in his masterful commentary, *Haamek Davar*.

The Netziv begins by insisting that Ibn Ezra's approach is untenable. He calls it "a wonder"; something that makes no sense to him. First of all, he argues, can we equate all who do not observe the Torah's laws and rules with worshipers of a pagan idol, Pe'or? With this argument, Rabbi Berlin once again demonstrates the tolerant attitude toward

unobservant Jews, which characterized his many decades of Je
community leadership.

He goes on to ask, "Are all idol worshipers in fact annihilated?"
He therefore rejects Ibn Ezra's commentary and takes an entirely
different approach. His approach is based upon his contention, supported throughout his prolific writings, that the meaning of the word
"life" in the Bible often means not just remaining alive biologically, but
something close to what we might call *joie de vivre*, the joy of living. As
he puts it, "The implication of the word 'life' is that of a full life, a happy
and meaningful life, replete with the delight one experiences with the
achievement of spiritual wholeness."

The Netziv enunciates a general principle: Religious emotions
enhance and intensify life. Just as intellectual achievements and experiences of prestige and honor stimulate the life force of all human beings,
so too do worship and expressions of faith nourish the life force within
us. Hence, the person who deprives himself of the opportunities to
experience spirituality is denying himself a healthier existence. He is not
fully alive, and in a certain sense, he is dead. As our sages taught, "The
wicked, even in their lifetimes, are considered dead."

Rabbi Berlin is saying that our religious experiences invest us with
a tangible and genuine (which, in more modern terminology, is called
improved) mental health. This takes the observance of the Torah's laws
and rules beyond the theological sphere into the realm of psychology.
There is psychological benefit to religious belief and to religious behavior. Rabbi Berlin concludes:

> In our verse, Moses is telling us that heeding the Torah's laws and
> rules can bring about a fuller measure of life. This is the mean-
> ing of the Mishna in the second chapter of Tractate Avot, which
> declares that, "He who increases Torah increases his life (*marbe
> Torah marbe ḥaim*)." This does not mean that he lives longer
> than others, or that his allotted life span is extended. Rather, it
> means that he expands the emotional repertoire of his soul and
> can thereby live a much more pleasant life…. Thus, we say in our
> Sabbath liturgy that those who taste the Sabbath earn life. They
> literally feel a psychic joy during the Sabbath day.

We can take away from the Netziv's interpretation a lesson which is so necessary in contemporary times. Religion is not psychically harmful as many are convinced. It has pragmatic value, not just metaphysical value. Religious faith, observance of ritual, and authentic spiritual experiences, can help us cope with the emotional problems of living.

Yes, there are more idealistic reasons for adhering to Judaism. But we are taught that it is sometimes acceptable to follow the Torah for ulterior motives because those motives will ultimately become transformed into far purer motives (*mitokh shelo lishma ba lishma*).

Our faith can help us deal with anxiety and depression and can enable us to better cope with the challenges and stressors that are unavoidable nowadays. These might not be the best reasons for adopting a religious lifestyle, but they certainly provide a place to start. Religion *is* good for you!

Discipline and Suffering

As a parent, grandparent, and psychologist, I am often considered to be something of an expert on parenting and child-rearing. In that capacity, I have frequently been asked to review or give an opinion about any of the plethora of books on the subject of raising one's children.

As in any genre, there are better books and worse books in this category. I have noticed that many of them fail to include a chapter on one of the most important components of child rearing: discipline. With few exceptions, the most that these books contain on the subject of discipline is a chapter on "setting limits." In my opinion, and certainly in my experience, discipline is an essential component of all parenting and teaching relationships. And discipline is not just about setting limits. It is also about setting goals.

My reading on the subject of dealing with children, whether as a parent or as a teacher, has taught me the importance of setting clear and achievable goals and objectives for children to reach, and then to show recognition of the achievement of those goals.

My experience as a parent, as a teacher for many years, and as a psychotherapist for much of my adult life, has borne out the wisdom of these two steps: First, lay out the expectations that you have of the child and clearly define the nature of the task at hand. Second, when the child has accomplished the task, even if not totally successfully, give him or her feedback and recognition, whether in the form of a verbal compliment or a nonverbal gesture.

Discipline does not just involve setting limits. Indeed, saying "no" and issuing restrictive commands may not, at all, be what discipline is about. Rather, it involves setting goals. It is about extending a challenge, with the implicit confidence that sends that child the message, "You can do it!" This to me is the essence of discipline. It is not synonymous with punishment. It is synonymous with learning and personal growth.

And this is what I think is meant by the passage in *Parashat Ekev*, "Bear in mind that the Lord your God disciplines you just as a man disciplines his son" (Deut. 8:5).

The Torah has much to say, even if the parenting books do not, about discipline. It takes for granted that parents will discipline their children and that teachers will discipline their students. After all, that is why students are called disciples.

The Torah insists, moreover, that the Almighty too disciplines us. And He does so in much the same way as successful parents do. He sets clear expectations for us and He shows us His favor when we meet those expectations and His disfavor when we fail to do so. The Lord really is a Father in this sense.

It is no wonder then that the Book of Proverbs cautions us to "heed the discipline of your father, and do not forsake the instruction of your mother." Notice: first discipline, and then instruction. First *musar*, and Torah only afterwards.

As usual, there is an even deeper message in the word that the Torah uses for discipline. The root containing the Hebrew letters *yud-samekh-resh* is the root of both "discipline" and "suffering."

Judaism teaches us that there is a meaning to our suffering. Sometimes that meaning is obvious to us; more typically though, the meaning eludes us and we desperately search for it. But one thing is clear. We learn through discipline and we also learn through suffering.

The words of Victor Frankl, the psychologist and Auschwitz survivor, who certainly knew a thing or two about suffering, are very instructive here:

> On the biological plane, as we know, pain is a meaningful watcher and warder. In the psycho-spiritual realm it has a similar function. Suffering is intended to guard man from apathy, from psychic rigor mortis. As long as we suffer we remain psychically alive. In fact, we mature in suffering, grow because of it – it makes us richer and stronger.

It is through the processes of discipline and suffering that we develop and are transformed. Both processes are painful, sometimes profoundly so. But through both, we widen our horizons, enhance our spirits, and attain a deeper understanding of our life's purpose.

Discipline and suffering are important to us all as individuals, as part of the Jewish people, and as mortal humans, struggling to cope and ultimately to grow.

How Am I Doing?

I f your child, employee, or colleague asks you that question, you can be sure that he or she is sincere, wishes to learn, and will succeed. The person who asks, "How am I doing?" is asking for constructive feedback. That person is expressing a need to know whether or not he is doing a good job, and if not, what he can do to correct his work.

The art of giving effective feedback is very important. In all human relationships, where there is mutual feedback, a relationship pattern is established that can self-adjust, advance, and thrive.

For feedback to truly be effective, it needs to be solicited. That is, the recipient of the feedback must ask the observer to tell him how he is doing. This signals a readiness to receive criticism, to modify behavior, and to change. Without that readiness, feedback is doomed to failure.

Feedback also needs to be specific. It is not helpful to say, "That was stupid," "You'll never be good at that," or even, "Great job!" It *is* helpful to say, "You turned left when you should have turned right," or, "When you softened your voice and smiled, it was easier to listen to you." The description of behavior is what is necessary, not evaluation.

Human nature is such that it is the rare person who asks for feedback and that few of us are comfortable in delivering criticism. However constructive and well-intended, it is hard to give feedback to another person. We are afraid of confrontation, of possibly embarrassing the other, and so we avoid giving feedback even at the cost of assisting the other to change in a positive way.

And yet, there is nothing more helpful to anyone learning a new task than to have feedback delivered to him or her in a useful, nonjudgmental, constructive manner. As the Talmud puts it, "No one has ever mastered Torah study without having first erred and made mistakes." Mastery is only achieved when mistakes are pointed out to the student so that he can correct them.

In *Parashat Re'eh*, we read at length about false prophets. We often mistake the nature of the mission of the prophet, assuming that it is to predict the future. But that is certainly not the mission of the great biblical prophets. Rather, their mission was, in our terms, to give constructive feedback to the people, pointing out their faults, and guiding them in a more positive direction.

The false prophet not only gives false guarantees about the future, complacently predicting peace and tranquility, but assures the people that they are doing nothing wrong, that they need not change their behavior. The false prophet gives no feedback.

These words of the Book of Lamentations, which we read in the synagogue on Tisha B'Av, are incomparably instructive here:

> Your seers prophesied to you
> Delusion and folly.
> They did not expose your iniquity
> So as to restore your fortunes,
> But prophesied to you oracles
> Of delusion and deception.

The false prophet cannot give proper feedback. He avoids telling the truth if he thinks it will offend. He is unaware of the positive value of effective feedback. Those who follow him will never benefit from words of correction and guidance. They cannot change and they will not grow.

I encourage the reader to reflect upon his or her own experience and to recall those occasions when a few words of corrective feedback were of immense benefit. I personally remember my own first days as a teacher, when a crusty veteran colleague sat in my classroom and gave me the benefits of his experience by pointing out the numerous things I did that were ineffective, and suggested alternatives to me. I cannot say that I enjoyed his deflating critique at that moment, but I know that I and a lifetime of students are profoundly indebted to him.

All the more do we cherish those occasions when we receive positive feedback from an observer. I can never forget the times when a mentor or senior rabbi approached me after a sermon with a warm handshake and a whispered, "*Yasher koakh* – job well done." That was enough to teach me that I was on the right track and could confidently continue on my path.

As an old Spanish proverb has it: "Self-knowledge is the beginning of self-improvement." And an old Chinese proverb says it even more incisively: "A man who knows he is a fool is not a great fool."

One of the lessons of our *parasha* is that the true prophet gives feedback, sometimes in a way that is hard to hear. But that prophet is extending a hand to us to bring us back to a better way of life, and has instructed us in an improved set of behaviors. If we attend to the feedback of the prophet, we "will be heeding the Lord your God and doing what is right in His sight."

Personally, I appreciate feedback for everything that I write. And so I ask you, dear reader, "How am I doing?"

Parashat Re'eh

The Thief of Blessing

I am sure that you, dear reader, have had the occasion to come across a book that you simply could not put down. Something so fascinating, so gripping, that you were compelled to read it cover-to-cover in as short a time as you could manage.

I came across such a book, a Hebrew book, the biography of a rabbi named Dov Cohen. Rabbi Cohen passed away at the advanced age of ninety four. He was one of the last, if not the last, of the students of the Yeshiva in Hebron that experienced the horrible massacre in the summer of 1929.

The book is entitled *Vayelkhu Shnayhem Yaḥdav (And the Two of Them Walked Together)*. Much of Rabbi Cohen's story is encapsulated in that title. For, you see, he was born in Seattle, WA into a family of Lithuanian Jewish immigrants. The family faced all of the challenges of Americanization in the early decades of the twentieth century.

Rabbi Cohen's mother witnessed the inexorable process of assimilation with which her older children were involved. She was determined that her youngest child, Dov, would receive a Jewish education as intensive as the one she witnessed back in the old country. So, in 1926, she took her then fourteen-year-old son from Seattle eastward across the United States, across the Atlantic Ocean, through the straits of Gibraltar, and ultimately to the then totally primitive and isolated village of Hebron. She committed him there to the tutelage of the famed Rabbi Nosson Tzvi Finkel of Slobodka. Indeed, "the two of them walked together."

I cannot possibly share with you all of the ensuing adventures in Rabbi Cohen's life. But there is one episode that I must relate. Dov visited the United States several times during the eighty years that followed his first days in the Land of Israel. And each time, he experienced a sort of "culture shock." Once, on a Sunday morning, he found himself in a taxi with the radio on. He soon realized that the radio was playing a sermon being delivered by a Christian minister in his church. He was unable to have the taxi driver change the radio station. And so, quite uncomfortably, he listened to the preacher's sermon. And this is what he heard:

> The group in charge of increasing the enrollment in *gehenna*, or hell, was discussing ways to get more people to sin. One suggested encouraging them to steal. But the others all protested that the laws against theft were too strict and not enough people would sin by stealing. Another suggested encouraging people to lie. Again, the others protested that lying would make people feel too guilty. Finally came the suggestion with which everyone agreed, "Let's encourage people to do good deeds, acts of loving-kindness, acts of charity, acts of courage and justice. But let's tell them not to do those things today. But rather, tomorrow!"

Rabbi Cohen was moved to the core by that story and was inspired by it. Indeed, he shared it with Jewish audiences whenever he could. The lesson he learned and shared was one that Judaism also teaches, albeit not with that particular story. It is the lesson of the dangers of procrastination, of the importance of doing things as soon as possible and not putting them off for tomorrow.

This lesson is conveyed in the opening verse of *Parashat Re'eh*, "See, I set before you today blessing and curse." Homiletically, the stress is upon today, this day and this moment. Do the right thing today and it will be a blessing. Put it off until tomorrow and the result is cursed.

We have all heard the advice, "Never put off until tomorrow what you can do today." This advice is useful in all aspects of life, but it is especially useful in the context of religious behavior and spiritual service. Postponing until a tomorrow, which may never come, can be, as the gentile preacher's story suggests, nothing less than sinful.

You may also have heard the adage, which originates with the eighteenth-century poet Edward Young: "Procrastination is the thief of time." The opening words of the *parasha* suggest that procrastination is not only the thief of time, but it is the thief of life and of blessing: "See, I have given you today, this day, now and not later, to perform the good deed, and if you do it now it will be a blessing. If you procrastinate you may never do it at all, and the result may be quite different from a blessing."

This is the lesson of the opening verse of *Re'eh*. And how ironic it is that the subject of the engrossing biography that I just finished reading, Rabbi Dov Cohen, a yeshiva boy and eventually a well-known Jewish rabbi, learned this lesson from a Protestant preacher on a Sunday morning long ago!

Idealism and Reality

It was another one of those park-bench discussions. I hadn't seen my old friend Eli for quite some time. We would run into each other every couple of years, not because we planned it, but because we lived in the same city. We both loved to take long walks and the frequency with which our paths crossed constantly amazed us. We also both enjoyed long talks, and the beginnings of some of those discussions went back to our sophomore year in high school.

Eli was a self-described utopian. He had a clear picture in his mind of what an ideal world would look like. Although I too am somewhat of a utopian, compared to my old friend, I am a hardnosed realist.

Many of our past discussions concerned what we both believed was the unfair distribution of wealth in the world. Personally, we were both acquainted with stupendously wealthy individuals. We also had mutual friends who were totally destitute.

Our most recent chance encounter found us reviving that old familiar topic. The news media that particular day were bemoaning the widening gap in the United States and many other countries between the very rich and the very poor.

Lo and behold, almost simultaneously, we were quoting chapter and verse from *Parashat Re'eh* (Deut. 11:26–16:17). Ironically, each of us found a proof text to support our positions about societal ideals and social reality.

Eli had served for many years as the *baal koreh* in his synagogue. He had no trouble precisely recalling the following verse, and even chanting it aloud for all in the park to hear,

> There shall be no needy among you – since the Lord your God will bless you in the land that the Lord your God is giving you as a hereditary portion – if only you heed the Lord your God and take care to keep all this Instruction that I enjoin upon you this day. (Deut. 15:4–5)

Eli thumped his hand down on the park bench triumphantly. "Clearly, the Torah envisions a world in which there are no poor people. That is unarguably the Torah's ideal," he said.

I could not resist reminding my good friend that he had used that very text so long ago when we were both members of our high school debate team. He argued the cause of socialism, while my duty was to defend capitalism. We had both outgrown the simple assumptions of adolescence, and, at this point in life, Eli was no socialist. But he still nurtured a penchant for an ideal world, a world without man-made discrimination.

I did not have to look very far for a verse that countered Eli's source. Although it has been very many years since I served as a regular Torah reader in the synagogues I attend, I had sufficient experience as a *baal koreh* in years gone by to attach the traditional mellifluous chant to the words, "Give to him readily.... For there will never cease to be needy ones in your land, which is why I command you: open your hand to the poor and needy kinsman in your land" (Deut. 15:10–11).

After all these years, we both must have reached a new level of maturity, for we soon decided that to continue debating the issues of idealism versus realism would be pointless at our age. I granted him that we were indeed encouraged by the Torah to try as best we could to construct, if not a perfect world, then a vastly improved one. If we could not achieve the ideal of "there shall be no needy among you," we could at least "open our hands" to those who were needy.

And Eli conceded that until we can attain an ideal world in which there are no needy, we had better scrupulously follow the Torah's urgent plea that we "open our hands" to those who seem to "never cease to be needy." "Until we achieve the ideal," concluded Eli, "we had better face the reality and be fervently charitable."

We parted ways and were each fairly certain that it would be a while until chance brought us together once again to revive old arguments on a common park bench. Was I in for a surprise!

The very next evening, I received a rare telephone call from an unusually excited Eli. He opened the conversation by exclaiming loudly that he had discovered a story that he had to share with me.

It seems that he had come across a relatively new book, in Hebrew, on the weekly Torah portions. It was simply entitled *Parashot, Portions,* and subtitled *A New Look at the Portions of the Week.* The author, Rabbi Haim Navon, compiled the book from the weekly columns he had written for the Israeli newspaper, *Makor Rishon.*

Eli was particularly impressed by an old story that neither of us had heard before.

It was back in the early years of the twentieth century when extreme socialism was in vogue and many believed that it would be the new world order. An old socialist leader was walking along the street with one of his devoted disciples. They passed a beggar pleading for alms. The master walked right by the poor man, but the disciple paused and gave him a few pennies. How shocked was the disciple when his master reprimanded him severely and called him a traitor to the cause.

The disciple objected, "All I did was help a poor person! Did you not teach us about the plight of the poverty-stricken worker?"

The master replied, "We are expecting the revolution, which will be a comprehensive and absolute solution to the problem of poverty. By relieving this man of his desperation for even a moment, you were providing a temporary solution to his situation. That will delay and postpone the ultimate Revolution."

I was deeply impressed by this story and thanked Eli for sharing it with me. We spoke a little bit further about it and came to the following conclusion: It is natural for humans to desire perfection, but they cannot allow that desire to get in the way of dealing with the ugly realities of life.

Our *parasha*, in verses that are separated by a few mere lines, drives home this important point. We must strive with all our might for a society in which poverty (and for that matter all forms of human misery) is eliminated. But in our striving, we cannot lose sight of the realities. Poverty exists and we must ameliorate it. We must expect that, at every step along the way to the ideal world, which we are commanded to create, there will be pressing problems that must be addressed immediately, even if that means that the long-term larger goals must be temporarily postponed. A lesson for the ages, and a lesson for today.

Parashat Re'eh

All That Glitters

I t is difficult to tell you much about my high school friend without disclosing his identity. He is now world-famous, having become a major figure in the field of high finance. So in the interest of protecting his privacy, I will alter some of the facts of the story I am about to tell. For starters, let's call him Eugene.

Our friendship began in our freshman year. I was new to the school, but he had attended grade school in the same institution. He reached out to me and showed me the ropes. We were pretty close friends for a year or two, but then our paths diverged. His intellectual interests were in the areas of economics and politics; I was more inclined toward the fields of literature and philosophy.

By our junior year, the bond between us was ruptured. He chose to abandon religious observance at precisely the time that I was becoming much more committed to religion. We found ourselves in entirely different social circles, and by the time we graduated, were barely on speaking terms. He chose not to continue his post-high school Jewish education and enrolled in a very prestigious business college. Within five years, he was a millionaire.

Had it been just up to me, I probably never would have seen him again. But in those years, I was under the influence of a very unusual, creative, and compassionate rabbinic mentor. Let's call him Reb Shmuel.

Reb Shmuel approached me one morning and asked whether I had any ongoing contact with Eugene. When I answered in the negative, he reproached me. "He was once a good friend of yours and he helped you acclimate to a new school. You owe him a visit."

My forceful attempts to argue that such a visit would be futile did not impress Reb Shmuel. "There are many things that one must do in life," he said, "even if they indeed turn out to be futile."

To make a long story short, I did visit Eugene. I came to his office in the financial district of Manhattan. He greeted me warmly, but the conversation soon deteriorated into a raucous argument about religion. We covered some of the usual ground of such arguments until he pounded his fist on the table and said, "I have absolute proof that the lifestyle I have chosen is correct."

I looked at him quizzically and asked incredulously, "Absolute proof? I am eager to hear that."

With a wave of his hand, he drew my attention to all of the luxurious trappings of his office and to the view of the New York Harbor that he could see through his window. "This is just one of my offices," he said. "And I have two homes, which are even more lavish. Not to speak of my sports car and extensive financial portfolio."

"I am successful. Hence, I am obviously correct in my beliefs." I have heard this argument countless times since that visit, sometimes by those, like Eugene, who have rejected religion. But it is also sometimes used by religious people who point to their material success as evidence of God's favor and of the correctness of their theological stance.

This was not the first time I encountered the argument that material success carries theological weight. The first time I encountered it was when I first reflected deeply on a passage in *Parashat Re'eh* (Deut. 11:26–17:17). The passage reads:

If there appears among you a prophet or a dream-diviner and he gives you a sign or a portent, saying, "Let us follow and worship another god" – whom you have not experienced – even if the sign or portent that he named to you comes true, do not heed the words of that prophet or that dream-diviner. For the Lord your God is testing you to see whether you really love the Lord your God with all your heart and soul.

Many of the students in the numerous Bible classes that I have taught over the years are put off by the above passage. "What relevance," they ask, "can there be in a passage that tells of a false prophet who can make all sorts of signs and portents happen? Perhaps he is a sorcerer? Is that what the Bible is teaching us?"

My confrontation with Eugene provided me with an answer that I have used again and again to respond to such a question.

"Truth to tell," I would argue, "this is one of the most relevant passages in the entire Bible, especially in our modern times. What we can learn from this passage is that the truth of a religious message is not at all related to whether or not material success is attached to that religious message. We cannot judge a prophet's authenticity by his ability to produce facts in the so-called real world."

Reb Shmuel taught me another way of expressing this lesson. "Human beings," he would say, "live in two worlds. We live in a world of values, and in that world our beliefs reign. We also live in a world of facts, and that is where your friend Eugene resides. For us, however, facts do not determine values."

For a religious person, values are determined by sacred texts and time-honored traditions. The Jewish people, especially, have confronted nations and cultures that were economically, politically, and militarily successful and powerful, while we were weak and impotent. Our greatness lies in the fact that we remained immune to the glitter of the success of those nations and cultures. We resisted the temptation to base our values upon facts, however strong and powerful those facts seemed to be.

Our *parasha* teaches us that we can often expect to see successful signs and convincing portents all around us, but we are not to follow them if they are inconsistent with the essential messages of our Torah. God tests us by exposing us to the glitter of success. Our greatness throughout our history is attributable to our ability to avoid the seductive trap of that glitter. We have learned, and we must teach our children, that material success has no bearing upon religious truth.

Parashat Shofetim

Justice, Justice

Like any good grandparent, I have seen my share of little-league baseball games. One summer, I sat through an all-day tournament of four five-inning games. Not too excited about what was happening on the playing field, I found myself slipping into a half-dozing, half-contemplative mood.

Watching the kids, from a dazzling diversity of backgrounds, playing by the rules, abiding by the umpire's calls, and lining up to shake hands with their opponents when each match was over, it occurred to me that more than mere recreation was taking place here. Rather, by fully engaging in this quintessential American pastime, these children were learning about justice, fairness, and the resolution of conflict. And they were learning about these vital principles in a manner far more effective than any classroom lesson.

They were learning that there are rules and that one must know them and abide by them. They were learning that their own judgments could be flawed, and were subject to a higher authority to whom they had to submit, albeit not without proper protest, if the game was to proceed successfully. They were learning to compromise, to adapt, to respect others, and to acknowledge the dignity of their opponents, in victory and in defeat. No trivial lessons, these.

I soon realized that I too, and most of us who grew up in the American culture, had similar experiences. Perhaps not as regimented, certainly not as well-organized, my peers and I learned about justice and fairness by virtue of the games we played. Whether or not we integrated these lessons into our ultimate adult standards is another matter, which depended upon a variety of circumstances far removed from the playing field.

As my philosophizing continued, and as the innings dragged on, with my grandson's team continuing its uphill struggles, I reflected on how basic was this human need for justice and fairness, and in how many ways our search for these simple principles is frustrated. I believe, along with a host of philosophers including Plato and Kant, that human beings are "programmed" to expect justice. We all have a built-in sense of what is just, and what is fair, and we are bitterly disappointed when our experiences in life do not match our expectations for justice.

A common reaction to bitter disappointment, especially expressed by the young but not absent from the adults' response repertoire, is the plaintive cry, "It's not fair!" We respond this way to the minor letdowns of everyday life, but also to truly grievous tragedy. Those of us who have had to break bad and unexpected news to another have heard the protest, "But that is not fair!" I know that I have heard this expressed by those who found out about the rejection of a lover and also from those who were notified of the sudden death of someone close.

I vividly recall my father-in-law's description of his first encounter: He and his father were fleeing the advancing Nazi army, together with an acquaintance who had just narrowly escaped the aerial firebombing of his entire village, and had witnessed the instant death of his parents, wife, and children. He collapsed into the arms of my father-in-law's father, a hasidic rebbe, wailing, "*Les din, v'les dayan!*" "There is no justice, there is no judge." In this moment of unutterable grief, he could only cry hysterically about the absence of fairness and justice in God's world.

How wise is our Torah in *Parashat Shofetim* to prescribe a thorough system of justice to be installed in "all your gates." Justice is the primary objective of a Jewish society, although the Torah fully recognizes that it is an elusive objective indeed. It requires unstinting diligence and painstaking persistence. It requires trained, qualified, and dedicated judges, and a cooperative attitude from all members of society. Justice is never perfect but must ever strive to approach that ideal. "*Tzedek tzedek tirdof* (Justice, justice, you must pursue)!"

I refer you to Reverend Martin Luther King's more famous insights, "The arc of the moral universe is long but it bends toward justice." I am a great fan of Dr. King and stand in awe of his eloquence. And my Jewish faith also foresees the "bend toward justice." Hence, "Zion will be redeemed through justice and by those who return to her in righteousness" (Is. 1:27).

But there is an aspect to the Jewish vision of justice that is much too impatient to passively await the curve of that long arc. Our *parasha* insists on the urgency of justice and the necessity to implement it swiftly and comprehensively.

Two of our weekly *parashot, Mishpatim* and *Shofetim*, are named for justice, and a full quarter of our Code of Jewish Law, *Ḥoshen Mishpat*, mandates its thorough implementation.

Yes, we believe that the course of history, ultimately divinely-guided, bends ever so slowly toward justice, but it is our responsibility to exert every human effort to hasten the pace of that course.

We Are All Judges and Kings

Ⅰn mid-August, when summer is waning, school children begin to experience the anxieties that come with the anticipation of the return to school, vacationers hasten to relish the last of the "lazy, hazy days," and the baseball season is at the stage when the pennant and wild-card races begin to really heat up.

Spiritually too, there is a change going on inside of us. The month of Elul, the last month before the New Year, has begun, and with it comes the sound of the shofar, which literally signals the fast-approaching High Holidays and Days of Awe. The shofar simply gives voice to the inner feeling of "the fun times are over, it is time to get serious."

It is precisely at this season that we read *Parashat Shofetim* (Deut. 16:18–21:9). We open our Bibles to this *parasha* in anticipation of some words to edify each of us as individuals. We hope to find verses that will goad us toward introspection and inspire us to improve ourselves in many ways. But that is not what we find in *Parashat Shofetim*. We are disappointed in our search for a deeply personal message.

What we find, instead, are laws and narratives that seem to be meant for someone else, not for us mere struggling ordinary mortals. The passages we read are directed toward the elite stratum of our society, to the leaders, the judges, and kings.

The *parasha* opens with a description of the judicial and legal institutions, and with the establishment of a locale, which we are to visit if we wish to consult priests and Levites and experts in the law. The *parasha* proceeds to speak of kingship and royalty, of the privileges and responsibilities of the priestly class, of the role of prophets, and even of the structure of the military.

Where is the role of the individual in all of this? At this time of year, when those of us who are serious about our religious responsibilities are searching for personal guidance and spiritual illumination, what lessons can we learn from these texts, which seem to be addressing a more lofty audience? What is a humble person to gain from laws of societal governance? Of what relevance are the responsibilities of judges and priests and kings to those of us with pedestrian concerns?

There are, of course, numerous approaches to resolving this quandary. But there is one approach that I would like to suggest and that seems to me to be of great practical utility.

To explain this approach, I must remind you of an important movement in the history of the Jewish people that had its roots in the middle of the nineteenth century. A man named Rabbi Yisrael Salanter was disturbed at the superficiality of the religious life that he observed even in the most traditional and observant communities of the Eastern Europe of his time. He felt that people were numb, or at least indifferent, to the important ethical issues that he considered to be the core of our faith. And so he initiated a religious revolution known as the Musar movement, which was designed to once again place ethics and spirituality at the center of Jewish religious life.

This is not the place to describe in detail the development of this movement over the course of the last century and a half. Suffice it to say that this movement, like so many similar ones, splintered into a number of different streams. One of these was centered in the small Lithuanian village of Kelm and another in a suburb of the large city of Kovno, Slobodka.

The "old man" of Kelm, Rabbi Simha Zissel, emphasized man's limitations, his frailties and vulnerabilities. His followers would spend the days of Elul in fear and trepidation, hoping to overcome the burdens of their sins.

The other "old man," Rabbi Nosson Tzvi Finkel of Slobodka, had a very different spiritual strategy. He encouraged his disciples to recognize the greatness of man (*gadlut haadam*). He urged his followers to recognize their strength and near infinite potential.

Far be it from me to decide which approach is correct. I believe they are both correct, but I feel that each is designed for its own time and place. In our time and in our place, I am convinced that the Slobodka approach is preferable.

Nowadays, paradoxically, our external demeanor of arrogance and hubris is but a mask for deep inner feelings of inferiority and inadequacy. We fail to understand that we are capable, as individuals and as a nation, of gigantic accomplishments. We need to be reminded not of our limitations, but of our capabilities.

Perhaps it is for this reason that we read *Parashat Shofetim* at this time of year. It reminds us that we are all "judges and kings." We all need to take our responsibilities seriously. Each and every one of us is a leader, if not over throngs of thousands, then over our communities, neighborhoods, and families, or, at the very least, over ourselves.

We are reminded that from our very beginnings, we were given the appellation "a kingdom of priests, a holy nation." The road to *teshuva*, to authentic repentance, is not a private and solitary road. It is not a road that we travel as isolated individuals, with the puny tools of introspection and contemplation.

Rather, with the approach of the New Year, we must regard ourselves as part of a great nation, and imagine ourselves as leaders of that nation. That is why *Parashat Shofetim*, with its emphasis upon large social institutions and systems of governance and military defense, is read at this time of year. It is to remind us, nay to persuade us, that we are all "judges and kings."

Anarchy or Utopia?

W hom would you consult if you wanted to know a thing or two about the perfect society? Would you ask a politician? A professor of government? A philosopher expert in theories of utopia? Or perhaps a historian familiar with successful societies across the ages?

Would it even occur to you to ask an entomologist, a scientist who studies insect life? But it is precisely such a person whom the Bible suggests we consult if we want to learn a thing or two about the ideal society. In fact, it is the wisest man in the Bible, King Solomon, who suggests that we observe insect life. I refer to the following passage in the Book of Proverbs:

> Lazy bones, go to the ant;
> Study its ways and learn.
> Without leaders, officers, or rulers,
> it lays up its stores during the summer,
> Gathers in its food at the harvest. (Prov. 6:6–8)

In antiquity, men were already observing colonies of mere ants, and noticing how remarkably efficient they were. Today, we would attribute that efficiency to the power of instinct. But those of us who retain a sense of the wondrous ways of nature are impressed by the complexity of tasks that ant colonies perform, without an instruction manual, without training, and, above all, without leaders.

The Midrash on *Parashat Shofetim* is not only in awe of the complexity of the ants' tasks, but is astonished at the moral lesson that we can learn from this lowly creature:

> Behold the ethical behavior of the ant as it avoids theft. Said Rabbi Shimon ben Ḥalafta: "I once observed an ant who dropped a kernel of wheat, which then rolled down the ant hill. All the ants came, one by one, and sniffed it. No ant dared take it, until the one who dropped it came and took it for herself. Behold the wisdom of the ant, which is to be praised, for it did not receive instruction from any other creature, and has neither judges nor policeman." (Deuteronomy Rabba, Judges, 3.)

There are many ways to understand the verse in Proverbs and the midrashic passage just quoted, and each time I personally encounter these texts, I understand them differently. But this year, I found myself fascinated by the possibility that King Solomon and Rabbi Shimon ben Ḥalafta ask us to take a glimpse of what a perfect society might look like.

It would be a society that had no leadership hierarchy and in which all were truly equal. It would be a society in which everyone contributed to the extent that he could, and would do so diligently and industriously. Furthermore, it would be a society in which each individual respected the other and would not dream of taking something that belonged to someone else. In short, it would be an efficient society and an ethical one. And it would have no leader, no need for judges, and no necessity for policemen to assure that crimes were not committed.

Parashat Shofetim describes a society that is far from that ideal. It opens with the command that we "appoint magistrates and officials ... who shall govern the people and do justice." The Torah insists upon a judicial system and personnel to enforce its laws. It speaks of a judicial hierarchy with lower courts consulting higher ones. It speaks of a king. It describes a military system and outlines the roles of priests, sergeants, and generals. It describes a system of government comprised of several different institutions, each with its own set of responsibilities and privileges.

Our *parasha* leaves us with the following question: is it the ideal society that is being described herein, or do the systems elaborated upon in the *parasha* reflect the Torah's concessions to human frailty? Perhaps the long list of laws is a response to the tragic fact that real societies do not resemble the utopian ideal and therefore require judges and policemen, overseers and enforcers, kings and generals.

Taking the latter approach – and understanding that the royal, military, and judicial institutions described in detail in this *parasha* are necessary because mankind is not perfect – enables us to understand a puzzle that confronts every careful reader.

For you see, there is one passage in our *parasha* that just doesn't seem to fit. It is the subject of chapter 19, in which the Children of Israel are commanded to set aside three cities to serve as sanctuaries for a person who was guilty of killing another unwittingly. How does this unspeakable calamity, unintentional manslaughter, fit into the rubric of the other passages of this *parasha,* which deal with institutions of government?

This is a question asked by numerous commentators, beginning with Avraham ibn Ezra in the early Middle Ages, and including Ovadia Sforno, who lived in Renaissance Italy; the Safed Kabbalist, Moshe Alshikh; and the German Jewish twentieth-century scholar, David Tzvi Hoffmann.

I recently came across an answer to this question that appeals to me in a book on the weekly Torah portion. The book is entitled *MiSinai Ba*, by Rabbi Yehuda Shaviv, a contemporary rabbi. Rabbi Shaviv suggests that the passage describing in detail how to treat an unintentional murderer illustrates the simple human lesson that accidents will happen. "It would be wonderful indeed," writes Rabbi Shaviv, "if people would never blunder or err, and could control all of their actions rationally and with great caution. But our Torah relates to human beings in all of their frailties and faults, and gives us ways of coping and rectifying those shortcomings."

To me, the difference between the harmonious social organization, which characterizes the colony of ants, versus human groups, which require intricate systems of control and management, is the difference between creatures guided by instinct versus humans blessed by free will. It is the very freedom that we as humans enjoy that compels us to be on guard against evil in all of its forms.

The lesson of our *parasha* is that human beings require external controls in the form of law, systems of justice and enforcement, kings and political leaders, and even militias and generals. King Solomon's call to witness the ants is really his invitation to envision an ideal society, but one that is nearly impossible to achieve, given the human condition.

Until that ideal is achieved, we are well advised to study all that the Torah has to say about safeguards against human faults. *Parashat Shofetim* provides excellent examples of the Torah's lessons in this regard. It recognizes the reality of crime, dishonesty, and violence. It even copes with inevitable unintentional violence.

Anarchy must be avoided, but utopia is not realistic. The Torah is designed to help us deal with the realities of existence, which are typically far from ideal. Nevertheless, the Torah holds open the possibility that a utopia might one day emerge. After all, if the ants can achieve an efficient and ethical society, why can't we?

Parashat Shofetim

The Participant Observer

Ihave had a long and abiding interest in the process by which we
make decisions in our lives. Long ago, I was taught that the best way to
make a decision is to impartially examine all of the relevant available
facts. Impartiality guarantees objectivity. Sadly, however, we are seldom
truly impartial and therefore our ability to make objective decisions is
impaired.

This lesson was first made clear to me in one of the first courses
I took in college. It was an elementary course in cultural anthropology,
a subject that I have found fascinating ever since. I remember reading
the works of anthropologists Ruth Benedict and Margaret Mead, who
studied exotic and primitive Native American and South Pacific societies, although they eschewed the term "primitive." They believed that, as
trained social scientists, they could observe these societies in a neutral
fashion, as one would study laboratory phenomena. They felt assured
that their descriptions and analyses would be objective.

However, subsequent social scientists severely criticized these
studies. They attacked the assumption that one could live in a society
for months and even years, yet remain impartial and neutral toward that

society. One could at best be a "participant observer," and participants in social interactions can never be totally objective.

The lesson that one cannot be fully objective when he has a personal stake in a situation is the central lesson that Sherlock Holmes tried to teach Dr. Watson in Arthur Conan Doyle's classic detective stories. Sherlock's amazing ability to see details that no one else saw, thus drawing his astounding deductions, was a function of his ability to detach himself from the situation at hand and observe it with total impartially. This is something that the more emotional Dr. Watson simply could not do.

Our self-interests hinder our ability to clearly see the facts before us, and, hence, cloud our capacity for clear judgment. This critical life-lesson is alluded to near the beginning of *Parashat Shofetim* (Deut. 16:18–21:9), "You shall not judge unfairly; you shall show no partiality; you shall not take a bribe, for bribery blinds the eyes of the wise and upsets the plea of the just" (Deut. 16:19).

The Torah instructs judges regarding how they are to handle their professional responsibilities. What application does this have to the vast majority of us who are not professional judges?

Rabbi Yisrael Salanter, the influential rabbinic scholar and insightful social critic who founded the important nineteenth-century ethical school of thought known as the Musar movement, asks this question. I have taken the liberty to rephrase his answer in contemporary terminology. This is what he says:

> All of us are judges. We may not be ordained scholars, wearing rabbinic robes. We may not be appointed by the community to adjudicate differences between plaintiffs and defendants. We may be unqualified to sit in judgment of those accused of crimes or sins. But we are all judges because we all face situations that call for personal decisions on our part. We face such situations countless times each day. A judge is but a person who must decide. In that sense, we are all judges, and we must all be guided by the directives that the Torah issues to the professional judiciary.

Following this line of thinking, we must all be careful not to take bribes, for bribes will blind us to the facts we need to know in order to make moral and practically effective decisions. But what are the bribes that threaten to undermine our objectivity in our daily life? Surely, we do not meet up with shady characters, sneaking up on us with envelopes full of cash, attempting to influence the numerous decisions that confront us moment to moment in the course of our daily routine!

Here too Rabbi Salanter has an answer, and here too I resort to my own paraphrase of his profound insights into the human psyche:

> There is a force within us called self-interest. This force pressures us to seek our own comfort, to procrastinate, to find excuses not to act, to avoid risk and flee from challenge. We all tend to prefer the easy way out. This inner force is "bribery," for it blinds our ability to see the facts as they really are. We choose creature comfort over ethically correct action and are tempted by the promise of immediate gratification instead of the difficult road that would produce long-term achievements.

This is one of the ways that Rabbi Yisrael Salanter defines the "evil inclination" of which the rabbis speak. But for him, this *yetzer hara* is not a demon or Satan or some other such personification of evil. Rather, it is a normal component of human nature, one with which we all struggle. It is part of our existential condition.

The shady character with the envelope full of cash is within us. It urges us to repress our moral inclination and to deny the sublimity of our souls. It persuades us to settle for less, to ignore our conscience. It frustrates our God-given idealism and it mocks our values and ideals.

How do we combat this "bribery?" Rabbi Salanter has suggestions in this regard as well, and they include serious study of traditional Jewish ethical works, introspection, humility, and self-discipline.

But there is another type of resource more readily available to most of us, and it is epitomized in this familiar teaching of one of our earliest sages, "Yehoshua ben Peraḥya used to say: Get yourself a teacher and acquire a companion" (Avot 1:6).

Too often, especially these days when society pressures us to exercise our moral autonomy, we make decisions without consulting others. We are loath to seek out the advice of wiser men and fail to heed their counsel when we do seek it. We are reluctant to discuss our decisions with friends, peers, and colleagues. We avoid those in our circle who could serve as mentors, and our competitiveness prevents us from requesting guidance from others who have confronted our very dilemmas.

King Solomon, the wisest of men, advised us, "Salvation comes with much consultation (*uteshua berov yoetz*)" (Prov. 11:14). Just as we have an evil inclination (*yetzer hara*), we also have a good inclination (*yetzer tov*). And that good inclination drives us to the company of other human beings. We can discuss our dilemmas with those in our environment who view them more objectively than we can on our own. That is the path to wise decisions, both in the moral and practical spheres of our existence.

Words Can Never Harm Me?

F or many of us, the first pieces of wisdom we learned were from nursery rhymes and schoolyard jingles. Sometimes these childish lessons had value, but more often they were off the mark and had the effect of distorting a truer perspective on life.

Take, for example, this ditty, "Sticks and stones may break my bones, but words can never harm me." The implicit message, which had some utility on the playground, is that we can safely ignore insults to our emotions and feelings, and need to only be concerned about physical injury. The truth, however, is quite different.

Obviously, we want to protect ourselves from physical harm. The trauma of bodily injury is something none of us wishes to bear. But we cannot minimize the harmful effects of psychological trauma, whether it comes in the form of insults, embarrassment, or shame.

During the years I spent as a psychotherapist, I dealt with quite a few victims of domestic violence. I saw the effects that abuse could have upon people, but I noticed that those who suffered emotional abuse were less amenable to successful treatment than those who were physically battered. Let's face it. Words hurt.

The power that words have to do damage is recognized by our Torah. That emotions can be grievously wounded, reputations ruined, and relationships damaged beyond repair through "mere words," is illustrated in biblical narratives, talmudic tales, and hasidic stories.

In *Parashat Ki Tetzeh*, we are instructed to "remember what the Lord your God did unto Miriam, on the road out of Egypt." The Torah is referring to the fact that Miriam was punished by a leprous infection.

The full episode of Miriam's sin and its consequences appears in an earlier portion of the Torah, at the very end of *Parashat Behaalotekha* (Num. 12:1–16). There, we learn that Miriam and Aaron spoke against Moses because of his Cushite wife. They went on to belittle Moses' importance and spoke condescendingly about him.

It seems from the context of the story that Miriam, as the instigator of this critique, did so privately. Nevertheless, the Almighty was angry with her and she was healed, ironically, only because of Moses' prayerful intervention. Thus, our sages understand this command to remember Miriam as an injunction against *lashon hara*.

Much closer to our time, at the beginning of the last century, the sage and saint Rabbi Yisrael Meir Kagan of Radin, became convinced that the central evil of modern times was the abuse of words. So confident was he of his diagnosis of the social ills of our time, that he devoted a major work to the subject of *lashon hara*. The name of that work is *Ḥafetz Ḥaim* (*Desirous of Life*)," after the verse in Psalms that reads, "Who is the person who desires life? Let him guard his tongue against speaking evil."

Recalling Miriam's misdeeds and taking seriously the comprehensive teachings of the author of *Ḥafetz Ḥaim* is especially valuable today. Because, you see, words have become even more powerful and potentially destructive than a rabbi living a hundred years ago could possibly have imagined.

Nowadays, through the power of electronic instant communication, words can be sent to millions of people in microseconds. If these words are negative, they can harm individuals instantly, without even the possibility of recourse or recall. The power of words has exponentially increased in scope and effect in our day and age.

Our tradition teaches that using words to offend another human being is akin to a snake and its venom. The snake's venom kills, yet the snake has no benefit from its fiendish action. So too human beings usually benefit from every other sin imaginable, but gain nothing by harming others verbally. Because of this, *lashon hara* is the least justifiable of sins.

Not a day goes by when we do not receive e-mails or read internet reports that damage reputations of individuals, and there is neither due process, nor any possibility of mounting a defense against such assaults. This goes against both our Jewish heritage and our democratic ideals in a very fundamental way.

In the month of Elul, the last month of the Jewish year, it behooves us to introspectively examine our faults. It is the season of *teshuva*, which precedes and heralds the imminent High Holidays. We must give thought to how we have offended others with words and with deeds.

Although the unimaginable spread of verbal abuse that postmodern technology has instigated is beyond the capacity for any one of us to correct, we have no option but to try, individually, to control the way we use words and the words we use. None of us is innocent of *lashon hara* and none of us is exempt from sincerely addressing this weakness.

In conclusion, I call to your attention the rabbinic dictum that the power of Good exceeds the force of Evil manifold. Thus, if words have the ability to harm, they have the infinitely greater ability to soothe and to heal. The way to undo our sins of the negative use of language is to resolve to use language positively.

Imagine if e-mails were limited to complimentary statements and words of praise. Imagine if the blogs and websites were replete with stories of human accomplishment, altruism, and heroism. It would be a happier world for sure. And it would be a world closer to that which the Almighty intended. Elul, the month preceding Rosh HaShana, is the ideal time for each of us to commit, in a deeply personal way, to bring about that better world.

Parashat Ki Tetzeh

And the Winner Is...

I t was the first time I announced a contest from the pulpit. It felt like a risky thing to do, and probably was. But it worked, and I tried it several times over the ensuing years.

It was on the occasion of *Parashat Ki Tetzeh*, but it was many, many years ago. What prompted me to launch the contest with confidence was a discussion I had one Friday morning with a group of teenagers. They were frustrated by the fact that they could find little relevance in many of the biblical passages that we were studying. So many of these passages seemed to be speaking of events and circumstances that were unrelated to those prevalent in the lives of these teens.

Instead of offering my own ideas about this issue, I told them that I would challenge the entire congregation to find relevance in some of the passages of that week's *parasha*, which happened to have been *Ki Tetzeh*. They felt excited to be in on what they viewed as a conspiracy, the planning of a sermon in which the rabbi would turn the table on the members of the congregation and require a response from them.

I stood up that Saturday morning and began by quoting the following verse, "If you see your fellow's donkey or ox fallen on the road,

567

do not ignore it; you must help him raise it" (Deut. 22:4). Rashi, following the explanation of the Talmud, understands this to mean that if the donkey's pack falls off his back, you must help your friend replace it there. This is the mitzva known as uploading (te'ina).

I challenged the audience with the following question, "Of what possible relevance is placing a fallen burden back on a donkey to us in our daily lives? When is the last time you met a donkey or an ox on the road, with or without a pack on the ground beside it?"

I then asked the audience to take out their Bibles and turn back to a passage in *Parashat Mishpatim* that we had studied together during the previous winter. There, we read, "When you see the donkey of your enemy lying under its burden and would otherwise refrain from helping him, you must nevertheless help him" (Ex. 23:5).

Rashi, again following the Talmud, sees this as the mitzva of *perika*, of helping to unload the donkey of its burden, and helping even one's enemy in the process. "Now I understand," I argued to the congregation, "that the lesson of helping one's enemy may be a relevant, if unpopular, one. But unloading a donkey? When was the last time anyone here did that?"

Then I announced the contest. "I am not going to provide my own suggestions to answer these questions," I said. "Rather, we are going to have a contest in which each of you can write your own answers to these questions."

I had done some preliminary work before Shabbat and enlisted two well-respected members of the synagogue to serve along with me on a panel of judges to evaluate the submissions and to decide upon the top three responses. I must confess to having been delighted by the number and quality of the answers that were handed in. It was by no means a simple task to decide upon the three most creative ideas.

As the second runner up, that is, the third of the top three, my two judicial cohorts and I chose the answer submitted by our *shul*'s resident *yeshiva baḥur*, a young student who found the answers to most of his questions in the Talmud. He reminded us of the passage in Tractate Bava Metzia, which imagined a situation in which a person would have to choose between the mitzvot of uploading and unloading, between *te'ina* and *perika*.

The Talmud describes the dilemma of the person who encounters not one, but two donkeys. One donkey has its fallen cargo on the ground next to it; the other is bent under its burden. You have time for only one donkey. Which one do you attend to?

The Talmud answers that your priority is to unload the overburdened donkey. The Jewish value of sensitivity to the suffering of animals (*tzaar baalei ḥayim*), trumps the mitzva of *te'ina*. "Surely teaching about the need to avoid cruelty to animals is a relevant lesson," argued the budding talmudic scholar.

The runner up, number two in the contest, was our local psychologist. "Every day," he asserted, "I help to unload peoples' burdens. I try to listen to them and to somehow lighten the weight that they feel. That's *perika*. And then there are those whom one must encourage to 'upload' the packs on their backs and to 'keep on truckin',' to get back on the road, and to get on with their lives. That's *te'ina*."

Our panel of judges was in for a surprise when it came to the contestant who won the grand prize. Of all the many members of the synagogue, it was the aging cantor who was clearly the winner. We all knew that his voice was far from what it once was and that he had trouble reaching the high notes as well as the lowest notes on the musical scale. But we kept him on, and indeed cherished him, for his genuine piety and sincere humanity.

"Whenever I stand in front of the congregation," he said, "and anticipate the difficulty I am about to have in reaching the high notes, I appreciate those of you who sing and chant along with me and help me achieve those high notes. You uplift me. When you do that, you fulfill the mitzva of *te'ina*. And as I falter in trying to descend the musical ladder to those lower notes, and you, the congregation, come to my aid with your voices, you help lower my burden, and you perform the mitzva of *perika*."

We are told that there are seventy facets to the Torah. We had about seventy contributions to our contest that Shabbat. I have shared only the top three with you, dear reader, and challenge you to come up with others on your own.

He Is Not What He Is

There is a phrase that one hears quite commonly nowadays, "It is what it is." There is something that has always disturbed me about that phrase. To me, the phrase seems to be stating that things will remain as they are and that there is no possibility for change. It conveys a sense of resignation and suggests that one must accept the status quo. The implicit lesson is that one should not expect circumstances to change for the better or, for that matter, for the worse.

In spite of its popularity, the phrase contradicts everything we know about the human experience. We know that things change. People change, circumstances change. Our social surroundings, and even our natural environment, change all the time. Heraclitus was certainly correct when he said that one cannot step into the same river twice.

I would not bother to protest the statement, however false I think it is, were I not convinced that it is more than untrue – it is quite dangerous. I base this conviction on a fundamental distinction, which goes back to the early Greek philosophers, and which is reflected in traditional Jewish works as well.

I refer to the distinction between *actual* and *potential*. This distinction is especially significant when we assess ourselves or judge other individuals. We can consider that we, or they, are overlooking the potential for us and them to develop into quite different sorts of people.

I sometimes ponder this distinction when I consider contemporary military situations. For example, the State of Israel today faces a serious military threat from Iran. At this very moment in time, there may be little, if any, *actual* danger, but the *potential* for very great danger certainly exists. It is the *potential*, in this case, that might very well justify a preemptive strike against future capacities of a hostile Iran. The moral justification of a preemptive war necessitates that we reject the implications of "it is what it is," and instead imagine what things might be like if the current *potential* became *actual*.

In *Parashat Ki Tetzeh* (Deut. 21:10–25:19) we encounter an example of a preemptive strike – not against a vicious enemy, but against a mere child. Just several verses from the beginning of our *parasha*, in verse 18, we read of the *ben sorer umoreh*, the "stubborn and rebellious son, who will not hearken to the voice of his father, nor the voice of his mother, and though they chasten him, he will not hearken unto them."

Which parent has not encountered some stubbornness and rebelliousness in even the best behaved of his or her children? But the son who is described in our *parasha* goes a bit too far. He raids his mother's purse or his father's wallet, steals some money, and purchases a small quantity of meat and consumes it, and a half measure of wine and imbibes it, perhaps becoming a bit tipsy in the process.

Are we not astonished to read that this young boy is to be stoned to death, that the evil he represents is to be eliminated from our midst, and that we all must learn the lesson of his behavior and its consequences? Of course we are astonished, as were the rabbis of old. They responded with two teachings: first of all, this boy's punishment is not the result of his *actual* behavior, but rather because of the inevitable *potential* that he would one day "become a bandit, and lie in wait at the crossroads and steal from wayfarers."

They further insisted that the entire passage of the "stubborn and rebellious son" is totally hypothetical. "It never happened and never will happen." They instruct us that the passage was written just so that we reflect theoretically upon its implications, but not that we actually administer such harsh punishment.

If the "stubborn and rebellious son" provides us an example of how we must take a person's potential for evil into account, the story of Ishmael provides an opposite lesson, namely that we must assess a person in terms of his current behavior and not anticipate his potential.

Thus, in Genesis 21:17, where the young Ishmael is about to die of thirst in the desert, his mother Hagar is assured by the angel that God has heard his prayers and that he will survive, "For God has heard the voice of the lad where he is."

Our rabbis note that, despite the fact that Ishmael was destined to become an arch foe of the Jewish people, he was judged as a young boy dying of thirst in the wilderness. He was judged "where he is," in terms of the *actual* Ishmael and not in terms of the *potential* one.

Numerous commentators, Ḥizkuni and Rabbi Ovadia Sforno among them, have offered explanations as to why the "stubborn and rebellious son" was judged in terms of his *potential* for evil, whereas Ishmael was given the benefit of being judged in terms of his *actual* innocence. These commentators suggest that Ishmael demonstrated, by the honor he gave to his mother Hagar and to his father Abraham, that he possessed *potential* for both good and bad, whereas, in the words of *Sforno*, "the very rebelliousness of [the wayward son] removed all hope that he would one day change his stubborn ways."

The biblical texts discussed above are open to various interpretations. As we saw, the rabbis of the Talmud instructed us to reflect well upon the lessons of the "stubborn and rebellious son," but they did not clearly enunciate what those lessons are. That, they left for us to ponder.

From a pedagogical and parental perspective, it is clear that we must always consider the *potential* that our students and children possess. That master pedagogue, who preached in the darkest days of the Warsaw ghetto and eventually perished at the hands of the Nazis in the Holocaust, Rabbi Kalonymous Kalman Shapira, would meet with his young adolescent students as they entered his yeshiva and encourage them to envision who they might be in a year, in two years, and in five years. He would then gently tell them that he would not be dealing with them as they were then but, rather, as they might be in the future.

Sadly, in his case, both the master and the majority of his numerous disciples did not survive long enough to realize the *potential* that they each envisioned, but we, children and grandchildren of survivors, can take the lesson to heart.

When dealing with others, we must forget about the slogan "it is what it is." It is a false and invidious slogan. I offer an alternative slogan, "It is what it could become."

The Duty of
Civilians in War

I

t seems that war is one of the most common of all human activities. Study history of the human race, and you will not find many years that were not blemished by warfare. Read the literature of the world, and you will find very few books whose pages are not blood-stained. Study the Jewish tradition, beginning with the Bible itself, and you will find very few narratives that do not contain the images of battle.

When I think back upon my own life, I immediately realize that I was born but several months after Hitler invaded Poland and that my most outstanding early memories are of the men in my family in military uniform and of the parades celebrating victory at the end of World War II. The wars of Korea and Vietnam dominated my high school and college years.

Of course Israel's many wars, major and minor, preoccupied me and my peers throughout our lives, and continue to do so. My wife and I have been in Israel during wartime, which, except for several brief periods of uncertain cease-fires, was punctuated by missile bombardments, ground invasions, and the heart wrenching loss of life, which inevitably accompanies warfare.

Parashat Ki Tetzeh is no respite from the descriptions of war. The previous *parasha* of *Shofetim* contained lengthy paragraphs that could easily have been part of a military manual. "When you take the field against your enemies, and see horses and chariots – forces larger than yours – have no fear of them…. When you approach a town to attack it, you shall offer it terms of peace…. If it does not surrender to you…. You shall lay siege to it."

Parashat Ki Tetzeh (Deut. 21:10–25:19) begins and ends with themes of war. The opening verse reads, "When you take the field against your enemies." The closing verses of the *parasha* enjoin us to remember the surprise attack launched against the Jewish people by Amalek and command us to "blot out the memory of Amalek from under heaven."

Not only does our *parasha* begin and end with martial themes, but about halfway through the *parasha*, we find the following words, "When you go out as a troop against your enemies, be on your guard against anything untoward…. Let your camp be holy; let Him not find anything unseemly among you."

What is striking about all of these citations is that they are instructions to soldiers, to men who are actively participating in battle. They are the ones who are instructed to be brave and to follow the codes of conduct mandated to men at war. There is no mention of commands for those not engaged in battle. What is the civilian population supposed to be doing while their brethren are risking their lives on the battlefield?

In the military operation in Israel against Hamas, I witnessed the extent to which civilians were involved in providing assistance to those who were engaged in the actual fighting. Indeed, those on the Homefront who simply went about their business and tried to maintain a sense of normalcy also contributed to the morale of those in the military service. As the signs said along Israel's highways, "A brave Homefront ensures a strong battlefront."

Certainly, those who engage in special prayer sessions, who devote their hours of Torah study and charity activities to the merits of those on the battlefield, also contribute to the war effort and, when victory comes, are able to say that even as civilians they helped achieve the desired goal.

I must share with you, dear reader, a most inspiring conversation that I read in one of the weekly leaflets available in great variety in every Jerusalem synagogue on the eve of Shabbat. The conversation was between a young woman, who was just a girl when her older sister's husband fell, many years ago, in one of Israel's wars, and her friend. It was at a memorial service for that hero that the conversation was initiated.

"I find it difficult to absorb," the young woman said to her friend, "that he died so that I could live. Every time I see the pictures in recent newspapers of fallen soldiers, I can't help but be haunted by the fact they were willing to die, and actually did die, just so that you and I could live our lives."

Her friend responded, "I too find it difficult to absorb. It is a simple fact that these young men, only one or two whom I knew even vaguely, gave their lives so that I might live. But I take it one step further. I ask myself whether my life is worthy of that soldier's ultimate sacrifice."

She continued, "What disturbs me is that in all honesty, I must say that the life I have been living is far from worthy of his sacrifice. What is my life? Another mall, another insipid television program, another flirtatious relationship. Surely these boys did not have to die to preserve such an empty life. I find myself searching inwardly in ways that I never had before. I want to redefine my life so that I can somehow justify that soldier's indescribable heroism."

The first young woman concurred. And so does everyone to whom I have related this inspiring conversation. There is a growing consensus, and it is a profoundly introspective one, that our lives must change so that we can collectively deserve the kinds of sacrifices we are asking of our young soldiers. They must feel certain that the risks they are taking are on behalf of a people who are devoted to the highest ideals, and who are living lives that are so meaningful and upright that they deserve defending, even at the cost of tragic losses.

So civilians have a duty too – not just soldiers. Civilians have the duty to examine their lives and to improve them fundamentally, so that the soldier on the battlefield can say, "I am fighting to protect and preserve lives that are worth fighting for and worth dying for."

Parashat Ki Tavo

Walls Have Ears

We all have our secret lives. I don't mean to say that each of us has a sinister side, which we wickedly act out in some deep, dark, private world. What I do mean is that we all act differently when we are alone, or with a few close intimates, than we act when we are out in public, among others.

There is no one who is so behaviorally consistent that he is the same person in the privacy of his own home as he is in the workplace or marketplace. Nor do I suggest that there is anything wrong with the fact that we each are two persons, and perhaps even multiple persons, depending upon the social context in which we find ourselves. It is problematic, however, when we act hypocritically, presenting a pious and altruistic face to the world, while acting cruelly and crudely in our own homes and with our families.

In *Parashat Ki Tavo*, there appears a particularly piercing and perceptive verse, "Cursed be he who strikes his fellow in secret – and all the people shall say, Amen."

In no way does the Torah imply that he who strikes his fellow in public is to be blessed. Rather, the Torah recognizes the tendency humans have to reserve the worst side of themselves for their secret social settings, even when they behave meritoriously in their public social worlds. It is the façade, the contrast, between public demonstrations of righteousness and private acts of fiendishness that is cursed.

Sinning in secret is particularly offensive in the religious personality. He or she who believes in a God who is omniscient, and who yet sins in private, is guilty not merely of hypocrisy, but of heresy. If God knows all, how can you delude yourself into thinking that your secret misdeeds can go undetected?

The *Shulḥan Arukh* opens with a statement recognizing that a person's behavior, when he is alone at home, is very different from his behavior when he appears before a great king. And it urges the religious person to be aware that he is always in the presence of the great King of kings, the all-knowing God.

But it is not only from a spiritual perspective that it is wrong to act demeaningly in private. There is a practical aspect as well to the importance of behaving properly even in secret. There always is the very real possibility that our secrets will be "leaked" and that things we were sure would never be known will become embarrassingly exposed.

I know of no place where this is conveyed more cogently than in these words of caution, to be found in Ecclesiastes:

> Don't revile a king, even in your intimate thoughts.
> Don't revile a rich man, even in your bedchamber;
> For a bird of the air may carry the utterance,
> And a winged creature may report the word. (Eccl.10:20)

Indeed, as our sages say (see Rashi on Berakhot 8b), the walls have ears.

The passage in *Parashat Ki Tavo* that condemns secret violence also gives quite a comprehensive catalog of other sins that tend to be performed behind closed doors. They include elder abuse, criminal business practices, deceiving blind persons, subverting the rights of the helpless, incest and bestiality, and the acceptance of bribery. It is quite a list, and one that has certainly not lost its relevance over the centuries.

I am not so naïve as to think we are required to act in an absolutely identical fashion in our "secret chambers" as we do out in the "real world." To a certain extent, it is necessary and right that we maintain a façade of sorts when we interact in public. We all have, and need, our masks and personas.

But many times, we go too far and indeed split our personalities between the Dr. Jekylls of our external visible behavior and the Mr. Hydes of our inner sancta. How well advised we would be to set as an objective for ourselves the words of the Daily Prayer Book, "A person should always be God-fearing, privately and publicly, acknowledging the truth and speaking it in his heart."

Parashat Ki Tavo

In the Good Old Days

I t was the kind of thing you would hear from old men. "Things just ain't the way they used to be." "This new generation is going to hell in a handbasket." "I remember when things were different and better, back in the good old days!"

Now that I am becoming a bit older myself, I find that I sometimes parrot some of those phrases. Increasingly, my attitude has become negative and critical of the contemporary world around me. It is at such moments that I feel convinced that things were indeed much better in the past and certainly much different.

My tendency to value the past over the present is especially marked when it comes to reflecting upon leadership phenomena. It is easy to say that presidents and prime ministers were once great statesman and that the individuals now holding those positions are at best mediocre. Authors, poets, artists, and even the composers of days gone by definitely seem superior to individuals currently in those roles.

It is especially in the area of religion that the past took on an aura of holiness, grandeur, and purity, that seems to be totally absent in today's religious world. It is easy to come up with the names of fifteen or twenty outstanding rabbis in the previous generation or two, or even three. It is hard to find more than a few in today's generation.

Is this attitude, which I suspect is prevalent even among individuals far younger than I, fair? Is it correct? Or is it based upon nostalgic memories, which distort the realities of the past as well as the conditions of the present? Dare I even speculate that this attitude stems from a cynicism, which, some would say, is typical of older people?

Personally, I have found correctives for this attitude in my own experience and in my Torah study. My personal experience was fortunately blessed by my acquaintance with a number of older men, among whom I count my own and my wife's grandfathers, who all felt that the current generation was in many ways superior to the earlier generations that they knew. In their conversations, they not only did not glorify the past, but well remembered that past generations had their own blemishes, some of which were quite severe.

Parashat Ki Tavo opens with the mitzva to bring the first fruits of one's new harvest to "the place where the Lord your God will choose to establish His name" (Deut. 26:2), which we know eventually was designated as Jerusalem. The next verse continues, "You shall go to the *kohen* in charge at that time." After reciting the proper recitations, the fruits were given to that *kohen*.

Rashi notes how very odd it is that we are told to bring those fruits to the *kohen* "in charge at that time." To what other *kohen* could we possibly have given them? To the *kohen* of a time gone by?

To those of us who were paying careful attention to *Parashat Shofetim*, this question sounds very familiar. For in that *parasha*, we encountered two similar phrases, not with reference to the *kohen*, but with regard to the judges whom we consult.

Thus, we read that we were to "appear before...the magistrate in charge at that time, and present your problem" (Deut. 17:9). Later in that same *parasha*, we learned that "the two parties to the dispute shall appear...before the magistrates in authority at that time" (Deut. 19:17).

The Talmud derives a powerful lesson from these three phrases that all stress "at that time." The lesson is that we are not to denigrate the judges or priests of our time. We are not to say that the judges of yore were well-suited to their positions, but that the judges of our own times are inferior and indeed unqualified. Yiftah, the leader of a rag tag group of warriors, was for his generation every bit as qualified to be a judge as was Samuel, the prophet of a later time.

I have always understood this teaching to mean that it is futile to compare the leaders of one generation to those of another. Each generation has its own special character and unique requirements, and the leaders who emerge, especially in the religious sphere, are precisely the ones most appropriate for that generation. As Rav Kook put it, "Every generation shines with its own qualities."

If this lesson applies to what our attitude should be to the judges of our time, how much more it applies to what should be our proper attitude toward the contemporary *kohen*. We are not to say that the *kohanim* of yesteryear were spiritually worthy of offering the priestly blessings, whereas today's *kohen* is unqualified to do so. Rather, we ought to follow Maimonides' ruling that everyone born a *kohen* is fit to utter the priestly blessing, "even if he is not learned, not punctilious in his observance of mitzvot, and even if there are persistent rumors about him" (*Mishneh Torah*, Laws of Prayer 15:6).

I close by quoting the words of the wisest of old men, indeed, the wisest of all men, King Solomon:

The end of a matter is better than the beginning of it.
Better a patient spirit than a haughty spirit...
Don't say, "How has it happened that former times were better than these?"
For it is not wise of you to ask that question. (Eccl. 7:8–10)

Didn't You See Them?

Ilt is a question that I learned never to ask. I first learned this lesson in my training as a psychotherapist long ago. I was seeing a gentleman for a number of problems, including his marital difficulties. Despite the passage of the years, I still vividly remember the evening in which he came to my office extremely distraught. He couldn't contain his torment, even for a moment. Before he sat down opposite me, he blurted out, "She is cheating on me!"

He had discovered incontrovertible evidence of his wife's infidelity. He continued to disclose the fact that bits and pieces of the evidence were available to him for more than a year. Letters, phone messages, unexplained absences, and unusual expenditures from their joint checking account had accumulated and he had been aware of all of them. Yet, it was not until that morning that he actually saw what was in front of his eyes all the time.

Strangely, and I only later learned this, he typically shared none of these hints and clues with me during the course of our numerous counseling sessions prior to the day of the big "discovery."

I was a fledgling psychotherapist back then and I could not suppress exclaiming the question, "Didn't you see it coming? Didn't you notice what was in front of your eyes?"

I was not prepared for his tearful but angry response. "Of course I saw it coming, you dummy!" He was furious with me for my total lack of empathy. He clearly saw it coming, but he did not *want* to see it. One does not see what one does not want to see, no matter how blatant and obvious the facts are.

The lesson I learned from this interchange was not limited to the field of marital counseling. It is a lesson that I have tried to remember throughout my personal, professional, and religious life from that time forward. I learned that all the evidence in the world will not convince someone who prefers to be blind to that evidence. All the arguments in the world, however rational and forceful they may be, cannot persuade a person who is clinging to his preferred beliefs and who is not open to logic and reason.

In truth, I should have learned this lesson long before I embarked upon a career in psychology. I should have learned it when I first studied *Parashat Ki Tavo* (Deut. 26:1–29:8). I should have given more serious thought to the following passage:

> Moses summoned all Israel and said to them, "You have seen all that the Lord did before your very eyes in the land of Egypt…. The wondrous feats that you saw with your own eyes, those prodigious signs and marvels. Yet to this day the Lord has not given you a mind to understand or eyes to see or ears to hear." (Deut. 29:1–3)

To paraphrase: "You saw, but you did not see. You heard, but you did not hear. All that you needed to know was before you, but you did not have the mind to understand."

At about the same time that I sat face-to-face with the betrayed husband who struggled so hard not to see what should have been apparent to him, I became introduced to the writings of a great rabbi in Israel, who died tragically very young, almost fifty years ago. His name was Rabbi Elimelech Bar-Shaul, and a posthumously published collection of his writings on the Torah portions of the week was issued shortly after his death.

The name of this collection is *Min HaBe'er* (*From the Well*), which is a very apt title for a book full of insights drawn from the deepest sources of our faith. Rabbi Bar-Shaul reflects upon these verses and upon the phenomenon of blindness and deafness to the sights and sounds that are prominent in our surroundings. Let me translate some of his reflections for you.

> There is a magnificent teaching here in these verses for all generations and all situations. A person can see wondrous things, true revelations, and yet, paradoxically, not see them.... The Almighty, blessed be He, gives the person eyes to see and ears to hear and a heart to understand, but it is the person who must choose to see, and hear, and understand. It is the person who must open his eyes well to see, and even then he cannot see unless he also opens his heart to understand. For if a person just sees with his eyes alone, he may react emotionally. But as long he does not direct his mind to what he has seen, his emotional reactions will fall short of understanding and of knowing.
>
> It is not for us to have critical thoughts about our ancestors who failed to see. But the Torah here is giving us both a guideline and a warning signal. When Moses tells the people of Israel, "You have seen.... But you were not given a mind to understand, or eyes to see, or ears to hear," he is calling upon us, today, to think deeply and well about these words and to apply them to our own circumstances.

So many times in our history we have failed to see facts that were apparent to those who possessed understanding hearts. Most tragically, all of us who read about the events leading up to the Holocaust find ourselves asking the questions, "Did they not see what was coming? Did our enemies not warn us very clearly about their intentions to destroy us? Were the signals not sufficiently obvious? Why did so few take advantage of opportunities to escape years before escape became impossible?"

These questions haunt us today and will continue to do so forever. Perhaps, these questions are beyond our capacity. They are over our heads. But what we can learn, in less terrible and less tragic circumstances, is to do our utmost to understand what the Almighty has allowed us to see.

He has allowed us to see, for example, a thriving Jewish state. We must understand its significance. He has allowed us to hear the voices of children studying His Torah, and the sounds of yeshivas greater in size than ever before in history. Our hearts must celebrate these achievements.

On Rosh HaShana, we see throngs of Jews all over the world participating in services in our synagogues and we hear the sounds of the shofar calling upon us to become better Jews and better human beings. The Almighty lets us see these sights and hear these sounds. We must open our hearts and minds, not just see and hear them, but understand them, appreciate them, and grow from them. We must not permit these blessed sights and sounds to be ignored. Let others not be able to ask of us, "How could you not see them? How could you not hear them?"

Parashat Nitzavim

This Season's Leitmotif: Return

We have all been brought up to believe in the importance of progress. For the past several centuries, the goal of philosophy, religion, culture, and certainly science has been to develop ideas and practices that advance humankind beyond its present state.

Poets have acclaimed the superiority of progress. One of them, Robert Browning, put it this way:

> Progress, man's distinctive mark alone,
> Not God's, and not the beasts': God is, they are;
> Man partly is, and wholly hopes to be.

Browning is certainly not the only person who enthusiastically endorsed progress to the point of seeing it as the hallmark of humanity, and as that which sets man apart from and above the animal world, and even distinguishes him from the Almighty Himself.

So forceful has been the emphasis upon progress that any attempt to return to past ideas and methods is almost universally criticized as backward and primitive, and at the very least, old-fashioned. The antonym for progress, regress, is a word with strong negative connotations. No one wants to be seen as a regressive.

Just before Rosh HaShana, the theme of progress is definitely in the air. We all hope to progress to a better year, to a year of growth and development. Indeed, many synagogues conclude the old year and begin a new one with the refrain, "May this year and its curses be gone, and may a new year with its blessings begin!"

No one seems to wish that the coming year be one of status quo. Certainly, very few hope for a return to the past. And yet, it is precisely "return" that our Torah promulgates, especially before the New Year.

Parashat Nitzavim contains the following passage (Deut. 30:1–10). I provide a literal translation of some of the verbs, in accordance with their Hebrew root:

> When all these things befall you – the blessing and the curse....
> And you take them to heart [literally, and you *return* them to your heart].... And you will *return* to the Lord your God, and you and your children will heed His command.... Then the Lord your God will *return* you from captivity.... He will *return* you from all the nations.... You will *return* and again heed the voice of the Lord.... For the Lord will *return* to delight in your well-being.... Once you *return* to the Lord your God with all your heart and soul.

In the space of just several verses, the word "return" appears, in one form or another, at least seven times! It was in the writings of the great Nehama Leibowitz that I first learned the importance of a word that appears repetitiously in the course of a single text. We are to think, she wrote, of such a term as a *leitvort*, a leading word, a word which gives us a clue and leads us to the deeper meaning of the text at hand.

Even my limited familiarity with the German language was sufficient for me to draw the comparison between *leitvort*, a word that identifies the theme of an entire passage, and the word *leitmotif*, which is a thought or melody that pervades a literary work or a musical composition.

The ten days that begin on Rosh HaShana and conclude on Yom Kippur are known as the *Aseret Yemei Teshuva*, which is usually translated as The Ten Days of Repentance. But *teshuva* does not really mean repentance, and it certainly does not mean penitence, as it is frequently rendered. Rather, it means return.

The *leitmotif* of this entire season is the Torah's call for us to engage in profound introspection and to return to a place that we have lost, forgotten, or abandoned. It is not progress that is demanded of us during this period; it is, oddly enough, regress.

It can legitimately be asked, return to what? I would like to provide an answer or two to that question, inspired by the book that I find so personally meaningful at this time of year. It is *The Lights of Teshuva*, by Rabbi Abraham Isaac Kook.

Rav Kook emphasizes that over the course of time, we each develop as individuals, and in that process, isolate and alienate ourselves from others, from our families, and from the people of Israel. To return means to return from our self-centeredness to the collective, from the *prat*, or single unit, to the *klal*, or all-encompassing group. There can be no *teshuva* unless we reconnect with larger components of society. We all, in our heart of hearts, know the ways in which we have cut ourselves off from significant people in our lives, and each of us knows how to reconnect to those individuals.

My experience as a psychotherapist has taught me that there is another destination to which it would pay for us to return. I speak of our childhoods. As we mature and develop in life, we grow in many positive directions. But we also move away from our innocence, from our childish enthusiasm, from the hope and sense of potential that characterizes the young, but which older individuals cynically eschew.

People find it very rewarding, if only in their imaginations, to return to their youth and recapture some of the positive qualities that they left behind as they made their adult choices.

Finally, we all need to return to the Almighty, to His Torah, and to His Land. No matter how intense our worship of Him was during the past year, we can return to Him for an even stronger connection. No matter how studiously we explored His Torah, we can return to even deeper levels of its impenetrable depth. No matter how loyal our faithfulness to the Land of Israel was, we can return to even greater loyalty and more courageous faith.

And no matter what our relationship was with others in our lives, we can draw upon our own inner sources of generosity and compassion, and enhance those relationships in a spirit of genuine *teshuva*, of returning to those others, and in the process, to our truer selves.

Parashat Nitzavim

An Attitude of Gratitude

T hank you." I think those two words are the most important two words in our language. I often recommend to new parents that these two words become one of the first things their baby learns to speak.

The idea behind this deceptively simple phrase is the concept of gratitude. Every one of us, no matter how difficult our position in life, has much to be thankful for. And yet, few of us feel thankful, and fewer still express our gratitude to others. The world would be a much better place if we each could cultivate an "attitude of gratitude."

There are two factors that make it difficult for many of us to have this attitude and to articulate it. The first factor is the sense of entitlement that so many of us have, and this seems to pervade our contemporary society. We feel that we are owed all that we have, that it is somehow "coming to us."

We raise our children to believe that all their needs will be provided for and that they need not exert much effort on their own to achieve the necessities and even luxuries of life. It is no wonder that our children feel no sense of gratitude toward us. No one can appreciate the benefits of life if he or she feels entitled to them.

There is another factor that stands in the way of the "attitude of gratitude." It is a consequence of the stress our society places upon the value of autonomy. The totally autonomous person is convinced that he is the source of all his achievements and, therefore, is beholden to no one else. The delusion of extreme autonomy becomes translated into that powerful biblical phrase, "It is my strength and the might of my hand that brought about my success."

In *Parashat Nitzavim*, there recurs a frightening litany of phrases. "The Lord will not forgive him." "The Lord's anger and passion will rage against him." "In anger and fury and in great wrath."

These phrases are nothing less than the Almighty's reaction to ingratitude. "I have taken you out of Egypt...I have included you in My covenant...I have set before you life and prosperity...that you may thrive and increase." And yet, you do not thank Me. You are not grateful. You fail to appreciate the blessings I have bestowed upon you.

In these nearly final passages of His Torah, God reserves His harshest scorn for our failure to "count our blessings." What an important and relevant lesson this is for us today! How many of us feel, truly feel, gratitude that we live and breathe, that we are healthy, that we live in an affluent and free society, that we have friends and family about us? Quite the contrary. Are we not instead ridden with complaints and petty disappointments?

Gratitude is the very stuff out of which healthy human relationships are made. Grateful children are happy children and are a delight to raise. A husband and wife who feel grateful to each other and who express these feelings of thanks are a happily married couple. Our sense of wonder, so important for a full expression of our humanity, depends upon our gratitude for our natural environment and its beauty. The fact that we take the natural world for granted is the main reason that we so abuse it, ultimately to our own detriment. The great blessing of possessing good friends is something to be grateful for. And, ironically, one earns good friends through mutual expressions of gratitude and thankfulness.

From a religious perspective, gratitude toward God is a confessional statement. By expressing gratitude, we acknowledge that we are limited creatures, dependent upon the Divine, without whose support and sustenance we could not survive. We recognize that one can, in the last analysis, achieve nothing with "one's own powers and the might of one's own hands." Thanking God in prayer or in contemplation is an expression of humility and an acceptance of human limits.

No wonder then that in Hebrew, the word for confession (*hodaa*), is the same as the word for gratitude. No wonder too that the very word that identifies us, "Jew," derives from the name given by our Matriarch Leah to her son Judah, which she gave him because Judah means thanksgiving.

I remember nodding my head in assent when I heard Isaac Bashevis Singer deliver his Nobel lecture in Stockholm in 1978. Surely one of the greatest masters of the Yiddish language, Singer keenly observed that the Yiddish language is unique not only in its humor, but also in the theme of gratitude that pervades it, "There is a quiet humor in Yiddish," Singer told the world, "and a gratitude for every day of life, every crumb of success, each encounter of love."

Well said. But the British poet Thomas Gray perhaps said it even better:

> Sweet is the breath of vernal shower,
> The bees collected treasures sweet,
> music's melting fall, but sweeter yet.
> The still small voice of gratitude.

Parashat Nitzavim

Lessons of Equality

For some time, certain ideas have dominated my consciousness. Don't worry, these are not obsessive thoughts, and I am not a candidate for a psychiatric diagnosis. Rather, whenever I prepare a speech lately, or sit down to write a column, I can't help but think about a particular set of political principles.

The principles I ponder are the principles of democracy. The lessons of the equality of all human beings and the concepts of freedom and tolerance have been demanding my attention. Why now? Why at this time of year?

One possible reason immediately comes to mind. As I write this, I reflect upon the tragedies of September 11, 2001, the anniversary of which falls during this time of year. For me, this event was a day of grief and mourning for all the victims and their families, but especially for those several victims whom I knew personally. One of them, Abe Zelmanowitz, will be remembered by the world for his heroic attempts to rescue handicapped coworkers. Another, Nancy Morgenstern, was one of the most creative and vivacious women I ever knew. A third, Shimmy Biegeleisen, grew up just a few houses away from my childhood home.

But, beyond the grief and the mourning, is the recognition that this tragedy affected all kinds of people: old and young, great and not so great, Jew and non-Jew. It is almost as if our enemies knew that if they were to strike at the heart of our great democracy, they would have to aim at a target that would symbolize democracy because of the diversity and ultimate equality of the victims.

It was only natural that as an immediate after-effect of the events of that horrific day, so many of us came to a new appreciation of the great gifts of democracy in general, and of the privilege to live in these United States in particular. It is also to be expected that when we commemorate any anniversary of that catastrophe, which we will do as long as America stands, our appreciation for our country and for its democratic way of life will be renewed and reinforced.

If there is one *parasha* in the Torah that conveys the principles of democracy most eloquently, it is *Nitzavim*. "Today, all of you, stand before the Lord your God; the chieftains of your tribes, your elders, your leaders – every person in Israel. Your little children, your women, and the stranger who is within your camp; from your wood choppers to your water fetchers" (Deut. 29:9–10). I first became aware of the fundamental principles of democracy long, long ago, when I learned these words in the early grades of the Jewish school I attended.

As we approach the end of the Jewish year, it is natural that our memories reflect upon its beginning, indeed upon all beginnings. For me, and I'm sure this is true for most of you, thinking about beginnings means thinking about the lessons that my parents, may they rest in peace, taught me.

My parents, one born in America and one an immigrant from Poland, were both proud Americans and proud Jews. And they both inculcated in me and my sisters a profound appreciation for the values that our country and our religion had in common. They taught by example that we were not to discriminate between the extremely powerful and the lowly, between the rich and the poor, between the Jew and the stranger, between the doctor or lawyer, and between the wood chopper and water fetcher.

My father in particular would explicitly teach me these lessons. "The Days of Awe (*Yamim Nora'im*), are approaching," he would say. "It is time to learn what some of the melodies are these days." And he would sing them to me. "It is time to learn some of the lessons of these days." And he would teach them to me.

The lessons he taught were basically religious lessons, but in a deeper sense, were also political ones. For he stressed to me, and this is obvious to anyone who but glances at the words of the liturgy of the High Holidays, that God judges all of mankind on Rosh HaShana. He put it quite bluntly, "Rosh HaShana may only be celebrated by Jews, but it is not only a Jewish holiday. It is the birthday of the world, and the Master of the world judges us all, with no discrimination."

These words of the prayer book, quoted below, anticipated the source works of American democracy by many centuries:

> And therefore cast Your awe, Lord our God, upon all Your handiwork, and Your fear upon all whom You have created...let all creatures bow before You, and may they all together form one united group.

Indeed, in the words of the Mishna, which have been incorporated into the High Holiday prayer book, "All the inhabitants of the world pass before you like a flock of sheep (*kol ba'ei olam yaavrun lefanekha kivnei maron*)."

The Lord sits in judgment over all of us, whatever our nation, whatever our race, whatever our gender, and whatever our faith. May He judge us with mercy and compassion and guide us in His ways so that we find peace.

Parashat Vayelekh

Forgiven, but Not Forgotten

He was one of the greatest Talmud scholars of the last century, but outside of a small circle of disciples, he was never well-known. He was a tragic figure in many ways, and although few have heard of him today, he has not been totally forgotten. Interestingly, forgetting was one of the central themes of his many teachings.

His name was Rabbi Arye Tzvi Fromer, and he hailed from an obscure town in Poland named Koziglov. He served in the rabbinate of several towns with equally obscure names. His extreme modesty mitigated the spread of his reputation. Late in his life, he experienced the unique frustration of being called upon to succeed an individual who was unusually charismatic and world-famous. He was asked to fill the shoes of a great man, and his accomplishments were constantly compared, usually unfavorably, to the achievements of his glorious predecessor.

The man he was called upon to succeed as the head of the great Talmudical Academy in pre-World War II Lublin, Poland, was Rabbi

Meir Shapiro. Besides being the founder of the Yeshiva of Ḥakhmei Lublin, an innovative school for prodigious young Torah scholars, Rabbi Shapiro was an author, an orator of note, and a composer of hasidic melodies. He was a member of the Polish Parliament and is remembered best as the person who introduced the concept of *Daf Yomi.*

Rabbi Shapiro died of a sudden illness in his early 40s. The search for a successor was not an easy one, and the reaction of most people to the choice of Rabbi Fromer was one of astonishment. "Who is he," people asked, "and how could he possibly follow in the footsteps of the multi-talented Rabbi Shapiro?"

Destiny did not give Rabbi Fromer much time to prove himself worthy of his new position. Within several years, World War II broke out. He suffered the deprivations of the ghetto and was brutally murdered by the Nazis.

We do have some of the writings he published in his lifetime, and those few of his students to survive the Holocaust published some of his teachings on the weekly Torah portion. I have become enamored with these writings and am particularly taken by the fact that he returns again and again to the theme of forgetting.

In *Parashat Vayelekh* (Deut. 31:1–30), we come across the following phrase, "This song [the Torah] will proclaim itself as a witness, for it will never be forgotten from the mouths of its descendants." Here, the Almighty assures us that, despite the vicissitudes of Jewish history, the Torah will never be forgotten.

Rabbi Fromer relates this assurance to an interesting phenomenon. The reader may not be aware that many passages of the Talmud were censored by the Roman Catholic Church over the centuries and are today absent from most editions of this fundamental text. Jews have struggled in various ways to preserve these censored passages, and some modern editions do incorporate them, but by and large, they have been forgotten.

Rabbi Fromer was once asked by a student who had just completed studying a tractate of the Talmud whether he could make a *siyum,* a festive meal celebrating that completion. "After all," the student argued,

"I didn't really complete the entire tractate. I did not study the censored passages because I had no access to them."

Rabbi Fromer responded, consoled the student, and encouraged him to go through with the festive celebration. "You must understand," he argued, "that we have a guarantee in the Bible that Torah will not be forgotten. If some words were indeed forgotten, that is *ipso facto* proof that they were not authentic Torah to begin with."

Many will take issue with this concept and find it too radical, but the message is one that we can all affirm. That which is not Torah can be forgotten. What is trivial is ephemeral. Torah is not forgotten. Sanctity is eternal.

This lesson carries over to the wondrous day that typically follows the reading of *Parashat Vayelekh*. I refer, of course, to Yom Kippur, the Day of Atonement. Even Jews who have forgotten the rest of their Jewish heritage remember Yom Kippur. Yom Kippur does not allow us to forget who we are.

Stories abound about individuals who were on the threshold of apostasy, but who returned to our faith because of their experience of Yom Kippur. That fascinating Jewish philosopher, Franz Rosenzweig, is just one example of this phenomenon, and he writes in his memoirs of his readiness to accompany his close cousin to the baptismal font, only to reconsider after spending a Yom Kippur in a small synagogue somewhere in Germany in 1913.

"Israel, and the Torah, and the Holy One, blessed be He, are one." This statement of the mystical holy Zohar says it all. All three are bound together forever.

"Forgive and forget." That is a cliché with which we are all familiar. One of the messages of hope that pervades this season of the Jewish year is that the Holy One, blessed be He, forgives but does not forget. He does not allow his two most cherished objects, His Torah and His people, to be forgotten.

Tzvi Arye Fromer could easily have been forgotten, given the horrible circumstances in which he perished. But the Almighty did not allow him to be forgotten. Nor did He allow the Torah he taught to be forgotten.

The *Yizkor* service, one of the prominent features of the liturgy of Yom Kippur, is a method by which we do our part to see to it that those souls whom we knew personally are not forgotten. And our regular Torah study is the method by which we each see to it that the words of the Torah are not forgotten.

Denying Death or Facing It

All men are mortal. Yankel is a man. Therefore, Yankel is mortal.

You have just read a basic lesson in logic, one that appears in almost every textbook on the subject. It is undoubtedly true that all of us, Yankel or Yentel, are mortal and will someday die. Yet it is also true that we deny our mortality and live our lives as though death were not inevitable.

Our tendency to exclude our deaths from our awareness leads to some peculiar results. For example, in the graduate program that was designed to prepare me for a career as a psychotherapist, death was not part of the curriculum. The entire topic of death and dying was not something discussed in the graduate psychology programs of the late 1960s and early 1970s.

How well I remember attending a workshop by the then little known Dr. Elisabeth Kubler-Ross, which introduced me and numerous other mental-health professionals to the issues of death and dying. Her book, *On Death and Dying*, became the first in a flood of similar works designed to train professionals to be aware of the psychology of the dying person and of the ways in which people cope with the death of loved ones. That book continues to occupy a place of prominence on my personal bookshelf.

The Jewish tradition encourages us to contemplate our ultimate end. Especially before the days of awe and judgment, death preoccupies our consciousness. Those of us who are familiar with the Rosh HaShana liturgy can already hear the cantor chant, "Who will live and who will die?"

The previous *parasha*, *Parashat Nitzavim*, contains the last public address that Moses made before his death, disclosing his inner feelings as he prepared to die. He stands before a huge audience, all of Israel, judges and chieftains, and the lowly wood choppers and water fetchers, and delivers a powerful inspirational message.

Our *parasha*, *Parashat Vayelekh*, opens with the phrase, "And Moses went and spoke." The commentaries tell us that Moses left the podium from which he addressed the public and went down to the people, visiting each of them individually. He did this in order to take leave of each person, and to assure them that his death did not mean the people's mission would fail.

He told them that, like every other mortal, he was about to die and could no longer "go out and come in." He was exquisitely conscious of his waning powers and wanted to use his final moments to say his goodbyes to his people face-to-face.

Rashi tells us that by saying, "I can no longer go out and come in," he was indicating that "the traditions and wellsprings of wisdom" were no longer available to him. He sensed that he no longer had access to his inner sources of inspiration and creativity. What a lucid glimpse into the emotional experience of our great shepherd during his last hours on earth!

As you may know, Rashi is so great a biblical commentator that there are commentaries written upon his commentary. These are known as "supercommentaries," and one of them, *Siftei Hakhamim*, offers us an even more profound insight into Moses' psyche. This author suggests that, as Moses realized that his wisdom was failing him, he was better able to accept his impending death, for a life without wisdom would not be worth living.

Toward the end of *Parashat Vayelekh*, indeed just at the point where *maftir* begins (Deut. 31:28), we find Moses asking that all the elders again be assembled for him to address them. Here Rashi wonders why Moses did not simply call for the trumpets to be sounded, signaling that assembly was in order. After all, throughout the sojourn in the wilderness, Moses would gather the people to him by sounding the trumpets (*ḥatzotzrot*). Rashi suggests that at this moment, just before his death, Moses no longer had the symbols of power and authority available to him. He quotes Ecclesiastes 8:8, "There is no authority in the day of death."

One of the lessons I learned from Dr. Kubler-Ross so very long ago is the importance of the helper, be he or she a family member or a professional, to assist the patient in reaching this stage of acceptance of impending death. To help teach us about this stage of acceptance, she quoted the following poem by the Indian poet Tagore:

> I have got my leave. Bid me farewell, my brothers!
> I bow to you all and take my departure.
> Here I give back the keys of my door – and I give up
> all claims to my house. I only ask for last kind words
> from you.
> We were neighbours for long, but I received more
> than I could give. Now the day has dawned and the
> lamp that lit my dark corner is out. A summons has
> come and I am ready for my journey.

Studying *Parashat Vayelekh* gives us a unique opportunity to learn about what a man's life is like in his last moments, as he prepares for his death. True, that man is Moses, and we cannot all aspire to his example. But there is, nevertheless, much to learn from this greatest of men, not only about how to live, but about how to die.

Parashat Vayelekh

Reflections Upon the Year's End

On the last Sabbath of the year, we will soon usher in the New Year. Without a doubt, there is quite a bit of sadness attached to this Sabbath, and indeed, to this time of year. Sure, we look forward to a new year with new blessings and new opportunities, but we cannot escape the fact that the year was marked with frustrations, disappointments, and even, yes, tragedies.

It is in a state of physical and spiritual exhaustion that we find ourselves on this last Sabbath of the year. Our energies are spent, our vigor diminished. Amazingly, this mood is especially reflected in the opening verses of *Parashat Vayelekh*:

> Moses went and spoke these words to all Israel. He said to them: I am now 120 years old, I can no longer come and go. Moreover, the Lord has said to me, "You shall not go across yonder Jordan." (Deut. 31:1–2)

Who cannot hear resignation in the voice of Moses, and perhaps even a note of despair? Rashi notes the words of our sages, who are surely in tune with Moses' mood when they comment, "The traditions and the wellsprings of wisdom were shutting down for him."

Rabbi Chaim ben Attar, known because of his masterwork *Ohr HaHaim* as the "saintly" Ohr HaHaim, answers the question raised by the mystical Zohar, "Moses went? Where did he go?" He suggests that the phrase "Moses went" signifies that "he felt that his soul was leaving him, and that he was aware that his end was drawing near on that day."

And so, as the year wanes, so does the life of Moses. A cloud of sadness envelops us, and though there is the glimmer of the New Year's light upon the horizon, it somehow feels as if there is still a great distance between us and that light.

I once, in the grips of this mood of sadness during this time of year, paid a visit to my parents' grave. This act of homage was consistent with the ancient Jewish custom of visiting the graves of one's ancestors during the month of Elul, just prior to Rosh HaShana.

As I stood before my mother's grave, may she rest in peace, it was the fragrance of the sweet holiday meals she prepared that rose to my nostrils and the image of her kindling the holiday candles that appeared before my eyes.

As I stood before my father's grave, and he died quite a few years before my mother, I had a different experience entirely. My father was a prayer leader in the synagogue, a *baal tefilla*, literally a "master of prayer." I closed my eyes and remembered well standing beside him as he positioned himself before the lectern at the front of the small synagogue in which he habitually prayed.

At that poignant moment, there emerged from the recesses of my memory a teaching of the sainted Rabbi Levi Yitzchak of Berditchev. Although I had not seen that teaching in print for many years, at that moment I could recall the text verbatim. It was a teaching on the very text that we are now considering, "And Moses went and spoke."

Rabbi Levi Yitzchak pointed out that when our sages referred to the prayer leader, they sometimes said, "One goes down before the lectern"; but sometimes they said, "One passes before the lectern."

Rabbi Levi Yitzchak therefore distinguishes between two modes of the experience of prayer.

In the first instance, the person feels spiritually inadequate and turns to the words to lead him as he approaches God. Such a person "goes down before the lectern." This teaching has a greater impact when one realizes that the Hebrew term for lectern, *teiva*, also means "word." He "goes down before the word," relying upon the liturgy itself to compensate for his personal limitations.

In the second instance, on the other hand, we have the person who "passes before the lectern." This person "leads the words." He is, in a sense, spiritually independent of the text of the liturgy, so righteous is he. This, writes Rabbi Levi Yitzchak, was the level of Moses through most of his life.

"However," concludes Rabbi Levi Yitzchak, "when Moses was at the end of his days, and when the fountain of wisdom was no longer accessible to him, he regressed to the level in which 'words led him.' This is the meaning of 'And Moses went and spoke' – that he went to the word, which was above him."

As I stood before my father's grave, enchanted by Rabbi Levi Yitzchak's profound insight into the experience of prayer, I realized that my father's unique talent was his ability to begin the services he led as one who "went down before the lectern." But then, with the sweetness of his melodic voice and with the passion of his unadulterated sincerity, he rose to a higher level, and not only "passed before the lectern" himself, but inspired others to ascend with him to that higher sphere.

As the year ebbs away, we are overcome by remorse and we regret our failures and shortcomings. We certainly feel spiritually inadequate. But we can take solace in the fact that we have access to "the words." We are able to go "down before the lectern," and allow the sacred words of the High Holiday liturgy to lead us to a higher and purer place.

Moreover, we can all be hopeful that we will be inspired, if only temporarily, to rise above the rank of those who "go down before the lectern," and reach the spiritual heights of those who "pass before it."

Parashat Haazinu

Two Songs, Two Singers

How does the poet get started on the process of writing a poem or the songwriter as he sets about composing a song? Does he or she look at the environment, at what is going on in the world, and seek inspiration from things external? Or does the creative artist look within, using introspection as a tool to uncover emotions out of which the poem or song can be fashioned? These questions can be asked about all creative processes, not just writing. They can be asked of the graphic artist, of the composer of music, and of the sculptor.

My wife's grandfather was the renowned hasidic rebbe, Rabbi Shaul Taub, who composed hundreds of liturgical melodies. When he was asked about his creative process, he would say that he fashioned his music out of the feelings that "overflowed from his heart." As a Holocaust survivor, his heart overflowed with the full range of human emotions, from hope to dread and despair and back to hope again. And one can detect the full range of these feelings in his music.

There are years when *Parashat Haazinu* falls on the Shabbat immediately following the two days of Rosh HaShana. This *parasha* consists almost entirely of a song (*shira*), of words spoken by Moses "into the ears of the entire congregation of Israel" (Deut. 31:30). What are the emotions that inspire those words?

To answer this question, it helps to remember that on the first day of Rosh HaShana, we read another *shira*, and a very different one at that. I refer to the "Song of Hannah" (I Sam. 2:1–10), which is the *haftara* for that day.

Hannah's emotions are apparent. She is joyous, exhilarated, exultant. Her desperate prayers have been answered and she has experienced God's wondrous powers. Her song is a triumphant one.

Let us contrast this with the song of Moses. Like Hannah, he is confident of God's omnipotence. She sings, "The Lord deals death and gives life" (I Sam. 2:6). He sings, "There is no God beside me, I deal death and give life" (Deut. 32:39).

But the song that Moses sings is of a very different nature. Moses has a clear, if pessimistic, vision of what lies ahead for the Jewish people. He foresees the consequences of their disobedience and rebelliousness. He anticipates the wrath of God. He places the blame for that wrath on the people themselves, not upon God. God is justified in all that He does. "The Rock, His work is perfect...just and right is He. Is corruption His? No! His children's is the blemish" (Deut. 32:4–5).

Moses' emotions as he utters the song of *Haazinu* are complex indeed. For one thing, he feels a sense of dread of what lies ahead for these people whom he knows to be weak and sinful. He is certain that great suffering is in store for his people. That suffering pains him.

But he also finds it necessary to express a deeper emotion, one of confidence and trust in God in the face of suffering. He thus expresses, arguably for the first time in the Bible, the Jewish reaction of *Tzidduk HaDin*, of proclaiming God's justice even in the depths of tragedy.

The poem of *Haazinu* calls to mind a mélange of graphic images: excessive sensuality, sin, faithlessness, and, in reaction to all this, "a fire kindled in God's nostrils that burns into the depths of the netherworld." These are powerful images that ring true to the experience of every Jew who is even minimally aware of our history. But Moses sets the tone for all of us with his opening declaration: God is righteous, God is just, God is fair. *Tzidduk HaDin.* This is the Jewish reaction to every manner of suffering.

How apt are the words of Rabbi Joseph B. Soloveitchik, who would stress the centrality to our faith of the concept of *Tzidduk HaDin*, justifying God. He saw in this concept our assertion of "dignity in defeat": "If man knows how to take defeat...as the halakha tries to teach us, then he may preserve his dignity even when he faces adversity and disaster."

During these days of judgment and introspection, we prepare ourselves for a future year of difficulties and challenges and worse. We ready ourselves for the dreaded possibility of the need to express *Tzidduk HaDin*. But does this cause us to despair? No. For this solemnity is our best way to prepare for an entirely different set of alternatives.

Anxiety over divine judgment, *Eimat HaDin*, propels us to repent, to commit to be better persons and better Jews. This "fear of judgment" becomes the ground out of which sprouts optimism and hope: optimism that God will shine His countenance upon us, and hope that we will merit His favor and be blessed with a sweet and happy New Year.

We learn the lessons of the song of *Haazinu* so that we can merit the triumphs of the "Song of Hannah."

Repression of the Sublime

I t was advertised as one symposium at a major psychology conference. It was to be a discussion about memory and forgetfulness. But it turned out to be one of the most intense and instructive days that I have ever witnessed.

The first speaker began by insisting that the fact that we remember things is obvious. What requires explanation, he argued, is why we forget. We are hardwired to recall every event that occurs in our lives. The mechanisms of forgetfulness are a mystery and call for a program of scientific research.

The second speaker took a position diametrically opposed to the first. He believed that it is only natural that we forget. It is one of nature's wonders, he maintained, that we remember anything at all.

The third speaker took a middle of the road position. For him, the major challenge to the science of the psychology of memory was not why we remember, or why we forget. Rather, it was why we remember certain things and forget others, and why we distort even those matters that we do remember so that our memories are grossly inaccurate and unreliable.

It is the position of this third speaker that has kept my interest over the many years since that conference. And it was when we commemorated the tragic events of September 11, 2001, that my interest in this subject was revived.

Very many of my acquaintances were on or near the scene of the collapsed World Trade Center Towers on that fateful day. To this day, some have clear recollections of every moment of their experiences. Others claim that they only remember certain vivid episodes, fleeting ones, and can only draw a blank when it comes to the majority of the time they were exposed to the tragic scene.

Some have memories that are as accurate and as clear as the "flash-bulb memories" that psychologists have studied as far back as World War II. For others, the memories have been partially, and sometimes substantially, repressed and can no longer be recalled. Their powerful and poignant emotional reactions have wrought havoc with the ability to accurately remember the events of that day.

Remembering and forgetting are major themes in our Jewish religious tradition. We are commanded, for example, to remember the Sabbath, to remember the lessons to be drawn from the life of Miriam, and not to forget the enmity of Amalek. In *Parashat Haazinu*, there are at least two verses that relate to these themes. One reads, "Remember the days of yore, understand the years of generation after generation" (Deut. 32:7). The other states, "You ignored the Rock who gave birth to you, and forgot God who brought you forth" (32:18).

I have always been intrigued by the notion of forgetting God. Earlier in the Book of Deuteronomy, we were admonished to be careful, lest "our hearts become haughty, and we forget the Lord our God" (Deut. 8:14). I can understand agnostic disbelief, and I can empathize with those who have lost their faith, but I have always found it puzzling to contemplate forgetting God. Either one believes, or one does not believe, but how are we to understand *forgetting* Him?

Many years ago, I came across the writings of a psychologist named Robert Desoille, and it was in those writings that I've discovered a concept that helped me come to grips with the notion of forgetting God.

Desoille coined the phrase, "the repression of the sublime." He argued that we have long been familiar with the idea that we repress urges and memories that are uncomfortable or unpleasant. We repress memories of tragedy, we repress impulses that are shameful or forbidden. It can even be argued that this power of repression is beneficial to individuals and society. If individuals would not be able to forget tragedy and loss, they could potentially be forever emotionally paralyzed and unable to move on with their lives. A society whose members act on every hostile impulse, rather than repress them, would be a society that could not endure for very long.

It was Desoille's insight that, just as we repress negative memories, we also repress positive aspirations. We are afraid to excel. There is a pernicious aspect to us that fears superiority and avoids the full expression of our potential. This is especially true in the area of religion and spirituality, where we dare not express the full force of our faith and in the process, limit our altruistic tendencies. Perhaps it is the dread of coming too close to the Divine. Perhaps it is a false humility that prevents us from asserting our inner spirit. Or perhaps it is simply that we do not wish to appear "holier than thou" to our fellows.

However one understands the reasons for this phenomenon, for me, the concept of "repression of the sublime" explains the notion of forgetting God. It is as if we have faith in Him, but do not have faith in ourselves to express our faith in Him, in our relationships, and our life circumstances. We repress our sublime potential.

There are many impediments to thorough personal change and self-improvement. Desoille demands that we consider an impediment that never before occurred to us. We are afraid to actualize the inner spiritual potential that we all possess. We are naturally complacent, satisfied with a limited expression of our religious urges. We repress the sublime within us.

The High Holidays and their truly sublime liturgy enable our spiritual emotions full range. We dare to express the religious feelings that well up within us during the moments of inspiration that we all surely experience during this sacred season.

Now our faith demands that we loosen the bonds of the repression that limits us, and take the risks of more fully expressing our religious convictions. Thereby, we shall be no longer guilty of "forgetting the God who brought us forth."

May we be successful in our efforts to free the sublime within us, to act courageously upon our religious convictions, and thereby merit the blessings of the Almighty.

Parashat Haazinu

Nationalism: Good or Bad?

When I entered college many years ago, one of the concepts that was studied and heatedly discussed was the concept of *national character*. Many social scientists, the anthropologists Ruth Benedict and Margaret Mead among them, believed that members of specific cultures and homogeneous nations had a distinct personality by which they could be distinguished from members of other cultures and nations.

It was then still politically correct to speak of "primitive" cultures. Benedict and Mead studied the cultures of Native American tribes as well as denizens of the South Seas. Their theory – that members of these cultures had unique personalities, which lend themselves to research – was widely accepted. Furthermore, the theory was extended so that it applied to modern nations as well. Thus, a Frenchman was different from a German not only in the language he spoke, but in the underlying structure of his personality as well.

This theory has been challenged in many ways. One basis for opposing this theory comes from those who maintain the belief that the existence of a *national character* is one of the primary causes of nationalism and national fervor. These individuals identify with a long line of anti-nationalist thinkers who are convinced that nationalism is the root of all evil. They promulgate universalism, not nationalism.

This line of anti-nationalist thinkers goes back to nineteenth-century philosophers such as Schopenhauer who wrote, "*National character* is only another name for the particular form which the littleness, perversity, and baseness of mankind takes in every country."

The anti-nationalist trend in the political arena was one of the contributions of the communist ideologists Karl Marx and Frederick Engels, who preached universalism and whose motto was, "The working class have no country."

In our time, anti-nationalism has become the hallmark of Islamism, which preaches the unity of all Muslims. Shaykh Ayman Zawahiri, one of the most virulent spokesmen of Islamism, wrote that the success of extreme Islamism necessitates discarding the very notion of nationality.

Where does the Torah stand on all of this? Is there such a thing as *national character*? Is nationalism a good thing or a bad thing?

The answer lies in *Parashat Haazinu* (Deut. 32:1–52). Verse eight in this chapter reads:

> When the Most High gave nations their homes
> And set the divisions of man,
> He fixed the boundaries of peoples
> In relation to Israel's numbers.

Nahmanides, not in his commentary on this verse, but in his commentary on Leviticus 18:25, gives us this interpretation:

> His Glorious Name created everything and gave over the power of lower creatures to the higher beings. Thus, each and every nation has its own land and has a sign in the heavenly constellations known to astrologers. Each and every nation has its territory and has a corresponding ministering angel that influences it and guides it. Except for the Land of Israel – its territory is singled out for His Name.

Let's translate Nahmanides' words into modern language:

> The Almighty created a world in which there are many nations. These nations are distinct, have specific cultures of their own, and differ in a fundamental way from all other nations. Each nation has its own "angel"; that is, its own cultural character and unique traditions. The geographical and anthropological features of each nation are divinely ordained and are "supervised," so to speak, by angelic intermediaries. The Jewish people too have their own territory, the Land of Israel, but its geography and its culture are directly "supervised" by the Lord Himself.

Thus, from the perspective of Nahmanides' interpretation of our verse, there is indeed such a thing as a *national character*, and nationalism is not only a good thing, but is something that was implanted in mankind by the Master of the Universe Himself.

Judaism understands the Almighty to be not only the God of nature, but also the God of history. This verse, and its interpretation by the great medieval commentator Nahmanides, expands the notion of the God of history. Not only does God move within history, but He shapes it and guides it to the extent that He preordained the phenomenon of nations, each distinct from the other, and each with its own will and objectives.

The Jewish people is but one of these nations. It too has its own *national character*, but it has its own special mission.

A most perceptive understanding of the role of nations in a divinely guided world is provided to us by the philosopher and rabbinic scholar, Eliezer Berkovits, in his book, *God, Man and History*. This is how he puts it:

> The goal of nationalism is to serve the nation; a holy nation serves God…. From the point of view of a nationalistic ideology, the nation is an end in itself; the holy nation is a means to an end.
>
> In history, he who seeks universalism cannot bypass the concept of the holy nation…universalism is only an ideal…. It has – thus far – never been known to exist in reality. We have

individuals and societies, nations and classes, empires and other concentrations of power and interest, all existing largely at cross purposes with each other.

This world will be established as a kingdom of God when *all* nations submit to the will of God…. But before all nations will do so, one must do so.

In the sacred days of a new year, each Jew must reflect upon what it means to be a Jew. For one thing, it means to be a part of a nation with a special mission. That mission is directed unto all the world's nations, and the ultimate goal is indeed to transcend nationalism; not to blur the very real and very necessary differences between us, but to steer all the very different peoples of the world toward one supreme goal.

That goal is so very well expressed in the liturgy of Rosh HaShana and Yom Kippur, "And they will all unite in one great assembly, to do Your will with a complete heart."

Parashat Vezot HaBerakha

A Godly Man

We all have lifelong interests. For some of us, they are hobbies or avocations. For others, they may be art or literature. My lifelong interest has been philosophy, and more specifically, theology.

I ask you, dear reader, to ponder what your lifelong interests have been. I further ask that you try to identify the specific time in your early life that this interest began to develop. Was it in childhood, or adolescence, or not until adulthood? And where did these auspicious beginnings occur? In a classroom, in a library, or perhaps on the playground?

For me, my lifelong fascination with matters theological began on the beach. My parents, may they rest in peace, took us each year for summer vacation to Rockaway Beach, NY. We rented some rooms there in a large house that belonged to an old Irish Catholic couple, Mr. and Mrs. Fletcher. After spending an entire year in a totally Jewish environment, those summers exposed us to individuals of a very different religious background. Believe me, it was a powerful learning experience in many ways.

For me, but perhaps not for my sisters, it was where I first began to learn, not just about theology, but about comparative theology. This came about because of my introduction to the Fletchers' granddaughter, Judith. I was then eight or nine, and Judith perhaps a year or so younger.

We had long talks, Judith and I, and they were often about God and the subject of prayer. I remember the shock I experienced when I learned about Judith's conception of God, which she had of course learned in the Roman Catholic parochial school she attended. In the simplistic discourse of eight-year-olds, it became apparent that her God was once a man, of flesh and blood. My God was very much "without a body and without any semblance of a body."

I brought my discovery of the differences between my God and Judith's God to the teacher my parents would hire each summer to make sure that I did some daily Torah study. He told me that I had made a very important discovery at a much younger age than most Jewish boys. He told me that I had learned about the basic difference between Judaism and Christianity. That discussion with my teacher so long ago launched my lifelong interest in the nature of the Jewish belief in God, and the profound differences between that belief and Christian belief.

The final *parasha* of the entire Torah, *Vezot HaBerakha*, which we read on Simhat Torah, has always brought back memories of that summer long ago and of that profound early learning experience. This is because the opening verse of this *parasha* contains the phrase, "Moses, the man of God, bade the Israelites farewell before he died."

Moses, for the first time in the entire Pentateuch, is called "man of God (*ish haElohim*)," an appellation provoking the question, "Was he a man, or was he a God? Was he different from other men, perhaps more godly than they? Was he in some way himself a deity?"

How emphatically are our possible misconceptions about Moses dispelled by the second half of the phrase, "before he died!" (Deut. 33:1) Moses was utterly human, he was mortal, he died and, as we learn later in the portion, was buried. Right here, we have the essential difference between our faith and the Christian faith. There is one God, and to use the language of theology, He is incorporeal; that is, He has no body and no physical form whatsoever. He is totally different from all of His creations. God is not man and no man can be God.

The lesson that follows from the aforementioned basic principle of our faith is that the Jew prays to God alone, and does not pray to any human being, living or dead, however inspiring that person may be. We do not pray to men or women, and we do not even pray to angels. We need no intermediaries in our prayers; we pray to God alone.

Also in the process of *teshuva* – self-examination, confession, and repentance – we need no human intercessors. We introspect before God, we confess directly to Him, and we repent, or return, to Him. How unlike is our process of *teshuva* from the experience that Judith told me about: the confessional of the Roman Catholic Christian believer. She dreaded those confessionals and the requirement that she recount her childish sins to another person. How different was my childhood experience of confession (*viduy*), before an all-forgiving God who understood and tolerated my spiritual failings.

The end of our *parasha* drives home a related lesson. Moses was buried in a grave, and yet "no one knows his burial place to this day" (Deut. 34:6). Why has Moses' burial place remained unknown for all these millennia? Wouldn't it have been only fitting for him to have an impressive headstone, a monument that we could visit when we wanted to pay tribute to our greatest leader?

It has been suggested that the reason the location of Moses' grave has been hidden from us is precisely so that we do not go there to pay tribute. Had we been able to visit his grave, we might very well have begun to worship the monument under which he lies buried. We may very well have yielded to the temptation of our Christian fellows, and have turned a man into a God.

At the end of the long Holy Day period, it is imperative that we call to mind this basic lesson in theology, the lesson I personally learned so very long ago. In Judaism, all men are mortal, all are flesh and blood, all can sin, and all are subject to human shortcomings. We cannot lose sight of this basic lesson, the one which distinguishes our faith from its "daughter faith."

In the words of the composer of the *Yigdal* prayer, found near the beginning of every Jewish prayer book, of every siddur:

> Great is the living God and praised.
> He exists, and His existence is beyond time.

He is one, and there is no unity like His.
Unfathomable, His Oneness is infinite.
He has neither bodily form nor substance;
His holiness is beyond compare.

More than Just a Man

I have been an avid reader of books about the psychology of religion since I was an adolescent. I remember going to the local public library and systematically taking out every book on the shelves that related to the topic of the human phenomenon of religious behavior.

Until relatively recently, I had been convinced that no book on this subject had anything new to say. The various theories about the origins of religious faith had all been presented in detail. They ranged, of course, from those who believed, like Sigmund Freud, that religion was a neurotic illusion, to those who were sure that the Bible was literally correct, and that God Himself breathed life into man, and in that breath was religious faith.

Over the years, however, several books began to come to my attention that seemed to be saying something substantially new. These books maintained that religious belief is genetically determined, and that faith has evolutionary benefits that explain its persistence over the course of human history. The authors of these books introduced such concepts as the "God gene" and the "faith instinct."

If these theories are correct, then we are programmed, or hardwired, to believe in a divine being. I have been contemplating this possibility and have found myself asking many questions. Here are some of them:

Granted that a belief in a god is built into our genetic structure. But what kind of a god do we believe in? And how does the kind of god we believe in influence our understanding of the nature of man? It is precisely over such questions that religions have differed and religious wars have been waged over the millennia.

In antiquity, a mythological understanding of god-figures prevailed. Simply put, the notion of a god from this perspective was that of a being very much like man. As Homer, among other ancients, makes abundantly clear, the gods competed with each other, fought with each other, and fell in love with one another. Christianity promoted a very different view. Man, or at least one specific man, could be God.

Distinct from such approaches, Judaism insists on a sharp and unbridgeable differentiation between man and God. Nowhere in our sacred texts is this point emphasized as clearly as in the *parasha* that we read on the holiday of Simḥat Torah. For it is on this holiday that we read the last portion in the entire Torah, *Vezot HaBerakha*, and in it we learn of the death of Moses.

Jewish thinkers have long pointed to the last eight verses of the Torah as the source for the principle that distinguishes our faith from that of Christianity: Moses was a man, a mortal man, and not God. He may have been buried by God himself, but he was not God.

It is apparent that the Bible insists that Moses was not immortal, and that he certainly was not divine. It is therefore fascinating to consult some of the rabbinical texts in which matters are not quite so clear.

Take, for example, the first verse of this *parasha*, "This is the blessing with which Moses, the man of God, bade the Israelites farewell before he died" (Deut. 33:1). The verse stresses that Moses died. But it also calls him "a man of God." What does that term mean?

How shocking to the novice student of rabbinic literature is the answer provided by the Midrash, "From his midsection and below, he was a man; from his midsection and above, he was a God!"

I will refrain from quoting here other rabbinic texts that, at least in some way, indicate that Moses was immortal. Suffice it to say that that supreme rabbinic rationalist Maimonides wrote, "Relative to us humans, his absence could be termed 'death,' but relative to Moses himself, who was elevated in the process, it must be termed 'life.'"

How are we to resolve this paradox? Was Moses a mortal man, or was he in some partial sense god-like? For me, the resolution of this question is to be found in the talmudic injunction, "Just as He is compassionate, so must you be compassionate; and as He is merciful, so must you be merciful."

Man is merely man. He is limited both physically and intellectually by his mortality. But he has within him, perhaps as a gene and perhaps as an instinct, the ability to strive toward god-like behavior. Moses was the perfect example of a mortal being who acted in a god-like fashion from the moment he sought out his enslaved brethren in Egypt. But even Moses could not get more than halfway to God's perfection.

This lesson is a fitting one for all. I have tried my utmost to convey two major lessons to you: One, a lesson in theology; in this case, an appreciation for the great divide between the human and the divine. And, two, a lesson in ethics; in this case, the need to set for oneself the goal of emulating God's compassion and God's mercy.

Maggid Books
The best of contemporary Jewish thought from
Koren Publishers Jerusalem Ltd.